COMPASSIONATE CANADIANS

Rhoda E. Howard-Hassmann

Compassionate Canadians

Civic Leaders Discuss Human Rights

UNIVERSITY OF TORONTO PRESS
Toronto Buffalo London

ISBN 0-8020-3664-3

Printed on acid-free paper

National Library of Canada Cataloguing in Publication

Howard-Hassmann, Rhoda E.
   Compassionate Canadians : civic leaders discuss human
rights / Rhoda E. Howard-Hassman.

   Includes bibliographical references and index.
   ISBN 0-8020-3664-3

   1. Civil rights – Canada. I. Title.

   JC599.C3H66 2003   323'.0971   C2003-902293-5

This book has been published with the help of a grant from the Canadian
Federation for the Humanities and Social Sciences, through the Aid to
Scholarly Publications Programme, using funds provided by the Social
Sciences and Humanities Research Council of Canada.

University of Toronto Press acknowledges the financial assistance to its
publishing program of the Canada Council for the Arts and the Ontario
Arts Council.

University of Toronto Press acknowledges the financial support for its publishing activities of the Government of Canada through the Book Publishing
Industry Development Program (BPIDP).

*To the seventy-eight Hamilton civic leaders
whose views are discussed in this book.*

And to Grace.

Contents

Acknowledgments

Many organizations and individuals have helped to make this book possible. In particular, I must thank the Social Sciences and Humanities Research Council of Canada, which financed the major part of the research and writing. I must also thank McMaster University, both for its Arts Research Board grant, which financed the final stage of writing, and for the research leaves it granted me in 1996–7 and again in the last half of 2000, permitting me to conduct the interviews on which this book is based, and to devote six months to writing.

I am extremely grateful to the Netherlands Institute of Human Rights and its Director, Cees Flinterman. I wrote the antepenultimate draft of this book in the latter half of 2000, in the quiet yet supportive atmosphere of the Netherlands Institute in Utrecht.

For permission to reprint revised versions of articles I published in their journals, I am grateful to *Citizenship Studies* (chapter 2), *The International Journal on Minority and Group Rights* (chapter 3), *The Journal of Homosexuality* (chapter 5), and the *Netherlands Quarterly of Human Rights* (chapter 6).

Several research assistants helped me throughout the research, drafting, and writing stages. They include, in chronological order, Bernard Doucet, Jacqui Fraser, Rina Rodak, Jason Wakely, Nina Rabinovitch, Sarah Colman, and Anthony Lombardo. To all of them I am most grateful, not only for the work they did but also for their sense of humour and their patience. If this project succeeds at all, it is largely due to their collective effort. I owe special thanks to Anthony Lombardo, who in addition to his other duties was of enormous assistance in preparing the final manuscript.

Karen Rachner transcribed the interviews with great patience and care. I was very fortunate to find her, and I am very grateful for her assistance.

Many colleagues have commented on various parts of this book or on earlier articles emanating from it, either in writing or in conversation. They include, from my home university, Janet Ajzenstat, Caroline Bayard, Elizabeth Boetzkes, Daniel Coleman, Scott Davies, Colin Farrelly, Tim Fisher, Louis Greenspan, Neil McLaughlin, Charlene Miall, Julianne Momirov, and Vic Satzewich. At the Netherlands Institute of Human Rights, Peter Baehr, Baas de Gaay Fortman, and Hans Werdmoelder read draft chapters. Others who listened or offered comments are Abdullahi A. An-Na'im, Robert Brym, Keith Doubt, Bogdan Drakulic, Michiel Horn, Frederick Johnstone, Rainer Knopff, Phil Resnick, Rudolf Rizman, and Bryan Turner. Jack Donnelly read the antepenultimate draft of the book, treating me to his usual biting criticism.

I owe a special debt of gratitude to Robert Martin, Barrister-at-Law and Professor of Law at the University of Western Ontario. His legal advice sustained me through a very difficult reviewing process in which my own right to freedom of speech was threatened.

My husband, Peter McCabe, as always has offered me his advice and support on everything from logistics to analysis. Our son, Patrick McCabe, patiently suffered through yet another of my research projects before at last escaping to university.

I am most grateful to the seventy-eight men and women who so graciously, generously, and openly discussed their views on human rights with me. Their willingness to share their opinions – as well as to put up with my occasional incompetence with my tape recorder – made this book possible. This book is dedicated to them.

This book is also dedicated to a seventy-ninth compassionate Canadian, my most beloved friend, Grace Stewart. A recently retired teacher of high-school English, Grace gave most generously of her time to edit this entire volume in the summer of 2001. More than that, she has been a constant presence and comfort in my life for many years. Always thoughtful, always compassionate, she attracts around her not only her family, but also her many students and friends, all of whom lean on her as I also do. Grace is a woman truly deserving of her name.

COMPASSIONATE CANADIANS

Chapter One

Hamilton's Civic Leaders

Michael Ignatieff has stressed the need for the intellectual elites of the world to listen to the voices of ordinary men and women.[1] Ordinary men and women constitute the everyday moral universe. If they do not accept the principles of human rights, law alone cannot enforce those principles.

This book reveals how some Canadian citizens grapple with questions about human rights. I discuss their moral reasoning by analysing the opinions of seventy-eight civic leaders in Hamilton, Ontario, and its surrounding region, whom I interviewed in 1996 and 1997. These citizens considered themselves part of the Canadian community and believed their voices could be heard in the public realm; they were active commentators on Canadian human rights issues. I asked them questions about hate speech, hate crimes, gay and lesbian rights, the limits to multiculturalism, employment equity, indigenous peoples' rights, poverty, and Canadians' obligations to strangers. We also discussed the Hamilton civic leaders' feelings of identity as Canadians. We did not discuss the complicated question of language rights in Canada, or the division of responsibilities between the rest of Canada and Quebec, which might be considered to be an issue of 'collective' linguistic and ethnic rights, if not of the collective right to self-determination.

The human rights questions these citizens discussed were of two kinds. One kind dealt with the reconciliation of competing human rights interests among different categories of people living in Canada. The other kind dealt with dilemmas of principle between competing human rights obligations. Some of these dilemmas, such as those regarding hate speech rights and the limits to multiculturalism, address actual contradictions in legal and philosophical human rights principles. Others merely show how principles are changing in Canada, and how Canadian citizens both react to, and impel, such changes.

These Hamilton civic leaders thought deeply about human rights questions. As I have argued elsewhere, 'The activist ... citizen, translating private reflection about the common good into public action, protects his own and other people's human rights.'[2] I talked to a small group of people chosen on the basis of their participation in civic affairs. However, as the following chapters will show, their opinions are not untypical of the opinions of Canadian citizens as a whole, as shown in national opinion polls. The reasoning they employed as they worked their way through typically Canadian commitments to the values of equality, respect for others, non-discrimination, and multiculturalism is reflected in national debates in the mass media, in debates in Canadian religious communities, in modifications in school curricula, and in millions of private conversations.

These civic leaders are, therefore, a reflection, if not an absolutely reliable indication, of the 'collective consciousness' of Canadian citizens, that shared moral ethic that underpins law and guides individual actions and moral decisions. The nineteenth-century sociologist Emile Durkheim coined the term 'conscience collective' to describe 'the totality of beliefs and sentiments common to average citizens of the same society.'[3] This collective consciousness is 'the cultural idiom of social action.'[4] In so far as the Hamilton civic leaders exemplify the cultural idiom of day-to-day Canadian human rights morality, they also show how this morality is translated into social action.

Research Population and Methodology

I interviewed these Hamilton civic leaders from July 1996 to April 1997. Hamilton at the time was a medium-sized Canadian city with a population of 322,000, about seventy kilometres west of Toronto. (It has since been amalgamated with smaller surrounding municipalities to form a region of 468,000 people.) The average income of persons in the Hamilton census metropolitan area in 1996 was $27,556, just above the average Ontario income of $27,309.[5] Formerly known for the two steel mills that were for decades its chief source of employment, Hamilton in 1996 was also a medical and educational centre, and a bedroom city for the employees of the many light industries that sprang up in the 1980s and '90s along the Hamilton-Toronto corridor. In 1996, 25.5 per cent of those residents of Hamilton who had worked since 1 January 1995 had worked in the manufacturing and construction industries, while 72.7 per cent had worked in the service sector.[6] Seven point seven per cent of the working population was employed in the education sector, while another 10.7 per cent was employed in the health sector.[7] The unemployment rate in 1996 was 8.1 per cent.[8] Nineteen per cent of the population of Hamilton was classified as low income in that year.[9]

I call the people I interviewed civic leaders. By this term, I mean leaders of civil society at the local level. This is a term that I bestowed on the people I interviewed, not necessarily a term they used to describe themselves. These individuals both reflected and led public opinion in Hamilton and its environs. Most of them were, or had been, active in numerous civic associations. They were not individuals who 'bowled alone,' to use Robert Putnam's trenchant phrase for those in the United States who do not participate in community life.[10] Rather, most had very long and complex histories of civic activism. Many had been instrumental in forming or administering civic organizations. Some had also been instrumental in identifying and fulfilling mandates for reform in various social and political sectors. Finally, many had been responsible for raising funds and distributing benefits in a wide variety of service and charitable organizations.

The interviews with these civic leaders were semi-structured. I had a list of general questions to pose to each person, but I tried to treat the interview as a natural conversation, varying the questions and the order in which I presented the different sections to preserve a natural conversational flow. Soon after starting the interviews I realized that the civic leaders were most at ease with my questions about their identities as Canadians, and least at ease with my questions about gay and lesbian rights; thereafter, I started most interviews with the section on Canadianness, and ended them with the section on rights for lesbians and gays. I tried to ensure that each new topic I introduced made sense, in that it flowed naturally from the topic preceding it; accordingly, the order varied, as also did the need for probing or follow-up questions. Some people answered at length as soon as I introduced a topic, while others were more at ease with a set of questions about each issue. Follow-up questions, and probes of their answers, also varied according to the civic leaders' knowledge of or interest in a topic, or according to their propensity to be talkative. The interviews lasted from one and a half and two and a half hours, and generated on average forty transcript pages each. The appendix presents the questions I had drafted to guide the interviews, but readers are warned, as explained above, that I followed these questions only loosely in the actual interviews.

Such informal interviews, relying on open-ended questions, allowed the civic leaders to put their thoughts in their own words and to speak about an issue as long as they wanted. Open-ended questions avoid the absolute answers that opinion polls normally elicit. They give the individuals who are interviewed a chance to explain their views, and to argue with themselves within their own answers. The purpose of this type of interview is not to generate a sample of opinions that is statistically representative of the opinions of a wider group of people, for example, everyone living in Hamilton, or everyone living in Canada. This is qualitative, not quantitative, research. While quantitative data condenses information, qualitative data enhances it.[11] Its purpose is to delve deeply into the meanings and interpretations that research respondents give to their social worlds – in this case, as reflected in their views on human rights issues.

My research method, then, used a sociological technique to investigate ethical problems usually written about by philosophers or legal scholars. Qualitative sociologists often rely on their scholarly intuitions to formulate their beginning research questions. My intuition, later confirmed by the interviews, was that Canadian civic leaders often think quite deeply about moral issues. This deep and complex thinking cannot be captured in public opinion polls or even in formal, highly structured interviews in which respondents are confined to short answers to the questions posed. To ascertain the depth of their reasoning, respondents must be allowed to range freely, providing examples, personal knowledge, and reasons and justifications for their views as they see fit. The analysis of the interviews is then based on what respondents say; it is their responses that frame the topics to be discussed. For example, in chapter 5, on gay and lesbian rights, I discuss the fact that forty-four civic leaders told me they knew someone who was gay or lesbian. I had not asked them about this; they volunteered this information, which turned out to be very influential on their opinions on gay and lesbian rights. In chapter 7, I discuss the civic leaders' interest in employment equity policies in local firefighting and police forces; again, this is not something about which I set out to ask, but rather an issue they brought up.

To locate the civic leaders whose voices are heard in this book, I used a method known in sociology as theoretical sampling. A theoretical sample is one chosen with particular theoretical interests in mind. Normally, a sociologist will be looking for a group that will offer answers to her starting theoretical question.[12] As a scholar of human rights with a background in sociology, I was looking for a research sample of people familiar with the types of human rights questions in which I was interested.

Theoretical sampling is in turn a subset of what is known in sociology as purposeful sampling. Purposeful sampling is especially useful for finding 'information-rich cases' that can be studied in depth.[13] This type of sampling aims to give real voice to those who participate in the sociological study, to allow respondents time to frame and think through their answers, rather than to merely ask them to choose one of a list of preset options.[14] I purposefully sought out members of the Hamilton community who I knew would be thinking about the human rights questions I was addressing, avoiding other members of the community who might not be thinking about these issues. By purposefully identifying civic leaders, I managed to locate the kinds of people I sought and among the seventy-eight people I interviewed, only one was unfamiliar with the issues. By tape-recording (with their permission) and analysing their lengthy, in-depth responses, I was able to distil their key reasons, the disagreements among them, and the range of views they held. The complexity of their thinking became evident, not only between different groups but within groups that might be thought to have homogeneous opinions on issues such as hate speech or multiculturalism, such as persons of African descent, or gays and lesbians.

Thus, once again, this is not a random sample of Hamilton citizens or even of civic leaders, of the kind one would seek were one conducting a quantitative survey. I interviewed seventy-eight people. There are no rules regarding sample size in qualitative sociological research, but the size of my sample was sufficient to generate what sociological methodologists call redundancy and saturation.[15] As I reached the end of my research, I found that the opinions and the background reasons offered by the civic leaders became redundant; I had heard them all before many times. The interviews started to fold in on themselves, as it were, having reached the saturation point.

This book reflects the voices of the Hamilton citizens with whom I had discussions. After deciding at the beginning of this project to focus on civic leaders, I was left with the problem of how to recruit them. Since there is no official 'list' of civic leaders, I had no pre-selected group from which to choose people in a statistically random fashion. One approach might have been what sociologists call snowball sampling. I could have started with one or two known leaders, then asked them whom else to consult, in this manner eventually collecting many names, just as a rolling snowball gathers more snow. I decided on an approach between the two extremes of random and snowball sampling. I wanted to locate civic leaders who were themselves activists in some of the causes about which I presented questions, particularly feminism, multiculturalism, Aboriginal rights, and gay and lesbian rights. But I also wanted to locate civic leaders who were not involved in these causes. In the event, I found these latter civic leaders by approaching the members of two local committees, and by consulting a list of volunteer organizations published by a local Hamilton agency.

One of the local committees had been established by the Hamilton city government. Most of its members were representatives of various minority groups in the city, including ethnic and 'racial' groups, Aboriginal people, and gays and lesbians. The other committee was an advisory body established by a local media organization; the people on this committee were more likely to come from the mainstream white, Christian-origin population than from minority groups. From the list of local volunteer organizations, I approached the presidents or chief executive officers of service clubs, business associations, private clubs, sports organizations, and patriotic organizations. I eventually recruited twenty-two civic leaders because of their involvement in multicultural activities. I recruited three advocates of gay and lesbian rights, four advocates of aboriginal rights, and eight women involved in feminist causes. I recruited thirty-two people through service organizations, two through business organizations, two through private sports organizations, and five through patriotic organizations. Among these, three were also civic officials. These choices reflected my perceptions, as a sociologically trained observer and long-time Hamilton resident, of which organizations were influential in the city. However, it should be noted that many of the civic leaders had had multiple memberships in civic organizations over their lifetime careers as activists. Their activism was frequently not confined to groups with which they shared particular characteristics. A feminist woman activist, for example, might also have worked with a poverty group, or with a service club.

Of the seventy-eight civic leaders, I was known to twenty before the research began, primarily because of my membership from 1991 to

1996 in one of the two committees from which I recruited subjects. My prior acquaintance with some of these civic leaders had established a high level of trust between them and me. Gays and lesbians, Aboriginal individuals, and members of minority racial and ethnic groups were willing to speak openly with me, even though I was not a member of their communities. One might question, nevertheless, how open and frank the civic leaders were. Their responses might have been influenced by what social scientists call the social desirability bias. This is 'Bias in the results of interviews or surveys that comes from subjects trying to answer questions as "good" people "should" rather than in a way that reveals what they actually believe or feel.'[16] The civic leaders might also have been influenced by what they thought were the opinions I wanted to hear. Those meeting me for the first time saw a white woman in her late forties, who they knew was a university professor. Those who had known me before might also have known that I was a married woman with a child. Politeness might have tempered their responses to suit my appearance or what they knew or presumed about me.

Nevertheless, the civic leaders were responsible adults who were guaranteed anonymity, and who appeared to speak quite frankly to me. Only one indicated distrust of me before the interview, and I was quickly able to dispel that distrust by assuring him that I was not 'out to get him' for his perceived right-wing views. In general, the interviews flowed easily and the civic leaders appeared relaxed, and happy to share their views. Members of non-white minority groups appeared no less relaxed than the others I interviewed.

I believe, therefore, that the civic leaders did offer me their actual opinions about the questions I asked them. The language they used, however, might have differed from that which they would use in more intimate conversations. Although privately conducted, the interviews were a type of formal, public discourse, similar to the discourse these civic leaders used in the public realm. Since I was interested in their thoughts as active Canadian citizens, I offer their opinions as indications of how Hamilton civic leaders think through their public stances on matters that concern them.

Thirty-eight civic leaders were women; forty were men. Seventy-seven were citizens; the one remaining individual anticipated receiving citizenship within a month of the interview. All except one spoke English as their first language, or their language of adoption since moving to Canada; one had been raised in a French-speaking Canadian home but at the time of the interviews lived and worked in English. Reflecting the fact that I deliberately chose to interview leaders of civil society with long personal histories of civic activism, their average age at the time they were interviewed was fifty. The group was very highly educated, with fifty-seven of the seventy-eight possessing bachelor's, professional, or higher degrees (as opposed to the 10.3 per cent of the Hamilton population as a whole that possessed a university degree in 1996).[17] I did not ask the civic leaders questions about their personal incomes. Reflecting their age and educational attainments, most appeared to be middle class, although during the course of their interviews nineteen volunteered that they had grown up in poverty.

I also did not screen the civic leaders for occupation or profession prior to interviewing them. This resulted in the rather anomalous situation that twenty were, or had once been, teachers, as discussed further in chapter 3. When I interviewed them, I asked the civic leaders for their current occupations, or for their occupations before retirement, unemployment, or disability. Three civic leaders were or had been employed in the arts; seven were businesspeople; twenty-three were managers of some kind; three were manual labourers; and six had various 'pink collar' jobs (low-income, typically female jobs). Seven civic leaders were professionals, including lawyers, doctors, and architects; twelve were employed in the service sector; fifteen were teachers; one was a student; and one retired person did not specify any earlier occupation.

Of the group as a whole, thirty-six were immigrants, including eighteen from Europe and eighteen from elsewhere. Another eight identified themselves as children of immigrants. Twenty-three civic leaders were not of European ancestry; of these, sixteen were immigrants and seven, including four Aboriginal people, were Canadian-born. Among those neither of European nor of Aboriginal ancestry, eleven were black or of mixed (black and other) racial background; they included two native-born blacks, eight immigrants from the Caribbean, and one immigrant from Africa. Four people were South Asian immigrants, two were East Asian immigrants, one was from the Middle East, and one was Canadian-born of Japanese ancestry. Two white civic leaders identified themselves as parents of black children. Of those of European ancestry, nine identified themselves only as Canadian, without elaboration on the ethnicity of their ancestors, while eighteen identified themselves as of some variant of Anglo-Scots or 'WASP' (white Anglo-Saxon Protestant) background. Three offered no information at all on ancestry. Among the others (and allowing for multiple responses) were five of Irish background, five of Italian, four of Dutch, three of German, two of French, and two of Portuguese. The group also included one person of Danish background, one of Estonian, one of general 'Eastern European' background, one of Greek, one of Polish, and two individuals who identified their ethnic backgrounds by their religions, one Mennonite and one Jewish. It should be noted here, however, that these ethnic categories were the ones that the civic leaders offered as their backgrounds, not necessarily the categories they offered when asked what their own ethnicity was. I discuss the latter aspect of their self-identification in chapter 2.

In all, 46 per cent of the civic leaders were immigrants, compared to only 23.3 per cent of the population of Hamilton in 1996, and 17.4 per cent of Canada as a whole.[18] The overrepresentation of immigrants is deliberate: I was looking for a range of opinions on questions of human rights, and also wanted to discuss contentious cultural issues with civic leaders who had originated from societies outside Canada. Aboriginals and non-whites are also over-represented, constituting 5 per cent and 24 per cent respectively of the people interviewed, as opposed to 0.9 per cent and 7.8 per cent of the entire population of Hamilton in 1996.[19] I wanted to be sure to include Aboriginal people and to discuss human rights with individuals who might have had actual experience of racial discrimination.

Just as I deliberately sought out a disproportionate number of immigrants and non-whites in order to tap diversity of opinion, so I also sought out a disproportionate number of non-Christians. Christianity is the dominant religion in Canada. In the 1991 census 83.4 per cent of Canadians identified themselves as Christian, while 12.5 per cent said they had no religion. (There was no question on religion in the 1996 census.) Among the Hamilton civic leaders, fifty-eight, or 74 per cent, identified themselves as Christian, among whom were eighteen Roman Catholics, one member of the Greek Orthodox Church, and thirty-eight members of various Protestant denominations. Ten individuals, or 13 per cent of those studied, variously described themselves as atheist, agnostic, or of no religion. Nine people, or 11.5 per cent, practised minority (non-Christian) religions; this includes three Jews, two Hindus, one Sikh, two practitioners of the Aboriginal Longhouse religion, and one person who practised Buddhism and goddess-worship. After repeated delays, the one Muslim whom I had hoped to interview dropped out of the study. In Canada as a whole in 1991, 4 per cent of Canadians identified themselves as belonging to non-Christian religions, including 1.2 per cent who were Jewish and 0.9 per cent who were Muslim.[20] The figure for non-Christians is much lower than the figure for persons of non-European ancestry because many immigrants to Canada from non-European parts of the world are Christian. Moreover, many non-Christians in Canada convert to Christianity, either to conform to the dominant majority, for reasons of belief, or upon marriage.[21]

Finally, five civic leaders voluntarily identified themselves as gay or lesbian, among whom all but one were white. Other civic leaders may have been gay or lesbian, but did not identify themselves as such. In deference to their age and backgrounds, I did not ask the civic leaders their sexual orientation. Many, if not most, would have found such a question to be an unwarranted invasion of their privacy.

In what follows, the civic leaders are frequently identified by name; all names are pseudonyms as I had promised all the civic leaders anonymity when I interviewed them. The civic leaders are also frequently identified by race or ethnicity, place of origin, religion, and/or sexual orientation. That they are identified in this fashion does not imply that there was any observable pattern of responses that differentiated majority (white, Christian or Christian background, heterosexual) Canadians from others in this study. Quite the contrary. These identifications are meant to show how people who, on the basis of their personal identities, might be assumed to have very different opinions from each other often share the same opinions. With the possible exception of employment equity, there was no neat division of opinion on human rights questions among the Hamilton civic leaders corresponding with their social identities.

Multiple characteristics influenced how each individual thought through her or his answers to the various questions, resulting in answers that might be unexpected if one assumed a strict correlation between social identity and thought. An immigrant might be more demanding of conformity to dominant Canadian norms than a native-born Canadian, or a conservative black Christian might be more insistent on the need to conform to the law than a liberal, secular white. A lesbian might be more willing than a heterosexual to tolerate heterosexuals' reluctance to accept gay marriages. In justifying their opinions on various questions, the civic leaders rarely referred to their own identities or social status. Both what might be called the 'old stock' (white, of European and Christian background) and the 'new' Canadians had multiple identities and interests, and were motivated by thought about matters other than their group memberships. Almost all thought in terms of rights and responsibilities and in terms of religious and civic duty. Most wanted to show respect for those who were vulnerable, whether or not they themselves were members of such groups. They agreed that certain social groups needed rights, but the social groups they were concerned about were not necessarily those of which they were themselves members.

In discussion of the civic leaders' opinions, I frequently cite numerical figures to present a summary understanding of their views. To determine these numbers, I coded each interview, sometimes on my own and sometimes with a research assistant who separately coded it. Where a research assistant helped me, there was generally a high level of agreement between us, about 95 per cent. Nevertheless, the numbers are not completely accurate assessments of the civic leaders' opinions, as readers will soon discover. Some questions were not posed to all civic leaders, or an individual did not answer all the questions posed. In other cases, a civic leader might show such a wide variety of views within each answer, or argue so much with him- or herself while answering, that a coding choice had to be made that did not entirely reflect his or her views.

The numbers I cite have no wider statistical validity; they are merely a small part of a picture of the Hamilton civic leaders. The people I interviewed were not chosen according to a statistically reliable method of sampling. Therefore, the numbers do not represent variations of opinions among a wider population. Nor are the numbers large enough to reliably correlate opinions with personal characteristics such as birthplace (Canadian or foreign) or race, gender, or sexual orientation.

This book, then, is not, and is not meant to be, a statistically accurate survey of public opinion in Hamilton, Ontario, or anywhere else in Canada. A statistically representative study, including more rural, more Christian, less educated, and fewer racially and ethnically diverse people than those whose voices are reflected here, might well reveal a different range of opinions. It might show Canadians as a whole to be less liberal and open-minded about some of the issues discussed in this volume than the Hamilton civic leaders. Nevertheless, on some issues, as shown throughout the book, the Hamilton civic leaders' views closely resembled the views recorded in national opinion polls. The theoretical issues and the human rights dilemmas that arose from the interviews reflect discussions in which Canadians across the country engage.

This book is about the moral reasoning of some Canadian civic leaders confronted with human rights dilemmas. It is a qualitative, in-depth look at how some Canadians think about their moral world. In his own research on the opinions of four hundred American citizens, Alan Wolfe argued that we need to go beyond the stark choices offered in quantitative survey research to discover how people think and what their logic is.[22] That is what I am attempting to do.

Democracy and Citizens' Moral Reasoning

In a democracy, what citizens have to say can and does affect public policy. It does not do so in a straightforward way; citizens' views are mediated through social movements, interest groups, the mass media, and political parties. Citizens' opinions and interests may fall by the wayside when elite economic, bureaucratic, or political interests take precedence.[23] Nevertheless, governments in democracies, including in Canada, do pay attention to what citizens think.

Many citizens are capable of that communicative rationality that Jurgen Habermas identifies as central to the formulation of social principles. '[T]he process of actualizing rights is ... embedded in contexts that require [citizens'] discourses as an important component of politics – discussions about a shared conception of the good ... In such discussions the participants clarify the way they want to understand themselves as citizens of a specific republic.'[24] As James Q. Wilson explains, ordinary people are moral people: 'the daily discourse of ordinary people is filled with oblique references to morality.'[25] Yet evidence of moral reasoning by private citizens is rare in the literature on human rights.[26] The Canadians quoted in this study thought about moral issues. They took their interviews extremely seriously, worrying about whether they knew enough to answer my questions properly and demonstrating great concern that they expressed themselves clearly, some even making notes the evening before I interviewed them.

Nevertheless, one might query exactly how 'ordinary' these citizens were. They were civic leaders; moreover, they were civic leaders conversant on the whole with the moral issues I posed to them. They were informed citizens, actively engaged in public affairs and familiar with the debates going on in Canadian public life. Paul M. Sniderman and his colleagues, who conducted a large public opinion survey on questions similar to those posed in this study, suggest that such a group might better be considered part of the Canadian elite, comprising in their view 'everything from officers of fraternal organizations ... to leaders of the Parent Teachers Association to trade union officials to religious leaders.'[27] It would, however, be an exaggeration to call the Hamilton civic leaders members of the Canadian elite. They were certainly influential at the local level, where they might be thought of as opinion leaders. Except for the three individuals who were civic officials, however, they did not possess decision-making power beyond the actual organizations of which they were members. Moreover, they had little or no influence on society beyond their local level. If they were not 'ordinary,' neither were they elite.

Moreover, this study can be taken as a reflection of 'ordinary' people's thinking about human rights in as much as the Hamilton civic leaders were not human rights professionals. Unlike most published commentators on the various questions addressed in the present study, they were not learned in legal theory or in the philosophy of human rights.[28] Their opinions and comments arise from their own life experiences, discussions with others, and contact with the mass media.

Knowledge of what these civic leaders think, and how they reason, helps us understand the depth of support among citizens for Canadian human rights law. Law cannot be effective if it is merely a set of principles and sanctions unconnected to social life. It cannot function in a normative vacuum. Law both reflects and influences wider social norms. It needs the moral backing of the people it governs.[29] In a technologically advanced, literate society such as Canada, where freedom of speech and political democracy exist, social norms constantly change as citizens discuss what are, or ought to be, just ways of organizing social life. Understanding the moral reasoning of ordinary citizens helps illuminate the moral consensus in civil society around the formal human rights laws that govern a country.

The lines of connection between public opinion, public policy, and law cannot easily be identified, but the active participation of citizens can and does influence the direction that public policy takes. It does not do so in a direct manner; one cannot trace neat lines of influence from citizens to legislators to public policy. Nevertheless, legislators in pluralist democracies that respond to interest and pressure groups must pay some attention to what their citizens think. In pluralist democracies – that is, democracies in which more than one group influences government – citizens exert pressure on their legislators to adopt the policies they advocate. They are part of a 'participant culture [that] rests on an active political self-concept.'[30]

In Hamilton, these participating citizens include both the white, native-born Canadians of European and Christian background who in the mid-1990s constituted the dominant cultural majority in Canada, and members of other social groups, not necessarily white, native-born, or of Christian background. These members of new immigrant groups and religious minorities are as much citizens as anyone else. They are frequently highly educated, reflective citizens who think about how to compromise between their former and present cultures, how to fit in to Canadian society, or, alternately, what kinds of changes they would like Canadian society to implement to accommodate their presence.[31] Moreover, even the 'old,' or the native-born, Canadians are frequently the children or grandchildren of immigrants. They, too, reflect on culture and the demands that Canadian norms such as human rights make for cultural change.

The citizens I interviewed in the Hamilton region were particularly concerned with the rights of those whom I term vulnerable groups; that is, of minorities of various kinds whose equal position in Canadian society was not, or was not yet, fully established. These vulnerable groups included gays and lesbians, persons of minority racial status, immigrants and refugees, Aboriginal peoples, the poor, and the members of the various cultural groups whose presence in Canada underlines the need, in these citizens' eyes, for a policy of multiculturalism.

Rights for vulnerable groups impel theoretical questioning of the relationship between such rights and classic individual rights, and the place that individual rights should have in an increasingly multicultural world.[32] Discussions of the rights of visible minorities to employment equity, or of Aboriginal peoples to their own systems of laws, are common in the Canadian media and in governmental and non-governmental fora. Thus the citizens whose voices are heard in the present study are used to public discussion of collective rights, group rights, and possible conflicts between group and individual rights. With such a legal heritage as part of their everyday world, most of these Canadians do not rely on severely individualistic conceptions in their discussions of human rights dilemmas. Nevertheless, as the following chapters will show, individual human rights, especially to equality, take precedence for most of these civic leaders over collective or group rights.

Involvement in Civic Life

Most of the Hamilton civic leaders had had a high degree of involvement in local civic affairs, defined broadly to include all types of volunteer organizations and clubs. Some, indeed, had had lifetime careers as activists. I asked them briefly about these careers, but did not ask for detailed autobiographical accounts as they would have lengthened the interviews beyond a reasonable time limit. From the civic leaders' somewhat sketchy descriptions, however, some patterns emerge.

Some civic leaders were 'single-issue' activists, confining themselves to one specific commitment outside their family and work lives. Mothers with small children especially demonstrated this pattern, although even they were often also active in parent activities at their children's schools, or in their local faith community. Typical of this pattern was Nicky: 'I'm involved with my children's school right now ... parents' council and volunteering through their school ... I'm [a] full-time [worker] with two young kids. That's pretty much all we're able to deal with right now.'

Other civic leaders were involved in what might be called personal activism; that is, activism connected with their personal identities. This applied particularly to leaders of the various ethnic groups; Aboriginal activists; feminists; and gay and lesbian activists. Their pattern was to move from one organization relevant to their personal interest to another, setting up new groups as the need arose, or migrating from the local to the regional level.

Among leaders of ethnic minority or immigrant organizations, this pattern of personal activism was particularly common, in part because of their own memories of difficulties joining the wider Canadian society. As Jacqueline, an adult immigrant from the Caribbean, put it, 'I know how I felt as an adult coming to Canada ... I felt I was sort of cut off ... I was caught between two countries.' George, also an adult immigrant from the Caribbean, had a similar motivation: 'I was concerned with certain minority groups in the country ... [M]y own children ... were growing up ... and they came to me with different problems.' Aboriginal activists were also motivated by personal causes. Walter had been involved in a variety of organizations, only some of which were connected to his personal status; nevertheless, he noted that he 'saw a lot of discrimination and harassment, racial harassment at work.'

Members of ethnic minorities, however, did not always confine themselves to volunteer activities within their own communities. Some preferred general service activities to those that were ethnically oriented, even when they were immigrants themselves. The more general focus gave them a chance to be part of the wider Canadian society. As Adnan, an immigrant from India who had joined a mainstream service organization, put it, 'No matter what you are, each ethnic group you belong to is the same ... everyone's blood is the same colour of red.'

Several female civic leaders had had long careers of service to women. Some of these women might be regarded as feminists, such as those who adopted a pro-choice position on abortion. Others were involved with organizations frequently considered anti-feminist, such as those that opposed abortion. Frances, involved in a pro-life group, felt that she should assist those many women who 'were going through an awful lot of pain after the abortion ... [T]here's so many women who feel vulnerable when they're pregnant, and they don't have the support system behind them ... their family, or their church, or whatever kind of community they live in.' Linda was particularly concerned about non-white women. 'I'm a black woman, and I've faced some of the racism that a lot of women come to me and talk about.'

The pattern for gay and lesbian activists was similar to the pattern for other personal activists. As Bob put it, 'I suppose the ultimate goal is equality ... but I do feel that we have accomplished some things. I mean, the awareness level is higher ... [People] at least acknowledge that there's probably a gay or lesbian perspective to any given field.' In this and other cases, the ability to affect the public and political agenda was an important motive to continue in a career of voluntary service.

Some of the Hamilton civic leaders had dedicated their volunteer careers to one organization specifically designed for general community service. Elliott, a Canadian-born professional of Anglo-Saxon background, was a member of several professional organizations and one service organization. He found this work personally fulfilling, even though he had not chosen the actual projects he worked on; rather, he had worked on projects chosen by his organization as a whole. He gave as his reason for this work 'the people, the challenge, the growth, the opportunity to try to be of help ... There's an altruistic component, but there's also a large personal component which I don't apologize for. I think it's a very important part of volunteerism that the volunteer gets something out of his or her involvement with the organization as well as giving something. I find it fascinating, and probably the most interesting part for me is developing the people skills through my involvement at this level.'

Other civic leaders moved around a good deal, looking for variety in their lifetime careers as local activists. Some had been appointed to Hamilton municipal bodies such the Police Advisory Board, the Status of Women Committee, and the Mayor's Committee Against Racism and Discrimination. Some moved from one committee to another as terms expired or mandates looked more interesting elsewhere. A few civic leaders were members of organizations that might be called directly patriotic. They were interested in promoting political identification with Canada as a country, rather than promoting the needs and interests of various subgroups within Canada.

A small group of civic leaders worked mainly on international issues, such as Amnesty International. Several had been involved in development work abroad. 'Well, you know,' said Gerard, '[I had] childhood experiences that helped me become aware that there was a whole other level of existence, in terms of how other people live and survive, that was not in my ... middle-class milieu ... [A]nd then, in high school, I had the opportunity to belong to a youth organization that exposed me even more to other situations in the world ... becoming aware of poverty in the world ... [I was motivated by] the desire ... to be of service, to try to change some of these situations.' Individuals such as Gerard tended to have a more internationalist outlook than the rest of the civic leaders, who confined themselves to Canadian activities. Even among the latter, however, there were many who gave money to international charities, and several who donated money monthly to foster parents' schemes for children in poorer countries.

These civic leaders constituted an important part of civil society in Hamilton. Putnam argues that dense social life helps underpin civil society. Meeting together in groups, citizens discuss civic affairs in a free-flowing manner, interwoven with other topics of conversation.[33] Such discussions keep the individual anchored in the community, giving her a sense of involvement in civic affairs and obliging her to think about social issues beyond the private realm. The Hamilton civic leaders considered themselves members of the wider community. They had a variety of motives for entering civic life, and derived a variety of benefits from it. Their accomplishments as members of the community were a major reason they remained in civic life.

As noted earlier in this chapter, Putnam describes the phenomenon of 'bowling alone'; that is, of Americans becoming increasingly privatized in their everyday activities, so that even bowling, previously a group activity, is now an individual activity. Joel explained how he first became involved in the myriad, ethnically oriented activities that had occupied him for several decades: 'Bowling ... I wanted to go out and bowl. I was married at the time, and I wanted to be with some people just apart from my everyday work, and bowling was one thing that attracted me [to his ethnic organization].' For some people, then, the social aspect is the impetus to join in civic affairs. Aqil, a very recent immigrant originally from South Asia, said, 'Since I came here ... I did not have any friend or relative. So first thing you're always looking for is some committees, or you need friends and people to talk to.' The civic leaders also occasionally cited some version of a desire for 'personal growth' as a reason to be involved in civic affairs. They expressed a need to have some change, variety, or intensity of commitment that was missing from their private lives. Said Al, a quiet man involved in a range of service activities, '[I was motivated] simply [by] an interest in ... human nature, and in people, and in trying to understand differences. It was more a learning experience for myself, a need to learn and to understand people.'

For a few others, a straightforward sense of self-advancement was the reason for civic involvement. Zelda said, 'When I came [to her organization] right from when I started I wanted to be president ... [T]he skills and the knowledge that I've learned from the training and from being a member ... I've been able to use in my work.' In certain business and professional quarters in Canada, individuals are expected to demonstrate some commitment to the wider community. Also, profitable business or professional connections can be made through memberships in diverse types of organizations beyond work, religious community, and family.

For many civic leaders, the desire to give to the community was the chief impetus for volunteer activity. William, a very kindly older man active in a service organization, explained, 'When I recovered ... from the cancer operation in '94, I made my mind up that I didn't know what was down the road and how long I had down that road, but whatever it was, I was going to do as much for people ... as I could.' He elaborated: 'maybe "give back to the community" is kind of a hackneyed phrase, but I was looking for something to kind of help ... I kind of like people.' Greg, also an older man, who belonged to a wide variety of organizations, explained, 'I decided to go along with [a] Chinese philosopher ... do what I can, where I was, with what I had.' Colleen, raised a Roman Catholic but no longer practising, had a strong sense of obligation to the community and dedicated every Sunday morning to a service activity. 'I don't go to church on Sunday mornings so I ... should do something.'

In fact, being a civic activist offers a wide-ranging set of benefits. The altruistic motive is a genuine one; empathy and compassion motivated almost all the civic leaders. But altruistic acts offer other benefits. Kevin put this most clearly: 'All kinds of things factored into why I volunteered. To learn, have fun, to effect things, have an influence over things ... [I]t's all, I suppose, in a sense self-interest in that in some cases I felt I could make a difference, and [in] other cases it was just quite a bit of fun.' Kevin's statement confirms Alan Ryan's assessment of the importance of civic participation in buttressing democracy. 'It is an important paradox that we may join organizations for pleasure, companionship, or commercial self-interest but that in the process we acquire the skills of co-operation and the skills of leadership. We learn to trust one another and to make ourselves trustworthy in turn. We learn to allow others to take responsibility for us, and we learn to take responsibility for them.'[34]

Most of these Hamilton civic leaders felt that their work at the local level in civil society had been useful. Several spoke of their feelings of accomplishment as they identified problems that needed to be addressed and mobilized others, including government officials, to do something about them. Margaret, a woman with a very long history of social activism in several different sectors, said, '[T]he changes don't occur as quickly as I would like to see them ... but it certainly has improved a tremendous amount ... with the acceptance of people of colour, of different nationalities. I don't think there is as much bias nowadays as there has been in the past ... [P]eople are a lot more tolerant today.' The sense of accomplishment as different tasks were fulfilled encouraged these local activists to go on to new ones. Sylvia had had a very difficult early life, raised in almost unspeakable poverty, but then she was recruited for jury duty and found within herself a capacity to effect change. 'I never really knew that I liked working in groups, as part of a committee or anything like that, until I was called for jury duty, and I really enjoyed the deliberations.' Sometimes civic leaders defined new concerns that needed to be addressed in part to be able to justify continuing their activist careers. Others persisted in their activism even though, as Betty put it, '[Y]ou join with the sense of help-ing people, and you can never do enough. There's never enough money, you can never really do what you want to do.'

As the interviews progressed, I realized that many civic leaders referred to their religious beliefs in order to explain their civic activism, their stance on the ethical issues I posed to them, or both. Canada is a secular country, with very low rates of weekly attendance at religious services.[35] National surveys of volunteers, however, show that they are more likely than the general population to be religious.[36] Their spiri-tual beliefs, it seems, impel volunteers to become involved in commu-nity affairs. That a substantial minority of the Hamilton civic leaders referred to their religious faith in explaining both their actions and their thoughts confirms this national trend.

Explaining his own reason for participating in civic affairs, Jacob told the story of a rabbi and his student. 'One of the students of the Rebbe comes to him and says, "Rebbe, why did God make the world the way he did, so full of poverty and disease and hatred? I could have made the world better." And the Rebbe said, "You're right, that's your job. Go do it."' For other people, religion was a guide to ethical mat-ters, including the human rights questions raised in their interviews. Sylvia, one of the two Aboriginal civic leaders who adhered to the Longhouse religion, explained, 'I really believe in the principles of the religion ... [T]hat's where I look if I'm in a quandary.' Karl, a practising Protestant, said, 'I'm using the Scripture as a guideline ... I think that Christians are given the gift of revelation, and we're given wisdom to see things.'

Other civic leaders referred more generally to a spiritual orientation, sometimes having left their original faith communities but having retained a sense of spirituality and of religious commitment. Beverly explained, 'The work that I do does not come from the religion ... [It] is more spirituality, believing in, as human beings in this planet we need to be helping each other.' Sofia said, '[A] lot of activists that I came into contact with were ex-Roman Catholics, so I think there's something about being raised in the Roman Catholic faith that leads one to take a lot of responsibility for what's going on with other people ... So ... although I've left the Church, I do feel a real need to be involved in the process of change.' Dorothy referred to the Golden Rule as a good guide to life, regardless of one's official faith.[37] 'I believe the Golden Rule, I think that's a good way to live ... It doesn't have to be Christian; it can be Muslim ... it can be Buddhist, [but] I think people are richer and more stable and stronger in their lives if they have an understanding of themselves within society.'

These, then, are the individuals whose voices are heard throughout this book. They are local civic leaders, very involved in civil society, and very much aware of the human rights issues confronting Canada. Upon such individuals depends the creation of those taken-for-granted social norms and practices that buttress new laws written to promote human rights. The Hamilton civic leaders do not all speak with one voice, but (with perhaps one or two exceptions) they do speak with the same tone: one of compassion, empathy, and reason. They are citizen-philosophers, thinking carefully about justice, rights, and responsibilities. They do this thinking in the context of a rich and still evolving Canadian rights culture.

Canadian Human Rights Laws and Policies

Canada possesses a very weak historical tradition of human rights. No individual human rights were entrenched in the Constitution that formed the country in 1867.[38] British common law ruled the English-speaking provinces, including Ontario, and determined citizens' rights. Until the 1950s, the Anglo-Canadian elite assumed that the country was organized in a manner that was just, at least for those who counted. Among those who did not count were women, Aboriginal peoples, people of African descent, various immigrant groups not of British or Northern European background, Jews, and the poor. Gays and lesbians were not even acknowledged to exist until the 1970s. Canada was, that is to say, a typical Western democratic country, espousing a thin veneer of individual equality and rights that in fact pertained to very few people. Changes in social and political ideologies after the two world wars, pressures on elites from previously quiescent social groups such as unionized workers and Aboriginal peoples, and the increasing sophistication of social movements for human rights have changed Canada into a country that actively promotes an ideology of rights and that strives to live up to its international human rights obligations.

A well-known list of incidents in Canadian history illustrates how heavy-handed was the State until the 1960s, and how uninterested it actually was in human rights. During and after the Second World War, Jewish refugees from the Nazi genocide were denied entrance to Canada; even Jewish Canadian citizens were not permitted to bring into the country close family members.[39] People in Canada of Japanese ancestry – citizens as well as aliens – were interned en masse during the Second World War and had all their property confiscated in perpetuity. Four thousand even suffered 'deportation' (better thought of as exile) to Japan, a country many had never visited, after the war ended.[40] Canadians of African ancestry suffered discrimination in employment, housing, and schooling well into the 1960s. In Ontario, there were segregated schools until 1965, although some had originally been segregated by African-Canadians' own choice.[41] 'Africville,' a settlement outside Halifax, Nova Scotia, of people descended from freed slaves and black Loyalist soldiers, was brutally bulldozed in the early 1960s without regard for the community and the collective welfare of its inhabitants.[42] Chinese labourers who built the Canadian Pacific Railroad later found that under the Chinese Exclusion Act, passed in 1923 and not revoked until 1947, they were not permitted to bring wives into the country.[43] A boatload of Sikhs attempting to immigrate in 1914 was refused the right to dock.[44] Immigration policy was explicitly racist until 1962.[45] Canada's first refugee law, spelling out refugees' rights and Canada's obligations under international law, was not passed until 1978.

Aboriginal people suffered the worst abuses of their rights. Assimilationist policies obliged large numbers of children to reside ten months of the year in missionary-run schools, where some were subjected to physical and sexual abuse. Treaty rights to property and benefits such as health care were routinely ignored. Even Aboriginal veterans, like black veterans, discovered they were subjected to discrimination when they returned to Canada after the Second World War. Aboriginals who lived on reserves were denied the right to vote until 1960, and did not receive the provincial vote in Quebec until 1969: thus, it is accurate to say that universal suffrage was not achieved in Canada until that late date.[46] In 1927 a law was passed forbidding Aboriginals to raise funds to pursue claims to the property to which they thought they were entitled.[47]

Women obtained the right to vote in federal elections in 1918, but in all other ways they remained subordinate to men until well into the 1970s. Discrimination in education, employment, housing, and almost all other aspects of a woman's public life was endemic. Laws mandated discrimination in such areas as marital rights and nationality rights. It was considered unseemly for women to speak of 'private' matters such as birth control, abortion, or domestic violence. Gays and lesbians were hidden populations, despised, subject to arrest, and sometimes driven to suicide by the attitudes of families, friends, employers, and the larger world.

The poor were equated with minority groups or else with a group generally known as the unfit, thought to breed too much and work too little.[48] They eventually received some protection through the trade union movement and the activities of socialists and social-democratic political parties, although Communism was discouraged and both Communist and socialist activists were subject to police and political persecution.[49] By the 1980s Canadians enjoyed a universal right to (fiscally circumscribed) health care and basic welfare protections, but did not enjoy any constitutionally entrenched economic rights.

The province of Ontario, where the present study was conducted, followed general Canadian practice in denying rights to minorities well into the twentieth century. In 1924 a black man in London, Ontario, who accused a restaurant-keeper of refusing to serve him discovered he had no legal protection against such discrimination.[50] In 1933, the Ontario Legislature defeated a private member's bill that would have outlawed public signs in store windows, and at beaches and resorts, that proclaimed "'Whites only," "Gentiles only," and "No Jews or Blacks Allowed."'[51] Nonetheless, Ontario was one of the earliest provinces in Canada to protect individual rights. Ontario's 1944 Racial Discrimination Act was the country's first anti-discrimination statute.[52] In 1951 Ontario passed a Fair Employment Practices Act, prohibiting discrimination on grounds of race, national origin, or religion,[53] and in 1954 it passed a Fair Accommodations Practices Act.[54] In 1962, Ontario instituted a Human Rights Code and established a Human Rights Commission.[55] An expanded Human Rights Code replaced the 1962 version in 1996. Reflecting provincial and national discussions of the meanings of human rights during the preceding twenty-five years, the 1996 code included new prohibitions of discrimination on grounds such as age, disability, and sexual orientation.[56]

There was no national legislation specifically protecting human rights in Canada until the Bill of Rights was passed in 1960. This bill provided that federal laws had to recognize certain civil liberties, especially freedom of religion, speech, assembly, association, and the press. It also protected certain rights of due process. Nevertheless, very few laws were found to be in conflict with it.[57] In 1982 the Canadian Charter of Rights was promulgated.[58] This Charter, however, is a rather problematic document. On the one hand, in keeping with the Canadian debate of the

1960s and '70s, it entrenches certain language, multicultural, and Aboriginal rights, the latter two to be discussed in more detail in chapters 6 and 8. On the other hand, its entrenchment of fundamental civil liberties is very weak. Under Section 33 of the Charter, known as the 'notwithstanding' clause, the federal or any provincial government can override protection of fundamental rights for as long as five years; this override, furthermore, is renewable. This permitted override pertains to Section 2 of the Charter, protecting fundamental freedoms of conscience, thought, press, assembly, and association, and sections 7 to 15, which protect legal rights to due process.[59] There is a taken-for-granted attitude to these fundamental rights in Canada, a sense that they are unlikely to be violated, even though there have been quite egregious instances of their denial in the past, as discussed in chapter 3.[60] The provincial human rights commissions that have sprung up in Canada before and since 1982 are fierce protectors of non-discrimination rights, but most do not provide any mechanism by which a citizen can seek protection of her or his basic civil and political rights.[61]

Thus, when the Hamilton civic leaders discuss human rights, they do so on a foundation that is simultaneously strong and flawed. Economic rights are not protected as constitutional rights: even those civil and legal rights thought to be absolute in most liberal-democratic states are not so in Canada. The historic depth of human rights as they are now known – encompassing the rights of minority communities, Aboriginal peoples, women, and (more weakly) gays and lesbians – is not more than four decades old, if that. Nevertheless, by the 1990s there was a strong culture of human rights in Canada. Rights issues were frequently reported in the national media and discussed in educational institutions. Social movements and civic organizations frequently organized around rights claims. All levels of government established committees and commissions dealing with human rights, as indeed did many private organizations such as universities and corporations. The courts paid a great deal of attention to human rights, sometimes, in the eyes of critics, going so far as to usurp the law-making functions of government in their rulings.[62]

With regard to the evolution of international human rights law, Canada is often considered to have made a distinctive contribution through its entrenchment of collective or group rights. References in the Charter of Rights and Freedoms to the collective rights of French- and English-speaking Canadians, of the various ethnocultural communities, of Aboriginal peoples, and of women are considered to have added a level of protection to the equality rights of individuals.[63] Thus, Canada's rights culture differs from the more individualistic American and French culture, or indeed from the 1948 United Nations' Universal Declaration of Human Rights. Canada, it seems, takes the human need for preservation of language and culture – for the preservation of group life – very seriously, providing a model for multiracial countries such as South Africa that have written their own rights documents since 1982. As Ignatieff puts it, Canada has attempted 'to create a society where everyone has rights without flattening out the differences that give us our identity as individuals and as peoples.' Indeed, argues Ignatieff, Canada has gone further in attempting to institute group rights that 'protect those essential things – such as land and language – that can't be protected unless a group is guaranteed the right to have them.'[64] Canada is engaged in a rethinking of the individualistic liberal tradition, especially with regard to the rights of ethnic minorities, cultural minorities, and Aboriginal peoples.[65]

Evolution of human rights law in Canada is, therefore, most pertinent to the international debate on the nature of group rights and the possible conflict between group and individual rights. Canada is a country in which certain group, or collective, rights are now well established, and in which much thought has been given to the question of how to protect group or collective rights without undermining individual rights. Collective rights, indeed, are 'deeply embedded in our [Canadian] traditions.'[66] Provincial rights, the rights of French- and English-speaking minorities, and the educational rights of Roman Catholic and Protestant Christians have long been constitutionally entrenched. As noted above, the rights of indigenous peoples, the right to multiculturalism, the rights of women, and affirmative action programs are protected in the 1982 Charter of Rights and Freedoms, in Articles 25, 27, 28, and 15 (2) respectively.[67] The concept of systemic discrimination is accepted in law, and legal attempts are made to remedy it.[68] The rights of gays and lesbians have been gradually included in most jurisdictions' human rights codes, and in early 2000 they were the subject of an omnibus federal bill to give same-sex couples benefits and responsibilities equal to those of common-law heterosexual couples.[69]

The Canadian discussion of the relationship between individual and group rights, then, may help to inform other societies that are wrestling with this question. Many other countries are multicultural, or are becoming multicultural, and many are accepting large numbers of immigrants and refugees. Canada is a country built on immigration, like Australia and the United States; it is also a precursor of the likely future of most Western European countries, which are currently absorbing large numbers of refugees and legal and illegal immigrants. Debates on limits to freedom of speech, punishment of hate crimes, limits to multiculturalism, and proper construction of employment equity or affirmative action policies now occur in many countries, not only in the West but also in other multiracial or multi-ethnic countries such as South Africa. The Canadian debate on human rights might also interest any society now confronting gay and lesbian rights, a relatively new topic on the international human rights agenda. The debate on indigenous peoples' rights and what should be done about them is relevant to other settler societies in the Americas or Australasia in which governments and citizens are attempting to make amends for past wrongs. Finally, the debate about who is responsible for the poor is of interest to all advanced capitalist societies, where poverty still exists in the midst of great wealth.

To summarize, the Canadian experience with human rights demonstrates four stages. In the early period of Canada's history, Canadians lived in a state of legal human rightlessness. From the mid-nineteenth to the mid-twentieth centuries, civil and political rights were gradually entrenched. From about 1950 to 1985, the legal and activist communities were preoccupied with assuring individual rights to non-discrimination. In the last four decades of the twentieth century, Canada also enjoyed a rigorous debate about the nature and necessity of group rights.

During all four stages of evolution of Canadian human rights law, the public (such as it was at each stage) was involved in discussions about the rights that Canadians should have. The institution of a strong human rights regime in Canada by the mid-1990s depended on a high degree of public agreement with legal norms. The public's agreement emerged in part from discussions among citizens themselves regarding what was just, and what unjust. This book reports on conversations about rights that citizens of Hamilton, Ontario, had with me, reflecting their conversations with others in their families, their communities, and in the voluntary and civic organizations of which they were members.

Chapter Outline

Qualitative sociological research often generates its own theoretical preoccupations as it progresses. That is what happened in this study.

I started with a list of general topics and a list of specific questions about each topic. Only some of these questions eventually generated responses that would engage an audience primarily interested in debates about human rights. This book is organized around such debates. It does not report on the views of the seventy-eight civic leaders on all the human rights issues about which I asked. Rather, it reports on their opinions on questions and dilemmas that are of interest to other thoughtful citizens, to policy-makers, and to scholars.

Thus, there is no separate chapter on one topic that readers might expect, that of women's rights. Although there was a separate section in the interviews on women's rights, by and large the responses were uncontroversial. For the Hamilton civic leaders, women's rights were obvious and unproblematic. The principle of equality for women was taken for granted. Even when I probed for possible hostility to feminists or feminism, I found very little.[70] The only areas of controversy had to do with employment equity for women, reported on in chapter 7, and possible contradictions between multicultural rights or indigenous rights and women's rights, reported on in chapters 6 and 8 respectively.

The chapters in this book, then, discuss human rights questions about which there is significant disagreement among the civic leaders, or that illustrate changing social norms, or that illustrate how civic leaders try to reconcile competing human rights principles or demands. Some of these questions have to do with the conflict between group and individual rights. Chapter 3 examines the conflict between individuals' rights to unfettered freedom of speech and the need for vulnerable groups to be protected from harmful speech, while chapter 4 examines the debate about whether there should be special sentencing for hate-motivated crimes of violence. Some questions have to do with the need to accommodate Canada's earlier individualistic, liberal view of human rights to the increasing diversity of Canadian society. Chapter 6 examines debates about the policy of multiculturalism and chapter 7 debates about employment equity. Some chapters address the assertion of previously hidden, submerged, or disreputable identities: chapter 8 examines indigenous rights and chapter 5 gay and lesbian rights. Two chapters examine types of rights that I believe are important but do not receive enough attention in the current Canadian discussion of human rights. Economic rights, examined in chapter 9, frequently receive short shrift in a discourse that is overly concerned, in my view, with identity, diversity, and social discrimination, as against the injustices and inequities of economic class divisions. Obligations to strangers, examined in chapter 10, are meant to remind the reader that the world as Canadians knew it in the twentieth century is unlikely to last, as the realities of global inequalities cause more and more people outside their borders to make demands on Canadians.

Chapter 2 discusses what it meant to Hamilton civic leaders to live in Canada. Despite their diverse ancestries and origins, the individuals interviewed for this study considered themselves Canadian; even most of those who were fairly recent adult immigrants thought of themselves this way. They were deeply loyal to Canada, and their thinking on the questions I posed to them was in the context of a profound commitment to Canadian social life. No one refused to answer questions by stating that his date of immigration was too recent, or that his identification was not with Canada but with his ancestral culture. The civic leaders' identification with Canada becomes clear in their referral in subsequent chapters to fundamental Canadian values of liberal individualism, equality and non-discrimination, and multiculturalism. This research population consists of a group of efficacious citizens, who felt competent to generate change in Canadian social policies and to make their voices heard. They claimed, and they acted upon, their right to citizenship, no matter where they came from, or how recently they had arrived in Canada.

Canada is becoming an increasingly diverse society. With such diversity comes discussion of whether individual human rights, upon which the Charter of Rights and Freedoms is in part premised, are suitable for all types of accommodation of new minorities. I addressed this question by asking the Hamilton civic leaders about freedom of speech, discussed in chapter 3, and hate crimes, discussed in chapter 4. Most of the civic leaders were willing to entertain stricter controls on the individual right of freedom of speech, if such controls would result in vulnerable groups feeling more comfortable in Canadian society. They were not so sure, however, that they supported stricter sentencing for hate crimes. On matters dealing with actual personal violence, about half argued for equal individual responsibility, regardless of the social status of victim or perpetrator.

The rights of individuals acting in ways that deviate from established social roles are also an important issue in contemporary Canadian human rights discussions. Gay and lesbian rights were high on the national agenda at the time I conducted my research. I was interested in how Canadians brought themselves to accept equal rights for this social group, against whom many in the past had harboured prejudices. Chapter 5 shows that many civic leaders had revised their opinions considerably during the course of the Canadian debate. Most of them favoured gay rights, although many still balked at permitting gays and lesbians to marry or to adopt children.

Gay and lesbian rights are often repugnant to members of new immigrant or religious groups entering Canada, who may come from countries where gays and lesbians are still subjected to severe punishments, including imprisonment and execution, and where such treatment is still approved by the population as a whole.[71] Yet the promise of multiculturalism suggests that these new groups should not be expected to give up their ancestral cultural norms. Does multiculturalism mean that basic human rights may be undermined if a culture is oppressive to women or to gays and lesbians? I explore this question in chapter 6. Most of the Hamilton civic leaders answered no, though most qualified their answers by suggesting that new citizens should be educated into acceptance of basic human rights values, that their private religious and cultural beliefs should be respected, and that eventually social change would bring about the desired result of acceptance of Canadian human rights principles.

Putting the principles of multiculturalism and equal rights together, some Canadians might think that there is a clear case for employment equity policies, in order to promote the economic achievements of minority groups. I explore this question in chapter 7. Of all the questions I posed to the Hamilton civic leaders, on this alone was there a noticeable split between whites and non-whites. A substantial number of the whites believed that employment equity programs would deprive their own children of jobs, not an insignificant worry given the high rates of youth unemployment in the mid-1990s. On the other hand, several non-whites thought that employment equity was an important aspect of the Canadian government's commitment to ensure that they would be treated as equal citizens.

Multiculturalism in Canada is a separate policy from rights for indigenous peoples. The rights of indigenous peoples, explored in chapter 8, caused the Hamilton civic leaders a good deal of confusion. While most felt that Canada definitely had a debt to indigenous peoples, they were very unsure about what should be done for them. Twelve civic leaders, in fact, thought that individual assimilation and equality was the solution to indigenous peoples' problems, while the rest of the civic leaders easily accepted group accommodation. At minimum, they wanted all legal obligations to indigenous peoples, such as treaty rights, to be sorted out. They had not, however, thought through the implications of indigenous self-government or self-determination.

Another human rights debate in Canada concerns the question of individual responsibility for oneself, as opposed to reliance on the collectivity. This is a key question with regard to economic rights and protection from poverty. In chapter 9, the Hamilton civic leaders wrestle with the question of responsibility. In an open, competitive, achievement-oriented society, how much responsibility do the poor have to take care of themselves, and how much responsibility does the society as a whole have to take care of the poor?

Both employment equity and the question of responsibility for poverty refer directly to the economic interests of Canadians. So, also, does the serious question of Canadian obligations to people whom I term in chapter 10 'strangers,' those who live outside Canada's shores. Most of the civic leaders believed those whom Canada admitted to its territory as immigrants or refugees should be treated as well as Canadian citizens, but they also believed they had a responsibility to Canadians first. Therefore, they had a lesser obligation to people outside Canada's shores.

Chapter 11 concludes by discussing the issues of compassion and empathy, group rights and rights conflicts, and the nature of community in Canada.

Chapter Two

Being Canadian

I'm a very proud Canadian, disgustingly so ... I have my family here, my roots here, I admire the Canadian personality. I admire the values that are strong in Canada ... values of honesty and hard work, of giving everyone a fair chance, of opening doors rather than closing doors, of embracing change ... I think we're a rather gentle people.

Susan

The attitudes of the Hamilton civic leaders to the questions I posed were intimately bound up with their own sense of being Canadian. They felt themselves to be active members of the Canadian social and political milieu, capable of influencing events, mobilizing resources, and achieving policy reform. Even those who had arrived fairly recently in Canada insisted on their full membership in the local and national society as loyal Canadians citizens. They claimed, and they acted upon, their right to citizenship, no matter where they came from, or how recently they had arrived in Canada.

One section of the interviews probed what it meant to these civic leaders to be Canadian. I asked whether they felt Canadian and what it meant to be a Canadian; at what stage in their lives, if ever, they had developed a sense of being Canadian; what a typical Canadian might be like and how he or she might behave; and whether it mattered if people living in Canada felt Canadian. The results of this section of the interviews showed that there was a sense of citizenship, a moral sense of belonging, among the civic leaders. They considered themselves Canadians. They referred to the opportunities and freedoms available to them in Canada, and the day-to-day respect they enjoyed. To be

Canadian, and recognized as such by others, was meaningful to them. Even relatively recent immigrants among the civic leaders did not define themselves primarily as members of their ancestral cultural communities. The Hamilton civic leaders were for the most part comfortable being Canadian, being immigrants, being members or not of communities other than the English-Canadian mainstream. The only significant exception, as will be discussed later in this chapter, was the attitude of three of the four Aboriginal civic leaders.

Immigrant and Native-Born Civic Leaders' Views of Being Canadian

As mentioned in chapter 1, thirty-six of the civic leaders were immigrants; among them were five infant, twelve child, and nineteen adult immigrants. I defined infant immigrants as people who were brought to Canada between birth and three years of age, child immigrants as people who were brought to Canada between the ages of four and seventeen years, and adult immigrants as people who immigrated at the age of eighteen or older. Those civic leaders who had been infant immigrants had no memory at all of life before Canada, while those who had been child immigrants had experienced the majority of their education and socialization in Canada. Both groups generally felt themselves to be more Canadian than members of any other society, including their parents' ethnic society. Adult immigrants also often insisted on their Canadian ethnicity, but were more likely to have a 'half-and-half' ethnic and national sense of loyalty.

Despite these variations among the thirty-six immigrants to Canada, almost all the Hamilton civic leaders had a strong sense of Canadian identity. In answer to the question 'How would you describe yourself in ethnic or racial terms?' eighteen described themselves as Canadians, for example, as 'Canadian first and foremost.' Another twenty-six described themselves as 'Canadian and other', for example, as 'Portuguese-Canadian of a Latino background.' These responses are consistent with much other research, which shows that when given the option, people living in Canada will identify themselves as ethnic Canadians.[1] A few people named non-Canadian ethnic groups only because they thought that it was not possible to be ethnic Canadians, and that they were obliged to think back to their ancestors' ethnicity.[2]

Among native-born civic leaders, there was a taken-for-grantedness about being Canadian. Bob, a white Canadian who described his ethnic background as 'Canadian first, my heritage would be Scot and English,' said, 'I can't imagine defining myself any other way [than Canadian]. I was born in this country, raised in this country ... I participate in Canadian society, I pay Canadian taxes. I carry a Canadian passport. I dare say ... I'm as Canadian as you can get.' For the native-born civic leaders, the meaning of being Canadian was usually that their ancestors were of Anglo-Scots, Irish, French, or northern European descent, and that their parents were also native-born; the original family immigrants to Canada would have been their grandparents or even more remote ancestors.

When asked what being Canadian meant to them, native-born Canadians frequently said they had never thought about it. For several, though, the feeling of being Canadian was reinforced when they had children. They then felt they had an obligation to teach their children about what it meant to be Canadian. Explained Michelle, '[On Canada Day] we typically get the kids to sing "Oh Canada." We do all kinds of silly little things but we talk about the country. We took my girls on a trip down Highway 2 [a local, older highway] to show them all the buildings and the churches and teach them about the country.'

For the most part, immigrant civic leaders also had strong feelings of being Canadian and could articulate those feelings quite easily. Infant immigrants had no memory of their life before Canada, and sometimes even no memory of having spoken another language. As Al, who had been brought to Canada from Italy at the age of two, said: 'I haven't known anything other than being a Canadian ... I have always appreciated my Italian background but I really did not understand that much about it, other than my parents were different than the rest of the world ... [B]ut I've always felt more connected with outside of the house. And was able to identify and wanted to identify more as ... being of Canada more than anything else.' Child immigrants typically began to distance themselves from their parents and to think of themselves more as Canadian than part of their parents' community once they entered school or began to speak more English than any other language. Hannah, who had come to Canada from Germany at the age of eight, said: 'I think I felt pretty Canadian right away ... [L]earning English makes you feel very Canadian somehow ... [B]ecause we didn't have any accent so there wasn't anything to distinguish, well, my name, but not super-major. I felt pretty Canadian. Especially in contrast to my parents ... who had accents.' These quotations confirm Breton's analysis that 'Second-generation individuals generally seek to distance themselves from the culture of origin ... This is part of their search for full integration in *their* society – that is, the one in which they were born.'[3] Breton is here speaking about Canadian-born children of immigrants (known in some Canadian discussion as 'second-generation immigrants'), not people who immigrated at young ages, but his analysis certainly applies as well to the infant and child immigrants among the Hamilton civic leaders.

Most of those who had immigrated as infants or children, like most children of first-generation immigrants among the Hamilton civic leaders, identified strongly with Canada. They experienced no sense of being 'at home' once they returned to the countries where they were born. Some had never returned and had little or no desire to do so; others had returned once or twice but felt like foreigners, or tourists, when they did. Karl, brought to Canada from the Netherlands at the age of two, explained, 'I don't have any memories of the old culture ... I visited once as a teenager and it was nice to see where I was born and see my relatives and so on. I'd like to go back sometime with my kids, but it's not ... a burning desire.' In fact, immigrants often felt more Canadian the first time they went 'home' to their birthplace; this visit was the catalyst to realizing their Canadian identity. 'I probably felt Canadian the very first time I went back to Italy. I realized I am Canadian,' said Emilio, whose parents had brought him to Canada when he was fifteen.

Among infant and child immigrants and children of recent immigrants, however, the feeling of Canadianness did vary by the ethnicity of their ancestors. People of British and northern European ancestry generally had very little sense of being of immigrant background. As Kevin, the son of Scottish immigrants, put it: '[A]s a child, I would have thought of myself as a Canadian ... [M]y understanding of immigrants ... [was] that white people weren't immigrant.' Child immigrants from southern Europe, and from non-European areas of the world, had a stronger sense of separation from Canadian society as a whole. In part this was bound up with dominant-culture perceptions of ethnicity or race at the time they immigrated. In the period of massive post–Second World War immigration, the 'swarthy-skinned' immigrants from southern Europe were routinely thought by Canadians of British ancestry to be less capable of intellectual work, more likely to be manual labourers all their lives, than the more easily assimilable Dutch and Germans. Thus, as a child immigrant from Italy, Emilio had strong memories of discrimination in the school system.

Among more recent child immigrants of colour, there were even stronger perceptions of racism. Nevertheless, by the time of the interviews almost all of these child immigrants defined themselves quite comfortably as Canadian.

Among adult immigrants there was also a strong insistence on the identity of being Canadian. For five adult immigrants from Britain or Ireland, who already spoke English before they came to Canada, this had been an easy identity to assume. 'I feel at home. It feels comfortable. I like it ... I think basically Canada is a pretty benevolent, well-intentioned, nice place. And I think people generally ... live good lives in Canada,' said Kari, who came to Canada when she was twenty-five. While only six of the twenty white immigrants had arrived in Canada as adults, fourteen of the sixteen non-white immigrants, who were also from non-European countries, had done so. In general, these non-white immigrants also insisted very strongly on their identity as Canadians: 'I've always felt Canadian. The minute I docked ... I mean, other people might not have accepted the fact, but in my mind and my heart I've been Canadian ever since I came to this country,' asserted Barry, who came to Canada from the Caribbean at the age of thirty-one. When asked if they felt Canadian, though, some adult immigrants said that they still felt, as it were, 'half and half.' The more recent the date of immigration, the more likely this feeling of 'half and half' was to exist. Having children and buying their first house made immigrants feel more established in Canada and more Canadian.

Finally, these Canadians tended to identify themselves in contrast to Americans. Not being Americans – having better qualities than Americans, being accepted in Europe more readily than Americans – was important to them. Many of the Hamilton civic leaders held quite negative stereotypes of Americans, who were generally viewed as louder, more aggressive, more pushy, more arrogant, and more competitive than Canadians. Muriel called Americans 'outgoing and ... blatantly bizarre.' Canadians, said Laurence, are 'not ostentatious like our neighbours.' The civic leaders also referred frequently to the extent of inner-city crime and decay in the United States, as evidence that Canada is a better place to live. Several of the black immigrants specifically stated that Canada was a better place for them to live, as blacks, than the United States. Mabel, who had lived in the United States after leaving the Caribbean and before coming to Canada, recounted, '[A]ctually, I didn't really know too much about my black heritage until I came here. And then when I saw there were a lot of black people who were talking about their heritage, celebrating it and so on, it helped me ... I really feel really great about being a Canadian, 'cause that's the only place that I was allowed to do that.'

Travel also reinforced a sense of being Canadian. Some civic leaders noted that they had felt very Canadian when they were in Europe, and were proud to display the Canadian flag on their clothes or backpacks. For Joel, who had experienced anti-Semitism in Canada in his early years, this feeling was particularly strong: '[W]hen I took a ... trip to Europe ... we travelled around and I was so thrilled to be accepted as a Canadian.' Beverley, who was black, said that despite being very aware of racism in Canada, 'when I go away to Europe ... I feel very proud to be Canadian ... I see the flag and I want to cry.'

That Canadians recognize themselves as Canadian when they are abroad is not surprising. Ethnicity is often recognized in the breach. It is only when they are away from Canada that Canadians begin to realize that they have a particular way of life, a particular way of looking at things, that they share with other Canadians but not with foreigners. In addition, current Canadian public discourse stresses multiculturalism and diversity. Thus, individual Canadians are encouraged to think about what are often very small differences between them and their fellow citizens.[4] Many of these small differences disappear when they encounter other Canadians abroad; instead, they recognize more easily what binds them together.

Canadian Characteristics

In an effort to obtain a picture of what a Canadian was, I asked the Hamilton civic leaders about typical Canadians, both their physical characteristics and their attitudes. Most of the native-born Canadians were reluctant to reply. Schooled in tolerance and multiculturalism, most replied that there was no typical Canadian, that when they thought of Canadians a rainbow of colours would float across their inner mind. Many agreed, however, that in their youth their vision of a typical Canadian was people like themselves. In the case of those of British or northern European ancestry, this meant, as Susan said, 'my idea as a child of a typical Canadian was a blue-eyed, white-skinned Anglo-Saxon.'

Many of the civic leaders had been raised in relatively homogeneous communities and had not encountered any noticeable ethnic or racial diversity until they grew up. Those older individuals raised in Canada had experienced in their childhood and youth a highly conformist society, in which the vast majority of the population was of European and Christian descent and the social standard was that of the dominant, British-origin culture. As Jacob, who was Jewish, described it, 'When I went to public school we sang Christmas carols. It was a Christian world and the Orangemen [Protestant nationalists] marched down the centre of Toronto on Orange Day ... And my neighbours were thinking of themselves as British and our flag had the Union Jack on it.'

Non-British infant and child immigrants, and children of non-British immigrants, tended to view 'Canadians' as those among whom they had grown up. This was the view of Isaac, the son of European Mennonite immigrants. In his youth, he viewed the English-speaking farmers surrounding his parents' farm as typical Canadians. Adult immigrants frequently said their stereotype before arriving in Canada was of white people of British background. This stereotype was usually presented merely as a fact, without any particular rancour. Immigrants also occasionally referred to 'Canadians' as people who played hockey, skied, or skated.

Some non-white immigrants simultaneously insisted on their own Canadianness and referred to 'Canadians' as whites, or those of British descent. As Basil, a black immigrant, said, '[W]hen I'm asked what nationality I am I say proudly Canadian ... I'm married to a Canadian. [RH: 'By that, what do you mean?'] I am married to a Canadian of Scottish ancestry. Which means ... she's white.' Such a dual perception is neither surprising nor contradictory. When immigrants insist on their status as Canadian, they mean that they have the legal status of Canadians, that they belong in Canada as much as anyone else, that they are contributing to the society and should be recognized as such. At the same time, in so far as they retain a dual identify or a strong sense of having come from another society, they will simultaneously use the term 'Canadian' to refer to native-born people from the dominant culture.

The civic leaders were much more willing to speculate upon a typical Canadian character than upon a typical Canadian background. Here an almost uniform picture emerged. According to these seventy-eight people, the Canadian character is quite admirable. Canadians are characterized by moderation, compromise, and tolerance. Canadians are also cautious, conservative, and slow to anger. Several white, native-born Canadians presented this picture: 'I think we're cautious people ... polite and temperate and sober and tolerant, law-abiding type of people,' said Colleen. This is not, however, merely a self-congratulatory opinion of white Canadians. Immigrants of colour shared this view: '[Typical Canadian behaviour is] sort of a quiet confidence ... [Y]ou don't find Canadians sort of boasting of what they have or their wealth ... [T]hey tend to be introverts, they tend to be sort of low-key,' said George, a black adult immigrant from the Caribbean. Canadians, in the view of the Hamilton civic leaders, are friendly, gentle, and kind people, respectful of others and especially of those who are different. Two civic leaders illustrated this respectfulness by saying that if someone bumps into a Canadian on the street, the Canadian will apologize.

In their general approach to government, the civic leaders viewed Canadians as calm, willing to accept what is done without a fuss. They felt that the Canadian tendency not to make a fuss contributed to the peace and stability of the country, and of the world in general. Internationally, Canadians soldiers are well known as members of peacekeeping forces, and that is a role to which, according to these seventy-eight people, they are well suited: '[W]e're [a] middle-of-the-road group. We're not fanatical ... and we're ... sort of back-seat kind of people ... I think we get involved in world affairs in a good sense, in a peacekeeping sense,' Isaac believed.

Thus, the Canadian self-image is of 'very good people.' These seventy-eight people, looking at themselves as Canadians, were well satisfied with what they saw.[5] This very positive self-image assisted the Hamilton civic leaders in their careers as activists. Their own views on political and social matters were, to them, important and worthwhile. They had a right to speak, and to be heard.

Freedom and Opportunity

The seventy-eight Canadians interviewed for this study did not root their admiration of Canada in an experiential vacuum. Both immigrants and the native-born were well aware of the freedoms they enjoyed, which were not available to most people in most countries of the world. They spoke of these freedoms in explaining their loyalty to Canada. 'I consider myself a Canadian ... I'm free to choose what I want to do. I have probably unlimited opportunities ... I'm free to make my own choices, live where I want to live, speak whichever language I choose to speak in my own home. I feel safe. If I decide to go shopping or walk down my street I feel safe in my community. I feel safe in my government's decisions so far. I sort of feel like I trust,' said Betty, inadvertently confirming the recent emphasis that democratic theory has put on the need for trust among citizens, and between citizens and the state.[6] Safety and comfort made these civic leaders feel that Canada was their country, their home, the place that their voices could be heard.

Two women specifically mentioned the opportunities available to their sex. 'I feel a lot of privilege living in Canada. I'm ... grateful that I was born here rather than in some other countries where women's lot is a lot different,' said Sofia, the daughter of immigrants from Italy. Similarly, two immigrants from Britain mentioned that they had better opportunities in Canada than they would have had in the United Kingdom, given their class origins. Dorothy noted, 'I'm very happy my parents came out after the war; I would have had a very different life had they stayed in England ... [In Canada] you can ... go as far as you really want to go ... I'm the only member of my family that has gone to university.' Immigrants from other countries also mentioned the opportunities available in Canada.

Although there was a general perception that Canada is a country in which one is free to do as one wishes, few civic leaders specifically mentioned civil and political liberties as reasons to feel good about being Canadian. Yin, who had immigrated from an authoritarian country in East Asia, mentioned his 'rights and privileges under the Charter of Rights and Freedoms' as the chief meaning of Canadianness for him. Kathleen, who was native-born, mentioned 'freedom of speech, of ability to live wherever you want and do whatever you want to do.' Two civic leaders mentioned the freedom to travel all across the country without encountering any officials or any border crossings: 'there's the freedom of going where you please in this country,' said Margaret. There was, however, little reference to such basic freedoms among the majority of civic leaders. Perhaps, these civil liberties are so familiar to Canadians that there is little overt perception of how valuable they are. As chapter 3 will show, the civic leaders trusted government to protect their basic rights, even to the point of being quite unworried about the possible detrimental effects of stricter controls on freedom of speech.

Importance of Feeling Canadian

Almost all the civic leaders, whether immigrant or native-born, thought that it was important for people in Canada to feel Canadian.

Feeling Canadian, they said, gave people a sense of community, a sense of belonging, and a feeling of loyalty to the country. 'I think all people need a source of grounding. We need some sort of safety, [a] safe place we can ... retreat to ... I think you do need ... a country that you feel home in, you can say "Yes, I live in Canada, I belong in Canada, it's where I'm comfortable, it's where I belong, it's where I feel home, it's where I feel that my neighbours are people that I'm comfortable having as neighbours,"' said Bob. Sarah, like Bob born in Canada and of British extraction, agreed: 'If you live in Canada and you are Canadian and you don't feel Canadian, then you're feeling alienated or left out or excluded ... and that is not a good thing ... [P]eople need to feel that they're part of the country.'

Without a feeling of being Canadian, citizens would not want to contribute to the community or to change things that might need changing. As Catherine, who was born in Canada and identified her ethnicity as Canadian, said, 'I think it makes you a better Canadian if you care about the country. If you care about the values we have or changing something that needs improving. If you don't care about it, then you're not going to work to change it.' Natalie, who was also born in Canada and who identified herself as 'Canadian first and foremost,' connected the sentiment of being Canadian with the likelihood of civic participation. '[Feeling Canadian] improves the experiences that you have in this country, and I think that it makes you want to participate in things like the political system, even on a local level. If you know that you are part of the government, if you know that you are responsible for the government ... then you're more willing to go out and try and make improvements in it and you'll feel as if you have the right to do that.'

Both immigrants and native-born Canadians stressed this need to belong to the community. Some cautioned, nevertheless, that immigrants should not feel obliged to discard their language or their original culture because they had come to Canada; they should just go ahead and live their lives as they wished. For these civic leaders, obeying the law, living peaceably, and earning one's own living was all that was required of a Canadian citizen. Speaking of her Italian parents, Sofia argued, 'I'm not invested in making sure everyone feels Canadian ... [M]y mom and dad didn't feel Canadian ... But they were really good citizens. I mean, they didn't break the law or they weren't disrespectful in any way ... they did no harm to anyone else.' These civic leaders realized that non-English-speaking first-generation adult immigrants often do not easily assimilate into the larger Canadian community. Most of them assumed that becoming Canadian was a generational matter, and that even if immigrants themselves did not feel Canadian, their children would grow up Canadian: 'It's a process ... a generational thing,' said Gina, who had come to Canada from Italy at the age of twelve.

Symbols and Rituals

Raymond Breton mentions the 'symbolic poverty' of Western societies, a lack of '"the kinds of symbols which make a person's life meaningful."' Symbolic statements of belonging, according to Breton, include symbols and rituals such as 'the flag; historical figures, and emblems ... ; dedication ceremonies; national holidays and their public celebration.'[7] The Hamilton civic leaders were certainly receptive to symbols and rituals of Canadianness. They frequently mentioned particular holidays or special events that had made a lasting impression on their sense of being Canadian.

For a few immigrants, becoming citizens had been merely an practical matter. Two child immigrants reported that they had taken out Canadian citizenship for strictly instrumental reasons, in one case because of possible repercussions from left-wing political activity at university and in another because of a desire to join the Canadian army. An adult immigrant stated that he had become a citizen in part to be eligible for certain jobs. For other immigrant civic leaders, however, becoming citizens had had a real emotional meaning. Almost all the people who had become citizens as adults, or who could remember the citizenship ceremony as children, had some emotional attachment to the event. As Eugene, brought to Canada from Italy at age eight, described it: 'I kept [my citizenship certificate] to this day. They came out shortly thereafter with the little card, the wallet-sized ID card with your picture, and although I have that, I still keep the original card which looks like a diploma, has beautiful artwork on it, and that's my citizenship and I was very proud of that.'

Some native-born civic leaders also expressed an attachment to the rituals and symbols of Canadian citizenship. Through service clubs, two individuals were in the habit of periodically attending citizenship court to help welcome new Canadians into the country. Obtaining a Canadian passport also had an emotional meaning for some civic leaders. Melissa, born in Hamilton, recalled this event with pride. 'Getting

my passport. That's pretty exciting ... It meant that I was Canadian ...
Getting my passport was exciting for me, as was the first time I travelled out of the country and came back again.'

Certain special events or national holidays were also important to
quite a few Hamilton civic leaders. Canada Day, July 1, was one such
holiday. Some merely celebrated it by hanging a flag outside their
home or summer cottage and having a family dinner; two mentioned
attending local Canada Day events. Lynn, though, made a full-scale
celebration of Canada Day. 'We have Canadian flags hanging in our
house ... and we have fireworks in our backyard and we have a Canada Day barbecue and we eat Canadian food at our barbecue – moose
burgers! ... We're all Canadian and we say "eh" all day ... And we all
wear red and white ... We light our fireworks and sing "Oh Canada."'

Other ceremonial occasions were also important to these civic leaders. Several who had been children or teenagers in 1967, Canada's centennial year, remembered it well as a time when their sense of being
Canadian was re-enforced. Karl had been very excited by all the centennial events. 'I really felt Canadian the centennial year, 1967 ... [T]he
flag-waving, I collected coins and stamps and that kind of thing ...
They gave us some medallions at school ... I remember there was the
centennial train pulling into town and that was a travelling museum
and so on. When you're twelve years old, that kind of thing, you're
very impressed.' Maya, who had been immersed in a closed, non-
English-speaking immigrant environment, found that the student
exchange she went on to Quebec during centennial year helped her to
feel Canadian: 'I think probably it helped a lot in terms of my background that there was another culture that was also Canadian and
wasn't English but was still Canadian.'

Other individuals mentioned other ceremonial occasions as very
important to their sense of Canadianness. Alexander, who had come to
Canada from India as a young adult, had travelled to Ottawa specifically to be present for the ceremonies surrounding Canada's 125th birth-
day. 'I feel proud of the 125th year of Canada celebration in Ottawa ... I
stood on the Parliament Hill there for two, three hours, couldn't even ...
move my foot ... Hundreds and thousands of people from all walks of
life, they were. This included black and white, blue and green ... That
probably had given me the boost of being a Canadian.' Three civic leaders were veterans of the Second World War and spoke with obvious
pride of their service to Canada during the war; to them, the November
11 Remembrance Day services were particularly important.

Other events in recent Canadian history also had meaning for these seventy-eight civic leaders. One or two mentioned how proud they had been when Canada won the Canada-Russia hockey series in 1972. Several others mentioned their pride when Canadians won medals at the Olympics.[8] Said Zelda, 'This is our country and I think that you have to feel some loyalty to this country, this country that gives you this way of life. I think that things like the Olympics where you hear we had gold medal winners, those are sometimes the kinds of things that bring out people's sense of feeling Canadian, and hearing the national anthem.' The annual Grey Cup football tournament was also an occasion for civic leaders to show their pride. Civic leaders also mentioned other Canadian institutions such as the Royal Canadian Mounted Police and the Canadian Broadcasting Corporation as symbols of Canada. Nicky mentioned that she was 'very proud to sing the national anthem' at her children's school, though in general the anthem seemed to have little or no significance for these seventy-eight people.

For many civic leaders, though, overt patriotism was not an admirable trait, nor one that Canadians should demonstrate. As Desmond Morton has put it, 'flaunting symbols might be called embarrassing and therefore un-Canadian.'[9] Muriel agreed: 'I don't believe in bumper stickers.' Kevin said, 'My heart doesn't beat quicker at the sight of a Canadian flag.' Some referred to the perceived jingoism and flag-waving of Americans with some disparagement. These Canadians were sometimes willing to display the Canadian flag on their houses or cottages, but they did not think it a necessary part of being Canadian; indeed, Angela found such display bad form. 'Now, as much as I wanted to put a Canadian flag out and actually thought about ordering a Canadian flag I just think, I don't know. That's not the Canadian way of showing you are a proud Canadian ... to be demonstrative.' For a few civic leaders, the very notion of patriotism was distasteful, and they preferred to think of themselves as citizens of the world, or as people who would make a contribution whatever the society they lived in. As Anthony put it, 'patriotism is a fairly dangerous behaviour. It tends to be exclusionary and I don't think that's very good.'

Patriotism for some of these individuals was action, not feeling. Sometimes, the action was to be critical of the government, to try to change the society you belong to. 'Do you take part in any ceremonies?' I asked Bruce. 'Yes,' he replied, 'displaying my anger at Queen's Park [the seat of the provincial government] ... [M]y loyalty is that I'm willing to stand up and argue on behalf of Canada at any time.' Olga, who had suffered very severely in her native country, then Communist, before escaping to Canada, believed very strongly that she had a duty to take advantage of the political liberties she enjoyed. 'Why do I send out the letters [to newspapers]? Why do I write the politicians? ... I care where Canada is going ... I appreciate what Canada did for me. Canada accepted me when I left Communist regime ... I try to give back something.'

The sincere and quite strong emotions expressed by many of the civic leaders about Canadian symbols and rituals suggest that perhaps these aspects of Canadian life are overlooked as an aspect of instilling a sense of Canadianness. True to their characterization of Canadians as lowkey and reticent, the people I interviewed did not want to wear their hearts on their sleeves. For the most part, their patriotism was private. Strong demonstrations of loyalty to the nation were considered to be in bad taste. Nevertheless, this was not a group of people without loyalty. They took pleasure in various Canadian rituals and institutions, which symbolized their identity to them.

Feelings of Exclusion

The picture of the seventy-eight civic leaders presented above, as people mostly satisfied with their lot, should not be taken to imply that the problems of racism and prejudice in Canada have been solved. I did not specifically ask questions about racism or prejudice, leaving it to the civic leaders to raise the issue if they thought it pertinent. Among the twenty-three people not of European ancestry, thirteen mentioned the problem of racial discrimination. So did one white parent of black children. Two members of the Jewish faith also mentioned minor and relatively recent anti-Semitic incidents they had experienced in Hamilton.[10] For some of those who mentioned racism, however, the problem was not severe and was understandable. As Laurence, who was black, said patiently, 'Canada is not perfect. It seems very slow to accept people who aren't white. So, but I think that that's Canada.'

A few of the people of colour felt racism keenly. Roy, who had immigrated fairly recently from East Asia, made it clear that he did not blame his own problems since immigration on racism, but rather on his difficulties with the language. Nevertheless, he thought his children would suffer discrimination. '[M]y kids ... one day they brought their report card and got so good 95, 97 ... and my kid says, "Aren't you proud of us?" "Yes, I am, but I want you guys to remember no matter how good you are ... you are still, your face is yellow, you have a sharp eye, you are [Asian], you have an [Asian] figure ... [T]o stay on the top you better be twice better than the white people." That's what I keep on telling my kids.' Alexander was especially annoyed by European immigrants who felt themselves to be more Canadian than immigrants from other parts of the world. 'Canadians ... have an instinct to treat the different-looking person differently. They don't readily accept them as they are ... [It] takes time to acknowledge you.'

Jacqueline, an immigrant from the Caribbean of African heritage, spoke very strongly of racism in Canada. 'I feel Canadian more when I'm out of the country than when I'm in the country ... [W]hen you're in the country you're more aware that you are less equal ... [A]s a black person I never really felt truly or [was] made to feel truly Canadian ... I feel more like a black Canadian than a Canadian because as a white person you are privileged. Me, I'm Canadian, but so far as I'm allowed to be.' Lily, a child immigrant from the Caribbean of mixed racial background, felt strongly alienated from the white Canadian community, and was the only infant or child immigrant to feel more at home in her place of birth than in Canada. '[T]here's always a sense ... of being different, right? Of somehow always, always being alien and alienated so that I don't feel Canadian because to me, I think Canadianness means whiteness ... [Y]ou see it as sort of being white people's country.' Linda, who was of very remote African ancestry and whose family had lived in Canada for many generations, was particularly annoyed by constant inquiries from strangers about her original homeland: '[N]o matter where I walk into, people say, "Oh, which island are you from?" ... [Y]ou with a white face and me with a black face, you hold more power and that's the way our community sees it.'

Of the four Aboriginal civic leaders, three asserted quite strongly that they did not identify themselves as Canadians. They considered themselves Aboriginal people; when they crossed the border to the United States they crossed as Aboriginals, not as Canadians. As Walter said, 'Well, I always put Aboriginal first. When I say Canadian, that's the way of life I have been brought up in ... I don't know my native language. I had to go and search for my native identity ... I swore allegiance to the Queen when I was a kid in school, not knowing what I know now, the atrocities that went on against native people ... the put-downs for the native people by previous governments ... I would have trouble until I saw some justice towards the native people in this land.'

The views of these three Aboriginal people confirm Darlene Johnston's contention that Aboriginals in Canada have been subjected to 'compulsory citizenship'; they are citizens only in so far as the government has decreed them to be, at its convenience and not necessarily taking into account their own desires.[11] As Sylvia said, 'When I go somewhere and they say, "Well, are you a landed immigrant, are you Canadian?" .... I have a really, really hard time ... I have to talk to someone with authority and let them know what my dilemma is because I'm not a landed immigrant and I don't feel I'm a Canadian citizen.'

Eight of the civic leaders of colour offered no accounts of having been discriminated against in Canada. Rather, they stressed their material comfort, the opportunities their children had had, and their gratitude that they had been born in or come to live in Canada rather than the United States or Britain. With the exception of one younger person, however, these people were older and, for the most part, professionally successful. A study conducted in Toronto in 1972, at which time most of these older professional black immigrants were already in Canada, confirmed that highly educated, white-collar West Indian immigrants were more likely to feel satisfied with their new society than their blue-collar counterparts.[12] Similarly, a later study published in 1994 concluded that Caribbean migrants in Toronto 'were on the whole satisfied in Canada,' and that migrants who found a fulfilling job, who found educational opportunities for themselves or for their children, and who owned a home were particularly likely to be satisfied.[13] The immigrants and non-Aboriginal members of minorities I interviewed, either from the Caribbean or elsewhere, tended to fit this picture.

Expressions of feelings of exclusion do not mean that the minority Canadians who still suffer from racism – other than Aboriginals – do not identify themselves as Canadians. The black Canadian human rights activist, Glenda Simms, has suggested that there are actually three categories of people in Canada: '"Canadians" (white Canadians), "Canadian citizen" (non-white Canadians), and Aboriginals.'[14] While this reflects a common perception among both whites and non-whites that 'real' Canadians are white, it exaggerates the extent of racism felt by non-whites in this study. Expressions of alienation, indeed of strong anger at racism, may have caused some of the minority individuals to feel less Canadian than whites or (in the case of Jewish civic leaders) Christians. Aside from the three Aboriginal civic leaders, however, almost all the members of minorities insisted strongly on their legal status as Canadians and their membership in the Canadian community.

Finally, readers might wonder if others among the civic leaders who occupied statuses that still suffer social discrimination in Canada, specifically women, gays and lesbians, and people with disabilities, expressed feelings of exclusion. With the exception of Lily, none of the thirty-eight women, of the five individuals who volunteered that they were gay or lesbian, or the one obviously disabled person among the civic leaders, stated that they felt these statuses excluded them in any way from Canadian citizenship or from participation in the Canadian community. Some of the strongest statements of patriotism cited above were from members of these groups, such as the statement by Bob, who was gay.

Canadian Citizenship

Canada is a nation of non-kin, of biological strangers. Aside from Aboriginal peoples, it is a nation composed primarily of individuals and families who immigrated during their own lifetimes, or whose not very distant ancestors (parents, grandparents, or great-grandparents) immigrated to Canada. Very few of the Hamilton civic leaders were more than third-generation Canadians. Melissa, who could refer back to her family's ownership of land in her local community since the early nineteenth century, was very rare indeed.

Identity in Canada is not defined by the ethnicity of one's ancestors,' however much the ideal of multiculturalism might make it seem that ancestry is the defining feature of one's identity.[15] At best, the European-origin Canadians interviewed in this study might be called 'weak ethnics': their interest in the ethnicity of their ancestors is quite weak, in some cases non-existent, and a minor part of their identity.[16] That they are weak ethnics is no surprise. Other research confirms, for example, that in the United States, by the third generation of immigration (i.e., people whose grandparents immigrated to the United States) ethnicity tends to be mainly symbolic.[17] Symbolic ethnicity best describes the Canadian situation as well, where identification with ancestral ethnicity is voluntary, personal, and often of very little salience to the individual.[18] In Canada, as has also been noted for the United States, the conversion of ancestral ethnicity to a symbolic matter may even start with the immigrating generation.[19]

Even the non-white first-generation Hamilton civic leaders did not exhibit a strong identification with their original ethnicity. Immersed as they were in the Canadian economy, Canadian educational system, and Canadian community and politics, they maintained at their strongest a dual, 'half-and-half' ethnic identity that faded as they spent more time in Canada. In addition, except for those few who expressed strong feelings of exclusion, the civic leaders felt that they enjoyed dignity and respect. The stereotyped picture of Canadian behaviour presented by the Hamilton civic leaders was by and large positive. State ideologies of fairness, anti-racism, and multiculturalism contributed to this feeling of dignity and respect. The civic leaders valued the policy of multiculturalism, which made them feel that they were welcome in Canada, yet not obliged to become like 'Canadians' (of British or northern European origin). This was especially the case for immigrants of colour.

This group of Canadians suggests that Spinner's notion of 'pluralistic integration' is a better way to define the melding and growing together of people of different ancestral backgrounds than the idea of multiculturalism, which suggests a certain static nature to culture and identity, a formal coexistence of separated cultures that belies the Canadianness of even very recent immigrants.[20] In effect, there is a paradox in Canada: it is because there is a dominant monoculture of respect for human rights and individual freedom that multiculturalism – in the limited sense of voluntary ethnicity – can thrive. As Spinner has noted, 'the demands of liberal citizenship in the public sphere and in civil society make it hard, although not impossible, for liberal citizens to maintain robust ethnic identities.'[21]

The reality of day-to-day identity for these seventy-eight civic leaders was Canadianness. The ties that bind in Canada are civic ties, acknowledgment that a shared life, shared rights and privileges, and shared legal status create Canadians. Above all, as Spinner maintains, 'Citizenship is ... about standing ... To have standing, to be an equal citizen, is to be judged on one's actions. It means that others listen to you in public settings ... Equal citizenship means being given the opportunities to do what others can and to fail or succeed on one's own merits.'[22] Most of the Hamilton civic leaders felt that they had such standing and were indeed listened to in public settings.

Both immigrant and native-born Hamilton civic leaders were aware of the advantages of living in Canada, compared to other societies, yet the sense of loyalty or patriotism they exhibited was low-key. While they were willing to speak of the ceremonies and events that moved them as Canadians, they felt, for the most part, that it was in poor taste to be outwardly patriotic. The self-image of Canadians as quiet, compromising, and peace loving was important to them. They enjoyed being recognized as Canadians when they travelled, and certainly made large efforts to differentiate themselves from Americans. Most immigrants had adjusted quickly to 'being Canadian' and insisted on their identity as such. Their citizenship as Canadians was important to them, even when they had trouble expressing this feeling. These were not tepid Canadians, to use Kaplan's terminology.[23]

These seventy-eight people illustrate how one becomes a citizen, how one develops a sense of belonging in a society. Their personal experiences and life stories made them feel Canadian. Citizenship is not simply a matter of loyalty to an abstract entity, in this case the country of Canada. While the teaching of national history and geography, the creation of myths of nationhood through museums or school trips, and the creation of national ideologies through state symbols such as flags are all tools to create a sense of loyalty to the state, loyalty is also rooted in much more mundane matters.[24]

These mundane matters include the quality of life offered to Canadians. All Canadians benefit from a freedom that is not only permitted, but taken for granted. The basic civil and political liberties are well protected in Canada, especially for the essentially middle-class group of people interviewed in this study. Economic rights are also protected, although imperfectly, as will be discussed in chapter 9. All Canadian children are offered the right to tax-supported education, and all Canadians are protected by a national health care system. There is undoubtedly a class system in Canada, and life in poverty is not pleasant, but the Canadians in this study were aware that poverty Canadian-style does not approach poverty elsewhere in the world. Several of them had been raised in poverty either in Canada or abroad, in some cases quite dire.

Wealth and opportunity were and are among the major incentives for immigrants to come to Canada; they are also what make immigrants relatively satisfied with their lives in the country. Those non-white Hamilton civic leaders who did not express a sense of exclusion from the greater Canadian society had done well professionally. They, and often their children, had good jobs. The feeling that Canada is a free country, where opportunities are there for those who would avail themselves of them, permeated the views of almost all these civic leaders except, tragically, three of the four Aboriginal civic leaders.

The individuals interviewed in this study were also citizens in the active sense of the word. All were active in the community. They exemplified the idea that citizenship is practice, not merely a legal status.[25] As Morton has noted, 'a basic proposition of Canadian citizenship [is that] people acquire it by experience and commitment.'[26] These citizens, all civic leaders, felt strongly that they had an obligation to their community. Almost all stated that it was important for people in Canada to 'feel' Canadian, to feel that Canada is their home and that they belong there. A chief reason for feeling Canadian is that a sense of belongingness will enable the citizen to act, to change things that need changing.

Paul Martin, Sr, introducing the Canadian Citizenship Act into Parliament in 1946, stated that 'citizenship is the right to full partnership in the fortunes and in the future of the nation.'[27] Writing almost fifty years later, Kaplan contended that citizenship should mean 'belonging ... in the sense of participating in national purposes. Citizenship can serve as a focus of benefits from and obligations to collective projects and shared values and goals transcending one's race, religion, language, ethnicity, and region.'[28] For the Hamilton civic leaders, this is what citizenship did mean. Identity is a state of mind; to think of oneself as Canadian is to be Canadian. The Hamilton civic leaders were loyal to the country of Canada 'as a project'; they felt part of Canada and emotionally bound to it.[29] The single significant exception to this assertion was the three Aboriginal civic leaders, who said they had no reason to call themselves Canadians, even though they were active in Canadian society.

Mavis Gallant, the Canadian writer of short stories, said, 'A Canadian is someone who has a logical reason to think he is one.'[30] Most of the seventy-eight Canadians interviewed in this study had very good logical reasons to think of themselves as Canadian: social acceptance (despite some racism), freedom, opportunity, and the capacity to act in the public arena. They were citizens in the 'thick' sense of being efficaciously involved in the community, not merely in the 'thin' sense of legal status.

These very good logical reasons to think they were Canadian were also what equipped the Hamilton civic leaders to think about public policy issues such as the human rights questions to which this book now turns, and to express their opinions in confidence that they would count.

Chapter Three

Moral Circumspection and Freedom of Speech

You're never going to get moral circumspection without some legal impositions. People aren't going to control what they have to say, without having some measurable restrictive legislation ... All of these things ... have to be in balance.

Michelle

Freedom of Speech: A Problematic Right

As active citizens in their community, the Hamilton civic leaders were used to discussing question about justice and human rights that were reported in the media. One such recurring question in late-20th century Canada was what, if any, limits should be put on freedom of speech. This question especially addressed whether citizens should curb their tongues to avoid offending vulnerable groups. Discussion of freedom of speech in Canada often focuses on a few key legal cases, which have come to public attention because of legislation limiting hate speech. Many of the Hamilton civic leaders were aware of these cases, and had thought quite seriously about the limits that should be put on hate speech.

For most of the civic leaders, free speech was not a fundamental human right deserving of special protection, but rather one among a competing set of values, the most competitive being equality, nondiscrimination, and multiculturalism. Thus, this is the first of several chapters that show how the Hamilton civic leaders thought through ways to protect both individual rights and the rights of vulnerable groups. The majority of these citizens agreed that in Canada, certain types of freedom of speech should be curbed in the interests of the higher good of a well-functioning community, in which all groups feel secure and protected. At the same time, most did not worry that curbs on freedom of speech might undermine their own individual rights.

This chapter explores the Hamilton civic leaders' attitudes to freedom of speech by focusing on several specific issues. I frequently introduced examples that I thought might be familiar to the civic leaders; depending on the individual, I might introduce an example about racism, anti-Semitism, or homophobia. To assess their opinions on 'Canadian values' that in their view ought to be promoted by servants of the public, I also asked the civic leaders about the rights to free speech of teachers and politicians. To ascertain their ideas about conflicting rights – the liberty of individual free speech versus the equality of groups suffering discrimination – I asked about the right of the Ku Klux Klan to demonstrate, the right of citizens to blaspheme, and the right to make or use adult pornography. The Ku Klux Klan is an organization many Canadians perceive to promote hatred against identifiable groups such as blacks, Jews, and Catholics;[1] blasphemy can be construed to be offensive to members of minority religious groups; and pornography can be construed to promote hatred of and violence against women.

While it would be convenient to classify each of the seventy-eight civic leaders as having consistent pro- or anti-free-speech positions, it is not possible to do so. The civic leaders were seriously conflicted about the role of free speech in Canadian society. In the course of their interviews, many would move from a position favouring unrestricted speech to one favouring stronger restrictions than presently exist in law. Many had 'gut reactions' to well-known civil liberties cases regarding hate speech, but had not thought these cases through to any sort of consistent position. Some had not thought of pornography or blasphemy as freedom-of-speech issues at all, until questions were posed to them; thus, they were thinking through their positions on those issues as they spoke.

The way these Hamilton civic leaders think reflects the larger North American and Canadian debates on freedom of speech. This debate has been most strongly discussed in the university, as many books attest, but it is also part of public discussion.[2] 'Free' speech, in the eyes of many of its critics, is freedom to commit speech *acts* that are, or can be, harmful to the targets of that speech. Freedom of speech as an individual right is often thought to interfere with the collective rights of vulnerable groups to protection against threats of violence and demeaning group insults. In this view, there is no such thing as speech separate from its consequences.[3] The very principle of liberal democracy, built upon the ideal of equal, autonomous citizens, is a sham, in so far as it does not recognize the continued inequalities among many groups of people, most notably those identified by race, ethnicity, religion, gender, or sexual orientation. Stereotyping speech, such as the stereotyping of women or of persons of African descent, is an act of aggression and ought to be controlled, much as any other act of aggression against a specific group of people, or member of such a group, ought to be controlled. The term often used for this is 'offensive speech'; the principle proposed is that speech which a vulnerable group, or member of such a group, finds offensive ought not to be permitted.

In Canada, freedom of speech has always been insecure. After the Second World War, Canadians holding left-wing views suffered along with the victims of McCarthyism in the United States, not least as a result of the Gouzenko affair.[4] The right of Jehovah's Witnesses to criticize Roman Catholicism was prohibited in Quebec under the regime of Premier Maurice Duplessis in the 1940s and '50s; the Witnesses' struggle to obtain freedom of speech was a key political struggle defining that right in Canada.[5] Canadians tolerated with little protest the detention of hundreds of persons under the War Measures Act, imposed to combat terrorism in Quebec in 1970; many were detained merely because of what they had said or were believed to think.[6] The battle for academic freedom did not really begin until the 1950s, and it took some considerable time before that principle was firmly entrenched in Canadian universities.[7]

Freedom of speech is not a right that preoccupies human rights activists in Canada. Canadians take such fundamental liberties as freedom of speech for granted.[8] In its Article 2 (b), the Canadian Charter of Rights and Freedoms (1982) protects 'freedom of thought, belief, opinion and expression,' but under Section 33 of the Charter, as noted in Chapter 1, this clause can be overridden by Parliament or any provincial legislature for a renewable period of five years. Thus, freedom of speech in Canada is a 'soft' right, less protected than, for example, minority-language (English or French) educational rights, which cannot be overridden under Section 33.

Canada also has hate speech laws that prohibit both the advocacy and promotion of genocide, and, more generally, the wilful public promotion of hatred against any identifiable group.[9] In this, Canada follows international law. The International Covenant on Civil and Political Rights states explicitly, in Article 20 (2), that 'Any advocacy of national, racial or religious hatred that constitutes incitement to discrimination, hostility or violence shall be prohibited by law.'[10] The United Nations International Convention on the Elimination of All Forms of Racial Discrimination also says that States Parties 'shall declare an offense punishable by law all dissemination of ideas based on racial superiority or hatred' and 'shall declare illegal and prohibit organizations, and also organized and all other propaganda activities, which promote and incite racial discrimination' (Article 4, a and b).

In keeping with the tenor of both Canadian and international law, most of the Hamilton civic leaders were willing to tolerate some restrictions on freedom of speech, believing such restrictions add to the greater good of the entire society. In their view, the entire society will benefit if minority and vulnerable groups are protected by controls on unwarranted speech. A harmonious society requires moral circumspection in the exercise of individual rights.

Community Harmony and the Need to Balance Rights

I started each discussion of hate speech by asking the civic leaders, 'Should people be allowed to say or print anything they want?' I used this question as an indication of their summary views on freedom of speech. I coded nine civic leaders as holding strong pro-free speech views, and another eleven as being mildly in favour of free speech. Among these twenty individuals, seven people, or 35 per cent, had identities that might render them vulnerable to hate speech attacks: one was gay, one Jewish, one Aboriginal, two black, and two members of other minorities. This roughly reflected the percentage of the group as a whole that was constituted by members of such potential victim groups. Among the rest, forty approved of mild controls of speech, while eighteen wanted strong controls. Thus, 74 per cent favoured controls on freedom of speech, exactly the same percentage that Sniderman et al., in their much larger national survey, found believed in 'laws prohibiting speech or writing "that prohibits hatred toward a particular racial or religious group."'[11] I coded as strongly in favour of free speech those who expressed strong misgivings about limiting free speech. I coded as strongly in favour of controls on free speech those who argued explicitly for stricter legal controls. Those either mildly in favour of free speech, or mildly in favour of controls, were trying to balance the principle of free speech with their belief that some controls were warranted; whether I coded them as mildly in favour of freedom of speech or mildly in favour of increased controls depended on my judgment of the degree to which each of these two positions influenced them.

So few people were coded as having strong pro-free-speech positions that it is worth analysing their reasons in detail. Three who held this position were worried about their own right to free speech. Kathleen, a pro-life activist, believed in the right of anti-abortionists to picket abortion clinics, a right that had been legally restrained in the province of Ontario:[12] '[A] lot of people ... who were just gently, quietly walking in front of these places, were arrested ... and I think that a peaceful demonstration ... [should be permitted].' Henry, the oldest civic leader, held a variety of fairly extreme right-wing opinions: 'I think they'll be coming out with a new [hate speech] law ... And this scares me, because it's coming around to restricting the voice of freedom again.' Sylvia, who was Aboriginal, was aware that for many years there had been legal restrictions on Aboriginals' rights to freedom of expression and assembly in Canada.[13] '[I value freedom of speech] especially for my people, we've been silent for so long. We didn't have a valid voice, we weren't listened to, we weren't heard.'

Other civic leaders among those coded as either strongly or mildly in favour of freedom of speech expressed a general concern that the right to freedom of speech must be protected; of these, three were in professions such as journalism and law, and would be directly affected by controls. Nora, who was one of those, said, 'I think that we can ... have healthy debates ... and come to reasonable conclusions. I think Canadians are pretty good at noticing ... when it's a wing-nut statement.' Dan was the only person not in a profession directly threatened by restrictions on speech, and who also had no direct personal fear of such restrictions, who nevertheless strongly defended freedom of speech. He argued, '[P]eople have the right to disagree and to be offensive if they want ... I wouldn't want the speech police telling me what I could say and what I couldn't ... I don't believe in censoring any transmission of ideas: I think that's dangerous.' One or two civic leaders feared excessive government control: 'I just hate getting into a situation where the government controls everything, everything that you think, everything that you see, everything that you do,' explained Angela. Roy, who was a fairly recent immigrant from an area of the world where Communism was a real threat, was worried about Communist censorship.

Those mildly in favour of freedom of speech also worried about speech's harmful effects. Said Martin, a member of an ethnic minority, '[T]hat's one of the fundamental rights, freedom of speech ... you can give an opinion. But I hate to see people bash other people. You know, something that incites hatred to other people, that's not right.' The dominant viewpoint, held by the forty people who favoured mild controls on freedom of speech and the eighteen who favoured strong controls, was that such controls are necessary for community harmony. Such harmony meant that all individuals would feel comfortable in the community, regardless of their background, and also that all vulnerable groups would be protected. Speech might lead to harmful action. Even if it does not, offensive speech in itself is an act with harmful consequences, which upsets its victims, damages their self-esteem, and makes them feel that they are second-class citizens. Mabel, a black immigrant, argued, 'I think that our society is based on creating a safe environment for everybody, so we cannot say, "All right, some people in our society, and maybe the majority, feel that just because we are black or women or gays, that they can get away with insulting us." ... I don't feel that people should have freedom of speech in that respect ... That's [being] against a person for being who they are.'

A healthy society, in the view of these Hamilton civic leaders, is one in which there is a balance of rights. To 'give a little' on freedom of speech is to enhance a greater value. No one should take the right of freedom of speech to an extreme. As Gina, not a member of any identifiable minority and therefore presumably not at personal risk, said: 'I hate restricting freedom of speech ... But when it becomes hate literature and hatemongering, then it's wrong. Somebody has to put some kind of balance in society ... establishing balance is very important.'

These concerns about the harmful effects of unfettered free speech were so strong among eighteen civic leaders that they were willing to argue for very strict laws to prohibit what they saw as hate speech. Said Alexander, a South Asian immigrant, '[I]f anything that I see in print ... is objectionable to the basic human values, it should not be printed. If it should be against a certain group or a certain individual, it is again interfering with the other person's freedom of speech. To me, often, society, or [a] certain group in society, come[s] up with the certain titles like freedom of speech, and extend[s] it to such an extent that it doesn't even belong under that title.' Matthew, a native-born minority Canadian, reinforced this position: 'Certainly the degradation of people, the degradation of groups, the slandering of groups in our society isn't acceptable, absolutely not ... [P]ublic-type speeches, people in the public, written documents, things of that nature that [are] degrading any group should be reviewed, edited, controlled to some degree, absolutely.'

Nor were those coded as favouring strong controls on freedom of speech the only individuals willing to entertain the idea of stricter laws. Allowing for multiple answers, fifty-one suggested stronger laws. Yet when direct questions were put to them regarding how best to control offensive or hurtful speech, they replied in ways that suggested some ambivalence, a feeling that it would be unwise to go too far with the law, and perhaps better to rely on other ways to control speech. Fifty-nine people suggested either using 'good speech against bad speech' (a phrase I introduced directly into some discussions), or stronger moral controls on speech. Said Christopher, a white Canadian, 'I would have no trouble with verbal sanction or verbal sort of response. Probably more than I had done in the past ... I would encourage other folks to confront that kind of speech ... but legal sanctions ... I think that would be kind of extreme in its own right.' Eugene, also white, agreed: 'People should be better behaved. The laws are there already ... but we forget ... common courtesy ... [W]e've become very confrontational, and confrontation ... becomes violent.'

Thus, these civic leaders advocated both stronger legal controls on hate speech, and promotion of moral circumspection and tact in the social realm. Threats to freedom of speech by government or police worried very few. The more general view was that government could be trusted to strengthen controls on speech, in the interests of more important Canadian values.

'Canadian Values' and Freedom of Speech in Public Life

The legal prohibition on speech that incites discrimination is at the heart of the Canadian debate about what limits should exist. To many Canadians, freedom of speech may be a fundamental aspect of liberal democracy, but since liberal democracy is secure in Canada, perhaps some attention should be paid to the greater good. The greater good is often defined in terms of group rights or multiculturalism.

Multiculturalism is a key Canadian value, enshrined in Article 27 of the federal Charter of Rights and Freedoms, which states that 'This

Charter shall be interpreted in a manner consistent with the preservation and enhancement of the multicultural heritage of Canadians.' In
1988 the federal government introduced the Multiculturalism Act,
which states that it is the policy of the government of Canada to 'recognize and promote the understanding that multiculturalism is a fundamental characteristic of the Canadian heritage and identity.'[14] The
booklet that the government distributes to prospective citizens lays
great stress on Canada's multicultural policy.[15] In his majority judgment convicting James Keegstra of hate speech (this case is discussed
below), then Chief Justice Dickson also referred to multiculturalism as
a key Canadian value: 'Multiculturalism cannot be preserved let alone
enhanced if free rein is given to the promotion of hatred against identifiable cultural groups.'[16]

In the view of the Hamilton civic leaders, if Canada is to be a multicultural nation in which all races, ethnic groups, and religions are
equally at home and equally respected, then perhaps restrictions
on freedom of speech should be even stiffer than they are now. Perhaps offence should be something against which vulnerable minority
groups should be protected. In the new, heterogeneous Canada that is
a result of open (non-racially or religiously biased) immigration since
the 1960s, perhaps multiculturalism should be a value that overrides
individual freedoms.[17] This is the debate that the Hamilton civic leaders confronted.

This debate intersects with the wider international debate on the
meaning of individual, as opposed to group, rights.[18] The individual
right to unfettered freedom of speech is viewed by some Canadians as
a threat to the rights of vulnerable groups to live in peace and security.
Verbal offences against a group are a serious matter, likely to result not
only in psychological but also in physical harm. A public atmosphere
of deep respect for vulnerable groups is a necessary protection of their
rights, even if such an atmosphere requires stifling the free speech
rights of some Canadian individuals. In the opinion of those who
favour stricter hate speech laws, the liberty of freedom of speech must
be balanced against the equality of groups in Canada, especially the
equality of groups such as women, gays and lesbians, members of
'racial' minorities, and Aboriginal peoples.

Many of the Hamilton civic leaders thought that it was incumbent
upon public figures to show their commitment to the Canadian value
of multiculturalism. The need to exercise self-control in speech, in
order to avoid offending others, applied to no one more than to those

in public life. Representatives and servants of the public should not exercise their individual citizenship rights in an unrestrained manner while speaking in their official capacities. Both teachers and politicians, the civic leaders felt, should always be aware of and conform to general public beliefs about appropriate types of speech.

Teachers

Two freedom of speech incidents involving teachers had been in the Canadian public eye in the 1980s and '90s. One involved the long saga of James Keegstra, a high-school history teacher in Alberta who routinely taught his students that the Jews were responsible for some of the worst problems of European history. After long trials under Canadian hate-speech laws, Keegstra was convicted by the Supreme Court of Canada.[19] The other case involved Malcolm Ross, a high school mathematics teacher in New Brunswick who, outside the classroom, wrote and distributed literature construed to be anti-Semitic. The Supreme Court of Canada ruled that Ross should not be allowed in the classroom; he was transferred by his school board to a non-teaching job.[20]

With these cases in the back of my mind, I asked each civic leader whether teachers should be allowed to present their personal opinions in the elementary or high-school classroom. I presented three optional responses: that teachers should never express their own opinions in the classroom; that teachers could express their opinions, as long as they distinguished between them and fact; and that teachers should be free to express their opinions. Allowing only one answer per person, thirty-eight civic leaders said teachers should not express any opinions. Thirty-two said they could express their opinions as long as they distinguished them from fact, but most also advised that this applied only to older students. Eight said teachers should be free to express their own opinions.

The Keegstra and Ross issues brought out the dominant response quite clearly, as the opinion of Nicky, a white Christian parent of school-age children, shows. 'What that person [Keegstra] is saying might be something that he believes in, but there's certain guidelines and restrictions, in terms of what you're feeding into the kids' minds ... You really need to keep things within an acceptable boundary.' Those who thought that teachers could present their own opinions, as long as they made clear that they were only opinions, were nevertheless cautious about teachers' even going this far. 'I don't see how a teacher could not present opinions ... However ... they should be very cautious in an elementary school and in [a] touchy subject ... when it might affect on a person's view of another group of people,' said Melissa, like Nicky a white parent with children in elementary school. Most of those who said teachers should be free to express their own opinions nevertheless qualified their statements, saying, for example, as did James, that teachers' opinions had to be 'sensible.'

Twenty of the Hamilton civic leaders turned out to be teachers, former teachers who had entered other professions, or retired teachers.[21] They were particularly concerned, therefore, with the teachers' role in the classroom. Their most common response was that teachers should not use the classroom as a platform for their own beliefs. Rather, the teacher's duty was to reflect community standards. Susan said, 'I don't think ... [a teacher] should be allowed to present a moralist stance that is not mainstream.' In the case of the Catholic school board, the teachers' duty was to reflect the teachings of the Church.[22] Emilio, a Catholic teacher, said, '[T]eachers are there to impart in example and action and the actual teaching, the teachings of the Catholic Church.'

Underneath these opinions was the belief that there is such a thing as community values. In the case of Catholic schools, the community was circumscribed by religion and the values were clear, as they were laid down by the Catholic hierarchy. In the case of public schools, the civic leaders believed that there was a broad national consensus on values. Multiculturalism was a core Canadian value, which teachers were expected to impart to their students. Multiculturalism demands courtesy to others, tolerance, and respect for difference, in order best to ensure social harmony in the schools and elsewhere. This respect for difference was especially important for people of colour and Aboriginal people. A harmonious community was one in which all members felt comfortable, not only as individuals, but also as members of their multicultural ethnic or religious groups. These values were viewed to be just as much a part of the Catholic as of the officially secular, public educational system.

Therefore, within the community in general, speech that might be construed to be offensive to these multicultural groups or to any particular members of them had to be curtailed, either by moral suasion or by compulsion. The speech of public servants such as teachers had to be particularly circumspect, as teachers both represented the values of the wider society and transmitted them to younger generations. It was incumbent upon teachers to transmit the general value now known in Canada as multiculturalism; that is, non-discrimination and respect for those who differ.

Politicians

Politicians, even more than teachers, are responsible for transmitting community values. The Hamilton civic leaders were almost unanimous in their belief that public officials should be extremely circumspect and tactful in what they said. Again, they assumed a commonality of values among all Canadians, even though there are sharp debates about such matters as employment equity, homosexuality, or appropriate immigration and refugee flows among politicians of the left, centre, and right in Canada.

None of the civic leaders thought that public officials, either elected or appointed, should be free to say whatever they wanted. Most said that public officials had a duty not to say anything that might be offensive to any identifiable ethnic, cultural, or religious group. Their duty was to represent all members of the community.

This issue was current at the time of some of the interviews. In May 1996 Bob Ringma, a federal Member of Parliament from the then Reform Party (in 2000 superseded by the Canadian Alliance), was reported in the press to have said that if he were a shop-owner, and the presence of a black employee in his store drove away racist customers, he 'should have the freedom to say "Hey, I don't need you in my employ," or "I'm going to switch you to the back of the shop."'[23] Several civic leaders alluded directly to this incident in discussing the free speech rights of elected politicians, suggesting that it was the responsibility of the Reform Party to discipline its Member. 'I think if that Member of Parliament is representing the government and the government is saying it represents equal rights ... The government should make sure ... that its representatives also appear to support those values, in terms of if an M.P. were to say "nigger" then that should be something that's abhorrent to government, and they should be chastised by the government,' said Carol, a white parent of a black child.[24]

Most of the civic leaders said politicians making objectionable statements should somehow be controlled from within their own political party. '[S]ince he is in a much more responsible position [than ordinary citizens] he shouldn't do that ... [H]e has a higher responsibility, he would be expected not to say things that are going to injure a certain group of people ... He should be disciplined, yes,' explained Yin. Twenty-four people said that it was the duty of the voters to ensure that politicians guilty of such offensive speech lost the next election. Louise, like Carol a white parent of black children, argued, '[I]f you're saying that kind of stuff ... maybe the best place for you is not in the political forum ... [W]hen you decide to become a politician, you should be thinking about everybody that you're representing, not just the few ones like yourself.'

Once again, the civic leaders' viewpoint was that there is a consensus of values in Canadian society. Certain types of opinions are beyond the pale; they should not be expressed. By 1996 public expressions of racial opprobrium had been socially taboo in Canada for about thirty years, of prejudice against women for about twenty years, of prejudice against gays and lesbians for about ten years. While for some Hamilton civic leaders, expressions of prejudice might be tolerated among the public at large, Canadian politicians were thought to have a duty to express what the civic leaders saw as 'Canadian values.'

Freedom of Speech versus Group Protection

'Canadian values,' both explicitly in government pronunciations and in the minds of these civic leaders, include sensitivity to the needs of vulnerable groups in society, if not actual legal group rights. Several discrete issues show how the civic leaders reacted to speech that they thought could harm vulnerable groups. The rights of racists, blasphemers, and those who manufacture or use pornography all raised the possibility of such harm: in the first case, against blacks, Jews, and Catholics, but most specifically blacks; in the second, against minority religious groups; and in the third, against women.

The Ku Klux Klan

Related to the more general right to freedom of expression is freedom of assembly. Freedom of assembly is particularly problematic when it protects those who wish to assemble in order to express their discriminatory or hate-filled opinions. Several of the civic leaders referred to a case well known in both the United States and Canada. This was the attempt in 1976 by American Nazis to march through the town of

Skokie, Illinois, where many Holocaust survivors lived.[25] More well known to the civic leaders was the existence in Canada of the Ku Klux Klan, a group believed by most to hold explicitly racist views about blacks; some people also referred to the Klan's discriminatory views about Jews and Catholics.

I asked the civic leaders whether the Klan should be permitted freely to hold demonstrations, or whether it should be banned from holding them. I also presented a third option, that the Klan should be permitted to demonstrate, but only if demonstrators did not carry any signs with hate-filled messages on them. Fifteen individuals thought the Klan should be permitted complete freedom to demonstrate; thirteen thought it should be permitted to demonstrate as long as demonstrators carried no hate messages on their signs; and forty-nine thought that the Klan should be completely banned. This 63 per cent favouring a complete ban conforms closely to the two-thirds of Canadians that Sniderman et al. found believed that the rights to freedom of expression of groups they disliked should be restricted.[26]

Among those who thought that the Klan should be permitted complete freedom to demonstrate, the attitude was more a pragmatic than a principled defence of freedom of speech, although some contended that to curb the Klan's freedom might imply others' freedom could also be curbed. As Maya put it: 'I can think of other demonstrations people might also disagree with, but if you denied one you'd have to deny the other.' Several civic leaders thought that if the Klan were not allowed to demonstrate, it would just go underground. '[I]f they aren't allowed to be visible, if we drive it underground, it will cause ... a lot more damage to our society ... [P]eople should be allowed to see ignorance and hatred. Talk about it,' said Kevin.

Those who thought that the Klan should be allowed to demonstrate as long as members did not carry any hate-filled messages were similarly lukewarm about the Klan's rights. Some held the attitude that they could not stop the Klan, and if its members were foolish enough to want to demonstrate, without actual hate-filled messages they would probably do little harm. Some put the condition, though, that Klan members should not be masked: 'Why are they hiding their faces? ... If they wanted to come down the street ... with their faces shown, and saying this is the way we believe, then they're not hiding anything,' argued Walter, an Aboriginal activist.

Even under these restricted conditions, support for the Klan's right to demonstrate was typically ambivalent. There was some fear that even without any explicit messages, a Klan demonstration could be intimidating. 'They have a right to be what they are as long as they're not promoting, you know, they don't have it [racist messages] spelled out. But yet, I suppose it's a pretty potent symbol just in and of itself. But I don't believe in blowing out someone who hasn't broadcast themselves, I guess,' said Susan, arguing with herself as she answered. Colleen was willing to permit a demonstration, but only in a location that would not be likely to intimidate any vulnerable people. '[A] racist has a right to his point of view, just as my point of view as a gay person may be offensive to many. At the same time, I wouldn't want to see a situation where a white supremacist group is allowed to parade through a non-white ... or a Jewish [neighbourhood].'

Those opposing the Klan's right to demonstrate, under any conditions, generally believed that everyone knows what the Klan stands for, even if members carry no messages of hatred. The very sight of a Klan member in a white sheet (even with his face exposed), or the very knowledge that demonstrators are members of the Klan, is enough in and of itself to cause fright in members of a vulnerable group. For these civic leaders, Klan marches are a form of symbolic assault; they would agree with an official of Skokie, Illinois, who said regarding the American Nazis' proposal for a march, 'This was not an exchange of ideas. The presence of these symbols was literally an assault.'[27]

The most common reason given to restrict the Klan's right to demonstrate was simply that it had no purpose other than to promote hatred. '[W]hether they wore hoods, or whether they had placards, the individual, knowing that they were KKK ... and what they represented, you'd have to say, "I don't want them in my town,"' was Bruce's view. The Klan's very presence is enough to upset people, whether or not members carry messages or any blatant symbols such as white sheets.

For people opposed to permitting the Klan to demonstrate in Canada, hatred and negativity of all kinds are not values that Canadian society should tolerate. The emphasis, rather, should always be on positive values. '[W]e need to focus on what our society values are, and anything that is negative ... [and] goes against those values ... are not encouraged,' maintained Al. The way to promote community is to focus on positive messages. As much as its actual message of hatred, the Klan's message is that it is all right not to love one's neighbour. Community cannot exist if some of its members hurt others with deliberation and with enjoyment.

Blasphemy

In 1979 Ayatollah Ruhollah Khomeini (then Supreme Leader) of Iran issued a declaration calling for the death of novelist Salman Rushdie, whom he accused of blasphemy against Islam in the novel *The Satanic Verses*.[28] In Canada, one repercussion of this incident was an attempt by some Muslim Canadians to persuade Canada Customs to prohibit the importation of *The Satanic Verses*, on the grounds that it was hate speech. In the event, the novel was prohibited entrance for two days.[29] With this incident in mind, I asked the Hamilton civic leaders whether they thought that blasphemy should be prohibited in Canada. Many had not been aware of what blasphemy was until I raised the issue with them, and in some cases explained the meaning of the term. In this section of their interviews many civic leaders were therefore speaking off the cuff, as it were, having given the topic far less consideration than they had given to hate speech in general.

Thirty civic leaders thought that blasphemy should be permitted. Five thought that this was an issue that awaited judgment in a higher court than could be found anywhere on earth: 'They'll [blasphemers] be dealt with at the gates of Heaven,' said Beverley. Several others deplored blasphemy, but thought the appropriate response to it was to disagree and debate; in other words, to 'fight bad speech with good speech.' As Karl, a devout Christian, explained, 'We should not have rules against poor taste. Blasphemy is in the eye of the beholder, is in the eye of the faith community, and I think that it is wrong for any religious group to tell an individual to shut up because it [speech] goes against their religious beliefs. A healthy debate is core to a live religious exercise.'

Only five individuals argued that blasphemy, like other types of freedom of speech, should be protected because it was too dangerous to ask government to legislate any type of speech. 'I'm confronted with it [blasphemy] as a Christian ... every single day, and no, I don't think I would like laws. That doesn't work,' Leo said. Two individuals worried that any attack on freedom to blaspheme might harm their own rights to freedom of speech: of these, one was Kathleen, the committed anti-abortionist, and the other was Lily, a former Christian who wanted the right to criticize the religion she had abandoned: 'I have many insulting things to say about Christianity, and I feel I should have the right to say them.'

Fifteen civic leaders thought that there should be legal controls on what they defined generally as hurtful blasphemy.[30] Some differentiated between blasphemy that might be hurtful to members of a minority religion and ordinary blasphemy, for example, Christian swearing. '[I]f someone said God is [a] pig, right, I wouldn't find that too relevant in my life ... [B]ut again if the purpose is to attack the Muslims ... we have to be sensitive to that,' thought Emilio. For these individuals, blasphemy against a minority religion (usually defined as Islam) constituted hate speech. 'I think we have to be much more aware of what is not acceptable to other cultures, other races ... I just don't think we should be blatantly hurting one another because of our thoughtless speech,' Margaret argued.

Twenty civic leaders believed that all blasphemy should be banned. For some, it was just plain courtesy not to comment on someone else's religion. 'I don't see why I've got any right at all to come to a Hindu or to a Muslim and tell them whatever they believe is wrong ... There's always the possibility they may be right,' said William, himself of Christian background. Other individuals articulated their answers more clearly within the vocabulary of social harm; speech harmful, hurtful, or offensive to others should be avoided. Barry, a Roman Catholic, said, 'It's a form of harassment. It makes you feel uncomfortable. It removes the freedom from people to practise [religion] according to their conscience.'

While their opinions on blasphemy often evolved as they spoke, the civic leaders' opinions on pornography were much firmer. This issue needed no explanation on my part; it was a debate about which almost all the civic leaders had thought prior to their interviews.

Pornography

In presenting this issue, I explicitly excluded child pornography, asking only if adults should be allowed freely to manufacture or possess adult pornography. Seventeen civic leaders thought that all pornography should be banned or controlled; twenty-four said that violent pornography should be controlled, and twenty-three (not necessarily the same individuals) said that demeaning pornography should be controlled (multiple answers were permitted here); twenty-nine thought that pornography should be freely permitted. I did not ask whether the civic leaders personally used pornography; only one person actually volunteered that she herself used it. 'I've watched them [pornographic movies] myself, [it] didn't bother me, I just get a bang out of it.'

Of those who believed all pornography should be banned, some argued this position out of distaste, a feeling that pornography was 'not a natural thing' or 'dirty.' A less frequent answer was the belief that pornography resulted in crime or abuse. 'It promotes abuse of people. It promotes ... power and control of one person over another,' said Hannah, a feminist activist. For some, the chief evil of pornography was that it debased women. Nerinder thought that, 'it's degrading to women and it falls into ... exploiting women to make money ... So it should be banned altogether to make the society a little better place to live.'

Like Nerinder, most of those who wanted controls on violent or demeaning pornography used feminist rhetoric, rather than more general expressions of moral concern. Many believed the fictional degradation of women could result in actual physical harm against them by users of pornography. In this, they followed an important 1992 Supreme Court of Canada decision, the Butler case, which permitted censorship of pornography on the grounds that there is reasonable cause to believe it could result in actual harm in the community.[31] Said Graham, 'I don't think there should be violence [in pornography] because I think that will teach people to say, "Well, it's okay to tie the woman up and whip her," who knows what else?' The attitude that pornography could result in actual harm to women was also found to be persuasive by the Canadians whom Sniderman et al. studied: 'Opponents of censorship are disproportionately likely to give ground after their attention is called to the risk of degrading women.'[32]

Several of those who opposed any controls on pornography did so on the grounds of the right to privacy. 'I am a believer that what is done in the privacy of one's home is one's own business,' asserted Elaine. Here, the viewpoint on freedom of speech varied from viewpoints on the other issues discussed in this chapter. All the other issues had to do with public speech. For those who advocated permitting it, viewing pornography was not a public matter, and was therefore not a speech act. In this instance, the view that individuals have a right to privacy overrode the view that all Canadians should evince respect and concern for other citizens, especially members of vulnerable groups.

Moral Circumspection

This chapter opens with a quotation from Michelle, who used the term 'moral circumspection' to describe the type of speech she thought appropriate. This term perhaps best sums up the attitude of most of the Hamilton civic leaders to freedom of speech in Canada. To ensure that the society is genuinely multicultural, and that all individuals and all groups feel themselves to be comfortable members of the community, moral circumspection must be part of everyday discourse. The government has a duty to reflect society's views in this regard, not permitting extreme freedom of speech if its effect is to damage social harmony.

Trust in Government

Philippa Strum notes: 'While a sharp distrust of government and a concomitant emphasis on rights emerged from the American historical experience, most other nations emphasize rights as being exercised within the context of obligation to the community.'[33] This is certainly true of the attitudes of the Hamilton civic leaders. They viewed speech in the context of its effects on community. Speech could be construed as a physical act; insulting, offensive, or degrading speech could have harmful consequences, just as a physical act could. Thus, the American critic of freedom of speech Stanley Fish would be very popular among them, taking as he does the position that there is no such thing as 'free' speech, separated from its content and possible harmful consequences.[34] Indeed, these civic leaders undoubtedly epitomize the citizens possessed of 'goodwill and good sense' who would, according to Fish, know intuitively what kinds of speech would be likely to hurt others.[35] In their eyes, absolutist positions defending freedom of speech ignore the link not only between speech and action, but between speech and feelings, between one person's free speech and another person's hurt feelings or damaged self-esteem. These Canadians would agree with the residents of Skokie, Illinois, whose attitude toward Nazi marchers was summed up by Strum as 'some speech should not be uttered in a society where the government exists to protect the dignity of all.'[36]

That the majority of Hamilton civic leaders were so unconcerned about the possibly detrimental effects of stricter controls over freedom of speech suggests a high degree of trust in their government. All who favoured stricter controls seemed to assume that such controls would be implemented fairly and justly. The civic leaders had strong moral beliefs in the importance of social rectitude, and they were willing to trust government to enforce rules against harmful speech if they were necessary. Thus, they generally agreed with the approach to hate speech embodied in Canadian legislation. As Eduardo put his position regarding the right of the Ku Klux Klan to demonstrate, 'the rights of every individual should be protected under law, and if it's the right to outlaw hatred speeches, then I agree with that.' For Eduardo, 'rights' clearly meant non-discrimination rights.

By contrast, very few people were concerned about possible violations of the right of freedom of speech. Brian was the only person to refer to the fundamental historical nature of that right: 'A lot of people die[d] over a lot of centuries to get ... [the] free right to speak. It's more valuable than anything. It's probably the most valuable right. And to tamper with it, mitigate it, restrain it in any way, shape, or form would do incalculable harm in the future.' Brian's position was very unusual in its reference to the historical origins of freedom of speech and its place in preserving the entire range of human rights that Canadian citizens enjoyed. Most of the other civic leaders were very much concerned with the human rights issues of the moment. The dominant public human rights discourse in Canada in the mid-1990s was that of multiculturalism, anti-discrimination, and group rights.

Liberalism and Communitarianism

Hamilton civic leaders' opinions that freedom of speech should be controlled so as to avoid offensive speech evinced a form of communitarian thinking. The community should take precedence over the extremes of individualism and individual rights. All Canadians, no matter what their identities or backgrounds, should feel that they are members of the wider community. This would not be possible if others were given the right to insult them, hurt their feelings, and deride their origins or their beliefs. In particular, individuals should be protected from racist speech, speech that attacks their religions, and from homophobic speech. As George put it, '[I]t all comes back to the same thing, equality. And if you are looking for certain rights ... to the same extent that you want certain rights, I don't think that you should infringe on other people's rights.'

In this respect, Hamilton civic leaders resemble the members of the Canadian elite surveyed about human rights by Sniderman et al., who found that the elite generally supports freedom of speech, unless that speech is racist.[37] Sniderman et al.'s conclusion is confirmed by the views of Elliott, whose profession would classify him among their elite. Although Elliott was strongly aware of the dangers of curbing freedom of speech, he was willing to support stronger laws against racial hatred. 'I probably would consider myself to be anti-censorship, more of a civil libertarian than not, but I'm very concerned with attacks on racial groups. Maybe I would personally make an exception in this area, and say that the potential wrong is so great, it's so horrendous ... [M]aybe I would draw the line in favour of much stronger control in this area than in most others.' This also appears to be the dilemma of the average thoughtful Canadian citizen: most of the Hamilton civic leaders decided that non-discrimination was a higher human rights value than freedom of speech.

Hamilton civic leaders tended to be liberal on all the other human rights issues on which they were questioned. Classic liberalism lays heavy stress on the rights of the individual, and the right of privacy, both in political beliefs and in the conduct of personal affairs. The civic leaders believed very strongly in the right of individuals to conduct their private lives as they see fit; thus, for example, most were supportive of gay and lesbian rights, as chapter 5 will show. However, they also had a very strong belief that all citizens owe each other respect. This was evidenced in many of their discussions of gay and lesbian rights, Aboriginal rights, the rights of refugees and immigrants, and the rights of the poor. Probably the single word used most often in their responses was, indeed, 'respect.' Non-discrimination, in their view, meant not mere tolerance of difference, but respect for it. In this regard, the Hamilton civic leaders resembled respondents in an American study who, asked to rank different types of harms that hate speech could cause, ranked highest 'the psychological pain experienced when they [the targets of hate speech] lose their dignity.'[38] The Hamilton civic leaders had a strong sense that no speech should be uttered that violated another's dignity. Preservation of others' dignity, especially the dignity of others at risk of prejudice and discrimination, was necessary to community harmony.

To live in a community, for these individuals, was to remember to bite your tongue, to be as tactful in your public utterances as, presumably, a decent person would be in private conversations. They agreed with the two-thirds of the respondents of Sniderman et al. who believed that 'society has to forbid certain things from being published in order to protect its moral values.'[39] That which is hurtful should not be said. As Neil argued, '[W]e do have the right to say whatever we wish to say ... but we have to be able to do that tastefully, not maliciously ... and maybe we do need more laws, to make sure that people's rights and freedoms are respected.' Nor is it enough, when encountering 'bad (or racist) speech,' to fight back with 'good speech,' the usual civil-libertarian approach to verbal racism. While this is a useful tactic, it is not sufficient. A democracy that encourages respect among citizens makes sure that certain things are not said. Joel, who was Jewish, put this well in a discussion of Ernst Zundel, an alleged Holocaust-denier then living in Toronto.[40] '[W]hen it comes to people like Zundel and the rest of his group, to be able to say that freedom of speech covers them also, I think really takes democracy out of context.'

Stanley Fish's argument that harmful speech cannot be cancelled out by more good speech because 'the pain and humiliation caused by racial or religious epithets' would not therefore disappear, would resonate well with these Canadians.[41] They would also agree with Ronald Dworkin's famous prescription that all citizens are entitled to 'equal concern and respect' from their government; they would add that all are entitled to equal concern and respect from other citizens as well.[42] They would be far less likely to agree, however, with Dworkin's equally spirited defence of the right to free speech.[43]

The Politics of Harm

A consistent position that renders the rights of members of groups suffering discrimination more important than the rights of those who do not would permit some groups in society freedom of speech, and others not. The Hamilton civic leaders had not taken their thinking on freedom of speech this far. They exhibited a sense of unease with absolute freedom of speech, a desire for tact, kindness, and circumspection that resulted in their advocating not only stronger moral controls on speech, but also stronger legal controls. In this, they reflected the common Canadian practice of confining discussion of human rights to issues to do with discrimination, disregarding threats to fundamental civil liberties that still occur.

Linda, who was black, referred to the emotional and mental harm that a mere encounter with members of the Ku Klux Klan could engender in African-Canadians, succinctly summing up the attitudes of the majority of the civic leaders to freedom of speech. 'The problem I have is when it becomes very dangerous. Physically, emotionally, and mentally to people, which it usually does. So that would be the reason I would say no, you wouldn't be allowed [to demonstrate].' Academics still hotly debate whether vulnerable groups ought to be protected from speech that might cause them psychological harm. To the majority of these Canadian civic leaders, however, the issue was unproblematic. If speech is, or can be construed to be, 'harmful' to its hearer, or to those with whom the hearer might interact, speech should give way at minimum to circumspection, at most to actual government censorship. 'Harm' is defined very broadly, to include emotional distress or merely offence. Thus, these Canadians would be persuaded by the contentions of Evelyn Kallen's Jewish respondents that the perceived anti-Semitism of James Keegstra and Ernst Zundel constituted real harm to them.[44]

This definition of harm is part of the wider concern of most of the civic leaders to ensure that all citizens in Canada – and more importantly, all groups in Canada – are treated with equal concern and respect. The practical equality to which all Canadians are entitled can only be achieved by inequality in protection from harmful speech. Unequal situations require unequal remedies; vulnerable groups such as blacks, religious minorities, women, and gays and lesbians require protections from offensive or degrading expression that non-vulnerable groups do not.

As a Canadian government document proclaims, 'The accommodation of differences is the essence of true equality.'[45] Agreeing with this, most of the civic leaders believed that part of what it means to be Canadian, and a member of the Canadian community, is to be protected against the gross offences of racial and ethnic hatred, misogyny, or homophobia, even when that offence is in the form of verbal expression only. Freedom of speech is not a basic, fundamental value, requiring special protection. It is a value that must be balanced against equally, if not more, compelling values, namely, non-discrimination, multiculturalism and social harmony. In this respect, the Hamilton civic leaders confirm the observation of Sniderman et al. that 'To an alarming extent ... the general public in liberal, democratic societies remains ill-informed about essential, democratic practices, ready to applaud them as abstract principles but all too willing to violate them in the heat of specific controversies.'[46]

Chapter Four

A Note on Hate Crimes

A crime is a crime is a crime is a crime.

Linda, an African-Canadian opponent
of hate crimes laws

A crime is a crime.

Elwin Hermanson, MP, Reform Party

A Counter-Intuitive Finding

Just as there is an international debate about hate speech, so there is an international debate about hate crimes, especially whether they should be punished more harshly than 'ordinary' crimes.[1] The assumption behind the proposition that hate crimes should be punished more harshly is that they are crimes not merely against individual victims, but rather against entire groups of people, particularly religious and ethnic minorities, and homosexuals. An assault on one member of such a group is assumed to be a threat against all members. In this respect, it is argued, hate crimes differ from, and have far more serious social consequences than, 'ordinary' crimes directed against individual victims.

In June 1995 the Canadian Parliament passed Bill C-41, the Sentencing Reform Bill, which in section 718.2 provided for more stringent sentences in cases of crimes motivated by hatred than in ordinary crimes. The exact wording of this provision is as follows:

718.2 A court that imposes a sentence should also take into consideration the following principles:

(a) a sentence shall be increased or reduced to account for any relevant aggravating or mitigating circumstances relating to the offence or the offender, and, without limiting the generality of the foregoing,

(I) evidence that the offence was motivated by bias, prejudice, or hate based on race, national or ethnic origin, language, colour, religion, sex, age, mental or physical disability, sexual orientation or any other similar factor ... [s]hall be deemed to be aggravating circumstances.[2]

As discussed later in this chapter, Section 718.2 had been quite controversial and stirred much debate in Parliament. Therefore, as part of the section of their interviews on hate speech I asked the Hamilton civic leaders their opinions on hate crimes. I asked them two questions. The first, directly reflecting the Parliamentary debate, was whether they thought that hate crimes deserved more severe punishment than ordinary crimes. I focused on violent crimes against the person, although there are also other types of hate crimes, such as defacing houses of worship. The second question was whether the civic leaders thought that an individual who responded violently to a racist or homophobic slur deserved to have such a slur taken into account in sentencing for assault. This question was not part of the national debate. I asked it because of incidents of which I had heard, in which individuals did respond violently to racist slurs. There had also been a Canadian case in which a sixteen-year-old black teenager, subjected to constant racial taunts by a white boy during hockey games, responded by kicking him in the stomach. Tragically, the victim died, and the black youth was convicted of manslaughter.[3]

Given that the majority of the Hamilton civic leaders favoured stronger hate speech laws, I had expected that the majority would also favour stricter punishment for hate crimes. I had also expected that those who were personally at risk of victimization by such crimes would have a very strong propensity to favour stricter punishments. This is not what the interviews revealed. Instead, both members of vulnerable groups and members of non-vulnerable groups split fairly evenly in their opinions on stricter punishments for hate crimes.

'Vulnerable groups' is my term for those social categories who might be at risk of assault because of their race, religion, or sexual orientation. An understandable assumption about such vulnerable groups might be that they are quite homogeneous; that is, that within each group, all members might think much the same way on issues related to their vulnerability. Thus, one might assume that there would be a black, gay/lesbian, or Jewish perspective on hate crimes. It would also be understandable to assume that this perspective would favour hate crime legislation, as a means of protection for individuals within the group. Such an assumption would be borne out by the official positions of some voluntary organizations that represent some members of such vulnerable groups in Canada. Thus, EGALE (Equality for Gays and Lesbians Everywhere), the B'nai Brith League for Human Rights, and the Canadian Jewish Congress strongly favoured the legislation imposing harsher sentencing for hate than for ordinary crimes.[4]

Conversely, one might also assume that Canadians who are not themselves members of any vulnerable group would be less likely to support hate crimes legislation than those who are. Most hate crimes in Canada are against people of colour, Jews, and gays and lesbians.[5] Thus, one might expect that white, heterosexual Christian Canadians would feel themselves disadvantaged by hate crimes legislation.

These expectations were not borne out by my interviews. The counter-intuitive result was not that half of the white, (presumably) heterosexual Christian or Christian-background civic leaders supported the hate crimes legislation, given that many had also supported stronger hate-speech laws. Rather, the counter-intuitive result was that half of those civic leaders who were members of the vulnerable groups the hate crimes legislation was designed to protect did not support the law. Including the nineteen members of visible minorities, four Aboriginal people, five self-identified gays and lesbians, and nine members of minority religions in the count, of the seventy-eight civic leaders, thirty-one (or 40 per cent) belonged to vulnerable groups (four individuals fit two categories and one fit three). Moreover, one individual self-identified as a parent of a gay child, and two whites said they had black or mixed-race children. This raises to thirty-four the number who might be considered to have had a direct interest in hate crimes legislation, or 44 per cent of the entire group of civic leaders. This count of members of vulnerable categories excludes women who were white, Christian or Christian background, and presumably heterosexual, even though Section 718.2 of Bill C-41 also included the category 'sex.'

That there was not a homogeneous perspective on hate crimes, either among members of vulnerable groups or among non-members, is explained by the fact that both sets of Hamilton civic leaders had multiple identities and interests, and were motivated by thought about matters other than their group membership. These citizens, whether members of vulnerable groups or not, thought carefully about matters of personal responsibility and social equality, as well as the need that vulnerable groups had for human rights.[6]

A Half-Half Split: Opinions on Harsher Punishments and Mitigating Circumstances

Thirty-seven people – or 47 per cent of all those interviewed – argued for stronger punishment for an attack against a member of a vulnerable group than an ordinary attack. Of these thirty-seven, fifteen were members of vulnerable groups themselves, while two others were parents of children who were vulnerable. Thus, seventeen individuals, or 46 per cent of those favouring hate crime legislation, could be considered to have a direct interest in it, while twenty of those favouring stronger punishments for hate crimes, or 54 per cent, had no known personal or family connection to vulnerable groups.

Those who were members of or connected to vulnerable groups spoke eloquently about the collective threat posed by an attack against an individual member of such a group. Louise, a white mother with mixed-race children, argued, 'If it's motivated by hatred it should [be punished more severely] ... because the only reason you're attacking that person is the colour of his skin or the way he looks ... there's no other reason there than "I just don't like the look of you" ... What are you teaching people if you don't reprimand it more severely? Are other people going to go out and do the same thing?' Colleen, a lesbian, agreed: 'If I'm assaulted because I've just come out of a gay bar, and somebody has decided they're going to get their kicks by beating up a dyke tonight, that becomes an offence against my community ... And it is designed really to inspire fear in an entire community.'

Civic leaders who were not members of vulnerable groups referred just as eloquently and with just as much feeling to the threat against the group posed by an assault motivated by hatred. Patrick, white and presumably heterosexual, thought that one hate crime might inspire others. '[H]olding up a bank is one thing, but I don't think it produces a rash of bank hold-ups, but gay-bashing and racial intolerance seems to attract the worst elements, who perpetrate this sort of thing.' Graham, also white and presumably heterosexual, thought that hate crimes were a direct attack upon equality rights. '[H]ate crimes are more insidious than anything else ... [T]hey aren't just committed because you want some economic benefit out of it ... [Y]ou're doing it just because you feel superior to the other person, and one thing about rights are [sic], everybody has equal rights, they work equal.'

Forty civic leaders also believed that if an individual responded violently to a verbal provocation of a racist, anti-Semitic, or homophobic nature, that provocation should be taken into account as a mitigating circumstance in sentencing. Among these, sixteen were members of vulnerable groups. The two white parents of black children also agreed with this position. Thus, eighteen of the forty, or 45 per cent of the civic leaders believing that racist verbal provocation should be a mitigating factor in sentencing, were members of or connected to vulnerable groups. The other twenty-two, or 55 per cent, were not.

If someone was called a 'nigger' or 'faggot,' in the view of these Hamilton civic leaders, there was some justification in the victim's responding to this verbal assault with physical violence. Jacqueline, an older black woman, said, 'Although I do think people should try and exercise control ... I think things affect people in different ways ... It [violence] shouldn't be condoned, it shouldn't be pardoned, but I think it [provocation] should be taken into consideration.' Carol, the second white parent of a black child, argued, '[T]he courts need to understand what oppression does to people ... The kind of anger that builds up in a person and the kind of sensitivity that a person will have. How a person feels about himself affects their entire outlook and their entire ability to function in the world.'

Some of the strongest and most passionate statements that insulting speech is a form of assault were made by individuals who were not likely to experience any such verbal assault themselves, as they were not members of any vulnerable group. Said Gina, of Italian background, '[I]t's part of the crime when you call someone else a name, and lots of times we don't look at that. We don't look at things that cause the other person to become angry and respond with anger. [S]ometimes words are just as hurting as a knife would be in terms of ... the dignity of your person being hurt.' Dan, also white and of Canadian background, agreed: 'I think that to call someone a "nigger" really doesn't have much relevance to me as a white person, but ... it means something completely different to a black person ... [I]t means more than just words, it's more than an insult, it strikes to the very heart of who you are ... [T]hose are fighting words ... and they should take that into account.'

These opinions favouring special sentencing for hate crimes, and mitigated sentences for those who responded violently to verbal assaults, were in accord with the views of most of the Hamilton civic leaders that it is incumbent upon all Canadians to be aware of the effects of hate speech, to see such speech as an act with harmful consequences. Nevertheless, fewer people believed in special or mitigated sentences than people who wanted hate speech controlled. Perhaps the reason for the difference was the issue of physical, rather than merely rhetorical, violence. For half the civic leaders, whether or not they were themselves members of vulnerable groups, violence against the person was such a heinous offence that the identity of the victim was irrelevant. For these civic leaders, a white, heterosexual Christian male should have as much protection against physical violence as anyone victimized because of his minority status. His suffering and pain should be taken as seriously as anyone else's suffering and pain. Conversely, violent action was so reprehensible that no one should engage in it, regardless of provocation. Racist, anti-Semitic, or homophobic provocation was no excuse for a violent response.

Forty-one people, or 53 per cent of the civic leaders, opposed the idea of longer sentences for hate-motivated crimes than for other crimes. Of these, fourteen individuals were members of one vulnerable group, and one was a member of two. That is, 37 per cent of those opposed to special sentences were members of vulnerable groups. Put another way, half of the thirty-one people who were members of vulnerable groups opposed enhanced sentences for perpetrators of hate crimes.

Many of those who opposed hate crime legislation thought that the social status of the victim was irrelevant. Several of the black opponents of longer sentences for hate crimes held to the simple proposition that there should be no double standard in punishments. Linda, quoted in the epigraph to this article, said, 'It doesn't matter who is the victim. It is a crime and it shouldn't be acceptable.' This was also the position taken by several members of other minority groups. Charlene, who was Aboriginal, argued, 'I think it should be punished equally ... everyone should be punished for whatever they do.' Joel, who was Jewish, contended, '[I]t's wrong to have a racial situation enter into what is morally right or wrong about the law. If somebody is doing something wrong, they should be judged accordingly.' This point of view, that all crimes were equally severe and that there should be no double standard, was also the most common reason given by those who opposed special sentencing and were not themselves members of any vulnerable group. Everyone should be punished equally, because all victims were equal, argued Greg, an older white man: '[L]et people comply with the laws of the land. You don't beat up other people. He's a minority of one, you don't beat him up. That's all there is to it. Doesn't matter what colour he is.'

Several of the women who opposed special sentences for hate crimes did so for explicitly feminist reasons, under the incorrect impression that hate crime legislation did not include hatred against women, which some saw as the root cause of the violence perpetrated by men against women. (I did not correct civic leaders' misapprehensions during the course of the interviews.) They asked why a crime of violence against a member of a racial minority or a homosexual should be taken more seriously than a crime of violence against a woman. Nora said, 'I think if you take a good look at rape laws and assaults against women first ... why that should be any less than any other crime is beyond me ... [V]iolence is used against women as a weapon of control, probably not in that different a way than it's used against a person wearing a turban.'

Actual physical violence was so reprehensible to some civic leaders that the circumstances impelling it were never enough to excuse it. Thirty-six people thought that even in cases of extreme verbal provocation, a victim should never respond with violence; thus, provocation should not be taken into account as a mitigating factor in sentencing. Among these were fourteen members of vulnerable groups, constituting 42 per cent of all those who were members of, or parents of members of, vulnerable groups, and 39 per cent of all those who opposed such mitigation.

Some of the members of vulnerable groups who opposed taking verbal provocation into account in sentencing someone for a violent crime did so on the grounds of general social responsibility. As Lily, of mixed race, put it, 'No. I don't think anyone has the right to physically assault anyone because of something they called you. I mean, call them back something. You don't have to hit them.' Walter, an Aboriginal person, agreed: '[M]y reactions should not be towards violence. If I were to do that, then in effect I would be bringing myself down to your level. If you're calling me a derogatory name, I'm showing you that I'm equivalent, 'cause I'm going to beat the shit out of you.' This type of reasoning also influenced some who were not members of or connected to vulnerable groups. A crime of violence should be punished without consideration of the type of provocation, or the victim of that provocation. 'You can say whatever you want, and how I respond to that, whether I'm black, white, green, or purple, is my choice, and if I decide to hit you back then that makes me in the wrong, no matter what I am,' said Betty, a white woman.

Additionally, just as some feminists opposed special-hate crime legislation on the grounds that women were not included as a vulnerable group, so also some were strongly opposed to any violent acts, regardless of provocation. 'I would not support a black person beating the shit out of a white person because that white person has called him a name. Perhaps I would be a little more sympathetic towards the black person and his reaction, but I think that violence is wrong ... Much as I appreciate how angry he might have felt, or how offended, he could still have walked away,' said Sofia. For such feminists, violence in and of itself is extremely reprehensible, as evidenced in male violence against women. No provocation warrants a violent response.

Comparison to Parliamentary Debate

The debate in Parliament about Bill C-41 focused on whether a crime motivated by hatred toward members of groups identified in Section 718.2 was somehow 'worse' than a similar crime not so motivated. The then Reform Party argued strongly that there should not be more stringent sentences for hate crimes. To Reform, such legislation seemed to make a crime against a member of one of the identified groups more important than a crime against other Canadians. The governing Liberal Party rejected this argument and advocated more stringent sentencing. The debate was unusually acrimonious.

Reform had four arguments against the hate crimes section. First, it objected to the inclusion of sexual orientation as a protected category, arguing that this was a 'back-door' means for the government to eventually include sexual orientation in all human rights laws and to start giving gays and lesbians the full range of benefits available to heterosexual couples. Secondly, Reform argued that 'sexual orientation' should be restrictively defined, since according to psychiatric testimony necrophilia, bestiality, and paedophilia could be considered sexual orientations. The governing Liberals responded to this latter concern by introducing an amendment specifying that the bill would not decriminalize anything already a crime.[7] This debate about sexual orientation was widely reflected in the public arena, the conservative press in particular focusing on the issue of special rights for gays and lesbians.[8]

Reform's third objection to Section 718.2 was that inclusion of the terms 'bias' and 'prejudice' along with 'hatred' as motives for hate crimes would undermine Canadians' right to freedom of thought; one is allowed, in Canada, to harbour biases and prejudices. Finally, Reform objected to Section 718.2 on the grounds that it implemented a double standard; certain victims would be worth more than others in the courts' eyes.

Among the reasons presented by Reform for opposing Bill C-41, only the last, that certain victims would be worth more than others in the eyes of the courts, resonated with those Hamilton civic leaders opposed to hate crimes legislation. 'A crime is a crime' was a position articulated both by these people and by some Reform Party members, as shown in the epigraphs to this chapter. On the other hand, the civic leaders who supported the legislation agreed with the governing Liberal Party, which in introducing Bill C-41 argued that to be a member of certain identifiable groups is to be more vulnerable to crime, and that a crime against such an individual is a symbolic attack against the entire group. Allan Rock, then Minister of Justice and Attorney-General of Canada, spoke of 'growing concerns about hate motivated crime,' noting as well that 'hate motivated violence against individuals based on the offenders [sic] bias toward other sexual orientations has sparked public anxiety,' and that 'General concerns have been raised about the pervasiveness of racism in Canada.'[9]

Resembling the position of the Hamilton civic leaders who favoured hate crime legislation, the official Liberal position was that the particular categories of people to be protected by the legislation suffered far more serious consequences than 'ordinary' citizens who might be assaulted for private or idiosyncratic reasons. In the eyes of the Liberals, an attack against one member of the protected communities was an attack against all. Liberal MP for Halifax West Geoff Regan maintained that 'When people are attacked because they belong to a group, whether it is a religious group or whatever, it is a kind of terrorism against the group.'[10] Speaking of the Jewish members of his own constituency, where several of the Hamilton civic leaders lived, Liberal MP for Hamilton West Stan Keyes declared: '[I]f someone were to paint swastikas on one of the five synagogues in my riding of Hamilton West, the victims would include all members of the Jewish faith.'[11]

Thus, the Liberals explicitly accepted the idea that certain groups were more at risk than others in Canada. They asserted that there were consequences for a group that flowed from attacks on its individual

members, and they argued that the law ought to reflect these consequences in the way hate criminals were sentenced. The Liberals, however, were also at pains to point out that everyone was equally
protected, since everyone has a race, a nationality, a religion, and a sexual orientation. Thus, for example, homosexuals who assaulted heterosexuals with a motivation of hatred would be as liable to prosecution
as the reverse. In the Liberals' view, Section 718.2 did not promote inequality under the law. The Liberals also were unconcerned about
the possible expansion of gay and lesbian rights, pointing out that
although such rights were not yet formally written into all human
rights legislation in Canada, court decisions already protected them.

Aside from their other concerns, the opponents of Section 718.2
expressed a real fear that special protection of people threatened
because of their sexual orientation would imply approval of homosexuality, in turn threatening the heterosexual family. Roseanne Skoke, a
backbench Liberal MP who voted against her party, exemplified this
fear. '[A] special recognition of sexual orientation in our federal legislation is an overt condonation of the practice of homosexuality which is
being imposed on Canadians. It has the effect of legislating a morality
that is not supported by our Canadian and Christian morals and values.'[12] Skoke's concern was not found among the Hamilton civic leaders. Those who opposed special hate-crimes sentencing did not do so
because of fear of homosexuals' rights. As chapter 5 will show, they
were relatively at ease with gay and lesbian rights, which they did not
interpret, as did Reform, as 'special' rights.

Reform's consistent claim throughout the debate that it was more in
touch with Canadian public opinion than were the Liberals was incorrect; the Liberals more correctly judged the public mood, as far as such
'special' rights were concerned. Nevertheless, Reform was partly correct in its identification of 'special interests' behind social pressure for
hate crimes legislation. Such pressure was in part a result of a new
social movement to recognize hate crimes, a social movement whose
rhetoric appeared to have convinced many of the Hamilton civic leaders. This social movement had introduced 'definitions that bestow victim status upon select groups,' so that 'what was once a privately
injured individual is now an official victim of bias crime.'[13]

For Reform, such special status for some victims of crimes undermined the principle of equality before the law. '[Special sentencing for]
hate-motivated crime ... would promote a two-tiered system ... What
about equality before the law? Assault is assault regardless of motiva-

tion.'[14] Introduction of the principle of group rights into Canadian law was for Reform a fundamental mistake. '[I]t hurts just as much to get punched in the eye no matter what group I am from. The whole concept of identifying Canadians by groups instead of as individuals is a disturbing trend in Canadian society.'[15] On the whole, Reform members of Parliament were much less at ease with the idea of group rights than were the Hamilton civic leaders.

Personal Responsibility and Hate Crimes

About half the Hamilton civic leaders took a universalist and individualist position on crime and social responsibility. Crime was crime no matter who was the perpetrator or the victim. No one individual victim was worth more or less before the courts. Even a crime of violence committed as a reaction to severe racist provocation was illegitimate. Everyone is responsible for her- or himself; no one has the right to use violence.

That these attitudes were held even by some of those who were members of vulnerable groups reveals the complexity of their thinking, their motivations, and their identities. The Hamilton civic leaders were highly educated, mostly middle-aged people, most holding professional or semi-professional jobs. All of the black and mixed-race individuals held university degrees, and all the older blacks were professionals, semi-professionals, or businesspersons. Several of the more recent non-white immigrants were from countries where crime was severely punished, regardless of either the perpetrator's or the victim's identity. Their decision to immigrate to Canada had been impelled in part by Canada's offer of social order.

Yet other civic leaders, equally committed to social order and equally likely to be highly educated, middle-aged professionals or semi-professionals, took the contrary view. For them, social order required special attention to the threats that hate crimes posed against vulnerable groups. To be Canadian was, in part, to recognize the needs of such groups and to make provision for them in society as a whole, whether or not one was oneself a member of such a group. Thus, these civic leaders agreed that the 'social fabric' in general was adversely affected by hate crimes, an argument put forth by two justices of the Ontario Court of Appeal in 1990: 'An offence which is directed against a particular religious or racial group is more heinous, as it attacks the very fabric of our society.'[16]

The disagreements among the Hamilton civic leaders revealed the complexity of the entire group's thinking on the question of rights and responsibilities. A common theme throughout all the interviews was the need to respect every citizen and every social group. Another theme was the balance between the rights of individuals and the rights of groups. The civic leaders frequently alluded to the need to respect disadvantaged groups. Respect required acknowledgment of the uniquely vulnerable position of some Canadians; support for hate crimes legislation was a way to show such respect.

The notion of respect for vulnerable individuals infused many civic leaders' views on multiculturalism. Martha Shaffer, a legal scholar, referred to the multicultural policy of Canada as one important underpinning of her argument for even stronger hate-crimes legislation than Section 718.2 of Bill C-41. 'Hate-motivated violence,' she argued, 'constitutes an affront to minority communities and runs counter to Canada's core values of equality and multiculturalism.'[17] She quoted the 1977 statement by the Court of Appeal in *R. v. Ingram*, a case of a very vicious assault on a Tanzanian immigrant by two white males: 'An assault which is racially motivated renders the offence more heinous ... The danger is even greater in a multicultural, pluralistic urban society.'[18] The value of multiculturalism was mentioned very rarely, if at all, by the Hamilton civic leaders with regard to hate crimes, but certainly that value permeated the interviews as a whole. For many individuals, respect for others meant respect for multiculturalism and social diversity. Multiculturalism required equal legal protection for all, regardless of origin or group membership. Nevertheless, I could draw no link between the civic leaders' stronger or weaker support for multiculturalism, and opposition to or support for hate crimes legislation.

Belief in multiculturalism was not the only reason for social respect. Some of the civic leaders referred to their religious beliefs as guides to their opinions on hate crimes laws, whether they favoured these laws or not. They did not, however, refer to their religious beliefs to oppose 'special' rights for homosexuals, as Roseanne Skoke and some members of the Reform Party did in parliamentary debate. Rather, like some Liberal members of Parliament, they referred to their religious background as the basis for tolerance and understanding. Don Boudria declared, 'I speak in the House as a practising Roman Catholic ... I ask my colleagues to share with me in that kind of tolerance toward other people, as I was taught to do in the church of which I am a member.'[19]

Nevertheless, how the civic leaders applied their religious beliefs, either in favour of or against special sentences for hate crimes, could not be predicted by reference to the likelihood that they themselves might become victims of hate crimes.

The civic leaders believed that Canadians had responsibilities as well as rights. For some individuals, such personal responsibility meant that there should be no special sentencing for hate crimes. One's obligation to others meant treating each 'other' as an equal individual, and acknowledging the legitimacy of his suffering equally whether he was attacked because he was a member of a vulnerable group, or because he merely was in the wrong place at the wrong time. Nor, to those individuals who opposed special sentencing for hate crimes, should reaction to hate speech be a mitigating circumstance in the case of a person committing assault. Just as they accepted their own personal obligations not to commit crimes, and not to react violently when provoked, so they thought that other Canadians should act in a similarly circumspect manner.

For other civic leaders, however, personal obligation meant a responsibility to protect vulnerable groups. To show the respect such groups deserved required acknowledgment of the heinousness of acts committed against certain individuals merely because they were members of them. Respect required public moral outrage at acts of racism, anti-Semitism, or gay-bashing. For some civic leaders, this obligation also extended to understanding why a member of a vulnerable group might react violently to hateful provocation.

In philosophical terms, the Hamilton civic leaders differentiated between group and individual rights, although they did not generally use these terms in their actual conversation. Those who favoured hate crimes legislation thought of victims as members of vulnerable groups. They believed that Canadian society had an obligation to protect groups as such, not merely individuals. Whether or not personally members of such groups, they had a clear sense that an attack against one member of such a group was an attack against all. Hate crimes were particularly heinous because they sent a message of hatred to every member of the group; every member felt threatened by the crime. On the other hand, those who opposed hate crimes legislation insisted that all individuals were equal in Canadian society. As respect was a core value in Canada, so was equality. Respect for difference was necessary, but in matters of crime, all Canadians should be treated equally, whether as victims or as perpetrators.

The Crime and the Punishment

The Hamilton civic leaders reacted to the hate crimes legislation in a somewhat different way than the debaters in Parliament. Among those who opposed hate crimes legislation, there was little sense, as there was among Reform Members of Parliament, that such crimes did not harm an entire group. Rather, there was a sense that even if such group harm occurred, crime victims should be considered as individuals. As an individual, an assault victim suffered regardless of motive. Even when an entire group was threatened, the individual nature of the crime should be at the forefront. Therefore, special sentencing for hate crimes was unwarranted.

This distinction shows that it is possible to unpack the debate. For the Liberals in Parliament, recognition of the especially harmful nature of hate crimes against vulnerable groups meant of necessity that harsher sentencing measures should be instituted. For Reform, the justification for opposing harsher sentences was that hate crimes either did not harm groups, or might also harm groups not enumerated in the legislation.

Yet recognition that hate crimes are differently motivated from other crimes, and have different effects, is possible without necessarily advocating harsher punishment. More efficacious means of rehabilitation might be devised. For example, perpetrators might be obliged to apologize to and compensate the victims, or to attend educational programs. Recognition of the social factors that cause young white males to join anti-black, anti-Semitic, or anti-gay gangs might render more productive such educational or compensatory approaches. The symbolic meaning of hate crimes might be better addressed, and abhorrence to them expressed, by public education. Indeed, the Liberal Party's reasoning during the 1995 parliamentary debate might be considered to have constituted such public education.

Sylvia, an Aboriginal civic leader, favoured this type of rehabilitation over stronger punishments. '[T]here are certain things that we learn, and that's good because we can unlearn them, so I think rehabilitation would be something that would be ... more important than punitive measures.' Rina, who was Jewish, made a similar point: 'I think really you punish the crime, and the motivation is sad, and hopefully you can rehabilitate that or change it, but to punish someone for what they believe, or how they feel, I don't think that's humane.' Rina was the only civic leader to note the danger of punishing individual perpetrators for their beliefs, a danger noted by several Reform Party members in parliamentary debate.[20]

Sylvia and Rina both had extensive personal experience of racism, yet both rejected harsher sentencing in favour of a more complete understanding of the causes of hate crime, and an attempt to rehabilitate the criminals. Such understanding of hate crime as a social issue extending beyond the problems of vulnerable groups themselves was very rarely reflected in Canadian public discussion.[21] In fact, it is known that violent hate criminals in Canada are almost all male and tend to be very young. They are also linked to gangs.[22] Presumably, factors such as poverty, social alienation, and unemployment increase the likelihood that any particular young male will join such a group. As Petersen, a strong advocate of the need to recognize the particularly harmful nature of hate crimes against gays and lesbians, argued; 'The fact that hate crimes inflict greater injury has been used to justify the imposition of enhanced penalties in the interests of retributive justice ... [H]owever, we should not examine the legitimacy of retribution, but rather its efficacy in combatting heterosexist violence. If enhanced penalties are not effective deterrents, then we need not even begin to discuss their legitimacy. Deterrence must ultimately be our goal.'[23] Shaffer agreed that 'hate-crime provisions may be little more than symbolic gestures, incapable of contributing to the solution of deeply-entrenched social problems.'[24]

One can accept that hate crimes are not crimes merely against an individual. Entire communities are frightened or perhaps even terrorized by them.[25] Indeed, as Hamm suggests, it might be reasonable to designate hate crimes as nonstate domestic terrorism.[26] One can also accept that groups of vulnerable people who are at risk of hate crimes deserve special recognition and protection. This does not necessarily mean, however, that one must also accept stricter sentencing and longer prison stays.

Those who feel strongly about hate crimes might assume that all those opposed to special sentencing ground their opposition in generalized homophobia or in an unwillingness to stretch their minds to understand the effects of racism or anti-Semitism on their victims and their communities. Yet one should not be quick to assume that the views of those who disagree with enhanced sentencing for hate crimes merely reflect a self-centred identification with their own social group, namely, white, Christian, or Christian-background heterosexuals. That half of those civic leaders who were members of vulnerable groups opposed special sentencing shows that there is a real equality issue under the debate. Social respect might mean treating different groups differently, thus 'ensuring that the criminal law responds fairly to the different harms faced by Canada's minority groups.'[27] On the other hand, it also might mean treating all individuals the same way. There is a legitimate philosophical debate about this issue, a debate into which the Hamilton civic leaders tapped in their thinking about rights and responsibilities.

Chapter Five

The Gay Cousin:
Learning to Accept Gay Rights

My cousin's gay and I'm around him all the time, we do things together, but I still ... deep down in my soul feel that it's not right ... I sort of cop out of it. I mean, I support it and I support people and their choices as much as I can. I won't go out of my way to be disrespectful, but I can't celebrate it. And I evolve, you know, it's an evolving thing.

Beverley

The Gay Rights Debate

As the new century begins, it is useful to reflect on whether any social groups are still unprotected by international human rights law. Obvious candidates are gays and lesbians.[1] If 'Everyone is entitled to all the rights and freedoms set forth in this [Universal] Declaration [of Human Rights], without distinction of any kind, such as race, colour, sex, language, religion, political or other opinion, national or social origin, property, birth *or other status*,'[2] then it is incumbent upon those interested in protecting the rights of gays and lesbians to show that they occupy a status analogous to that of other social groups who suffer discrimination. This is not an easy task.

Gays and lesbians constitute a social group that is more difficult to protect than other weak social groups such as women or children, because they are often perceived as innately shameful. Because they assert a deviant identity that defies social norms and common morality, gays and lesbians are also often considered undeserving of respect. The debate is not only about sexual practices, however repugnant many opponents (and many supporters) of gay rights might find them.

The debate is also about morality, and especially about the role of that fundamental social institution, the family. Acknowledgment of the legitimacy of gay and lesbian families in Canada – symbolized by the rights to marry and to adopt children – is the last frontier of their rights.

In reacting against and attempting to understand homophobia, or dislike of gays and lesbians, little attention is paid to the opposite phenomenon: how do heterosexual citizens learn to accept gays and gay rights? How do they learn, in fact, to go further than a pure rights approach and treat gays and lesbians with respect? Fewer and fewer gays and lesbians today are willing to hide their sexual orientation or sexual activities; gays and lesbians want not only rights, but also social recognition, concern, and respect.[3] This requires from the dominant heterosexual population a change of attitude that in many cases is severe. To recognize and respect homosexuals requires many heterosexuals to adjust their ideas of what is appropriate sexual behaviour and to adjust their views of the purpose of marriage. It also requires them to reject or reinterpret their fundamental religious beliefs.

In this chapter, I analyse how the (presumably) heterosexual Hamilton civic leaders brought themselves to the position that they could accept gay and lesbian rights. I discuss only the opinions of the seventy-three civic leaders who did not identify themselves as gay or lesbian, leaving aside the opinions of the five self-identified members of the homosexual population. It is possible that some of the other seventy-three were also gay or lesbian, but in the absence of self-identification, I assume that all were heterosexual. This chapter reveals that the civic leaders were often conflicted about gay rights, wanting to do what they saw as the right thing but held back by religious views, heterosexual social norms, and disapproval of gay sexuality.

I asked the Hamilton civic leaders a number of questions about gay and lesbian rights, to be discussed below. The key set of opinions revealing division in their views concerned gay marriages and adoptions. Accordingly, I classified anyone who supported both gay marriage and adoption on the same basis as heterosexual marriage and adoption as strongly favourable to gay rights. Individuals who otherwise favoured gay rights but who hesitated to extend equal rights either to marriage or adoption, or to both, were classified as moderately favourable. Individuals who expressed strong hostility to gay marriages and/or adoptions were accordingly classified as opposed to full gay and lesbian rights. Twelve of the seventy-three civic leaders opposed gay rights, forty were moderately favourable, and twenty-one strongly favoured gay rights.

On the whole, the Hamilton civic leaders roughly reflected overall Canadian public opinion regarding gay rights at the time of their interviews, as evidenced in survey data. National attitudes to gay rights in Canada changed rapidly during the 1990s toward greater acceptance, especially of equal rights in marriage and adoption. In 1996, 49 per cent of Canadians agreed with legal recognition of gay marriages, compared to 24 per cent per cent in 1992. Similarly, 42 per cent of Canadians in 1996 thought that homosexuals should be allowed to adopt children who were not biologically theirs, compared to 31 per cent in 1992.[4]

The Canadian legal system is highly protective of gay rights. As of 27 December 1998, all Canadian jurisdictions but one prohibited discrimination on the basis of sexual orientation.[5] Sexual orientation was added to the Canadian Human Rights Code as a prohibited ground of discrimination in 1996. Discrimination against gays in the Canadian military was prohibited in 1992.[6] On 11 April 2000 (three years after my research was completed) the government of Canada passed Bill C-23, 'The Modernizing Benefits and Obligations Act,' giving gay and lesbian couples the same rights and responsibilities as common-law heterosexual couples.[7]

Given all these legal developments, the outstanding issues of public debate in the very late 20th and early 21st centuries were the rights of gays and lesbians to marry and to adopt children. As of December 1998, the provinces of British Columbia and Ontario were the only jurisdictions to permit adoptions by same-sex couples.[8] Rights of gays and lesbians to marry and to adopt are the key to a completely equal legal regime for heterosexuals and homosexuals. Debate about these rights, along with the question of whether respect for the gay lifestyle should be taught in schools, also acts as an indicator of whether Canadians are willing to go further than merely according equal rights to gays, to according them societal respect and acknowledgment that their relationships are as worthy of concern as heterosexual relationships.

To show how their thinking about these matters has evolved, this chapter discusses the Hamilton civic leaders' attitudes to equality rights and the disapproval of gay sexuality that some of them still expressed. It then proceeds to a discussion of marriage and adoption.

Equality Rights

The Gay Rights Movement

For purposes of analysing the Hamilton civic leaders' opinions, I interpreted equality rights as those that allowed gays and lesbians the same protections in matters of housing, education, and employment as were afforded to any other group that might suffer discrimination. In the eyes of many of the civic leaders, these rights were separate from those that actually affected the meaning of marriage, family, and child-rearing in Canada.

I asked the civic leaders what the gay rights movement meant to them, and whether they supported it. Thirteen people said they did not support the movement, thirty-nine indicated moderate support, and twenty indicated strong support. Many individuals interpreted the gay rights movement as a means for gays to obtain the basic equality rights available to all other Canadians. Frances's response was typical: 'I think that they would like to have the same rights as the rest of us Canadians.' Since the dominant social ideology in Canada lays strong stress on equality rights, adoption of this ideology makes it easier for Canadians who might otherwise be uneasy about homosexuality to agree that homosexuals should nevertheless have basic rights, regardless of their sexual orientation. Other civic leaders viewed the gay rights movement not only as one for rights, but also as one for social acceptance. Al speculated, 'I think the gay rights movement is trying to get recognition for being human like everybody else ... so that they don't have to hide anymore, and they don't have to feel negative. The community can be accepting of them and they can be accepting of themselves.'

Those who saw the gay rights movement as one striving for respect and acceptance did not always agree with it, some seeing the quest for respect as going too far, demanding from the 'normal' population a degree of recognition homosexuals did not deserve. Other civic leaders thought that progress from mere assertion of equality rights to the social claim to respect and dignity was a positive aspect of the movement. As Gina put it, 'I'd like to think that it's about regaining their dignity and self-worth as individuals who perhaps see the world in a different way.'

The majority view among the civic leaders was that the rights that gays and lesbians had attained in Canada at the time of the interviews were appropriate. Some who did not feel that they could actually support the movement nevertheless said they were tolerant of it. A few, however, like Eugene, saw the movement as one for special rights. 'I perceive it as being provided a special treatment.' According to a very few civic leaders, including some otherwise sympathetic to gay rights, gays had too much political and social influence. An example was the inordinate attention that one person thought was given to AIDS (seen as a homosexual disease). '[O]nce again we're being co-opted into uncritical support of a noisy minority. For instance ... breast cancer apparently accounts for about ten times as many deaths as AIDS. And the resources devoted to the two things are also about ten to one but reversed.'

Those who objected to the gay rights movement thought that sexual orientation should be irrelevant to one's behaviour in the social realm, not a matter requiring acknowledgment by the general public or by the law. Those doubtful about the gay rights movement, however, did not fear that with rights, gays would start to recruit children or engage in paedophilia. Most of the civic leaders favoured gay rights, even if some activities of the gay rights movement caused them concern.

Rights That Gays Still Needed

The civic leaders frequently differentiated between basic equality rights and rights to marriage and adoption on equal terms with heterosexuals. Most were much more comfortable with the former than with the latter. Indeed, many were quick to say gays and lesbians still needed more of the basic equality rights.

Forty people stated or implied that gays needed more rights than they had at the time of the interviews. Of these, at least eighteen volunteered that gays still needed the types of rights known in Canada as spousal benefits or same-sex benefits, e.g., pension benefits for surviving spouses, or health insurance for spouses (these are the rights granted to all gays and lesbians in the April 2000 omnibus Bill C-23). Since there had been a great deal of press coverage in Canada in the years preceding the interviews of various court cases in which such spousal benefits were claimed by homosexuals, it is not surprising that this particular right was most often mentioned. The idea of spousal benefits seemed to fit most civic leaders' sense of fairness. Spousal benefits as such, moreover, did not necessarily imply a recognition of gay marriage. While (as will be discussed below) many civic leaders viewed marriage as religiously ordained to be of a man and a woman,

there are no religious prohibitions against permitting same-sex financial benefits.

When asked a summary question at the end of the interview about
whether they thought that in general gays and lesbians had enough
rights, forty civic leaders replied that they did not, while eight thought
they had enough rights and another sixteen thought that gay rights
were going too far. However, the civic leaders who thought that gays
needed more rights focused more on the problem of respect and dignity for gays and lesbians than on legal rights problems. '[T]heir
[gays'] main problem now is attitude; it's not the law that's going to
help, it's attitude,' was Catherine's typical response.

Some civic leaders made stronger statements about the need for atti-
tudinal change, even going so far as to explicitly mention the problems
of homophobia and gay-bashing. Said Joel, '[Gays need] understanding. The ability to speak to someone who isn't afraid they're going to
turn. See, most men have difficulty talking to a gay man for fear that
he'll become gay himself. He thinks that it's a disease.' Dan said, 'I
think anyone deserves to be able to walk down the street and not be
called a name or be assaulted because of someone's perception that
they may be homosexual.'

Among those who thought that the gay rights movement was going
too far, the most common concern was the demand for marriage and
adoption rights, to be discussed below. Graham simply felt that gays
had too much power, a concern shared by a few others: '[T]hey're exert-
ing way too much influence in their society ... [T]hey've changed how
society looks, tremendous fear, politicians wouldn't say one word
against a gay now. Because this big machine would come down and just
shut you down.' Nevertheless, those individuals who actually feared
gay rights were few. This lack of fear reflected both overall Canadian
social attitudes to gays and lesbians, and the fact that, as community
leaders, even the recent immigrants from countries where gays and gay
rights were unheard of were attempting to adopt more 'Canadian' social
norms. Most of the civic leaders were satisfied with equality rights, even
when they disliked gay sexuality and disapproved of gay 'flaunting'
and militancy. Often such dislike coexisted with an explicit attempt
to live and let live, to overcome prior prejudices and adopt a tolerant,
open attitude that fit the prescribed Canadian liberal ideology of non-
discrimination. Disapproval of gays, as described in the next section,
did not always mean that the civic leaders opposed gay rights.

Disapproval of Gays

Gay Sexuality

A survey of American sexual habits conducted in the early 1990s showed that about 9 per cent of respondents who had had a sexual partner in the year preceding the survey had engaged in heterosexual anal intercourse during that year.[9] Yet anal intercourse is usually connected in the public mind with male homosexual behaviour, and many members of the American and Canadian publics find this sexual practice distasteful. Presumably, many such individuals also find other types of male and female homosexual activities distasteful.

I used a euphemism to ask the civic leaders what they thought about gay sexuality, referring to what gays 'do in bed.' Ten civic leaders said that they found gay sexuality repugnant, unnatural, or immoral in some way. Thirty-two said that whatever people did in private was their own affair, while twenty-six maintained that they had no difficulty with gay sexual practices. The way they spoke, however, and the kind of body language they used, suggested that many individuals were still working through this issue, overcoming an initial repugnance or prejudice to arrive at a view that was acceptable in liberal public discourse. Since at least forty-four civic leaders knew someone who was gay or lesbian, as discussed below, it is probable that they were also attempting to come to terms with the sexual practices of their relatives, friends, co-workers, and acquaintances.

To state that what people do in private is acceptable is to absolve oneself of making the moral judgments that one's early upbringing or religious beliefs might otherwise require. As Natalie said, 'That's something I'm still having trouble with, because of the religious issues. But I've had gay friends and I've worked with gay people and I mean, it's more or less not my business what they do. As long as they're doing their job, I don't care.' Others did not cite religious beliefs, but had difficulty with the 'unnatural' aspect of gay sexuality. Alexander, an immigrant from Asia, showed this ambivalence, clearly thinking gay sexuality unnatural yet trying to accept that it is a private matter. 'That's not how ... the nature intends of us as humans to behave ... [C]ommon sense prevails here. [Y]ou know, men and women ... if there was only men or only women, we can say, "Oh, there's no other way." Now, it's not so. What they do in bed, why should it be a public concern? I don't talk about my private life to other people ... [W]hy should we make it a national issue?'

Other civic leaders seemed to genuinely have no difficulty with gay sexuality. Kathleen explained her acceptance of gays largely as a consequence of becoming more at ease with her own sexuality: 'If they're both consenting and that's their desire I don't have a problem with it. I'm not interested either in what a lot of heterosexual people do ... [A]s long as both are consenting and both are okay and nobody's being injured, then that's their prerogative.' Several civic leaders felt that love was more important than the actual sexual act, as Hannah explained. '[A] loving expression of a sexual nature is fine. I don't think it's people's business what they do in a loving way.'

Among those who expressed strong disapproval of gay sexuality, some relied explicitly on biblical injunctions. Olga, a Roman Catholic, said bluntly, 'God created Adam and Eve, not Adam and Steve.' Karl, who was a conservative Protestant, also felt that he could not go so far as to endorse gay sexuality: 'Biblical standards speak out against it, and as a matter of principle I use God's word as a guideline on difficult issues. And so, while I have no problems with someone who is gay, I do have a problem with practising homosexuality.'

Sexuality between gays is difficult for many people to accept. Most of the Hamilton civic leaders had been raised within a religious tradition that in their interpretation explicitly forbade homosexuality. As older individuals, many had never heard explicit talk about homosexuals until they were well into adulthood. The modern tendency to speak openly about all sexuality, heterosexual as well as homosexual, was difficult for them to accept. Among some recent immigrants from the non-Western world, the Canadian openness about sexual matters was somewhat shocking, although other immigrants found it refreshing and adapted rapidly. Another shocking aspect, for some civic leaders, was that gays and lesbians are now open about their sexuality in public.

Flaunting

Much of the disapproval of gay sexuality among the civic leaders was expressed via concern that gays 'flaunt' their sexuality.[10] I did not pose a direct question about flaunting, yet twenty-seven individuals volunteered some concern about it, ten evincing strong disapproval, and seventeen milder disapproval. However, disapproval of gay flaunting was not an indicator of opposition to gay rights. Many people expressed support for gay rights in general, while expressing doubts about the more extreme displays of gay sexuality that they saw in the media.

One of Canada's largest Gay Pride parades is held every summer in Toronto. As they do with other events such as political demonstrations, the media routinely seek the most extreme image of this event to portray in print or on television. Thus, the people I interviewed were exposed to pictures, perhaps, of a male couple dressed in leather bikinis, rather than pictures of the tens of thousands of others in the parade dressed in an unremarkable fashion. As Brian noted, '[W]hen you're first exposed to it [homosexuality], it's the Yonge Street [Toronto] parade ... with a bunch of flaming fairies ... And it's like, "who the hell, what kind of sicko is that?" ... I find that abhorrent.'

In Hamilton, there was also a debate in 1991 when the gay community asked the mayor to declare a Gay Pride Week. The planned gay pride festivities did not include a parade, yet the common perception among the civic leaders was that such a parade had been planned. More conservative individuals saw this event as a plan for 'flaunting,' an 'in-your-face' activity. The general perception among those civic leaders concerned with flaunting was that a certain social decorum, the imperative to rectitude in sexual matters, was being violated by the gay community, as Edith explained. 'If I see a couple of fellows walking down the street with their arms around each other, laughing, that could be anyone, and I wouldn't think about it. But if they're perhaps cuddling up on the way down the street, then I'd probably think, "Well, they can keep that for home."' The civic leaders frequently noted that they themselves did not flaunt their own sexuality. '[W]hat really upsets me,' said Muriel, 'are these gay parades where there's all of this blatant physical contact and I think it's disgusting. I mean, my husband and I don't go walking down the street, taking off our clothes and hugging and kissing, and why should they?' Individuals from more sexually restrained cultures than Canada's also found public displays of affection upsetting. Said Yin, an Asian immigrant, 'I know that they are different, but do they have to behave and dress that way in the open? ... [T]hey can do whatever they like in the private life ... but sometimes I feel that it's just exhibitionism ... rather than [a] legitimate way of expressing themselves.' Thus, while trying hard to be nonjudgmental about the sexual activities of gays, some of these Canadians were still uneasy with them.

It should be noted nevertheless that although this section is entitled 'disapproval of gays,' the majority of the Hamilton civic leaders did not express disapproval either of gay sexuality or of flaunting activities. Even among those who did express such disapproval, it did not necessarily mean they were against gay rights. Such individuals tended, for the most part, to be moderately favourable rather than strongly favourable to gay rights. Working through the issue, these individuals had not yet brought themselves to the point at which they could completely accept gay and lesbian rights. They tended to be less willing to accept gay marriages and adoptions than those individuals less concerned by gay sexuality.

Family Issues

Gay marriages and adoptions were still contentious issues in Canada in the mid-1990s. The demand for equal rights of gays to marry and adopt goes beyond the national commitment to equality and non-discrimination. In matters such as employment, education, and housing, as several civic leaders pointed out, whether one is gay or straight is irrelevant. Being gay does not affect one's ability to do one's job, nor one's ability to avail oneself of educational opportunities, nor one's likelihood to pay one's rent. Gay marriage and adoption do, however, radically challenge the traditional picture of marriage and parenthood.

Gay Marriage

Sixteen civic leaders opposed gay marriages outright, nineteen agreed that a domestic partnership for legal purposes would be acceptable, and thirty-six approved of gay marriages on the same basis as heterosexual ones.

Gay marriages challenged the religious beliefs of many of the civic leaders, for whom religion was not simply a matter of formal affiliation; they frequently made clear that theirs was an active faith. In order to accept gay marriages, then, they had to work through their religious teachings. Christianity, Judaism, and most other religions teach that marriage is a union between a man and a woman for the purpose of procreation, sanctified by God. For example, two members of minority Asian religions noted their concern that marriage be between a man and a woman: in both cases, they were immigrants to Canada. Nerinder, the more recent immigrant, said, '[I]t's my religious background, just my upbringing, that marriage is a union between a male and a female, and that's how I look at marriage, so that you could be together and raise a family.'

The civic leaders who were opposed to gay marriages also stressed the responsibility of married people to procreate. Although many married people in Canada have no children, and indeed some are childless by choice, the religious principle that marriage ought to be for procreation was one that many people took seriously. As Margaret put it, '[T]he way the Bible says is, marriage is for the procreation. Well, two of the same-sex couples are not going to procreate.' Naimah, a recent immigrant from the Middle East, simply could not understand the gay and lesbian rights movement, stating that gay marriage was 'not productive,' meaning not productive of children. This concern evinces a common response in non-Western societies to homosexuality, that it is not the homosexual behaviour itself that is offensive, but rather the unwillingness to conform to social norms regarding the values of marriage and procreation.[11]

When I proposed it to them as an alternative, nineteen civic leaders were able to accept domestic partnerships, even though they could not accept gay marriages. I explained that domestic partnerships would provide gay couples with the same legal rights and responsibilities that heterosexual married people enjoyed, such as the right to act as each other's next of kin, the right to sponsor immigration of spouses from other countries, and the right to inherit from each other; in effect, what Bill C-23 later mandated. However, such a domestic partnership would not mean that the partners would marry. In the civic leaders' eyes, this implied that the holy aspect of marriage would be kept intact. The strongly symbolic nature of marriage, as a union and a commitment between a man and a woman, would be retained. Thus, perhaps, their own marriages, their own commitments to their opposite-sex partners, would not be threatened. Susan agreed with this proposal: '[A]s long as there was a distinction there that ... marriage ... still does have [its] basis in religion and in the Bible, and it was designed to sanctify the relationship between a man and a woman ... [I]f you can design another kind of ceremony or another kind of relationship, I'd have no problem with it.'

The largest number of civic leaders, however, agreed with gay marriages on the same basis as heterosexual. Some approved of gay marriages because of a basic commitment to equality in all respects. As Martin put it, '[I]f a person is gay he or she should be entitled to a quality of life in society, and if he's happier with a same-sex partner ... why should I say, "No, you can't do that?" That's not right.' Stability of relationship was also important in some individuals' thinking, as Elliott exemplified: 'I probably would [accept gay marriage] ... I probably would if the effect of such a marriage would be to provide additional stability to the relationship ... [P]articularly if there are children involved, I think that it would be desirable.' Others felt that homosexual love should be acknowledged in the same manner one would acknowledge heterosexual. Rina's belief in the loving quality of same-sex relationships was typical of this view: '[Marriage] means commitment, honesty, love, relationship, sharing ... and it doesn't necessarily have to be between a man and a woman ... I really believe that two [gay] people feel those things and can commit to each other.' This type of thinking reflects a change in contemporary society from thinking of marriage as a procreative duty, to thinking of it as a relationship between two companions.

That the majority of Hamilton civic leaders favoured gay marriage or domestic partnership may indicate a fairly recent development in their thinking. Some literally seemed to be considering the issue for the first time when I interviewed them. A few argued themselves through an initial hesitation about gay marriage to acceptance of it as they spoke. Many underwent a similar process in their discussions of gay adoptions.

Adoptions

A common-sense assumption is that anyone opposed to gay marriages is also opposed to gay adoptions. But in the Hamilton study, three people strongly opposed to gay marriage nevertheless accepted gay adoptions, as did ten people willing only to go as far as domestic partnerships. On the other hand, two of the thirty-six individuals favouring gay marriages opposed gay adoptions, and another six thought that gay adoptions would cause problems for the children involved.

Forty-two people favoured adoptions by gays on the same basis as adoptions by heterosexuals. This exceeds by six the number of people who favoured gay marriages on the same basis as heterosexuals. Most made this judgment on the assumption that gays and lesbians would undergo the same types of screening and legal procedures as heterosexuals would have to undergo. 'I think that they should have the same kinds of screening process that everybody else does ... But I don't see any reason why, just because a person is gay, that they can't make as good a parent as someone who isn't,' said Sarah. Many of those who favoured gay adoptions were most concerned with ensuring that children received good, loving care. In this, they argued, heterosexuals had not proved themselves competent, large numbers abusing or abandoning children. As Linda said, '[T]here's a lot of children right now in homes who are being physically, mentally, and emotionally abused badly by parents who are heterosexual. So I don't see why, if there's some loving lesbian couple ... that can take this child in and care for them, and give this child what they need, I don't see what the issue is. My first issue would be safety and love and protection for the child.'

For those favouring gay adoptions, it was not important that children have parents from both sexes. '[T]here can always be role models from the other gender through uncles or friends. You know, positive role modelling in that other way,' said Sylvia of lesbian adoptions. For those worried about gay adoptions, however, having a male and a female parent was very important. Fairly recent immigrants from Africa or Asia especially held this point of view. Aqil felt, 'Education ... it's not just sending a child to school ... [I]t takes man and woman, mother and father together of opposite sex ... [W]oman is different than a man is, so ... a lot of things go into day-to-day home life which the child has to be witnessing to become a full human being.' There was a general sense among those worried about gay adoptions that children raised in such a situation would be confused, not necessarily about their own sexuality, but rather about their own social situation.[12] As Nicky said, '[I]t makes it so difficult for the kids, at school, their peers, trying to explain that "I've got two Moms," or "I've got two Dads because my Dad fell in love with another man" ... [T]hat is not healthy for the child ... [I]t's very confusing.'

Eight civic leaders were concerned that children adopted by gays or lesbians would grow up gay themselves, or would be pressured to become gay to conform with their parents' sexual orientation. Adnan said, 'I've still got to see how do I think of their upbringing ... how they are going to identify their sexual identity, how they are going to come to terms with that.' On the other hand, eighteen people volunteered that homosexuality is genetic or biologically based, thus making it easier for them to accept gay adoptions. '[T]he genes will tell you whether that ... baby is going to be gay,' claimed Walter.

Finally, for a few civic leaders, gay adoption, like gay marriage, was wrong because it broke biblical norms. If the Bible prohibits homosexual relations, it also prohibits homosexuals, as sinful people, from caring for children. Neil, a devout Protestant, argued, '[S]ome people would say today, "You've got to get with reality and the twentieth century." I think the Scriptures have stood the test of time ... and the Bible never did adhere to it [gays raising children], so I don't think ... we should be adhering to it now.'

Teaching about Homosexuality in Schools

An issue under some public discussion in Canada at the time of the interviews was whether children should be taught about the gay lifestyle in school and, especially, whether they should be taught that the gay lifestyle is as morally valid as the heterosexual lifestyle. The civic leaders' opinions about whether children should be taught about homosexuality at all, or whether they should be taught about it in a morally neutral or a positive way, tended to parallel their opinions on gay adoptions. Twelve individuals preferred that nothing about homosexuality be taught in the schools, twenty-four said that children should be taught on a 'need to know' basis, and twenty-three said that homosexual unions should be presented to children as normal, and as morally valid as heterosexual.

Some people said it was important to teach about homosexuality in a respectful manner because some of the children might themselves be gay. Kari, the mother of a lesbian daughter, said, 'I remember talking to one gay man about his childhood in rural Nova Scotia and ... he said he really felt he must have been from another planet, because he knew he was different ... [H]e felt so alone ... And I think you should be taught at school about human sexuality in all its variety.' Some felt that teaching about homosexuality would lessen the chances for homophobia. Laurence had grown up in an area where many homosexuals vacationed and had always had a very tolerant attitude toward them. He believed, '[I]t [education] prevents that homophobia that we suffer from, because we didn't have that sort of education back there and then.'

Other individuals argued that, more generally, it was important in Canada to inculcate in children a sense of respect for homosexuals. '[I]t's valuable to teach children about all lifestyles in school ... [I]t's valuable absolutely that they learn to celebrate the differences in families, and to understand that families come in all shapes and sizes and ages and colours and cultures, and family is about people who love each other,' said Lynn. Natalie, the youngest of the civic leaders, had been a student in an experimental sex-education program in which the children were taught to respect homosexual relations as they would respect heterosexual. She appeared to be the only civic leader who had had such an experience. '[T]hey weren't showing pictures of what intercourse looks like or anything like that, but it was discussed in a very rational manner ... [I]t didn't bother us in any way, nor did it make all of us run out and become homosexuals. So I think if it's discussed rationally, fine, I've got no problem with it.'

Other civic leaders thought that children should be taught about homosexuality, but only on a 'need to know' basis. Homosexuality exists, and therefore students should be aware of it; this is especially necessary in the era of AIDS. Among this group of civic leaders were several who were reluctant to accept the gay lifestyle, although they were trying to adopt a more liberal approach to gay rights. 'I think we have to [teach about gays], with proper guidance ... no problem there ... [But] where I find it a little hard to accept [is] that it's, that they're [heterosexuals and homosexuals] both on the same footing, and I'm not condemning the gay existence. I'm saying that I don't put them on the same, exactly the same, footing,' explained Patrick, an older European immigrant.

Only a very few people thought that children should be taught nothing about gays and lesbians in school, other than that the gay lifestyle is wrong. Leo, a conservative Protestant, said, 'I would teach children ... my belief that the normal relationship ... between human beings is meant to be heterosexual, that gay tendencies are abnormalities, and from a Christian perspective something to be struggled with.' Henry, an elderly man who was the only civic leader who thought that gays actively recruit young people, said, '[I]t's not the norm ... [I]t's all wrong. You teach in a democracy, you go by the majority ... [W]hat two adults do together is their own business, but certainly [do] not teach an abnormality in school, no.'

It is striking, nevertheless, that very few of those people who still felt uneasy with gay rights were willing to state outright that children should not be taught about homosexuality, or that they should be taught it was wrong. Most of the Hamilton civic leaders accepted that homosexuality is a social reality, that children need to know about it both for their own protection and in case they themselves are gay, and that an attitude of tolerance, if not an attitude of acceptance, should be expressed in the classroom.

Changing Social Mores: The Gay Cousin

Exposure to the Gay Rights Debate

In Canada, acceptance of homosexuals increased rapidly in the 1990s, both in law and in social attitudes. Since the gay and lesbian population had become more socially and politically assertive, Canadians who might never have actually acknowledged in their earlier lives that there were such people as homosexuals were confronting their own attitudes, thinking about what and who a gay or lesbian person was, and deciding how they were going to react to gays they knew, or to gay claims for equal rights.

The Hamilton civic leaders were engaged in a process of rethinking their attitudes. I asked most if their attitudes to homosexuals had changed since they were young or, for the older people, in the last twenty-five years. Sixteen said they had had no change in their attitude, and one said his attitude had become more negative, but forty-one said their attitude to gays had changed from fairly negative to fairly positive.

A few individuals changed their attitude to gays as an explicit corollary to their attitudes to equality rights in general. As Jacob, who was Jewish, put it, '[I]f it is wrong to be opposed to an identifiable group that I belong to, when is it okay? ... [T]he answer is, it isn't.' Martin had become active in human rights issues in general: 'What made me change? I think my feelings on human rights. Being active in human rights involves everybody, not just me, and equality of each individual ... and gays are just individuals, they're not on a lower level or a higher level, it shouldn't matter.' Several individuals said they felt ashamed of the attitudes to gays they had had in their teens or youth, and of the tolerance they had shown of verbal gay bashing. Walter, who had grown up in a very rough part of Hamilton, said, 'Well, I did go through that phase [of verbal gay-bashing] ... when I was a child ... [W]hen I was with ... my friends and they were saying, "Look at that queer, look at that faggot." ... It's not something when I reflect back that I should have said.'

For other people, exposure to the problems of discrimination faced by homosexuals was enough to encourage tolerance and acceptance of gay and lesbian rights. Many of the older people, especially the immigrants, had grown up at a time was homosexuality was unknown, or rather, unspoken. Eduardo, who was from Portugal, explained, 'Well, this was non-existent when I grew up, to the age fifteen. There was no such thing as a gay or lesbian – so yes, I did change. I had to learn, I had to cope, and I had to adapt.' Exposure to gays resulted in the sometimes startling realization that the civic leaders had been living and working with gays all their lives.

'Some of My Best Friends ...'

The most important influence on the civic leaders' developing respect for gays and lesbians was actual contact with members of the gay and lesbian community, having, in effect, gay cousins. Forty-four people volunteered during the course of the interview that they knew someone who was gay.[13]

'Some of my best friends are gay,' like the phrase 'Some of my best friends are Jewish,' is often taken by social liberals to be a sign of underlying prejudice in the speaker. After all, those who had Jewish friends in Europe during the Hitler era seem to have done little to help them. To help a Jew in Hitler's Europe, however, was to incur a severe penalty. Canada is a democracy, not a dictatorship. To help a gay person is an act of choice, to which no legal penalty is attached. The ballot is secret, and one can vote for or against a party that favours gay rights. Freedom of speech is protected; one can debate gay rights in the public arena and give one's opinion to pollsters without fear.

In a liberal democracy, to know a member of what might be considered a strange group is not necessarily to fear her or him. To know someone, according to the Hamilton civic leaders, is to think about that person, what makes him tick, what makes her upset or sad. To know someone and then discover that he or she is gay or lesbian is often to feel obliged to rethink one's prejudices, to ask oneself whether the way one thought in the past was morally correct.

Two of the civic leaders had cousins who they knew were gay; another mentioned a lesbian daughter. Two others had known gays who committed suicide. Michelle recalled, 'I think it's going to take another generation or so to evolve to the point where there will be more openness ... And I really do hope that in the process we'll reduce the number of suicides ... [I knew] a young man, he threw himself in front of a train in Toronto because he was gay, and he couldn't deal with the backlash from his family.' Dorothy also had known an individual who later committed suicide. '[W]hen I was a little girl we had a babysitter and I didn't know, I'd never heard the word "lesbian" until I was an adult really, but I knew she was different ... and then when I was an adult my mom told me that she committed suicide and that she was a lesbian.'

Two civic leaders had been influenced by knowing people who contracted AIDS. William said, 'I've worked with two [homosexuals], one who died of AIDS ... And he wasn't any different than the rest of us, he wasn't any better and he wasn't any worse ... He kept up until he couldn't keep up anymore and ... I thought, "By golly, he's no wimp, he's got a lot more courage than I might have under the same circumstances."' Other people simply noted that knowing gay people had changed their attitudes. In some cases these were friends, as for Lynn. 'It was a very dear friend of mine who told me that she was a lesbian. And I had to really do a lot of thinking about that. My initial reaction was one of abhorrence. And then I was very angry at myself for feeling that way ... I had to do a lot of reading and a lot of thinking and a lot of talking, and fortunately she was a dear enough friend that she allowed me to do that process without being offended by it.'

In many other cases, although they knew of no one close to them who was gay, the new openness of the gay community meant that civic leaders met them in their everyday life, which they would not have done in the past. As Louise said, 'I know people now who are gay, whereas before I didn't. So it was always like, "Oh, those people." Now, when you meet people and you find that they're just the same as you are, just normal human being[s] ... you start to realize it's no big deal, they're just people.' The realization that homosexuals are individuals, that they have names, faces, social roles and relationships extraneous to their sexual orientation, has helped many heterosexual Canadians accept gay rights. Gays and lesbians are people they know, not merely strangers from a foreign (sexual) landscape.

Reinterpreting Religious Belief

One barrier that civic leaders felt to full acceptance of gay rights was religious belief. As discussed above, this barrier made it difficult for many to accept gay marriage, and made it difficult for a few to show any tolerance whatsoever toward gay sexuality.[14] Nevertheless, there have been recent changes in the way religious groups in Canada approach gays and gay rights that modify the unease felt by devout individuals considering questions about homosexuality.

Canada's United Church was formed by the union of Presbyterians,

Methodists, and Wesleyans in 1925, and had about 3.1 million adherents in 1991.[15] It underwent a soul-searching in the early 1980s, and eventually decided in favour of ordination of sexually active homosexual ministers.[16] The United Church justified this decision by arguing that it is the actual expression of physical love that is important in a Christian relationship, not whether such expression is heterosexual or homosexual. 'The closer we can get to a concept of sexuality, both in its physical and spiritual aspects, as a way in which we express our love of God, of one another and of ourselves, the better we will be able to evaluate the sexual activity of ourselves and others.'[17] Thus, biblical exhortations against homosexuals are disregarded in an interpretation that emphasizes Christian love and acceptance over the prohibitions and exclusions that characterized the Christianity of earlier times. To the United Church, what is important is not the physical sexual activities of homosexuals, but their overall Christian commitment.

Other Canadian churches have not taken as radical a stance as the United Church, but even the Roman Catholic Church accepts that homosexuals should be welcomed, although their actual sexual activity cannot be condoned.[18] This is a common attitude among Canada's Protestant churches as well. Even the small, conservative Christian Reformed Church (brought to Canada by Dutch immigrants), to which two Hamilton civic leaders belonged, has rethought its attitudes to homosexuals. One Christian Reformed committee concluded, 'It is one of the great failings of the church and Christians generally that they have been lacking in sympathy and concern for the plight of the homosexuals among them.'[19] These new religious attitudes makes it easier for Canadians who want to accept gay rights to do so. It is important to many Canadians that the religious authority to which they turn confirms the evolution of secular trends of tolerance and acceptance.

One difficulty experienced by religious people in learning to accept gay rights is the idea that active homosexuality is a choice. If it is a choice, then it is a choice to commit a sin. A good Christian, Jewish or other religious person may then believe that she or he has a duty to judge the sinner. The idea now frequently discussed in the press, that being gay is a genetic characteristic, helped some Hamilton civic leaders to overcome this moral disapproval of homosexuality.[20] Eighteen individuals mentioned a belief that being gay is a genetic condition. Muriel, an older native-born Canadian, reconciled herself to her gay cousin partly because 'I guess they were born that way. If it's in their genes then they're going to be that way ... You know they can't help it.'[21]

For other religious individuals, it was not necessary to convince themselves that homosexuality was a genetic condition in order to accept gays. Rather, the key was to reinterpret the religious tradition itself. 'Hate the sin, not the sinner' was a common approach. So also was the belief that Christianity is more interested in loving and accepting everyone than in rejecting those who sin. Nora rejected what she believed were explicit Roman Catholic teachings against homosexuality in favour of a more universal message from Jesus. '[T]he way I look at being a Catholic is, I look at ... what Jesus was trying to tell us ... I don't think certain Popes or priests have more understanding of tolerance than individuals who are trying to practise. They carry out their lives and their beliefs based on what Jesus has taught, and I've never found any place where He said we were supposed to exclude ... this group of people.'

Thus, some Christian civic leaders felt that they could not accept any religious teachings that obliged them to exclude from their community any sector of the population. Just as Christianity has rejected anti-Semitism and racism, so, they felt, it should reject homophobia. The wider secular liberalism of Canadian society influenced how they worked through their thoughts on religion. A democratic approach to authority enabled them to reject the teachings of priests and ministers, just as they would reject the advice of a politician or a teacher with whom they disagreed. 'Knowing' that it is wrong, in this day and age, to exclude anyone from respect and concern on any basis whatsoever enabled these civic leaders to maintain their religious faith while rejecting illiberal aspects of it.

On the other hand, not all Christians, and certainly not all Christians or other devout people interviewed for this study, are able to accept the recent liberalization of some Christian churches' attitudes to homosexuals. While many Christians consider acceptance of gay and lesbian sexuality, even to the point of sanctified marriage, to be a mark of progress to greater diversity and inclusivity, some others consider this diversity to be a moral outrage. In this view, pro-gay-rights liberals have so influenced public debate that there is no room for religiously based opinions.

Diversity versus Conformity

In the 1980s, the rhetoric of 'diversity' entered Canadian public discussion. The principle of diversity required that Canadian society go beyond tolerance to open acceptance of those deemed to be different, indeed, even to celebration of that difference. In the opinion of those who advocate diversity, the truly rights-protective society is one that is inclusive. Inclusivity requires the moral acceptability of the diverse family. A homosexual family is as worthy of concern and respect as a heterosexual family.

The language of inclusivity and diversity was at the core of the debate over Bill 167, 'An Act to Amend Ontario Statutes to Provide for the Equal Treatment of Persons in Spousal Relationships,' debated in the Ontario Legislative Assembly in 1994.[22] This bill, introduced by the ruling left-leaning New Democratic Party, was meant to ensure that all benefits and duties accruing to or incumbent upon heterosexual spouses should also be available to homosexual spouses. The debate on the bill reflected the divisions still existing in Canadian society in 1994, which had eroded sufficiently by 2000 for the federal government to pass Bill C-23. While the Ontario bill's sponsors used the language of inclusivity and diversity, its opponents evinced a discomfort with the idea of homosexual spouses, and a fear that the bill would undermine the Canadian family. In deference to its symbolic and religious meanings, the word 'marriage' was carefully eschewed in the bill, which was nevertheless defeated.

Introducing Bill 167, the attorney-general of Ontario, Marion Boyd, used terms familiar to sexual liberals of the 1990s. 'Tolerance, diversity, fairness, and respect: These are the main themes of this legislation,' she said, later arguing that 'it is our duty as legislators ... to bring our laws into accordance with this fundamental articulation of the core Canadian values of diversity and tolerance.'[23] This modern, inclusive interpretation of homosexuality was nevertheless upsetting for many members of the provincial parliament. Opponents of Bill 167 were very concerned that the traditional family would be undermined by it. Said one Liberal member of the legislature, 'Because of my upbringing and my religious beliefs, I believe firmly in the concept of the traditional family and I think of family as the traditional mother, father, and children ... In society today, every major problem we face ... can all be traced to the breakdown of the traditional family unit.'[24] This quotation illustrates the depth of religious and moral commitment of opponents of Bill 167. In the Ontario of the mid-1990s, not everyone believed that the concept of diversity included commitment to a diverse family, equally respectable whether heterosexual or homosexual. For the Hamilton civic leaders opposed to gay marriage or adoptions, acknowledgment of the gay family went further than their fundamental moral beliefs would permit.

Humanizing Gays and Lesbians

One of the most fundamental questions facing those who investigate human rights is how individuals come to think of those different from themselves as the same. How, beneath differences of physique and skin tone, clothing, customs, language, religion, indeed sexual orientation, does one recognize a common humanity with another? Each individual who becomes tolerant of difference, and who learns to respect it, has to recognize that the person she thinks of as different has something in common with herself.

The process that the civic leaders in this study went through was one of humanizing gays and lesbians. Forced to confront their existence by the previous twenty-five years of activism in Canada, the civic leaders attempted to reconcile their attitudes to gays and lesbians with their attitudes to general Canadian social values. A general social belief in the value of privacy helped them to come to terms with gay rights. Several civic leaders made reference to the famous statement by then Justice Minister Pierre Elliott Trudeau in 1967 when, legalizing homosexual relations between consenting adults, he said, 'The State has no place in the bedrooms of the nation.'[25] These strong pro-privacy views were buttressed by the strong pro-equality views that were part of the core ideological orientation of Canadians after the 1960s. Just as women and members of racial minorities should not be disadvantaged in the public realm in areas such as employment, housing, or education, so, in the eyes of the Hamilton civic leaders, homosexuals should not be so disadvantaged.

The rights to privacy and equality demand that deviant sexual practices be entirely overlooked not only in public but also in private decision making. The citizen who even in her private discussions takes homosexuality to be a deviant or despicable attribute is failing in her duty to respect other citizens. The Hamilton civic leaders were concerned with the need to be inclusive and respectful, to exhibit actual concern for gays, rather than merely to exhibit tolerance for private differences.

The process of accepting gays was eased when the civic leaders became aware that gays were not in fact so different from themselves, that they were their relatives, neighbours, students, co-workers, or clients. The new concern and respect that they were teaching themselves to feel was not for abstract strangers, but for members of their own families and communities. The civic leaders who earlier in their lives had been hostile to gays were, in the mid-1990s, confronting their previous beliefs. They felt obliged to change those beliefs to conform to their overall principles of equality and respect. In many cases, they also felt obliged to reconcile their evolving respect for gays with religious beliefs declaring homosexuality a sin. They did so, however, in an overall liberal and secular society, in which high social value is placed on non-discrimination, diversity, and respect. This eased their passage into a new social attitude of acceptance of homosexuality.

Chapter Six

Limits to Multiculturalism: Gay Rights, Women's Rights, and Minorities' Rights

You're here in Canada now, you're not in your own country. You have to practise what the law is here in this country.

Dan, a white native-born Canadian

Cultural Relativism and Human Rights

One question that arises in a multicultural country like Canada is whether minority religious or ethnic groups should be expected to adhere to human rights values that might not be part of their own belief system. In chapter 5, I discussed the opinions of the Hamilton civic leaders about gay and lesbian rights. Separate from their own opinions on such rights, however, is their opinion on whether members of such minority groups should agree with them. This is an issue to do with the thorny debate about cultural relativism, especially in the era of globalization.[1] As the world becomes more globalized, should the cultures of immigrant groups be preserved in Western societies, even if the internal practices of such cultures violate some internationally and nationally held principles of human rights?

The debate on cultural relativism spills over into the debate on multiculturalism in Canada. Some worry that an extreme relativist stance would undercut the moral fibre of the Canadian collectivity.[2] New immigrants must accept the extant laws: 'our country, our rules' is the slogan. Others believe that some attempt must be made to accommodate the beliefs, rituals, and customs of new immigrant groups. Thus, Canadians must learn to accustom themselves to the sight of Muslim women in headscarves or veils, or to the sight of Sikh policemen in turbans. Yet to some Canadians, these visible signs of difference are still upsetting and confusing.[3]

Many Canadian citizens are aware of the debate about the relationship between cultural relativism and human rights. Public discussion of obligations to minority cultures and religions occurs in Canada in places of worship, in many non-governmental organizations, and in the press. Yet there is little investigation of what citizens think the relationship ought to be.

This chapter probes the attitudes of the Hamilton civic leaders to this debate. It analyses their answers to two questions: 'Should all ethnic or religious groups in Canada have to support women's rights?' and 'Should all ethnic or religious groups in Canada have to support gay rights?' The meaning of 'support' in these questions is deliberately left open, to allow the civic leaders to distinguish between the obligation to obey the law and the obligation to render moral support to the principles of women's and gay and lesbian rights. Thus, the question leaves leeway to also discuss the obligation, if any, to respect minority cultures.

The chapter focuses on women's and gay and lesbian rights because the rights of these two categories of people are central to any notion of culture. Women are the primary carriers of culture. It is they who socialize the young, who exemplify their family's honour, and who are expected to conform to traditional social norms even when men adapt to social change.[4] Thus, the rights of individual women often seem to clash with the rights of cultures to carry on their own traditions. As Susan Moller Okin puts it, '[O]ne issue recurs across all contexts: ... what should be done when the claims of minority cultures or religions clash with the norm of gender equality.'[5] Similarly, as I discussed in chapter 5, gays and lesbians who openly express their sexuality challenge the centrality of the family in the culture of any society.

It is often thought, therefore, that the creation of a multicultural community, as in Canada today, might result in the erosion of the rights that the dominant culture has bestowed on women, or on gays and lesbians. Minority religions and cultures might not be as tolerant of rights for these two groups as the majority religion and culture. Although the questions posed for this chapter regarding women's and gay and lesbian rights referred to all ethnic and religious groups in Canada, most Hamilton civic leaders assumed that the questions referred only to ethnic and religious minority groups.

In a nutshell, the civic leaders come closest to the stance described by Jack Donnelly as 'weak cultural relativism,' in which 'the relativity

of human nature, communities, and rights serves as a check on potential excesses of universalism ... [W]eak cultural relativism would recognize a comprehensive set of prima facie universal human rights, but
allow occasional and strictly limited local variations and exceptions.'[6]
These Canadians agreed that respect for the cultures and religions of
new immigrant groups with customs or beliefs strange to the dominant European-origin Canadian of Christian background was important. One should actively demonstrate such respect. Customs that
strangers value, such as wearing the veil or arranging marriages, can
be accepted in Canada as long as they do not violate anyone's individual human rights. The excesses of universalism should be avoided.
Nevertheless, Canada cannot tolerate introduction within its borders
of customs that constitute what scholars would call gross violations of
human rights, particularly female genital mutilation.[7] Nor can Canada
tolerate violation of the principle of non-discrimination, at least as it
applies to women. Some civic leaders, still personally uneasy with gay
rights, would tolerate some discrimination against gays and lesbians.

The Response Continuum

As a group, the civic leaders revealed a continuum of opinions. I coded
as 'yes' or 'no' each answer to the two questions mentioned above,
namely, 'Should all ethnic or religious groups in Canada have to support women's/gay rights?' The coding was difficult, as most individuals hedged their answers, and many argued against themselves within
a single answer. The numbers discussed below do not total seventy-
eight as I did not pose each question to each civic leader, and some
people failed to answer one or both questions. The answers are in any
case only a crude indication of the actual opinions of the civic leaders,
as the complexity of most answers belied placement into simple yes/
no categories.

Of the twenty-nine immigrants who responded to the question
about women's rights, 17 per cent (five of twenty-nine), thought that it
was not incumbent on all ethnic or religious groups to support
women's rights. Among the native-born, 24 per cent (nine of thirty-
eight civic leaders) held the same view. With regard to gay and lesbian
rights, a somewhat larger percentage of immigrants answered no.
Forty per cent of the immigrants (ten of twenty-five) thought that it
was not incumbent on all ethnic and religious groups to support gay
and lesbian rights, while 31 per cent (eleven of thirty-five) of the

native-born civic leaders held the same view. Nevertheless, this difference is not large. More significant is the fact that both groups were more willing to allow leeway on gay rights than on women's rights.

It should not be assumed that those who thought there was no obligation on immigrant or minority religious groups to support women's or gay and lesbian rights personally opposed such rights. Many of the civic leaders separated their own views from those they felt that minorities should hold. Sensitive to what they saw as the need to respect multiculturalism, they did not think that they should 'impose' their views on others. Some others, however, were personally troubled by gay and lesbian rights, and therefore argued that minority religious and ethnic groups should not be obliged to hold views that they themselves did not. As Eugene, himself originally a child immigrant, declared, 'I don't accept them [gay rights] so why should they [immigrants]?'

It would be fairer to describe the responses to the two questions not as a yes/no dichotomy, but as a continuum, as shown in the accompanying figure:

Figure 1 Continuum of Responses

'Should all religious or ethnic groups have to support women's/gay rights?'

yes, via law __; yes, via education __; yes, but respect difference __; no, can have own opinion __

The strongest 'yes' answers were to the effect that the law is the law and must be obeyed, regardless of the personal, cultural, or religious beliefs of minority communities. Somewhat weaker 'yes' responses argued that minorities, like all other Canadians, had to accept women's and gay rights, but it was better to educate such minorities to acceptance of these values than to oblige them by law to accept them. The most typical weak cultural-relativist approach was one that said minorities should respect human rights laws, yet the majorities should also respect minorities' difference. Finally, some civic leaders argued that like anyone else, members of religious or ethnic minorities were entitled to disagree with women's and gay rights. This continuum might seem neat; however, it was impossible to code each individual's answer as only one of the four options, as many people discussed several options.

In another section of the interviews, not reported on in detail in this book, I had asked the civic leaders if they thought that immigrants made too many demands on Canadians. Most said they did not. Of those who did hold such views, some were themselves immigrants, and would contrast their relatively hard days as newcomers with the relative ease that they believed characterized more recent immigrants' entrance to Canada. Those few who did think immigrants made too many demands on Canadians usually referred to demands for social benefits or welfare payments, not to moral or cultural demands. Thus, they did not worry that new immigration patterns might fray the social fabric with unknown customs that violated Canadian values. They displayed more concern that the majority should respect the beliefs and customs of new minority groups in Canada than that those groups should uphold Canadian norms. Nevertheless, by and large both native-born and immigrant Canadians did express the view that once in Canada, all groups have to obey the law.

A 1993 national poll suggested that 72 per cent of Canadians believed that ethnic or racial groups in Canada should 'adapt to the value system and the way of life of the majority in Canadian society.'[8] Similarly, Sniderman et al. found in their survey of Canadians that 33 per cent strongly agreed, and 44 per cent agreed, with the statement 'While it is all well and good to celebrate one's heritage, it is more important for new immigrants to learn what it is to be Canadian than to cling to their old ways.'[9] Sixty-four per cent 'basically agreed' with the statement 'People who come to live in Canada should try harder to be more like other Canadians.'[10] Sniderman et al. refer to these findings as having about them 'the scent of xenophobia.'[11] It is difficult to interpret such results, however, unless the people who answer the questions are separated into immigrant and native-born categories.

Both these national surveys might be taken to imply that all those who believe immigrants should adopt the 'Canadian way of life' are native-born, whereas those who disagree with such a statement are more likely to be immigrants. The 'majority in Canadian society,' however, does not necessarily mean those born in the country and who are of European and Christian background. It can refer, rather, to the numerical majority, among whom may be immigrants or members of ethnic or religious minorities. Among the Canadians in the present study who thought that immigrants should adopt 'Canadian' values were many who were not of European origin, and many who were immigrants.[12] Given their own backgrounds, it would seem that the 'scent of xenophobia' is an inappropriate way to summarize their attitudes. Many of those who want immigrants to 'adapt' are afraid that they might otherwise hold intolerant views that could undermine the Canadian consensus on multiculturalism, non-discrimination, and respect for the rights of others. Such an interpretation is consistent with the 68 per cent of those surveyed in the 1993 national poll who also agreed that 'one of the best things about this country is that it accepts people of all races and ethnic backgrounds.'[13]

Our Country, Our Rules

For some civic leaders, whether native-born or themselves immigrants, respect for other cultures stops at Canada's borders, at least as far as human rights are concerned. Those who immigrate to Canada have to accept Canadian rules on matters that might offend their culture or beliefs. In so far as both women and gays and lesbians are protected from almost all forms of discrimination in Canada, members of minority religious or ethnic groups must also refrain from such discrimination. As Jacqueline, an immigrant from the Caribbean, put it, 'If you choose to belong to a country that has such laws [women's rights] ... you should have to follow the laws of the country.'

For these civic leaders, immigration to Canada means that Canadian laws take precedence over custom and culture. Underneath the tolerance for difference is a legal system that protects human rights and a state that backs up human rights laws. Jacob asserted, 'Is it the business of the state to protect the rights of its citizens? Absolutely and unequivocally. And if your religious group prevents a citizen who wishes to exercise his or her rights ... then the state has ... the obligation to intervene.' The sensitivity to cultural relativism otherwise displayed by the civic leaders does not mean that laws may be broken by members of religious or ethnic minorities. 'You are the citizen of the nation, you should be supported; it doesn't matter what, gay rights or religious rights,' said Eduardo.

This attitude, that the law is the law, was not generally presented in an aggressive or hostile manner. It was simply a fact; one should always conform to the law of whatever country one is in. As Carol, an activist in various international human rights causes, put it: '[T]here are certain laws that ... we all expect people to follow ... [T]o a certain extent you have to follow the laws of the country ... And the same thing if I were to go to Saudi Arabia; I guess I would have to wrap up and cover my face.'[14] Both immigrant and native-born individuals, non-white as well as white, accepted this principle. 'Our country, our rules' was not meant to suggest that people of non-European and/or non-Christian background were more likely to break the law than native-born, European-origin or Christian-background Canadians. Rather, the civic leaders were confident that Canada was a rights-protective society and that obedience to the law was, therefore, synonymous with human rights protection.

Unfamiliar Customs

While the civic leaders admired Canadian human rights law, they were well aware that elsewhere there were many customs that seemed to violate human rights principles and that were often protected by state law. They were willing to accept that some of these customs, such as veiling, were relatively harmless, but they found other customs intolerable and absolutely unacceptable in Canada.

Customs regarding Women

The civic leaders had an intrinsic sense of what constituted a gross human rights violation and what did not. Presumably through their exposure to the mass media, many were aware of some of the worst violations of women's rights in other societies, and were adamant that whatever their cultural or religious basis, such violations should not be permitted in Canada.

Female genital mutilation was explicitly banned in Canada in 1996, as part of a package of Criminal Code reforms. Prior to that time, it had been considered a crime under the general prohibition of assault against women and children.[15] The civic leaders had no hesitation in condemning female genital mutilation. As Michelle said, '[T]hat [female genital mutilation] sounded so awful to me; it would be a crime if that kind of behaviour seeped into this country.' Martin agreed: 'Well, things like that mutilation, Middle Eastern people have this ... female circumcision, that just turns my stomach ... That's a culture that ... once they come to Canada, these women should be protected ... If there is gender bias ... they should adopt our way.'[16]

Wife beating was another custom that the civic leaders singled out for condemnation. Edith expressed a typical view: '[W]hen in Rome, do as the Romans do ... I don't like to see ... someone abused because, "Well, that's what we can do at home, that's what we can do in the country we came from, so we should be able to do it here" ... We frown upon that here ... I think they have to become Canadian.' For Edith, being Canadian meant obeying Canadian laws regarding women. Walter also volunteered his strong condemnation of wife beating, going so far as to invoke the principle 'our country, our rules,' even though in another part of his interview he had spoken quite strongly about how as an Aboriginal person he did not personally identify himself as a Canadian. 'Should they have to accept women's rights over here? Eventually they'll probably be forced to ... [T]he violence against women, if they're still beating their wives, I don't agree with that. If that's what they're doing then I'll say they'll be charged, and justice will be meted out ... For the immigrant, the refugee ... we have laws that say they have to obey ... [W]hen they come to this country and they accept Canadian citizenship, they accept everything else that goes along with it.'

Sylvia, who was active in both Aboriginal and feminist causes, condemned wife beating but suggested, nevertheless, that some consideration had to be given to cultural beliefs and practices in trying to assist the victims of such beatings. '[T]hose women that are coming from places where they have pretty well no rights ... they kind of know what their role is, or where their place in society is, and they come here and perhaps they suffer from violence in the family. Well, you can't just go in there and say, "Well, you've got to leave this man" ... [T][here needs to be respect for where this woman is coming from.' Drawing on her own experience as an Aboriginal person, Sylvia was sensitive to the need for culturally appropriate corrections of human rights violations, but was not willing to forego the principle of universal women's rights.

While female genital mutilation and wife beating were most often referred to as examples of customs that should not be tolerated in Canada, regardless of the original cultures of those who practised them, the civic leaders also referred to other customs they found unacceptable. William mentioned reports of the Taliban practices in Afghanistan. 'What's happening in Afghanistan? Those people who have taken over Kabul? ... I see no reason why people like that should come to this country and treat their women in the same way that they do there ... So whether it's part of their culture or not ... it should not be part of ours.'[17] Brian mentioned the practice of dowry in India, which he equated with the sale of women.[18] '[I]n other parts of the world there are traditions ... Now, if they want to ... transplant something like that to Canada, i.e., the selling of the bride ... no. That's not a traditional Canadian mainstream ... societal norm ... If you want to continue to do that, well, go home and exercise it, not here.'

Thus, on the whole, the civic leaders were confident of the value of women's rights, and of the absolute necessity that they be respected by all immigrants to Canada. They were somewhat less confident of the value of gay and lesbian rights.

Customs regarding Gays and Lesbians

The civic leaders' somewhat weaker insistence on gay and lesbian than on women's rights reflects the weaker and more recent entrenchment of the former than the latter in Canadian law and customs. Moreover, as discussed in chapter 5, some individuals belonged to religious faiths that still questioned the equality of gays and lesbians, especially with regard to the right to marry. As members of faith communities, these civic leaders understood how gay and lesbian rights could conflict with religious principles. Colleen, herself a lesbian, argued, 'They [minority religious and ethnic groups] should have to support it [gay rights] in legal terms, but not in religious terms ... [I]t's part of their revelation ... that homosexuality does not fit in with their concept of what constitutes healthy or godly sexual relations. I don't think we can impose a point of view on people.' Other individuals were themselves so opposed to gay and lesbian rights that they could not conceive of any duty for religious or ethnic minority groups to support them. As Betty said, '[W]e're looking at an unnatural thing. It's just not natural that women be with women and men be with men.'

The civic leaders' weaker support for gay and lesbian than for women's rights might also have been a consequence of lack of information. They were not as aware of the mistreatment of homosexuals in some foreign countries as they were of the mistreatment of women. They did not seem to know that such mistreatment is often tantamount to gross human rights violations. No one mentioned laws such as the death penalty in Sudan for a third conviction of homosexuality.[19] Nor did they mention other practices such as denying homosexuals employment, schooling, or housing, or imprisoning them for long stretches of time as punishment for engaging in anal intercourse.[20] Part of the tolerance the civic leaders showed for violations of the rights of homosexuals was, therefore, probably a result of ignorance. The relative lack of debate in Canada on such basic rights for gays and lesbians as non-discrimination may have influenced the civic leaders' perception of the kinds of human rights abuses homosexuals experienced abroad.

The lack of outrage over persecution of gays and lesbians was also a result of the belief that Canadians need to learn about, and respect, unfamiliar religions. The civic leaders worried about how freedom of religion would conflict with other human rights.

Freedom of Religion as a Human Right

The unease some civic leaders felt about 'imposing' women's or gay and lesbian rights on religious or ethnic minorities reflected, in part, their belief that it is incumbent upon 'mainstream' (white, European-origin, Christian or Christian-background) Canadians to understand the religions of new groups entering the country. Some individuals who personally supported gay and lesbian rights did not believe that they should require those beliefs of others. As the process of acceptance of gay and lesbian rights had been gradual for many of them, and for the religions to which they adhered, so it had to be gradual for others, including new Canadians from unfamiliar parts of the world. As Alexander, a non-white foreign-born Christian, said, 'I think it's an individual choice, in terms of recognition of certain groups [gays] ... [R]eligious teaching has a lot of value and a lot of strength to certain people, and I think we can respect each other's religious thoughts, religious teachings.' Kathleen, a white native-born Christian, agreed. '[I]n religion you can choose your beliefs. And so ... if the religion says you cannot be part of this religion if you are gay, then you can choose another religion that would support you ... And to try and force a religious group who feels that way to accept gays ... would probably cause more damage than it would do good.'

On the other hand, some civic leaders were not so forgiving of unfamiliar religions that discriminated against women. While Kathleen was relatively flexible regarding gay and lesbian rights, she was less flexible regarding women's rights. '[I]f they're doing something ... I consider to be wrong ... we should be able to intervene in that ... [I]t would depend ... on what the right is ... If they are putting a woman at danger ... and she chooses that, do I have the right to tell her, "No, your religion can't do that?" My heart says, "Yes, I want to tell her that to get her out of that relationship," and then my mind says, "Well, doesn't she have a right to make her own choices?"' Here Kathleen was wrestling with three principles: respect for cultural diversity, respect for Canadian human rights laws, and respect for personal autonomy. Although she wanted to encourage women adhering to discriminatory religions to rebel against ill-treatment, she also wanted to respect their right to make their own decisions. Kathleen's internal debate shows the seriousness with which many Canadian citizens take the whole range of human rights, which they accept as intrinsic to their society. It is possible that, had she been aware that minority religions might also put gays and lesbians 'at danger,' as they sometimes do women, Kathleen would have revised her answer regarding the tolerance that should be shown toward those whose religions oppose gay and lesbian rights.

Many civic leaders debated with themselves whether the rights of members of minority ethnic and religious groups to freedom of religion must be taken into account in determining what their obligation was to respect human rights laws. Some thought that in the end, no matter what the religion, the laws had to be respected. As Yin, an adult immigrant from East Asia, said, '[A]s long as they [minorities] want to be ... in Canada, they should follow the laws here, and that means that women should have the same rights, regardless of where they come from or what religion they are from.' Patrick shared this view. 'I think of the rights of Muslim women being very restrictive ... and [when] they move to this part of the world ... I would hope they could adapt some changes ... [I]f that's a religious situation, that they feel they have a right to exercise ... [nevertheless] it's against our present laws ... [T]hey have to conform.'

Other civic leaders were not quite as adamant about the law's taking precedence over religious beliefs. Anthony, an adult immigrant from Africa, could not decide whether in cases of conflict, minority custom ought to give way to human rights law. '[T]he Charter of Rights guarantees people freedom of religion, and this is where sometimes there's a clear conflict ... I don't know how true this is, because I didn't see this in the Islamic people that I knew [in Africa], but they said Islam has ... little regard for women. If this is true, this would be in clear conflict with that law ... [H]ow does a legal system handle that? Freedom of religion and yet equality, and their religion may not necessarily be preaching equality; that's a tough one.' Karl, a deeply religious Christian, speaking of gay rights, argued that religions must be respected. 'These are matters of the heart and of the soul. These are deeply held beliefs, and I think that one cannot legislate a belief system; then a government oversteps its bounds.'

Rina, however, had a somewhat different perspective on religion and rights. She argued that women within minority religions, among whom she was one, should have the right to make up their own minds about what practices they would follow. '[I]t's really up to the woman ... [I]f the woman is Orthodox [Jewish] and she wants to have an abortion, I think she should be able to have an abortion. I don't think religious groups should have any say or control in that area.' Her perspective was shared by Naimah, an immigrant from the Middle East, who saw Canada as a country that would protect women against abusive customs from their home countries. 'I know so many women [who] ... want to have a career, they get into divorce because the man looks at it ... like humiliation for him because he's supposed to be head of the family ... [People] ... are living in old experiences. It's different environment, different country ... you should change ... [T]his [women's rights] is part of the ... Canadian culture.' Rina and Naimah both referred to feminist beliefs, generally accepted in the Canadian population, as overriding the need for female members of minorities to conform to their own group's beliefs.[21]

To some Hamilton civic leaders, freedom of religion meant that one cannot impose one's majority customs and beliefs on minorities. Equally, however, it did not mean that new minority religious groups can impose their beliefs on other Canadians. As Sarah, a Christian feminist activist, argued regarding gay rights, 'I think everybody should get off everybody else's back ... [W]hat I allow for myself on the basis of my religious background, I can be as strict as I like with myself, or as liberal as I like ... [I]f they [immigrants] feel that homosexuality is wrong for them, then they have to deal with that themselves, whether they are gay or straight ... But for them to be telling me with a different religious background that it's not right for me to be gay ... that's another issue ... I'm not prepared to have other people oppress me.' This is a rather libertarian principle that sits uneasily with many of the more conservative members of new ethnic and religious minorities. Yet it is a common tenet among many Canadians, who believe that what one does in one's private life is one's own business, as long as it does not violate anyone else's rights. '[T]he basic human right is, I should be able to do whatever I want to do, as long as I don't hurt anybody else. I think everybody else should respect that of other people,' said Isaac.

Learning to Accept the 'Canadian Way'

The 'Canadian way' is one of respect for difference, but such respect must be a two-way street. This means that minorities who think homosexuality is evil have to learn nevertheless to respect homosexuals, even as other Canadians simultaneously respect minorities' rights to hold views they find abhorrent. Sofia, a lesbian, asserted, 'That [respecting gay rights] doesn't mean that ... you need to be forced to like it, but your behaviour better not be disrespectful or inappropriate, and you keep your opinions to yourself.' Nevertheless, several civic leaders believed that learning to respect gay and lesbian rights is more of an ideological wrench than learning to accept women's rights. 'I would expect everybody to abide by the laws of the county ... [But] ... I think respecting gay rights is a bigger job for most people than respecting women's rights ... I personally would give people a bit more leeway, a bit more time to open up their eyes,' said Carol.

Just as freedom of religion was an important principle that the civic leaders discussed when assessing minorities' religious views of women and gays and lesbians, so they frequently referred to freedom of thought as part of the Canadian way. Aqil, a recent immigrant who was personally very uneasy with gay marriages and adoptions, referred to the democratic process in discussing freedom of thought. 'Some people may be very strongly against it [homosexuality] ... It should be left to them ... accommodating it or really saying yes, to a vote that it should be done, it should be left to an individual.' Even those individuals who were very active in Hamilton's feminist and gay rights communities deferred to the overarching value of freedom of thought in discussing minorities' obligations to accept Canadian human rights practices. Said Lily, a lesbian and feminist activist, about women's rights, 'I guess it comes down to a freedom of expression and speech and belief, and I certainly don't believe anybody should be[lieve] something they don't believe. If they want to have whatever their belief is ... that's their choice.'

Many of the civic leaders referred to the social value of education in persuading members of minorities to accept the 'Canadian way' of women's and gay and lesbian rights. Elaine, an Aboriginal activist, thought that such education for immigrants should occur before they came to Canada, so that if they found they could not accept Canadian principles, they could be rejected as immigrants. '[T]hey're pretty strict when someone's coming into this country ... [T]here should be something as to what our expectations are, or this is the way the laws are ... [A] lot of it is educating people because then that way they can make their own decision [to obey Canadian laws], and if not, then don't come into the country.' Other individuals were more lenient, merely arguing for education once immigrants had arrived in Canada. Regarding gay and lesbian rights, Nicky, a native-born white, said, '[I]t's ... not pushing someone's values or beliefs down their throat, but I think if we really help educate ... [T]hey might not have had those opportunities [to learn] back in the countries they came from. It wasn't recognized, it wasn't discussed.' The assumption here was one of goodwill on both sides. Members of new minorities were presumed to be willing to change their values to conform to the Canadian norm, while members of the dominant Canadian society were presumed to be equally willing to respect those who were different, and use persuasion, not compulsion, to inculcate rights-supportive ideas.

At the same time, some civic leaders pointed out that Canadians sensitive to other cultures should remember that whatever the formal position of women is in Canada, many from the dominant community suffer the same types of abuses that are often connected in the public mind with minority religions and immigrant cultures. Respect for others requires that mainstream Canadians acknowledge their own faults, and not stereotype the behaviour of new immigrants. As Sofia, of Italian background, note, 'I don't think that immigrant and refugee groups ... disrespect women more than Canadians ... It's not okay for a Canadian man to hit his wife ... and it's not okay for a man who comes from Sicily ... Women are entitled [to rights], regardless of culture or religious background.'

The 'Canadian way' included a strong sense among the civic leaders that there is a known Canadian culture. Canada has a certain way of life, which includes a strong commitment to the human rights of everyone, including women and gays and lesbians. Immigrants and minorities need to conform to that way of life. As Bob, who was gay, said, '[T]hey [immigrants] should understand ... that in this country, this is how we organize our society, and I think as a Canadian, it's the kind of society I want ... and yes, I think they should have to support it [gay rights].' Cran, who had a very strong sense of loyalty to Canada, had the same views. 'If we choose as a society to adopt certain values, then yes, I think that people who choose to become Canadian should also.' These civic leaders defined belief in human rights principles as part of what it meant to be Canadian. They were more interested, therefore, in protecting human rights than in tolerating diversity.

Those civic leaders who favoured adoption of Canadian culture were more likely to answer 'yes' to the question of whether all ethnic or religious groups in Canada should support women's and gay and lesbian rights. Their position was not an absolute one, however. It was more a hope that as immigrants assimilated into Canadian society, acceptance of Canadian culture and basic human rights norms would automatically follow. '[P]eople coming into our country should be encouraged to adopt our culture. Not perhaps as a precondition to entry, but I think that our society has a lot to offer. I don't know if I would want it to be diluted by the growth of divergent cultural views,' maintained Elliott, a white native-born Canadian. To Elliott, diversity could undermine basic human rights principles; therefore, diversity had to be curtailed, for the greater good of Canadian society.

Culture, Rights, and Social Change

The references made by Hamilton civic leaders to Canadian culture, Canadian values, or the Canadian way suggested a cohesive view of the country. The civic leaders did not articulate their respect for minority ethnic and religious groups in terms of a fractured multiculturalism, or a lack of a common core that could bind all Canadians together. Rather, they argued that as individuals they ought to respect other individuals who had come from different cultures or religions and whose beliefs differed from their own.

The civic leaders were aware of the capacity and propensity of immigrants and members of minorities to adopt Canadian values and ways of life. For them, minority cultures were not static. Even the seemingly most permanent alien custom would eventually be modified by absorption into Canadian life and adoption of Canadian social norms. As Susan, who was white and native-born, put it, 'I think in many cases that just being immersed in Canadian society is going to make the difference. I don't know that you can insist that people change cultural values and religious values that are really intrinsic to them, but I think inevitably they will change.' In the minds of these civic leaders, education was particularly important to ensure that immigrants, or at least their children, adopt Canadian norms of rights protection. As Mabel, a Caribbean immigrant, put it, 'Well, they [minorities] have been given equal rights. And their children are going to be learning this in their schools, equal rights ... And the only kind of thing that's going to make them change is for them to see that their children are getting along well with the new things.'

A multicultural policy that would support static cultures, rather than accepting that all cultures change, was not appropriate in the eyes of these Canadian citizens. Ruth, an adult immigrant from Britain, argued that Canadians should not assume that values are static in the home countries of ethnic or religious minorities. Just as Canadian human rights values have changed significantly over the past several decades, so values in other countries have also changed. '[L]ook at India. The dowry has been outlawed, bride burning has been outlawed, so are we really that much different?'[22] Here, there is a clear sense of social change, and an understanding that it affects principles held by immigrants coming into the country. Some immigrants come to Canada precisely because they agree with Canadian values and want to take advantage of them, whatever their original culture may have been. As some civic leaders realized, the non-European societies producing Canadian minority groups are not as radically different from Canada as is sometimes thought in the public imagination.

The capacity and desire of immigrants to adapt to Canadian ways, combined with the willingness of native-born Canadians or long-time residents to be patient and to respect the different views of minority groups, suggest that the country will be able to continue its rights-protective path into the twenty-first century. Even as the world becomes more global and there is increased migration and intermixing of peoples, strong human rights values and laws can ensure that clashes or misunderstandings of cultures do not result in the undermining of basic principles. The vast majority of Hamilton civic leaders accepted all rights for gays and lesbians except the right to marry and adopt children; all, similarly, accepted full human rights for women. They expressed these views no matter where they came from, and no matter how long they had been in Canada.

Part of the willingness of the more recent, adult immigrants to adopt these norms was undoubtedly a result of their opinions and values before coming to Canada. Canada accepts immigrants according to a point system that gives preference to highly educated, professional or business-class immigrants, who tend to have a more cosmopolitan view of the world than the less educated.[23] Even immigrants who are not highly educated or professional have already chosen to take what Michael Walzer, speaking of immigrants to the United States, calls the 'cultural risk' of moving to a new society. '[T]he communities they [immigrants] have created here are different from those they knew before precisely in this sense, that they are adapted to, shaped significantly by, the liberal idea of individual rights.'[24]

Another part of the willingness of members of minorities to adopt Canadian human rights values is a result of socialization, a normal consequence of living among people whose values may differ from those of one's ancestors. While for strict multiculturalists socialization might seem a form of assimilation that should be resisted, for most of the Hamilton civic leaders change in values consequent upon residence in Canada was normal and acceptable. Indeed, many had changed their own values in their own lifetimes. Their memories of how they had adopted new norms of human rights and discarded old ideas of disgust with homosexuals, or beliefs that women should stay in the home, helped them to assess the process newer Canadians were likely to undergo.

Hamilton Civic Leaders and the Academic Debate on Multiculturalism

The way that the Hamilton civic leaders articulated their answers showed that while they were aware of some of the polemics surrounding issues of multiculturalism and cultural relativism, they were unaffected by its extremes. As thoughtful citizens, they tried to balance a number of conflicting principles, including the right to preservation of culture and religion, freedom of religion and thought, and the individual rights and autonomy of women and gays and lesbians. They used the ideas and principles they encountered in everyday Canadian life to make sense of the competing rights Canadians enjoy and the concomitant duties incumbent upon them.

Some advocates of the rights of minority cultures argue strongly that any loss by minority groups of their culture is an illegitimate exercise of cultural hegemony by the 'dominant' group in a society. For such advocates, ancestral cultures must be preserved by immigrant ethnic and religious groups. It is incumbent upon the state to preserve cultures by promoting the right of a group to exist as if it had never changed geographic locations and as if its members had never encountered the social norms of the wider society.[25] Such espousal of extreme multiculturalism was not attractive to the Hamilton civic leaders.

A softer type of multiculturalism is espoused by Will Kymlicka. This softer view would try to ensure that minority cultures do not disappear, but would also preserve the individual rights of persons living in multicultural societies. '[A] liberal conception of minority rights will not justify (except under extreme circumstances) "internal restrictions" – that is, the demand by a minority culture to restrict the basic civil or political liberties of its own members ... [I]ndividuals should have the freedom and capacity to question and possibly revise the traditional practices of their community.'[26] This is the type of multiculturalism that seemed to appeal to the Hamilton civic leaders. They would agree with Kymlicka's statement that 'I do not think it is wrong for liberal states to insist that immigration entails accepting the legitimacy of state enforcement of liberal principles, so long as immigrants know this in advance, and none the less voluntarily choose to come.'[27] Immigration is a choice: the immigrant has chosen to leave old customs behind if such customs violate human rights.

To the Hamilton civic leaders, multiculturalism was an important Canadian social value, but not so important that it could override fundamental human rights. They would agree with Jeff Spinner's approach to liberal citizenship. 'An unfamiliar practice that does not violate liberal ideals should not be discouraged. Religious practices that appear strange but harm no one should be respected ... [But] practices that violate liberal principles should be either discouraged or forbidden ... Respecting all cultural practices and values means accepting racism and sexism.'[28] The civic leaders, therefore, did not adhere to any extreme view of cultural relativism. They simultaneously espoused a universalist vision of human rights and a particularist vision of the need to respect different religions and cultures. Because many were themselves immigrants or the children or grandchildren of immigrants, they understood how strange Canada might seem to foreigners, and how security of custom and traditional belief might help new immigrants adjust to Canadian life. Cultural relativism did not mean that cultures could not change, nor that members of minorities were so wrapped in their indigenous cultures that they were unattracted by wider Canadian social norms. Rather, cultural relativism meant to 'give a little,' to respect beliefs and customs that differed from one's own, as long as they did not hurt anyone else, either outsiders or insider members of the minority group.

In this respect, the individualist, somewhat libertarian view of rights so often decried by non-Western critics of human rights was, in fact, an advantage for non-Western, minority immigrants.[29] If a citizen can do whatever he or she wants as long as it does not hurt anyone else, then citizens can believe what they want to believe and dress and act however they want, however outrageous those beliefs, clothes, or customs may seem to the majority. Freedom of religion and thought impel multiculturalism; Canadians must not only tolerate, but also respect, differences in belief and opinion. Liberal principles protect illiberal practices, as long as those practices do not violate basic human rights.

In the end, then, these Canadians are soft liberals. Whether immigrant or native-born, most adhere to the liberal premises that underlie international human rights. Their liberalism is soft, however, because they do not expect everyone in Canada to automatically share their liberal views. They want room for diversity. Extreme universality of human rights, if enacted not only into law but also into social behaviour, would erode that diversity. On the other hand, extreme cultural relativism would erode the Canadian culture – rooted in equality, non-discrimination, and adherence to human rights – that many Hamilton civic leaders held dear.

In the view of these civic leaders, what Donnelly called weak cultural relativism was the best way to respect difference while simultaneously ensuring that human rights remains a fundamental Canadian value. A stronger insistence on difference, at the expense of universal human rights, would result in a non-democratic society in which the fundamental Canadian values of equality and non-discrimination would be subjected to the no less fundamental, but nevertheless not absolute, value of multiculturalism. The Hamilton civic leaders did not want a multicultural Canada to become 'a mosaic of tyrannies,' in which cultures could determine individuals' rights.[30] Liberalism for them meant equality, and perhaps even autonomy, for all individuals, rather than merely tolerance of differences among groups.

These Hamilton citizens, engaged in thinking through questions of rights conflicts and the need to protect both individual equality and cultural minorities, were part of the global human rights culture now characterizing world society.[31] Their capacity to think about the position of minority cultures (often their own cultures) in a multicultural liberal democracy is part of the capacity for humanitarian, cosmopolitan empathy that in the new global society is one counterweight to the dangers of ethnocentrism and social exclusion.[32] These citizens were the contextualized individuals that Brems suggested should be taken as the starting point in the analysis of the conflict of feminism and cultural rights.[33] They felt connected to their fellow citizens, and they were connected. They understood the connectedness of the individual to the group and society as a whole, but they also understood that there are multiplicities of connections, and that anyone living in Canada was as much a Canadian as a member of any other society. The

Hamilton civic leaders were real people, living with and working with other real people. Knowing those real people, they worried about their rights and freedoms, both the freedom to maintain their cultures and the freedom to be protected from individual harms.

Chapter Seven

The Sins of the Fathers: Employment Equity

I'm worried about my grandson ... I'm a little tired of [people] ... saying, 'Well, we're discriminating against you now because your grandfather was ... or your great-grandfather did this.' I don't really feel I should have to ... answer for my forefathers.'

William

The Policy Debate

Several of the preceding chapters have addressed Canada's policy of multiculturalism, both indirectly through discussion of hate speech and hate crimes, and directly through discussion of human rights-based limits to multiculturalism. Employment equity can be viewed as another aspect of the policy of multiculturalism, in so far as it is designed to ensure that all groups in Canadian society have a fair chance for employment and promotion. As such, one might expect that the Hamilton civic leaders' opinions about employment equity would reveal the same high degree of consensus as the previous chapters demonstrated, or at least that disagreements would not be characterized by obvious splits among different social categories. Not even in their opinions on hate crimes was there an obvious split between members of vulnerable categories such as blacks and gays and non-vulnerable categories such as whites and heterosexuals. The questions I posed to the civic leaders on employment equity, however, did reveal such a split.

In Canada, the term 'employment equity' applies to government policies whose aim is to remedy discrimination in employment against certain disadvantaged categories of people.[1] Canada's Charter of Rights and Freedoms protects such policies in its Section 15.2, which states that equal protection under the law 'does not preclude any law, program or activity that has as its object the amelioration of conditions of disadvantaged individuals or groups.' Employment equity is an official policy at the federal level. It is designed to facilitate entry into employment and fair promotion through the ranks of four designated groups of Canadians: women, Aboriginal peoples, people with disabilities, and 'visible minorities,' the last term referring to non-whites other than Aboriginals.[2] There is much debate about what employment equity actually means. Does it mean simply the removal of barriers to equal opportunity for individual members of these designated groups, so that they can compete on equal terms with white, able-bodied men? Alternately, does it mean minimum hiring and promotion quotas for members of designated groups?

The two types of policies have different implications. The first looks only to equal opportunity for individuals, with the outcome for social groups dependent on their individual members' own efforts in a society in which there is no discrimination against them. The second appears to imply some form of social engineering, or what the critics of employment equity Rainer Knopff and Thomas Flanagan call social technology.[3] In this view, employment equity attempts to equalize outcomes for the federally designated groups. It does so by mandating that their members be hired and promoted proportionate to their numbers, even if their individual members do not possess the requisite qualifications for the various positions for which they must be hired. Since their inception, employment equity programs in Canada, like affirmative action programs in the United States, have thus been criticized for unfairness towards individuals not included in the groups that would benefit from them.[4]

Disagreements about the aims of employment equity are exacerbated by the fact that the Employment Equity Act does not specify whether workplaces should reflect the social composition only of those who might be qualified for particular occupations; whether workplaces should reflect the social composition of the geographic area in which they are located, regardless of the qualifications of the people living in the area; or whether they should reflect the social composition of the entire Canadian workforce.[5] All three of these appear in the eyes of critics to require some sort of quota system, ensuring that minimum quotas of members of each of the four designated groups are hired.

Although the Employment Equity Act specifically prohibits the setting of quotas (Article 33.[1].[e]), the hiring goals that it does permit seem like quotas to many Canadian citizens.

In short, the debate is about equal opportunity for individuals versus equal outcome for groups. This, in any case, was how the Hamilton civic leaders interpreted the debate. Most approved of measures that encouraged or protected hiring and promotion strictly on the basis of merit. The idea of quotas, however, was contentious. Indeed, the idea of quotas sufficiently disturbed the Hamilton civic leaders that thirteen of them raised the issue independently in the section of the interviews about women, as well as responding to my formal questions about employment equity in the section of the interviews on multiculturalism. Almost all the discussion centred around two of the designated groups, women and visible minorities, with a little discussion of Aboriginal people as well. No one questioned that people with disabilities needed protection under employment equity programs.

Of sixty-four individuals who believed that employment equity policies meant equal individual opportunity, fifty-two favoured them. Of fifty-nine who discussed group quota systems, however, only twenty-one favoured them, with thirty-eight opposed. These figures reflect almost precisely the findings of Sniderman et al. in their national survey that 'Ordinary Canadians are opposed to affirmative action [employment equity] quotas in hiring by a margin of two to one.'[6] Of the twenty-one civic leaders favouring quota systems, only four were white males; in the study as a whole, twenty-seven were white men. Ten of those favouring quotas were white females, six were members of visible minorities, and one was an Aboriginal person; all of these might conceivably benefit from quotas. Of the thirty-eight opposing quota systems, sixteen were white males and thirteen were white females, the remaining nine being either Aboriginal or members of various visible minorities. That white females would oppose policies that might be construed to be in their interests was not surprising; many thought of their husbands' or sons' opportunities, rather than their own. A story William told illustrates this attitude: 'My daughter-in-law was a ... feminist until it hit her in the pocketbook. She was ... women's rights for this and women's rights for that until my boy [son], who should have got a job, was finally told when a promotion came up, "You can put in for it, but I'll save you a little bit of embarrassment by telling you you're not going to get it, because there's a woman that has to get that job."'

The disproportionate number of white males opposing quotas (four times as many as supported them) tells a tale. That tale is of a feeling that the social bargain between government and ordinary citizens had been broken by the introduction (as they saw it) of quota systems. In Ontario, the debate on the purpose of employment equity – whether it meant individual opportunity or group quotas – was sharpened in 1993 when the then New Democratic Party (NDP) government introduced a sweeping employment equity law, Bill 79, 'An Act to Provide for Employment Equity for Aboriginal People, People with Disabilities, Members of Racial Minorities and Women.' This act required that hiring by any corporation with fifty or more employees reflect the demographic composition not of those qualified for the available positions, but of the community as a whole.[7] Article 2.2 stated, 'Every employer's workforces, in all occupational categories and at all levels of employment, shall reflect the representation of Aboriginal people, people with disabilities, members of racial minorities and women in the community.' This provision seemed to go beyond mandating equal opportunity by using the rough rule of thumb that the proportion of members of the four designated groups hired by any employer should approximate their proportions among those qualified for the employer's positions. Instead, it seemed to require that the proportions of members of the four designated groups hired by any large employer should reflect their numerical proportion in the community, whether or not they were actually qualified for the positions available. Thus, it appeared to mandate group outcomes over individual equality of opportunity.

That there was sharp public disagreement with this act was revealed in a December 1993 Gallup Poll showing that 75 per cent of Ontarians believed that 'Government should ... hire new employees based solely on their qualifications,' only 20 per cent believing that 'Government should ... actively hire more women and minority group members.'[8] The NDP seems to have sharply misjudged the public mood in this instance. A poll conducted in 1987 showed that even among supporters of the NDP, only 38 per cent answered 'Yes, have quotas' to the question 'Do you think large companies should have quotas to ensure a fixed percentage of women are hired, or should women get no special treatment?' On the other hand, 68.5 per cent of NDP members of federal and provincial legislatures answered 'yes' to this question.[9] The Ontario NDP decision-making elite, then, seemed to believe that the public would accept a form of group rights even though opinion polls showed the public sharply opposed to this type of right.

Bill 79 was rescinded when the Progressive Conservative government was elected on 8 June 1995. This government had won the election partly on the basis of its slogan, 'The Common Sense Revolution.' The title of its repeal act, 'An Act to repeal job quotas and to restore merit-based employment practices in Ontario,' succinctly reflected public concerns.[10] For many Ontarians, common sense meant the best qualified person should get the job, regardless of her or his group membership or that group's historical or contemporary disadvantage.

The Hamilton civic leaders were interviewed shortly after the Ontario Employment Equity Act was rescinded. For those white men who opposed group quotas, as well as for some of the white women who did so, this recently introduced and then rescinded law could be construed as a direct threat to their or their children's economic interests. Non-white, Aboriginal, disabled, or female members of the community might have had a better chance of obtaining a job than they or their husbands or sons had. In the eyes of these white men and women, membership in groups designated by the NDP legislation seemed to give some Canadians privileged and unwarranted access to a scarce commodity, namely, a job.

Barrington Moore, Jr, speaks of a universal social belief that everyone is entitled to enough property to play a 'decent' role in society.[11] In advanced capitalist society, the right to work – to hold a job – is often a substitute for property.[12] For some of the white civic leaders, an employment equity program that appeared to deprive individuals of the right to compete for or hold a job merely because they were not members of certain designated groups constituted a violation of the social bargain between ruler (government) and ruled (citizens). The Common Sense Revolution gave back to them the right to enough property to play a decent role in society. On the other hand, for some of the civic leaders who were members of the designated groups, the social bargain to make sure they had enough property (access to employment) to play a decent role in society could not be honoured unless some sort of minimum quota for hiring were in place.

The Meaning of Employment Equity

Some Hamilton civic leaders thought that employment equity meant equal individual opportunity, without any privileges to members of the four designated groups. Others thought that the term implied a quota system. Still others distinguished carefully, stating that as long as employment equity meant equal opportunity for individuals, they approved of the policy. If it meant, or became, a form of quota employment, then they disapproved of it.

As noted above, sixty-four civic leaders offered definitions of employment equity as equal individual opportunity; of those, fifty-two volunteered that they approved of such policy, while only six said they disapproved. Those who approved believed such employment equity policies removed barriers that previously had existed to the hiring of members of the four designated groups. Nor did they quarrel with the categories that had been designated. Those of African descent were most likely to stress the importance of employment equity to their own careers. George, a black immigrant, saw the policy as one that helped him to obtain fair treatment. '[I]f you do a day's work [the same] as another guy, there's no reason why you shouldn't be treated the same way ... it encourages fairness.' Women also referred to the advantages of such a policy. Sarah, a white native-born woman, said 'The laws that attempt to bring about employment equity are attempts to remove barriers to everybody having the same shot at the same job.' Given their average age of fifty, many of the women had entered the labour force or sought higher education at a time when there was still active discrimination against them.

Equal opportunities for individuals struck the Hamilton civic leaders as a fair policy. It supported the implicit social bargain that everyone in Canada should have an equal chance to work and to be remunerated fairly for that work. The civic leaders' understanding was that such a policy was necessary because until the recent past the four categories of protected people had been denied equal opportunity to obtain work and to be fairly remunerated. No white males, or wives or mothers of white males, objected to this policy on the grounds that their past privilege, or the past privilege of their husbands and sons, would be eroded.

For some civic leaders, though, employment equity meant extra incentive for employers to hire members of the four designated groups, or extra privileges for members of those groups seeking employment. Fifty-nine civic leaders discussed the possibility that employment equity might become a quota system. Some of these raised the possibility of a quota system on their own; in other cases, I asked whether their approval of employment equity programs would go as far as approval of a quota system. As noted above, twenty-one said that they would approve of a quota system, while thirty-eight said that they would disapprove.[13]

A typical viewpoint of those approving of quotas was that it is always best not to have to resort to them, but if necessary, quotas should be set. Al, one of the few white men who approved of quotas, believed that '[I]f there were to be quotas, if it's to correct an injustice ... I would agree with that, yes. My preference would be to try and do it without quotas ... but if we had to have an imposition of quotas to get there [to employment equity] faster, then I don't see anything wrong with that. And I don't think it waters down the merit principle at all.' Dorothy, also white, agreed that quotas were sometimes necessary, although it was always best to retain as much as possible the principle of strict equality of opportunity in hiring. 'It's not fair to say, "Well, you don't have the job because you're white, and you should get it because you're Hispanic" ... [M]erit has to go first ... [W]hen you're hiring someone they must be able to do the job that you're wanting them to do, but I also understand that we do need a variety of groups of people involved in decision making in our society.'

Among the thirty-eight people who disapproved of a quota system, there were two main objections. The first was that any quota system was unfair to those who did not fall within the quota: there should be strict individual equality in hiring. Matthew, who was white, argued, '[E]quitable employment ... means that any individual that has the capability for any type of position should be considered fairly. As opposed to what I believe some people interpret equitable as being – you must have X number of people of this ethnic origin or that ethnic origin in this ... level of management and position, because there happens to be that percentage of those people in your neighbourhood. I don't believe in that.' Edith, an older white woman, pointed out the necessity for all Canadians to try to better themselves. 'I don't think it should be held against him, that he's a white male, if he's got better qualifications than the black female. I think the white male should get the job. It's just that we all have to better ourselves, education-wise.' Nor was this a viewpoint that only whites argued. Aqil, a recent South Asian immigrant, stated, 'I'm not a firm believer of ... there should be a reservation of quota for the minorities. I ... say it should be open for everybody, and the right candidate should get the job.'

Another, secondary objection to group quotas was the danger that such a system would backfire, with members of designated categories in positions of authority assumed by their colleagues or clients to have obtained those positions merely because they were members of visible minorities. They would be tokens, not acknowledged as qualified for their jobs. Kathleen, a white woman, argued, 'I don't think it [employment equity] actually works to break the barriers down ... [P]eople my age group, that are my friends, often tend to see it more as a forced [policy]; they never give credit to the people who have made it there ... [T]he immediate response is "Well, you know, they're the token female or the token black," and so I don't think it's working to do what it was supposed to do.' For some non-white Canadians, public perception that there was a quota system did cause their qualifications to be questioned, or cause hostility from whites. Martin, a native-born member of a visible minority, related, 'I've been accused of [benefiting from] reverse discrimination ... [W]hen I got promoted one time, this guy was really bitter, so I said, "Why are you so bitter?" He says, "Well, you stand out in a crowd; when they assess me, they don't really know who I am." I says, "Well, I can't help that."'[14]

Thirty-three civic leaders discussed the 1993 Ontario Employment Equity Act in their interviews, some bringing it up on their own, while others responded to my question as to whether they were familiar with it. For many, employment equity meant the strong provisions of this act, mandating that employee pools reflect the demographic composition of the community. Some civic leaders considered this act to be highly preferential to woman and non-whites. 'I'm not impressed with it [the former NDP law] ... People should be judged on their abilities and their qualifications, not on what race they are ... When it comes to the point that one person is more qualified than the other, but because ... the more qualified person is not from the [preferred] race ... she or she cannot be hired, I don't agree with that,' said Angela, who was white. The provisions of this act seemed to be an important cause of the 'backlash' against employment equity in Ontario in the mid-1990s.

Police, Firefighters, and the 'Backlash' against Employment Equity

For both white and non-white civic leaders, males and females, employment equity and the possibility of group quotas were a real, lived issue. Many believed that there was a white male backlash against employment equity in Ontario. Of sixty-four people who said such a backlash existed, fifty-one said so on the basis of things that they had heard about. Their assessment may well have been affected by the media, which tend to report sensational cases that appear to be gross injustices, rather than focusing on the day-to-day operations of employment equity policies.[15] Several individuals mentioned a local talk show with a host reputed to be quite hostile to attempts to ameliorate racial injustices in Ontario. As Barry, a black civic leader, put it, 'Just listen to the talk shows ... [Y]ou know they [whites] are bitter. They're really bitter. They say some awful things.' Only eleven people, however, said they had personal experience of such a backlash. Carol, herself very approving of employment equity policies, said about the white males she knew, 'Snorts, they snort an awful lot!' describing their attitudes to employment equity.

Some of the white civic leaders were part of this backlash. They were worried that their own sons, nephews, or other family members were being obliged to pay for previous social discrimination in Canada, for the sins of their Canadian fathers, so to speak. They were familiar with controversial employment equity programs in the Toronto firefighting force and the Royal Canadian Mounted Police that seemed to exclude white males from any chance of employment.[16] Several also mentioned a controversy over the decision by the fire department in Kitchener, Ontario, a city close to Hamilton, to set 'differential qualification thresholds: seventy [per cent] for [designated] group members, eighty-five for able-bodied white males.'[17] There had been much public discussion about these programs, much of it deeply emotional and generally focused on rhetorical questions along the lines of 'Would you want a Vietnamese firefighter to rescue you from your burning house, when you could have a strong white male?'

Eighteen people mentioned the debate about firefighters and police in their discussions of employment equity. Jacob, generally approving of moderate group quotas, argued, 'On the other hand, do I want to have someone who's a fireman ... do I want to have a ninety-eight pound, four-foot-eleven woman doing that ...? ... I don't think so ... I think in order to be a fireman, you have to be able to carry someone down a ladder.' The issue of the police and firefighting services was particularly salient for the fourteen white civic leaders who said that they or family members had been directly, and adversely, affected by employment equity policies. Leo was particularly angry about this.

My son wanted to become a police officer ... [Yet he] had the deck stacked against him when he went ... to take the test because he was told ... that the police departments were seeking whatever the qualified minority groups were ... [B]y inference it was very clear that the standards for the people in those groups were lower ... I don't have a problem with seeking broader representation, especially in the police force, which needs to deal with the many facets of society, but I think when you start to lower standards in order to impose certain quotas ... then I have a problem. It bothers kids my son's age ... that they see themselves as sort of citizens of the world, and at the same time being discriminated [against]. My son has a real hard time with that, because he was always very fair-minded about racial and ethnic differences ... [H]e now isn't a police officer and he's not going to be, he was completely demoralized.

Not all white people had these concerns, however. Ruth believed that preference for the designated categories was just the price her sons would have to pay. 'My understanding ... is ... that if there are two people who are equally qualified for a job ... and one was a visible minority, the minority get[s] the job ... I don't really have too much of a hard time with that ... I have had my sons argue this with me because they felt, as white, educated men, that they've been discriminated against. However, my husband is not their father; he can argue on the other side of the story, where he feels he hasn't had opportunities because's he's from [identifying country omitted], broken English, etc.' Ruth's perspective was influenced by the fact that she had both white and non-white males in her immediate family. Such was not the case for most of the whites who worried about quotas.

Like Ruth's husband, Hamilton civic leaders who were members of visible minorities had reason to support special programs to recruit minority firefighters and police. Despite her awareness that quota systems might result in rumours of tokenism, Lily, who was of mixed racial background, nevertheless supported them. '[T]here was this big concern that they were letting in a bunch of ... non-white firemen who wouldn't be able to do the job, when that actually wasn't the case ... [T]here had been a standard set ... [B]ut there's always this sense ... that the ... white cultural narrative becomes, "Well, they all got in because they were black." [Y]ou [blacks] often operate in a work environment that is a little less than welcoming, when quota systems and things like that start to happen.'

Lily was correct in referring to some whites' perception of special privileges for women and members of minorities seeking to enter the police or firefighting units as a 'cultural narrative.' In an era of high youth unemployment, the debate about policemen and firefighters focused a general concern among whites, that white males might not be able to find jobs at all.[18] 'I think white males feel like they are really under the gun right now,' said Betty, who was white. 'They're feeling if there's a job to be had, it's not going to be gotten by a white male ... and it's upsetting when you hear [of] them working hard to go to university, getting degrees, no job, getting more degrees, no job ... [I]f there's a job to be had, because of the equity ratios and so on it would probably be filled by a visible minority.' The specific targeting of non-white groups for what seemed to some white civic leaders to be preferential hiring contributed to their overall concern about employment prospects for male family members.

Whites and Social Power

To gauge the Hamilton civic leaders' interpretations of the past history of Canada, and the position of visible minorities in it, I asked them whether they thought white Canadians had too much social power. Of the sixty-eight individuals who responded to this question, forty-nine agreed that whites did indeed have too much power, among whom thirty-five were white. Nineteen disagreed that whites had too much power, among whom five were members of visible minorities.

Twenty-five of those who agreed that whites had too much power posited a relatively benign explanation for this phenomenon, maintaining that it was merely a consequence of whites having been in Canada first, before any significant non-white immigration flow, although obviously not before the arrival of the indigenous peoples. James, an older white man, said whites held the power they did 'by virtue of being here that much longer, and they probably know their way around [better] than the new immigrants, whether they're new whites or new anything. I don't think the new white has got any more power than the new black. They've got to ... establish themselves, get a job.' Other civic leaders felt that whites deserved their authority. Many of the white males who held power had worked hard for the positions they presently held; with the equal opportunity that was now Canadian law and increasingly Canadian social practice, others could work just as hard and attain just as much. Said Cran, a younger white man, '[T]o a certain extent, those people are older white males who ... have worked hard for a long period of time throughout their career, and probably deserve to be where they are ... [H]opefully over [the] years [we will see an] increased number of women and multicultural people participating.'

On the other hand, twenty-one civic leaders were of the opinion that the power that whites held was a direct consequence of racism. Bob, a younger white man, said, 'I hear the racist talk, I see the lack of black people and racial minorities ... in politics ... in the boardrooms ... even in volunteer boardrooms.' Basil, who was black, disagreed explicitly with the 'whites were here first' argument, noting that blacks had also been in Canada for a very long time. 'Blacks have been in Canada for almost four hundred years ... It's racist ... slavery and loss of power, being treated as property, and with the end of slavery we immediately moved to a ... labour condition that there was no equality ... And then there was racism, and maintenance [of] power by denial of the things that would give people, black people, the power.'

Only nineteen people thought that whites did not have too much power. Henry, the oldest white male among the civic leaders, thought, 'Anything that white people got, they've earned. The majority have earned.' Nor was it only whites who held this type of opinion. Yin, an Asian immigrant, took a tolerant view of white Canadians who still had difficulty accepting non-whites in positions of authority. 'The fact that ... in the public service or in the higher level of government is mostly the white people ... doesn't really mean that ... all the power is in them. For instance, if I want to run for office, legally I could. Now, whether people vote for me is a different thing ... Maybe it has to do with tradition, maybe it has to do with custom, maybe it has to do with being familiar and being at ease with someone who looks like you.' This tolerant view of the foibles of whites not yet used to non-whites was not unusual among the more recent non-white immigrant civic leaders. Native-born non-whites and those who had lived in Canada for longer periods of time, however, were generally less willing to accept prejudices as an inevitable part of whites' coming to terms with the new composition of Canada's population.

These differing views on whether and why white people held too much power affected the Hamilton civic leaders' opinions on employment equity. Those who did not think whites had too much power, but rather believed that the dominance of white males was primarily a historical accident, were unlikely to be strong supporters of quota systems. In their view, no special compensatory measures were needed to help visible minorities on the road to success. Rather, anyone could

succeed in Canada as long as equal individual opportunity was protected. For those, however, who attributed both the past and the
present predominance of whites in positions of power to racism,
employment quotas were necessary, both to overcome past discrimination and to protect non-white individuals against racism in the present.
For these latter civic leaders, such quotas were a form of compensatory
justice.

Compensatory Justice and Group Rights

Among the civic leaders, the argument for compensatory justice took
three forms. One was that the designated groups protected by employment equity were presently suffering discrimination in Canada. Equal
individual opportunity had not solved their problems; therefore, programs imposing hiring quotas had to be implemented instead. This
was the opinion of Jacqueline, a black civic leader who compared her
chances in life to my own, arguing that as a white person I possessed
privileges unavailable to her. The purpose of compensatory programs
was to help her get to the point where she could compete on equal terms
with whites. '[I]n many instances, a so-called immigrant or visible-
minority person has to be twice as good or better than other people in
order to get half as much, and I don't think that's right ... Sometimes in
order to be fair to me, you might have to give me a little more ... Because
you are white you are up there, and me, because I am black, I am here,
and in order to even things up I will have to be given more than you to
reach this spot ... You just need one step. I need nine steps in order to get
there.'

A second argument for compensatory justice did not maintain that
minorities or women were suffering discrimination in the present.
Rather, because minorities or women had suffered discrimination in
Canada in the past, white males should give up contemporary privileges to compensate for those abuses. As Kari, who was white, argued,
'I can see that if you're a white male, and you feel you're going to be
discriminated against because a white female or a black female gets the
job over you, because she's as good as you but not necessarily better,
you're going to feel peeved. But for a very long time a woman has had
to be infinitely better than a man, in order to be employed ... [T]his is
only a very small bit in the balance to redress a great inequity.' Isaac,
also white, took a similar approach. '[F]rom my background ... all you
had to be was male to be promoted ... and if two people came, one was

male and one was female, qualifications didn't have much of a bearing ... [I]n that sense I see employment equity as, if two people are
equal, the female gets the advantage, as justness over time.' Thus, by
this logic, the current generation of whites or men should pay the price
for the sins of their fathers, even if the current generation of non-
whites or women was not suffering discrimination.

A third justification for employment equity was even less worthy,
in the eyes of its opponents. This was the justification that argued, as
did the 1993 Ontario Act, that affirmative measures must be taken to
ensure proportional representation of the entire population in all
employment categories, even when in some categories the population
was not proportionately distributed among those qualified. Disproportionate distribution might be the result of personal preferences; for
example, despite affirmative policies to recruit women into engineering schools in Ontario since the 1980s, in the 1990s they still registered
in very small numbers, compared to their registration in other disci-
plines.[19] Another reason might be the relatively recent arrival of certain
minority populations in Canada, sometimes as the result of sudden,
large refugee flows.[20] There was some resentment among white civic
leaders against what they viewed as claims for compensatory justice
for groups who had arrived very recently in Canada and could not
have been subjected to discrimination in previous decades. Susan compared her son's chances for employment with the chances of those new
to the country. 'I have this lovely young man, twenty-one years old,
Canadian, that I've raised, who, as a result of these [employment
equity] policies, may have less of a chance, less of an opportunity
employment-wise, than someone new to the country.'

The most typical attitude of the civic leaders to employment equity
policies was to favour those that enhanced individual opportunity by
preventing discrimination, but to express concern about policies that
promoted one group of people over another, even if the ancestors of that
group had suffered discrimination in Canada. Fairness and merit were
issues preoccupying civic leaders who were members of visible minorities, as well as those who were white. No one argued that merit, as traditionally defined by 'objective' standards such as intelligence tests,
should be entirely discarded in favour of hiring a labour force representative of the community. Rather, those who supported group quotas
usually suggested that once minimum standards had been reached, an
effort should be made to hire members of groups that had previously
suffered discrimination. As Nerinder, a South Asian immigrant, ar-

gued, '[A]ny company or, say, the police force or the military ... have set standards. I don't think they should change those standards ... If a white person gets in with one hundred, any other person should be able to get in just with one hundred, not with seventy-five ... [Otherwise] that would be lowering the standards ... [M]erit should come first. You should have typical set standards, and then from there you should look at the quota ... and then pick that person.' Individual merit, in Nerinder's view, was more important than group membership, but once merit was satisfied, group membership should be taken into account.

Some civic leaders replied to the questions about employment equity in vocabulary specifically articulating individual versus group rights. Nora, who was white, said, 'I think it's only fair that everyone be given, as much as possible, an equal chance, and I think the history of excluding groups of people is something that should be redressed.' By contrast, Kevin, also white, reasoned against group rights. '[I]n some ways, we're coming full circle, in that in the sixties and seventies social policy was focused on the individual and individual rights, and then with employment equity ... [we] talked about removing barriers. And for the sake of identifying barriers, we were speaking in groups. But then the groups became so very important that the focus ... became on whether or not you were a member of this group or that group or the other group. To the point where the notion of the individual was getting lost in the group.' Like Kevin, some other civic leaders objected to group rights, although their objection was usually implicit, not explicit. The existence of groups as such, occupying different positions in the status hierarchy, was a notion with which many civic leaders, white and non-white alike, were uncomfortable.

Disagreements over the justification for employment equity policies that go beyond strict equal opportunity to hiring and promotion quotas constitute one reason why the debate seems so sharp, and at times rancorous. If the justification is to ameliorate present discrimination against certain social groups, then perhaps it can be accepted by those, mainly white males, who might consequently have to give up some privileges. If, on the other hand, it is to compensate groups that historically suffered discrimination but no longer do so, then to white males and females the policies seem vengeful and unfair.[21] Further, if it is to guarantee equal opportunities to groups that have only recently arrived in Canada, then there seems no reason for white males to give up any of their own equality rights for groups that have never suffered discrimination in the country. Failure by governments to sort out historical and sociological fact contributed to Hamilton civic leaders' unease with policies meant to ensure that everyone in Canada enjoys equal opportunities.[22]

Poverty and Group Rights

A common-sense understanding of the need for employment equity programs is to remedy the contemporary economic disadvantage of some groups in Canadian society. If some groups are significantly less well off than others, then perhaps strong programs might be necessary, including minimum quotas on hiring members of disadvantaged groups. If there is no such strong disadvantage, however, it is difficult for many people to see what need exists for group quotas. Equal opportunity can protect individuals from discrimination, regardless of the social group to which they belong and whether that social group is, in the aggregate, better or worse off than Canadians on the whole.

I addressed this aspect of the debate by asking the Hamilton civic leaders which social groups they thought were poor in Canada. The civic leaders were almost unanimous in their belief that Aboriginal people were significantly poorer than everyone else. No such unanimity existed, however, in perceptions of the level of wealth of visible minorities, of blacks alone, or of immigrants. For the purpose of analysing this topic, I divided the civic leaders who discussed this question into two groups. The first group, of twenty-five people, comprised all the non-white civic leaders (nineteen members of visible minorities and four Aboriginal people) as well as the two white parents of black children. The second group comprised all the other white civic leaders, or forty-six people. Eleven of twenty-one people from the first group (or 52 per cent) thought that members of visible minorities were generally poorer than other Canadians, while twenty-three of forty-six from the second group (or 50 per cent) shared this opinion. Twelve of nineteen civic leaders in the non-white group (or 63 per cent), and twenty-one of thirty-nine in the white group (or 54 per cent), thought that blacks were poorer than other Canadians. Only two of twenty-three individuals in the non-white group (or 9 per cent), and eight of forty-seven in the white group (or 17 per cent), thought that immigrants were more likely to be poor than native-born Canadians.

The civic leaders did not conflate immigrants with non-whites, as often seems to be the case in popular discourse. They were aware that many immigrants were white. The majority believed that over time,

new immigrants' earnings would 'catch up' to those of other Canadians.[23] A common perception was that immigrants were much more
hard-working, ambitious and family oriented than native-born Canadians. As Eduardo, himself a European immigrant, put it, 'I believe
that certain minorities ... even though they make less money ... make a
good living for themselves because they live frugally.' The stereotype
of the hard-working, twenty-four-hour-a-day Korean shopkeeping
family was cited approvingly by several people, among them Muriel,
an older native-born white. 'I see them [immigrants] as being more
willing to work than the Canadian. They don't mind getting down and
slugging it out, and working long hours, like the Korean store people.'

This perception of immigrants also carried over to a perception of visible minorities as a whole. Many of the white civic leaders who had had
contact with members of visible minorities mentioned their devotion to
hard work. Michelle said, 'I'll just cite my exposure to the Filipino community, where the people I ... came to know all had two and three jobs
each ... [whereas whites] tend to have some negative habits ... and they
also tend to view working as not positive.' Some members of visible
minorities contrasted their own behaviour to the poor work ethic of
white, native-born Canadians. Roy, an East Asian immigrant, attributed
poverty in Canada to 'all the lazy people. They are able to work, but
they don't want to work.'

Statistical evidence supports those Hamilton civic leaders who
believed that not all visible-minority groups suffer from poverty, or
even from a lower income than Canadians as a whole. Summary data
from the 1996 census shows that all visible-minority populations
except Japanese earned less that the national average income: the average visible-minority income was $20,158 while the average national
income was $25,196.[24] However, Derek Hum and Wayne Simpson have
shown that once the data are controlled for such variables as education
and work experience, members of visible minorities who are born in
Canada do not earn less than members of the native-born white Canadian population. Immigrant males who are members of visible minorities do suffer a 13 per cent wage gap compared to all Canadian males
and to immigrant males who are white.[25] More disturbingly, Hum and
Simpson also show that native-born black males suffer a 24 per cent
wage disadvantage compared to all native-born males.[26]

Hum and Simpson conclude from their evidence that perhaps
employment equity policies as currently designed in Canada should be
modified. '[O]ur findings should sound a note of caution in treating

visible minorities as a homogeneous group for public policy purposes, particularly employment equity strategies ... [I]t may now be time to rethink Canada's emphasis for achieving equal opportunity in the labour market.'[27] Another conclusion that could be drawn from their data is that employment equity policies are definitely necessary for black men, but not for black women or members of other visible-minority groups. Alternately, the focus might be on other social means of ensuring that black males are better prepared for the labour market.

Laurence, himself black, felt that the children of black immigrants had difficulties in Canada. '[W]e immigrants ... came with the idea that "I'll do anything to succeed," but I don't think ... [our] children have got that same sort of psyche. Especially if they were born here ... It's ... possible that the children may not hold the same values as their parents ... [E]ducation is ... very high on their [the parents'] list. Now, this may not hold the same for black children.'[28] Natalie, whose father was black, had a similar perception. 'I know specifically from my father's side of the family ... they weren't necessarily encouraged ... to reach. If they could hold down a minimal job that sort of paid the rent and paid for the booze and paid for a good time, then that was enough.'

In contrast to these self-critical remarks from within the black community, many of the civic leaders who believed that blacks were less well off than whites attributed this difference to racism. Beverley, a black immigrant, attributed black poverty to 'the way society is structured, and perceptions of stereotype[s] that prevent people from climbing the economic ladder.' Bruce, who was white, also thought prejudice was the cause. '[T]he black colour seems to be associated with the slave mentality for so long that we've [whites] become engrained as individuals in that thought process, so that we ... put them into a category outside of even the Asians.'

If racism is the principal cause of the very large wage disadvantage of native-born male blacks, then a strong quota system in hiring for black men might be a legitimate public policy measure. It also might be one that would cause less resentment among whites than a quota program targeted at all visible minorities, including those whose earnings are the same as or greater than the earnings of white Canadians. If, however, the reasons for the gap in black male earnings can be attributed to causes other than racism, as both Laurence and Natalie suggested, then it is difficult to justify quotas-based programs. The Hamilton civic leaders who opposed quotas did so in part because they were aware that the causes of such earnings gaps as did exist were complex. Given that complexity, the solution offered by quotas seemed very arbitrary, as well as personally costly to those who were white males or parents of white males.

For those civic leaders opposed to those variations on employment equity programs that they saw as quota systems, one reason may very well have been that their personal experiences confirmed the data that Hum and Simpson presented. The personal experience of many white Canadians suggests that visible minorities such as Indo-Canadians or Chinese-Canadians are not poorer than whites are, as a collectivity. These white Canadians have difficulty understanding why they or their sons should be expected to relinquish opportunities to members of these particular visible-minority groups. Such group rights seem to require white Canadians to sacrifice individual equality, for no good purpose if some of the designated groups do not actually need special protection.

Real Costs, Symbolic Insults

Debates about employment equity bring together two issues that apply both to whites and non-whites.

The first issue is the real cost to private citizens of employment equity. Many white civic leaders felt that they, or more commonly their children, would be economically disadvantaged by such a policy. Youth unemployment was very high in Ontario in 1996–7. A policy advantaging visible minorities or women was therefore perceived by some civic leaders as a policy disadvantaging whites and males. Government attempts to promote equality and non-discrimination, especially the Ontario NDP government's employment equity act, caused many people unease. Unlike other human rights policies discussed in this book, these policies appeared to impose a direct economic cost on able-bodied white males.

The second issue is symbolic. To some of the Hamilton civic leaders, quota-oriented employment equity policies seemed a form of group insult to ordinary, hard-working, law-abiding white citizens of Canada. These policies told such citizens that the normal rewards of hard work and law-abidingness would no longer be available to them. This constituted, in their view, the end of an implicit social bargain: 'Obey the rules, work hard, and you will be rewarded.' To these Hamilton civic leaders, the new rules of employment equity seemed to prevent white males from achieving their just reward by not permitting them to compete for scarce jobs on the basis of merit and equal individual opportunity.

This feeling of symbolic insult was compounded by the social backgrounds of many of the white civic leaders. Most did not come from wealthy backgrounds; some, in fact, had been raised in quite severe poverty. If they, or their elders, had benefited from what some activists call 'white skin privilege,' they were not aware of it. What those who opposed quotas saw was that they were being individually punished for the collective sins of previous generations. These were not sins of their own fathers; they were the sins of Canada's rulers, a political elite to whom they and their own fathers often felt little or no attachment. They did not feel responsible for past or present discrimination against visible minorities, Aboriginal people, and women – at least, not responsible enough for them or their sons to incur real economic costs. In their view, it should have been possible for governments to rectify situations of discrimination without requiring direct payment from them as individuals.

On the other hand, discrimination against non-whites, women, and Aboriginal people was severe in Canada until the mid-twentieth century, when legislation finally was introduced to try to ban it.[29] There was no social bargain between government and Aboriginal people or visible minorities prior to the 1960s. Myriad types of legislation excluded them from what was considered to be the Canadian community, from the denial of voting rights to Japanese-Canadians in British Columbia to segregated schools for Canadians of African descent in Ontario and Nova Scotia.[30] White women were considered part of the Canadian community, but their roles as subordinates to white men were taken for granted and superseded what formal rights they might have enjoyed as Canadian citizens, such as the franchise.

To ignore the sins of the (white) fathers, then, could arguably be taken to suggest that Canadian citizens who are not white males are only weakly incorporated into the present social bargain. Consequently, they should not expect remedies either for the present consequences of past legal discrimination, or for the continued practical discrimination that many of them suffer. Rather, they should rely on individual merit alone in seeking employment or promotion. Yet 'merit,' the capacity to compete for a job, depends in part on family and community background, on possession of social capital. Glenn Loury defines social capital as 'nontransferable advantages of birth which are conveyed by parental behaviors bearing on later-life productivity.'[31] Such advantages can include positive attitudes to education or disciplined attitudes to time management. Drawing on Loury, Putnam further defines social capital as 'features of social organization, such as trust, norms, and networks, that can improve the efficiency of society by facilitating coordinated actions.'[32] For individuals, possession of social capital means possession of personal networks that can help them obtain employment; socialization into the norms of behaviour approved by the dominant, employment-granting sectors of the population; and both trust in and trust by those who hold the keys to social advancement. In these respects, those Canadians whose white grandparents, enjoying the racial privilege of their time, did well in life may have an advantage over non-white Canadians whose grandparents did poorly.

For Canadian authorities to ignore the intergenerational effects of past discrimination, assuming non-whites of the present can simply compete as individuals with whites, may well be taken as an indication that the social bargain now incorporating non-whites as formally equal citizens is a permeable one. Similarly, women might well feel that without special attention to the continued discriminatory expectations of their social roles, expectations that were pervasive and debilitating until the 1970s, Canadian authorities ignore their very recent incorporation into the community as full citizens. To deny their needs for protection is both a real material matter and a symbolic insult to many members of these groups.

How then, to reconcile the social insult that both sides of this debate feel? The attitudes of some of the Hamilton civic leaders suggest that it might be wise to stick to policies of equal individual opportunity in Canada, but to take great care not to go beyond them to group quotas. Employment equity programs based on the principle of equal individual opportunity can remedy some of the harms of past and present discrimination in Canada. They can ensure equal opportunity to compete for jobs, and can go beyond that to take special measures to encourage members of groups that previously suffered, or even still suffer, discrimination to so compete. Quotas, however, seem to go farther, undermining the equality rights of members of groups not protected by employment equity legislation.

There is a danger in permitting the search for remedies for group inequalities to obscure the cost to equal opportunity for individuals of imposing minimum quotas for hiring and promotion. As Sniderman et al. put it, this type of rhetoric constitutes an 'effort to immunize equality conceived as equality of outcome from equality conceived as equal-ity of opportunity.'[33] The NDP government's 1993 law in Ontario did not acknowledge this conflict. The law pretended that the legitimate rights of able-bodied white males in Ontario to compete for jobs only on the basis of their qualifications were not undermined by legislation requiring workforces to reflect the demographic composition of local populations. This pretense suggested that Canada's human rights laws were no longer based on equal opportunity for individuals, but on unequal opportunity for various social groups.

Ordinary Canadians – and given that they were not a wealthy or otherwise privileged group, the Hamilton civic leaders in this study were ordinary – believe that they have a right to make their own way in the world through hard work and obedience to the rules. This is part of the social bargain between government and citizens. If this social bargain is violated in order to compensate for sins of the fathers, not for one's own sins, then some ordinary white Canadians feel insulted, and excluded from the government's concern. On the other hand, other equally ordinary, hard-working Canadians who are not white – and many of whose ancestors suffered overt, systematic, and brutal discrimination – also feel insulted, and excluded from the govern-ment's concern when they are told that they need no special protec-tions in the labour market. Like their white fellow citizens, they too would like the opportunity to make their own way in life, so that they can play a decent role in society.

This is not an easy problem, and it cannot be solved within the body of this book. Suffice it to say, however, that the feelings both of those who support and those who oppose quotas need to be taken seriously. If citizens feel excluded from the social bargain because of group char-acteristics not under their own control, whether they be white or black, male or female, this constitutes a political and social problem.

Chapter Eight

The Duty to Respect: Aboriginal Rights

Respect. Respect more than anything else. I don't know what a treaty is, how they were separated from the land they owned. I really don't understand these things. but ... I think we really owe respect to them.

Barry

Collective Rights

Previous chapters dealt in part with the conflicts between individual and group rights. For the purpose of analysing conflicts of rights, there is no satisfactory definition of a group. When an aggregation of individual human beings becomes a group for the purpose of the assignment of rights, or whether such group assignment should ever be made, is deeply debated.[1] So also, as preceding chapters have shown, is the issue of whether any individual rights should ever be sacrificed for the sake of the group.

With regard to Aboriginal peoples, however, the situation is slightly different. In law and philosophy, they might better be regarded as collectivities than groups. A collectivity is a group of people that shares a particular culture, language, religion, and lifestyle, connected to its occupation of a particular territory and to a historical memory of being a group. Such a collectivity has a common feeling of identity.[2] Its culture is 'indivisible,' that is, if others in the collectivity do not enjoy the culture, the individual cannot enjoy it. 'It would be impossible or lacking in meaning ... for an indigenous individual to ... alone speak an indigenous language or engage in a communal religious ceremony.'[3]

Languages and cultures can only survive in a collective setting, usually tied to a territorial base.

Aboriginal activists in the physical territory of Canada claim that they are a collectivity (or group of collectivities) separate from the collectivity 'Canada.' They have discrete cultures, religions, languages, and ways of being; they therefore have, or should have, self-determining or self-governing territorial land bases. For Aboriginals, to respect their rights is to respect their collective rights to self-determination. 'Self-determination means the right to choose ... how you will organize and govern your own nations. It means that the choice belongs to the people.'[4]

In this chapter, I discuss how non-Aboriginal Canadians regard Aboriginal collective rights. I investigate how non-Aboriginals confront an unfamiliar set of rights for people with whom most have few or no ties, and very little contact. In so doing, I rely on the opinions of the seventy-four non-Aboriginal Hamilton civic leaders, excluding the opinions of the four Aboriginals. The Hamilton civic leaders' views on these questions cannot be separated from their general attitudes to Aboriginal people, which are also discussed. The majority of the civic leaders favoured collective Aboriginal rights, including self-determination. The minority did not favour collective rights, preferring to focus on the individual Aboriginal person's rights to assimilate into the wider Canadian society.

The civic leaders' views on some of the issues discussed in this chapter were very hesitant, especially regarding self-determination. This was the only section of the larger study in which they frequently mentioned their own ignorance, an ignorance which appears to be characteristic of the Canadian population as a whole.[5] On all the other issues, they were confident about their opinions and did not evince any feeling that they were ill-informed. Perhaps this was because of the complexity of the topic. All the other issues to do with minority rights required a willingness to absorb former outsiders into the larger, mainstream community. By contrast, sympathy for Aboriginal peoples seemed to require support for their desire to stay outside the mainstream, and possibly even to remove themselves from Canada. The civic leaders were ill at ease with this requirement, not knowing how to balance their sympathies for Aboriginal Canadians with a general sense that everyone is better off acting as an individual and taking advantage of individual opportunities.

Attitudes towards Aboriginal Rights

Although their situation did improve during the last quarter of the 20th century, standard indicators of well-being showed that Aboriginal people lagged behind other Canadians in many respects. As of 31 December 1996, there were 610,874 registered Indians in Canada. At 68.2 years, their life expectancy was 7.5 years shorter than the all-Canadian expectancy of 75.7 years. Their infant mortality rate, at 11.6 per 1,000 infants, was almost twice as high as the all-Canadian rate of 6.1. Their tuberculosis rate was 35.8 per 100,000, compared to the much lower all-Canadian rate of 6.5. Their unemployment rate was 27.2 per cent, compared to 10.1 per cent for all Canadians, while their median household income, at $25,602, was more than $15,000 less than the all-Canadian median of $41,898.[6] The crime rate for Aboriginal bands in 1991 was 1.8 times the national average, while the rate of violent crime was 3.67 times the national average.[7] The suicide rate of registered Indians in the mid-1990s was estimated to be 3.3 times the national average, and 5 to 6 times the national average for youths age ten to nineteen.[8] These facts, moreover, understate the extent of the problem, as they refer only to 'status' or 'registered' Indians, and do not refer to non-registered Indians, or to many Canadians of partial Aboriginal ancestry, who also experience disadvantages compared to non-Aboriginal Canadians.

Recognizing these distressing disparities, some non-Aboriginal Canadians wonder what could be done or ought to be done to ensure the rights of their indigenous compatriots. To gauge their overall levels of concern, I asked the Hamilton civic leaders a series of questions about Aboriginal rights. I then coded each person's opinion of Aboriginal rights as 'strongly positive,' 'weakly positive,' 'neutral,' 'weakly negative,' or 'strongly negative.' Twenty-five individuals had very positive views of Aboriginal rights, and another thirty-four had weakly positive views, for a total of fifty-nine of the seventy-four, or 80 per cent of the civic leaders. Those classified as strongly or weakly positive mentioned few if any negative stereotypes of Aboriginal people, and sometimes mentioned positive stereotypes, such as that they were closer to nature, or had more community spirit, than non-Aboriginals. The positively oriented civic leaders also favoured special rights for Aboriginals as a group, and generally said that they felt they had some sort of personal duty to them. Their belief was that without a high degree of control over their own affairs, Aboriginal people would never be properly treated. It was the duty of other Canadians to respect Aboriginal people, but not to impose their way of life on them. As Beverley, a Caribbean immigrant, said, 'I think Aboriginal people have just been dealt a bad deal in this country, and it's about time that we started to ... give them more say in their life overall.'

Seven civic leaders held strongly negative views of Aboriginal rights, and five held weakly negative views, for a total of twelve, or 16 per cent of the total. (Three civic leaders were classified as neutral.) I classified as strongly negative anyone who expressed hostile stereotypes of Aboriginal people, for example, that they drank too much or refused to pay taxes. I classified as weakly negative those who favoured strict equality for Aboriginal individuals, but no special measures for Aboriginals as a group.

I ranked those who favoured strict equality as weakly negative because the issue under debate in Canada is not equality and equal opportunity for individual Aboriginals, but rather collective (and possibly compensatory) rights for Aboriginal peoples.[9] Those civic leaders who thought that strict equality was the best path to rights for Aboriginal individuals denied the need for collective rights. They tended to think that legal treaty rights should be settled in the courts once and for all, and that Aboriginal individuals should then get on with their own lives, just as other Canadians did. As Matthew, a child immigrant from Europe, put it, 'A lot of them probably want to maintain their Aboriginal backgrounds and their culture and things of that nature ... I think a lot of them, though, are hiding behind it, not wanting to get out into society, and doing something more successful or more useful.'

Almost all of the civic leaders were aware of the extreme Aboriginal poverty documented at the beginning of this section. Only two ventured the opinion that Aboriginal people were no less wealthy than other Canadians. The reasons proffered as to why Aboriginal people were poor, however, revealed a division among the civic leaders.

Some civic leaders thought that the poverty and social disorganization of Aboriginal Canadians was rooted in racism, colonialism, and paternalistic state policies.[10] This position was most common among those who favoured collective Aboriginal rights, such as Natalie, the youngest civic leader, who was angered by the history of Aboriginal peoples. '[T]here is a group of people who were shafted, kicked around, abused by the country's government.' This perception of the effects of colonialism was also shared by some of those who favoured individual Aboriginal assimilation. Leo argued that 'They were ... conquered ... peoples ... who were perceived of as savages by us when we conquered them, and relegated to basic non-existence and non-participation in the development of this province, and so they simply never had a chance to assimilate.'

Isolation on reserves was seen as a major cause of Aboriginal poverty,[11] but some civic leaders felt that such isolation was necessary in order to preserve Aboriginal culture. Isaac lamented, '[T]hey're shut out ... from so many positions because they don't have the training, and ... it's really tough ... for them on their reservations ... because their culture's different ... [I]f they're to gain much of anything, they have to leave their culture behind and become one of us.' On the other hand, Olga, an adult immigrant from Poland, thought that Aboriginal people stayed on reserves because they lacked ambition and self-restraint. '[M]any of them are drinking, and that is what makes them poor. And they should have a chance to get some education, and maybe move from [the] reserve.'

Those who, like Olga, thought ambition and integration were the key to resolution of Aboriginals' problems were also likely to view them as voluntarily choosing dependence on state handouts. Nicky thought that Aboriginal people had plenty of opportunities, but did not take advantage of them. '[T]hey're on welfare, and they're drinking, they're not working, and they have free education; they're not taking advantage of it ... [T]here's a lot of opportunities for them, but I don't think they capitalize on them.' On the other hand, Catherine thought that the dependence was bred into Aboriginal people by whites like herself. 'The attitude problem of the welfare, bleeding welfare ... it's part of their culture now. We did that, we gave them the welfare and said, "This is the way you should live."' Jacqueline, who was black, believed that this dependence bred psychological traumas. 'A lot of Aboriginal people ... have this low self-esteem and self-worth.' For Jacqueline, dependence was a consequence of racism and paternalism, not a voluntarily chosen cause of poverty.

Those civic leaders who looked to racism and paternalism as causes of the current situation of Aboriginal people were likely to perceive themselves as having a personal duty to Aboriginals. On the other hand, those who thought that individual integration would solve Aboriginals' problems were less likely to perceive themselves as having such a duty.

Duties towards Aboriginal Peoples

I asked the civic leaders whether they viewed themselves as having any personal responsibility or duty toward Aboriginal people. I was interested in the level of consciousness they possessed of what might be taken as their ambiguous position as resident on land taken from its original occupants by means that would now be considered morally questionable. I wanted to know whether the civic leaders held themselves responsible for the actions of those who were if not their actual, then their official, ancestors; that is, the government of the country in which they now resided.

Twenty-two individuals said that they had no personal duty toward Aboriginal people. Ten offered some variation of the view that 'the past is past.' As Cran, a white old-stock Canadian, put it, 'Do I have a personal responsibility? No ... My ancestors were United Empire Loyalists, and I suppose maybe I should feel some responsibility ... because that's part of my heritage, but it was a long time ago.'[12] Aqil, a very recent South Asian immigrant, agreed: 'I don't think we should live in the past: past is finished ... Whosoever has done to whom, whatsoever, we should forget it, otherwise we will never improve.' Five individuals offered an answer along the lines that, as they were not yet born at the time that Aboriginal people suffered rights violations, they were not responsible for them. Surprisingly, given the number of recent immigrants among the Hamilton civic leaders, only one person said that he was not personally responsible to Aboriginal people because it was not his own familial ancestors who participated in their original mistreatment.

Those who said they had no personal duty to Aboriginal people were not necessarily those who had negative views about Aboriginal rights as a whole. Some held positive views of Aboriginal rights, but separated their personal duty from what they expected Canada, as a country, to do. Among those who held negative views of Aboriginal rights, however, some argued that they had no personal responsibilities because Aboriginal people already had many privileges. 'As far as I can see, they have the same opportunities that we have, that anyone in Canada has ... Maybe in some ways more, with tax exemptions and ... those kinds of thing ... I don't think there's any reason why they should have problems, unless they bring the problems on themselves,' was Betty's view.[13]

Most civic leaders, however, felt that they did have a personal duty to Aboriginal people, fifty-two answering this question in the affirmative. Seventeen specified that they held such as duty as an individual. Lynn, a white native-born Canadian, believed, 'Yes, I really do [have a duty] ... [W]e each as Canadians have a responsibility, to look at what has been done ... [I]f we're the part of history that has begun to realize the damage that we've done, we also have an obligation to begin to reverse that.' Other people believed that as members of Canadian society, they bore such duties, even if they did not do so individually. Twenty-six people offered such a perspective. Bruce, an adult immigrant from Australia, asserted that 'as a Canadian taxpayer' he bore such a duty. Naimah, an adult immigrant from the Middle East, agreed: 'I don't know much about it ... but as a Canadian, yes, I feel like it's everybody's responsibility to help and improve.'

Thirty of the 74 civic leaders volunteered that their first duty to Aboriginal people was to offer them respect. This was the word that they themselves chose; it was not a word that I offered them in my questions. Linda, a native-born black Canadian, put it this way: '[P]eople ... owe them respect ... They need to acknowledge who they are ... They [Aboriginals] feel they've been stripped of everything and that people won't respect ... where they came from, and that they were here first ... They've somehow been lost in all the shuffle ... I think they just want to be heard.' So also agreed Emilio, who was a child immigrant from Italy: '[We owe Aboriginals] respect, right to citizenship, right to make a living, respect of the treaties that we signed with them ... [W]e used, abused them ... I'm not sure what can be done right now but certainly at this point, respect, right of opportunity, maybe compensation.'

Twenty-seven individuals thought that they had a duty to know more about Aboriginal people, twenty-two also saying that they had an actual duty to become involved in Aboriginal affairs. Frances, a younger native-born Canadian, said, 'I think that it would be good to be educated about them [Aboriginal people] and what has gone on till now, and how we could help them.' Nerinder, a child immigrant from South Asia, agreed. 'I think if I'm in somebody's house I owe them something ... [I]t's their house, it's their country, and they let all the immigrants in ... I personally think I have a responsibility ... for their well-being and [to] help out as much as I can.'

That more than two-thirds of the civic leaders felt that they had some sort of duty toward Aboriginal peoples can perhaps be explained in part by the fact that they were already activists in the Hamilton community. They acted upon their civic duties more readily than Canadians as a whole. Nevertheless, there was also a sense among the civic leaders that in the case of Aboriginal peoples, non-Aboriginal society had been particularly at fault. Other matters to do with discrimination in Canada were being remedied; the problem of Aboriginal peoples, by contrast, seemed intractable. Combined with a sense of duty was a sense of confusion, of not knowing what to do, other than offering support or learning more.

On the other hand, among those who did not think they had a duty to Aboriginal peoples, the issue was much clearer. They believed that the only necessary remedy was to provide Aboriginals with equal opportunities in the wider society, of which they could then avail themselves as individuals, much as did self-reliant non-Aboriginals.

Assimilation versus Cultural Particularism

Some Canadians believe that Aboriginal people should merge into the wider Canadian society much as various immigrant groups do, while others believe Aboriginals occupy a unique place within the country. To get a sense of whether the civic leaders thought that Aboriginal people had a special status as the country's first inhabitants, I asked them whether they thought that Aboriginal people were just like other minorities in Canada, or whether they were a different type of minority. Twenty-nine individuals said that Aboriginals resembled other minorities. Of these, twenty-two said that the similarity consisted in the fact that both Aboriginals and other minorities faced discrimination. Sofia put this problem forcefully: '[T]here are similarities with all marginalized and oppressed groups ... [Y]ou could look at all of those groups and say that there are inaccurate stereotypes about each ... [T]here's a process whereby each of those groups internalizes some of the messages about themselves ... The fears we have about them may be different, but it's the same process that's used to keep oppressed groups in their place.'

These answers reflected many people's concerns that discrimination still plagued both Aboriginal people and immigrant minorities in Canada. Nevertheless, most of the Hamilton civic leaders believed strongly that the situation of Aboriginal people was very different from that of other minority groups. Of fifty-four who believed that Aboriginal people were different from other minorities, thirty-three reasoned along the lines that 'they were here first.' '[T]hey did not immigrate here;

they were always here. We were the ones who imposed our values, our laws, our society on them ... They didn't enter into any social contract with us ... [W]e forced it on them,' said Ricardo, a child immigrant. Canada was the Aboriginals' actual home, whereas all other minority groups chose to migrate to Canada. Said Maya, 'The difference is that there's a greater wrong because we came in and took their land, and we've got a longer historical tradition of abusing them.' Aboriginal people deserved special rights, compensatory treatment as it were, to make up for the unique and devastating wrong of having been deprived of their own homes.

Several civic leaders suggested that the difference between Aboriginal people and other minorities consisted in Aboriginals' retention of, or attempt to retain, a different way of life. Canadians had a special obligation to Aboriginal people because Canada had tried to destroy that way of life. 'We, as Canadians, have forgotten the price paid by the Aboriginals to protect their land and their part of the country, and we just figure that they need to be the same as what we are ... [but] they feel that, "Hey, this is the part of the land that we want to protect and keep our own people together, and we should have a right to do that,"' explained Neil.

The view that Aboriginal people were different from other minorities tended to be expressed by those civic leaders who also thought that it was important for them to maintain their own way of life, or at least to have a choice as to whether or not they should assimilate into the wider community. I asked the civic leaders directly if they thought Aboriginal people would be better off integrating into the wider mainstream society, or if they would be better off maintaining their own way of life. Allowing for multiple responses, twenty-nine thought that Aboriginal people should integrate more into mainstream society, twenty-six said they should be free to make their own choices one way or the other, and thirty-six said they should retain their own way of life.

Some civic leaders thought that Aboriginal people should integrate as fast as possible into the wider society, and forget about retaining their way of life. For them to try to preserve their way of life would do them more harm than good. James, an older native-born white Canadian, explained, 'We'd never ... say [to] a great big group of Koreans ... put them all in a great big reservation and say, "Here, now, you carry on with all the cultures you had, wear all these funny outfits and everything, and we'll give you all you need, you don't ever have to come out and encourage your children to be part of the mainstream or part of the schools" ... To my mind it creates such a stilted, stunted version of life.' For some civic leaders, attempts by Aboriginal people to maintain their own way of life were merely a perpetuation of the unjust reservations system of former times. Only equality and integration could help them. '[T]he reserves are a fundamental inequity. The people are squirreled away there in hopes that we wouldn't notice them, and they wouldn't notice us, and out of sight, out of mind,' lamented Greg, like James an older native-born white Canadian.

Some civic leaders, especially immigrants, took the view that Canada in general should be more integrated. They viewed multiculturalism as a policy that excluded immigrants from the mainstream, forcing them to remain perpetual outsiders. They then transposed this concern onto Aboriginal people, thinking that they too would benefit more from integration. '[W]e have to learn to live together as a common entity, really, as Canadians, really ... It's a fragmentation of shutting them off,' said Adnan, an adult immigrant from India. These immigrants adopted the strict equality approach to indigenous rights, just as they opted for and asked for strict equality in their own treatment.

The figures above on integration versus maintenance of Aboriginals' own way of life total more than seventy-four, indicating that some people gave multiple answers to this question. Most of these people thought that Aboriginals probably would be better off in a material sense if they were to integrate as individuals into the wider society, but they also thought that this was a choice that Aboriginals should not be forced to make. Yin, an adult immigrant from East Asia, argued, '[I]f they insist on practising exclusively their own culture, their training and their language and so on, then how are they going to make a living ...? So if they wanted to go ahead I would say ... they would have to do what the other Canadians ... do. I think they would be better off if they maintained their heritage, but at the same time get the training, get the education that is needed for modern society.' Many of the civic leaders also argued, however, that the price for such integration would be deterioration of the distinctive Aboriginal way of life. These individuals tended to think that it was up to each Aboriginal person to make her or his own choice, balancing individual mobility against collective solidarity. 'I'm sure they could get ahead better in the mainstream way. But I would imagine for each one of them there has to be a [question], "Which is more important to me?"' said Kari.

Those who thought that Aboriginals should definitely retain their own way of life were very preoccupied with land rights. Anthony had immigrated as an adult from Africa, from a society in which it was still the cultural norm for each family to have access to a plot of land. He felt that '[the best solution is] integration into the Canadian population, without necessarily losing the land that they currently own ... [A]t the end of the day, you have to have access to land.' For most of those favouring Aboriginals' retention of their way of life, though, actual property rights were less important than the way of life that went with Aboriginal landholding. This way of life included a sense of self-worth that could not be attained by integration. Ruth, an adult British immigrant, worried about Aboriginals' need for an identity. '[M]any Aboriginal people really feel that their culture has been taken away from them, and they want to recapture that, and they want to nurture that, and they want to develop that. So ... integrating into the mainstream would not necessarily assure that ... [The] integrity of who they were as a culture ... may be lost.'

Strict Equality versus Collective Rights

In the course of our discussions, many Hamilton civic leaders answered my question about whether they had a personal duty towards Aboriginal people by immediately discussing what had gone wrong in the past, and what needed to be done now by the government.

The types of solutions they suggested followed the pattern discussed in the section above. Some favoured the approach of strict equality, most frequently mentioning individual rights, education, and equal access to jobs as the solution to Aboriginals' problems. Some who took this approach were immigrants who had worked their way into relatively prosperous lives in Canada, and thought that Aboriginal people should have the same opportunities they had had. Eduardo, from southern Europe, argued, 'I believe that everyone should be for themselves, should be an integration into the society as a whole.' Others adopting this viewpoint were native-born Canadians who acknowledged past injustices to Aboriginals, but thought that the solution to contemporary problems was to put the past aside, at the same time making sure that all Aboriginal individuals had the same rights and opportunities available to them as to any other Canadian. Said Melissa, 'We owe the Aboriginal people the same opportunities, the same education and the same rights as what we have ... The thing I have a major problem with is compensation in dollars. I think we owe them ... but the compensation should not be in the form of handing over dollars. It should be in the form of education.'

In the opinions of these civic leaders, with equal rights come equal responsibilities. If they are to be equal citizens of Canada, Aboriginal people should no longer enjoy any special privileges. In particular, the tax exemptions that some status Indians enjoy should be removed. '[W]e owe them full rights as we enjoy. I think they should be given the right to vote. I think they should have every right and they should pay tax, income tax, like everybody else,' asserted Joel. Implicit in this view was a belief that special privileges and compensatory measures discouraged both individual and collective Aboriginal self-reliance. Collective compensation or national measures meant to preserve Aboriginal identities would merely discourage necessary individual initiative.

This strict equality approach was not favoured by the majority of the civic leaders, who believed that Aboriginals needed to have their rights preserved as viable collectivities. For many of them, the government and the general non-Aboriginal population owed the Aboriginals compensation for past historic injustices, among which land theft, violations of treaties, and compulsory residential schools (with attendant sexual abuse) loomed large.[14] Elliott, who was white, had lived next door to a residential school in his youth, and had witnessed the harm done to Aboriginal children. '[L]ooking back ... I can see how we failed those people miserably ... We physically and emotionally tried to separate them from their families and their culture. We thought we were doing a wonderful thing by bringing them to the south ... providing them with heating and housing and food and clothing ... [yet] almost none of them made it out of elementary school ... because they couldn't ... adapt to our culture.' Laurence, a black immigrant, rooted Canadian responsibilities toward Aboriginal people in the imposition of Christian religion and European civilization. '[Our] responsibility lies in the fact that they were treated pretty badly by Canadians, the conquerors. They were sort of hindered in carrying out their culture ... [T]he missionaries called them ... savages ... and that is a good example of how the perceptions of Indians work.'

The civic leaders who grounded their analysis of Aboriginal Canadians' problems in the deprivation of their land, livelihoods and culture believed that innovative solutions were necessary in order to preserve Aboriginals as peoples, as First Nations, to use the Canadian phrase. They believed that individual equality of opportunity had to be made available to all Aboriginal people, who were, after all, Canadian citizens (even in cases where, as three of the four Aboriginal civic leaders in this study said, Aboriginals did not view themselves as Canadian). They also believed, however, that such equal opportunity could undermine Aboriginal culture and community, if members of First Nations were to lose contact with their Aboriginal identity. They therefore opted for solutions that would help Aboriginal peoples to maintain their identity, culture, and language.

These solutions, then, suggested some civic leaders' acceptance of collective rights. Aboriginal peoples had to be treated as collectivities, whose collective identity had to be preserved and strengthened. Aboriginal identity made sense only within the context of membership in such a collectivity. By contrast, those who favoured equality of individual opportunity and insurance of individual basic rights did not agree with the concept of collective rights. A clear demarcation between the two views existed. This demarcation was also reflected in the civic leaders' discussions of self-determination.

Self-Determination

An unresolved issue at the international level in the mid-1990s was the meaning of the right to self-determination, as applied to indigenous peoples. The right of self-determination is enshrined in the International Covenant on Civil and Political Rights (1966) and in the International Covenant on Economic, Social and Cultural Rights (1966). In both Covenants, the text of Article 1.1 reads 'All peoples have the right of self-determination. By virtue of that right they freely determine their political status and freely pursue their economic, social and cultural development.' Furthermore, Article 1.3 reads in part 'The States Parties [those countries that ratified the Covenants] shall promote the realization of the right to self-determination.' At the time these covenants were written and ratified, the right of self-determination applied only to countries that were still colonies of European powers.[15] However, since that time the text of the Covenants has been used by indigenous peoples worldwide to suggest that they too have the right to self-determination.[16] The United Nations Draft Declaration on the Rights of Indigenous Peoples enshrines this right in its Article 3: 'Indigenous peoples have the right of self-determination. By virtue of that right they freely determine their political status and freely pursue their economic, social and cultural development.'[17]

There has been much discussion in Canada of self-determination as a necessary solution to Aboriginals' problems. For many of the Hamilton civic leaders, the notion of Aboriginal self-determination rang true. Self-determination, in a philosophical sense, meant to them the right both of individual Aboriginals and of Aboriginal collectivities to determine their own destiny. No longer should Aboriginals be under the rule of white Canadians; they should have their own 'space,' both in the psychical and the physical sense. The idea of self-determination had been given real teeth in Canada in the early 1990s with plans for the establishment in 1999 of the new northern territory of Nunavut, a self-governed entity populated by about 17,500 Inuit and 4,500 other Canadians.[18] Nevertheless, on the whole the civic leaders were very unsure about what exactly self-determination would mean, in legal terms. Like many academic commentators who are wary of self-determination for substate entities, they also tended to confuse self-determination with complete legal sovereignty.[19] They were not familiar with the position of the government of Canada that the right to self-determination is an 'internal right, for groups living within existing states, that respects the territorial integrity of states'; that is, that self-determination does not imply legal sovereignty or the right to secede from an already established state.[20]

The civic leaders' misunderstanding of the meaning of self-determination, and their confusion of the term with political sovereignty, was evidenced in their replies to my questions. When I introduced these terms, asking them what they thought they meant, many replied by asking me to define them. When pressed for their own definitions, half the civic leaders took sovereignty to mean what is meant by the sovereigntist movement in Quebec, to which they often referred. That is, like Natalie, they took sovereignty to mean complete political independence. 'I think they [aboriginals] deserve it [sovereignty]. Now, of course, that would only be if Quebec got sovereignty. If Quebec was allowed to leave [Canada], for reason with regard to preserving its own culture, then the Aboriginals should have the right to do so too.'

In all, forty-four civic leaders mentioned their opinions on sovereignty. Of these, twenty-three thought that Aboriginal peoples did have the right to sovereignty. A common answer was that after what other Canadians had done to Aboriginal peoples, they ought to be free to go their own way, as Louise argued. 'I think it may be that they want their own little country ... It means to rule themselves, which wouldn't be a bad idea. They couldn't do any worse than we've been doing ... I

think that might just make up for some of what we've done to them.'
Twenty-one people disagreed with sovereignty, defined in their terms
as complete political independence for Aboriginal peoples. Those who
adopted the strict equality approach to indigenous rights also tended
to argue that whatever their treatment, Aboriginals were still Canadians, first and foremost. Others worried about the breakup of Canada;
in this regard, their fears reflected their concern that the province of
Quebec might secede from Canada, resulting in political instability
and consequent personal insecurity.[21] Basil, an immigrant from the
Caribbean, took this point of view: '[Aboriginals want] responsibility
for determining their own decision making and economic policies and
all that kind of stuff. [But] if I say yes to that, then I'm going to have to
say yes to Quebec ... I don't know what the answer is. I think we have
to work out systems within the Canadian structural framework.'

The civic leaders were more willing to accept the principle of self-
determination than sovereignty. Self-determination suggested to them
some level of government for Aboriginal peoples short of full political
self-rule; in this, they followed official Canadian government policy,
although they did not realize it. Colleen grounded her support for
Aboriginal self-determination in Canada's need to compensate
Aboriginals for their colonization. 'I'm a white person ... I'm part of the
group that conquered and the group that benefited by the conquest ...
and that conquest has led in many cases to Third World living standards on reservations ... [W]e're still imposing white man's modern
culture on these people. They have to have self-government, and it has
to be the self-government that they desire, and not forms of self-government that we deem appropriate.' Like other of the Hamilton civic
leaders, Colleen was more familiar with the term 'self-government'
than 'self-determination.'

In discussing self-determination, some civic leaders referred to the
types of powers conferred on provinces in Canada. Canada is a decen-
tralized federal state, and Canadians are used to the idea of three levels
of government, federal, provincial, and municipal, with various powers allocated to each. Twenty-seven individuals explained Aboriginal
self-determination by analogy to provincial governments. '[W]hat I
think they mean is ... their own set of laws and their own territory or
province or country or however they want to formally call it ... [I]f they
want sovereignty [self-determination], yes, it should be granted,'
argued Bob. The civic leaders were familiar with various attempts over
the preceding decades to grant more independence to Aboriginal

bands in matters such as education and policing. For many, the idea of a separate Aboriginal order of government seemed just and feasible.[22]

Fifty-one civic leaders made specific reference to Aboriginal police or justice systems, thirty-nine saying they agreed with attempts to institute Aboriginal justice systems, and twelve saying they disagreed. Margaret, an older immigrant from the United Kingdom, argued, '[T]hey don't want the white man ... They don't want ... government officials saying, "This is what you must be doing and this is where you must be living." The Indian nation wants to govern themselves, and make their own laws, do their own policing, and I agree because we ... are living in their country; they're not living in ours.' Several civic leaders referred favourably to an Alaskan case, in which two young Aboriginal males had been sentenced by an Aboriginal court to solitary exile on two separate islands for a year.[23] They approved of what they saw as a better punishment than locking up young men in jail. Some civic leaders also approved of sentencing circles, in which Aboriginal community members would decide on the appropriate punishment for delinquent individuals.[24] They felt that community involvement might tailor the punishments of young offenders to more accurately fit the crime. 'They've got a system of punishment which is better than our system ... and I've always ... thought they do things a heck of a lot better than the white society has done,' argued Eugene.

Also reflecting their concern for young people, fifteen civic leaders mentioned attempts by Aboriginals to develop their own school systems, fourteen agreeing that they were a good idea. '[They want] their own education system ... [T]hat has a very big influence on people growing up ... they should have more control over that,' said Nerinder. There is a high level of awareness in Canada of social problems among young Aboriginal people, both on many reserves and among urbanized Aboriginals. Many Canadians believe that these problems are a consequence of the treatment of Aboriginal peoples in the past. In particular, there is a widespread belief that by removing Aboriginal children from their parents and communities, the system of residential schools that existed from 1872 to the 1970s inflicted severe psychological damage on many individuals.[25] These individuals are now the grandparents and parents of young Aboriginals. Yet they were prevented from learning adequate parenting skills because of their removal from their own parents and grandparents, and by the often brutal treatment meted out to them by the white adults who were supposed to be their caretakers.[26] For Canadians who favour Aboriginals' control over their own schools, it is imperative that they be able to rebuild their family and community structures, and recover their own indigenous language and culture. An independent educational system is seen as one way to achieve this goal. 'I wouldn't want them to ... see themselves as not Canadian, or not part of Canada. But I think what they really want is to be able to control their own destiny within Canada, and to revitalize their culture and their language and be accepted ... I think that's important ... I understand that,' said Dorothy.

Thus, a fairly coherent picture of the Hamilton civic leaders' views on Aboriginal rights emerges, despite their unfamiliarity with the legal meanings of sovereignty, self-determination, and self-government. Those who advocated collective rights for Aboriginal peoples were more likely to favour self-determination than those who favoured the strict equality approach to Aboriginal rights. Within both groups, nevertheless, many wanted to encourage experiments with aspects of self-government, such as Aboriginal police and justice systems, and a separate Aboriginal school system. These were seen as measures that could be safely left in Aboriginal hands, without threatening the structure of the country as a whole. Moreover, even some of those most in favour of strict equality thought the wider society could learn some lessons from the Aboriginal way of life, especially as far as young people were concerned.

Self-Determination and Canadian Human Rights Law

If Aboriginal peoples are actually collectivities with the right to self-determination, then perhaps they should have the right to determine with what aspects of Canadian and international human rights law they agree. All sovereign states can choose whether to ratify international human rights treaties. For some Aboriginal activists and scholars, the very principle of individual rights as enshrined in the Canadian Constitution is anathema, as they consider it to violate their collectivist orientation to life.[27] For other Aboriginal activists and scholars, some individual rights may be acceptable, but each self-determining Aboriginal collectivity would have to ratify international documents as a sovereign state, just as, for example, Canada has done. That Aboriginal self-determination is not understood by the Canadian government to mean political sovereignty does not deter some activists from the view that they ought to have the right not to adhere to Canadian human rights law.[28]

I chose to investigate this aspect of self-determination by asking the Hamilton civic leaders about women's rights, for reasons to do with the centrality of women's rights to culture already elaborated in chapter 6. For some Aboriginal people in Canada, preservation of traditional men's and women's roles is an important affirmation of self-determination, as well as of difference from the Canadian mainstream.[29]

In 1992, there was a national referendum in Canada on the Charlottetown Accord, an agreement worked out between the federal and provincial governments to make some important changes in the way Canada was governed. Among these changes was a proposal to amend the Canadian Constitution 'to recognize that the Aboriginal peoples of Canada have the inherent right of self-government within Canada.' The accord stipulated that 'the *Canadian Charter of Rights and Freedoms* should apply immediately to the governments of Aboriginal peoples.'[30] Despite this stipulation, there was a lively national debate about what would happen to the rights of Aboriginal women if Aboriginal peoples were to achieve self-government. Some Aboriginal women feared that self-governing Aboriginal communities might revert to a type of 'traditional' rule in which men had ultimate authority over women, and women's rights were not protected.[31] In the event, the accord was defeated. The debate then lay dormant, but it was not forgotten.

I asked the Hamilton civic leaders about this question because I wanted to know how far they would go in allocating self-determination to indigenous peoples. Would those who thought that indigenous peoples should enjoy self-determination agree that there should be no human rights conditions put on Aboriginal self-determination by the Canadian government? Or would the civic leaders support the condition that self-determined Aboriginal nations should protect human rights as defined in Canadian law? In the Charlottetown accord, this question was left ambiguous, as the word 'should' rather than 'will' was used in the clause on the application of the Charter to Aboriginal governments.

In chapter 6, on the limits to multiculturalism, the majority of the civic leaders said that immigrants should accept and conform to Canadian human rights law, regardless of how culturally offensive they might find it. Women's rights in Canada should not be modified or undermined out of respect for the religions or cultures of new immigrant groups. In the case of Aboriginal peoples, however, only the minority held this position. Twenty-three individuals said that self-governing Aboriginal collectivities should be subject to Canadian human rights law. Of these, eighteen gave reasons along the lines that 'we are all Canadians.' 'It ... [the Charter of Rights and Freedoms] [is] part of Canada and you bought into it ... You are part of Canada ... Plus you are participating ... 'cause you can vote for federal Members of Parliament ... So you're a Canadian, just like anybody else, when it comes to the basic law and the basic governance of the country,' maintained Brian, a white native-born Canadian.

Among those who interpreted self-determination as political sovereignty and felt that sovereignty implied complete political independence, however, the idea that one should avoid imposing his or her ideas about what Aboriginals should or should not do was very strong. '[W]e can't grant them sovereignty and then tell them how to be sovereign ... I suppose you'd negotiate that ahead of time ... But once granted sovereignty, it would be up to them ... [S]overeignty is sovereignty,' said Sarah, a native-born white. The most that other Canadians could do would be to try to persuade sovereign Aboriginal governments to stick to Canadian human rights principles. Karl, an otherwise fairly conservative person, said, 'I am reluctant to impose a Western model of human rights ... I think that there is a [belief in] cultural superiority built into that ... [T]he Aboriginal group should be able to define for themselves what their human rights are ... No one should tell them what to do.'

Four people said that all Canadians, including Aboriginal people, were subject to international law. Yin explained, 'That's universal. I don't see why, even if they are self-governing, they should drop all these human rights.' This rather sophisticated viewpoint is one that would certainly solve Aboriginal peoples' desires to both conform to human rights principles and assert their self-determination, since it would require them to accede to international, not Canadian, human rights law. It is not a point of view that most of the Hamilton civic leaders had encountered, however.

Among those who said that Canadian law regarding women's rights should not be imposed on Aboriginal people were a few who said that such an imposition would be unnecessary. They believed that Aboriginal peoples already granted more rights, respect, and autonomy to women than did Canadian society; that, in effect, all Aboriginal collectivities in Canada had a matriarchal element. 'There are some of the native groups that I am familiar with ... it's a matriarch society, it's not a patriarch society. So the women's rights are already there,' said Margaret. This was also the opinion expressed by all four of the Aboriginal civic leaders, whose responses are otherwise not reported in this chapter. According to them, women in their indigenous communities already enjoyed equal rights, so Canadian human rights law would be superfluous. 'I'm from an Iroquoian background. In the Iroquoian background the women had very strong say; when there was European contact ... the men were taught ... "Well, your women have too much say." So ... traditionally back in history we had equal say. So ... that law would not be necessary if ... things were left the way they were,' explained Elaine.[32]

On this issue, then, most of the civic leaders were comfortable with the complete independence of self-determined Aboriginal peoples from Canadian law, at least in theory. How they would react in practice if a self-determined Aboriginal nation within the boundaries of Canada were to deny a female her equal rights, or were to refuse to ratify international women's rights conventions, is another matter. The hypothetical nature of this question may have made it easy for the civic leaders to agree to self-determination with regard to women's rights. Had the civic leaders understood that according to official Canadian policy, self-determination did not mean sovereign independence, they might also have replied differently to this question.

Canadian Public Discourse and Collective Rights

For the majority of those Hamilton civic leaders who held positive opinions on Aboriginal rights, the notion of 'special' rights for Aboriginal people was not problematic. Since the rejection of the federal government's 1969 White Paper suggesting integration as the appropriate path for individual Aboriginals, the dominant discourse in Canada concerning Aboriginal rights has been a discourse of collective rights. In official discourse, it is now accepted that the various Aboriginal groups that inhabited Canada at the time of early European settlement had as much right to be called nations as any peoples elsewhere who controlled physical territory.[33]

Only a few Hamilton civic leaders espoused a point of view about Aboriginal rights that might be called a strict equality approach. These few thought that indigenous people were just like any other Canadians, and that the important thing was to make sure that each Aboriginal person, as an individual, was not disadvantaged. Even these civic

leaders, however, generally argued that all treaty rights and outstanding land claims had to be satisfactorily resolved in the courts.[34] Thus,
like the civic leaders who favoured collective rights, they agreed that
there were historic injustices to Aboriginal people. Only once these
injustices had been rectified could one expect that Aboriginals would
enter the mainstream of Canadian life as individuals, availing themselves of the opportunities on offer.

In their discussions, many civic leaders stressed the need to respect
Aboriginal people. This key word, 'respect,' also appeared frequently
in other parts of the interviews, especially with regard to gay and lesbian rights, multiculturalism, and hate speech laws. The notion of
respect both reflects and contributes to the evolution of Canadian
human rights law and philosophy in the last thirty years. Respect now
means not only respect for all individuals, but also respect for collective identities. Moreover, respect entails an active commitment to preserve such identities, especially the identities of those collectivities that
might otherwise disappear.

As part of their commitment to respect Aboriginal peoples, most of
the Hamilton civic leaders supported some version of self-determination. Autonomy analogous to that enjoyed by Canadian provinces,
allowing Aboriginal peoples control over justice, police, education,
and other such matters, was not problematic for most civic leaders.
Nor, for some, was the idea that more land might need to be turned
over to Aboriginal peoples, as Nunavut was to be turned over to a pre-
dominantly Aboriginal population in 1999.[35] Overall, the civic leaders
were willing to approve of any concrete solution to the problems of
Aboriginal peoples that did not threaten Canada as a country, though
some were much more adamant than others that Aboriginals must be
loyal Canadians.

Thus, the notion of collective Aboriginal rights was not problematic
for the majority of these Canadian civic leaders. Compensation for past
injustices loomed large in their analysis of what ought to be done.
'What's past is past' was not a popular attitude, nor was the idea that
Aboriginals ought simply to get on with their lives as best they could,
without seeking compensation for injustice to their ancestors. The
majority of the Hamilton civic leaders believed that there was something dreadfully wrong, and that the solution lay in preserving and
renewing Aboriginal collectivities. Oppressed peoples, in their view,
must be respected and compensated as collectivities. To focus only on
individuals would be to destroy the collectivity; yet the collectivity

itself, with its own distinctive language, culture, and tradition, was what must be safeguarded. To do less than protect and renew the collectivity, to do less than ensure that First Nations became self-confident, national entities, would be to continue the historic injustices perpetrated against Aboriginal peoples.

Nevertheless, one word of warning must be added to this picture of the willingness of Hamilton civic leaders to accept the principle of collective rights, even the right to self-determination, for Aboriginal peoples. Hamilton is not a region in which Aboriginal rights seriously conflict with the rights or legal perquisites of non-Aboriginals. Whereas elsewhere in Canada there have been disputes over land and over logging and fishing rights, no such disputes have occurred in the Hamilton region.[36] Claude Denis maintains that 'Canadians are favourable to native claims so long as they themselves are not affected ... There should be no cost to Canadians, who should not be expected to change anything about themselves.'[37] This is the situation in which the Hamilton civic leaders found themselves. As chapter 7, on employment equity, has shown, when the institution of a group right results in a perceived direct cost to Hamilton's civic leaders, opinions on that right are not so easily approving.

Chapter Nine

Short Bootstraps: Poverty and Social Responsibility

You hear about remarkable people who drew themselves up by their own bootstraps ... but you shouldn't have to be a hero on that scale in order not to be poor.

Sarah

Economic Rights

In a book about human rights, it might seem odd to include a chapter about poverty. Yet one could argue that in Canada, poverty is the greatest human rights violation of all. It also presents a dilemma, namely, how to resolve the problem of poverty in the midst of great wealth.

Even in a wealthy country, to live in poverty is to suffer violations of one's economic rights. The international law of human rights includes a Covenant on Economic, Social and Cultural Rights. Among the economic rights are those such as the rights to food, clothing, housing, social security, education, and health care, which might be considered basic to any national legal system purporting to uphold human rights.[1] These economic rights also include the right to work. Canada ratified this Covenant in 1976. Moreover, Canada has ratified the 1989 United Nations Convention on the Rights of the Child, whose Article 6.2 requires states party (to the Convention) to 'ensure to the maximum extent possible the survival and development of the child,' implying a positive duty to ensure that children are not raised in poverty.

In Canada, all citizens and others with legal standing in the country have the right to health care. They also have the right to tax-supported primary and secondary education. They do not, however, have justiciable rights to food, clothing, or housing; that is, they cannot go to court to claim these rights. Those familiar with the state of the poor in Canada worry about homelessness: 'an estimated 1% of Canadians are homeless at some point over the course of a year.'[2] There is also much concern about the necessity for food banks, where the poor can be given free food; in March 2000, according to a survey by the Canadian Association of Food Banks, 726,902 people (or about 2.5 per cent of the entire population) used food banks.[3] Poor nutrition is also characteristic of the Canadian poor.[4] Under these circumstances, the poor can be considered victims of human rights violations, just as an individual suffering discrimination because of his or her race, ethnicity, gender, or sexual orientation is a victim of a human rights violation.[5] One can, indeed, argue that the right to adequate nutrition is a core economic right, to which familial, social, and state resources must be devoted.[6] Yet, the Canadian Charter of Rights and Freedoms does not protect any economic rights. If they exist at all, economic rights are 'soft' rights in Canada; the state does not have a constitutional responsibility to ensure them to all citizens.

If poverty were a consequence only of racial or ethnic discrimination, then the poor in Canada would be protected both by the Charter and by provincial human rights codes. In 1996, 17.5 per cent of Canada's total population was poor.[7] As was discussed in chapter 7, however, the assumption that poverty falls mainly on members of racial or ethnic minorities is quite problematic. Poverty is primarily an issue of social class, not of race or even of gender. Even though poverty does tend to be feminized in Canada, with young never-married mothers at a severe disadvantage, the poor include men as well as women, families as well as those who live alone or without other adults. In 1997, 42.8 per cent of young Canadian families (with a head of family under the age of twenty-five) were poor, as also were 18.7 per cent of Canadians over sixty-five, and 39.6 per cent of all unattached individuals.[8] In 1998, 17.5 per cent of Ontario's children were poor.[9]

Social class is based to a large extent on whether or not one has work, and the type of work one has. That in its turn is based on other factors, such as one's educational level, and whether one possesses the social capital to be part of the workforce. The Hamilton civic leaders were well aware of this problem. They often referred to the cycle of poverty, or the welfare cycle – the notion that while some people could rise out of poverty by obtaining employment, others were stuck in poverty for life, as were their children and grandchildren. These civic leaders were also aware of the multiple consequences of poverty that can result in multigenerational social exclusion. Such consequences include family breakdown, poor social services, inadequate public space, and inferior education.[10] Denial of economic rights is not merely denial of the basic material goods that one needs in order to survive; it is also a denial of the capacity to enjoy other rights, as Henry Shue notes in his argument for the right to subsistence as a basic right. 'It is fraudulent,' he maintains, 'to promise liberties in the absence of security, subsistence, and any other basic rights.'[11]

If within a particular society a certain level of material security is considered necessary for a dignified life, then denial of that level can be a profound personal hurt. Living below a certain level of material security can also signify denial of the right to participate in the community, as a letter to the *Hamilton Spectator* in June 2001 made clear. Ken Platt pointed out that disabled people who might want to engage in volunteer work might well be prohibited from doing so by their tiny personal allowances of $112 monthly, not enough to pay for transportation. As he wrote, 'Consider having to choose between trying to make a difference in your community through volunteerism or buying some desperately needed new clothes.'[12] A poor person who cannot properly present herself, or who lacks the resources to take a bus to a meeting or a class, cannot participate in society as a whole. Sofia noted this problem regarding clients who came to her place of work for counselling. 'We see women coming in ... who can't pay their bills, are in fear of being evicted from their shabby apartments and are going hungry. Who desperately need to receive counselling ... and can't, because they're ... caught up in this process of surviving, and putting food on their table, and they can't [afford to] get buses here.' That one may physically survive in Canada, in the sense that one's life is not at risk from absolute poverty, does not negate the spiritual and social poverty that arises from exclusion from the larger society.

Probably the biggest social division among Canadians is between the comfortably well-off and the poor. The vast majority of Canadians have enough resources to ensure through their own initiative the fulfilment of their basic economic rights. Most individuals have enough money to provide themselves decent shelter, clothing appropriate to the season, and reasonably nutritious food. There are various programs to support those who are out of work or unable to work, including unemployment insurance, old-age pensions, welfare, disability payments, and mother's allowance. It might, therefore, be argued that anyone living in poverty is simply not spending her or his income wisely.

To say this is to invite discussion of whether Canadians whose economic rights are not realized lack what they actually need to survive, or merely lack what they want. Indeed, this is an issue that a few Hamilton civic leaders raised. Olga, who had immigrated to Canada from a very abusive Communist regime, felt that the poor could manage quite well if they used their money wisely. Referring to a woman she had seen at the hairdresser's whom she assumed to be on welfare, Olga said, 'This woman having her hair tinted in two colours, does she deserve help?' Olga's point of view, a minority viewpoint among the civic leaders, was that the poor could rise out of poverty, if they would only be sensible. Her point of view also reflected that fact that she herself had lived in poverty when she first came to Canada, but had risen out of it.

Olga's comment raises the issue of the responsibility of the poor to help themselves. If some can manage their economic affairs well while earning very little or receiving very little by way of social benefits, why cannot all? How much poverty is a consequence of social irresponsibility? A frequent observation made by immigrants is that 'Canadians' (white native-born citizens) appear to be extremely lazy. As Aqil, from South Asia, observed, 'I've seen more poor people outside of visible minorities than [inside] the visible minorities. The [white] people take it for granted, welfare for example. They don't think twice going to welfare.' Roy, from East Asia, thought that many welfare recipients were undeserving of assistance. '[T]hey're lazy, and the governments, they allow them their way ... [A]ll the lazy people, they are able to work, but they don't want to work.' Although in this study the comment about laziness tended to be made by non-white immigrants, there is a general sense among Canadians that laziness is at least part of the problem regarding failure to fulfil economic rights. In a survey by Totum Research conducted in the late 1990s, 63 per cent of respondents attributed the use of food banks in part to 'laziness,' presumably referring to the personal laziness of the users.[13]

The laziness that many Canadians observe reflects, in their eyes, a breakdown of the work ethic. That breakdown, in turn, seems to reflect the general moral laxity of Canadian society. A standard reference in public discussion of such moral laxity is the perceived increase in the numbers of very young, never-married mothers. Some of them, it

appears, have babies in order to collect family benefits, the social benefit provided by the state to mothers who are unable to work as they
must care for their children.

In the underdeveloped world, it might be considered patronizing or
specious to discuss the responsibility of the poor to help themselves.
There, poverty is overwhelming, and often the resources the poor need
are not only unavailable, but actively withdrawn from them by agents
of the state, the military, or local elites. In Canada, the problem is much
more complex. Canada is one of the world's richest countries: its 1998
per capita Gross National Product was U.S.$19,170.[14] Who, in such a
wealthy, industrial society, is responsible to whom? How far does the
responsibility of society go to provide for those who will not, rather
than cannot, provide for themselves? Such social problems have a reso-
nance not only with the international debate on the legal status of economic rights, but also with the international debate on the meaning of
social responsibility.

This latter debate pits the individualist, seemingly 'me-first' attitude
of advanced capitalist societies against the more communitarian attitudes of less wealthy societies. For well over two decades, there
has been an active debate between 'Western' advocates of individual
human rights and advocates from the Asian, African, and Islamic
worlds of more collectivist attitudes toward rights. It seems to these
non-Western commentators that individual rights have contributed to
the breakdown of social order and collective responsibility.[15] This
debate is not merely one between the West and the 'Rest.' It is also one
that takes place within Western societies and is reflected in government policy-making.[16] The Progressive Conservative government of
Ontario pledged in 1995 to oblige recipients of welfare payments to
either find work or participate in some sort of training program. 'The
centrepiece of this government's strategy to convert welfare from a
handout to a hand-up is mandatory workfare and learnfare ... Those
who refuse to participate will lose their benefits.'[17] The government's
view reflected that of Ontarians as a whole: in a 1994 survey, 89 per
cent favoured making welfare recipients go to work.[18] To many Canadians, part of the social bargain referred to in chapter 7 is that all citizens do their fair share. No one should impose him- or herself
unnecessarily on the public purse. In return for equal opportunity, citizens must avail themselves of such opportunities as come their way so
as not to burden others.

The Hamilton civic leaders wrestled with the problem of poverty and the question of what citizens supported by the state owed their fellow citizens. What do those in financial distress owe to those who pay the taxes to support them? What is the social meaning of work? What is to be done with children who bear children – who ought to bear the costs of such births? Is sexual restraint a social obligation, or merely a choice that some people freely make but that others avoid? The 'non-Western' criticism of Western social breakdown is also one that concerns many in the West.

Social Responsibility for Poverty

Since Canada is such a wealthy country, the cause of poverty has to do at least in part with social arrangements. This, at least, was the view of the Canadians who responded to the Totum Survey on causes of the hunger problem. Allowing for multiple answers, 78 per cent identified 'government cutbacks and inadequate social programs' and 72 per cent identified lack of jobs; these were large-scale structural problems. Seventy-three per cent identified family or marital breakdown and 66 per cent identified unplanned pregnancies or pregnancies out of wedlock; these are problems that can be attributed to social breakdown.[19] Like the Canadians who answered this survey, the majority of Hamilton civic leaders also thought about these issues. When I asked them who was responsible for poverty, forty-eight civic leaders said society as a whole was primarily responsible, while eighteen thought that the poor themselves were responsible, the rest suggesting a balance of the two.

The reasons the civic leaders gave for blaming society as a whole were generally the lack of concern and care that society shows for the poor. For Dorothy, there was something wrong in a system that allows great wealth, yet at the same time great poverty. '[A]t this point, it looks like the "haves" are becoming "haver" and the "non-haves" are certainly becoming "non-haver" ... [The] tremendous wealth that a very few people have seems to me wrong ... [I]t's morally wrong.' Emilio also thought that society denies its own responsibilities to make sure everyone can function as a contributing citizen. 'I think it's the village allegory, that we do create conditions that sometimes oppress people ... We create environments where people can succeed or not ... [T]he powerful group is really oppressing [the] helpless group of society that maybe is not as educated, doesn't know which buttons to push.' For Dorothy and Emilio, as for many others, the 'village' has disappeared when the haves can dominate the have-nots, without thought to the haves' greater responsibility to society as a whole.

A small minority of civic leaders blamed capitalism, or the corporate economy, for poverty, some thinking that the extreme wealth of a tiny minority in Canada was dependent on the poverty of many others. Hannah, who had been a left-wing political activist in her youth, represented this point of view. 'I'm thinking along the lines of corporations or the rich [as responsible for poverty], to tell you the truth ... [T]he corporations feed on poverty. Because the corporations' modus operandi is based on making profit ... There's that ... mechanism that ... has to have poverty as one of its inputs in order to give out the profit.' Carol, who had also been a social activist before having children, agreed with Hannah. '[Y]ou have people who are working at low wages so that you can have a profitable company. You're benefiting off of those people's poverty ... [I]f you have a pool of people who are ready and willing to do work at a crummy level of pay, then you've got a nice security [system] so you never have to raise wages.'

Both Hannah and Carol reflected a left-wing discourse that blames poverty on corporate profit. This attitude was less common in Canada in the 1990s than in the 1970s, when economic nationalism and socialist rhetoric were common among many members of the Canadian intelligentsia.[20] Nevertheless, it influenced the view that the poor cannot be blamed for their own lack of economic well-being, trapped as they are by a capitalist system supported by Canada's wealthy elite. In the national poll on causes of hunger taken in 1996, 33 per cent of Canadians identified food companies as a cause, while 27 per cent identified private industry.[21]

In contrast to the approach blaming government or the corporate economy, some Hamilton civic leaders simply saw poverty as a condition, like disability, to which all were susceptible. Rina had grown up poor and remembered that life well; she viewed her present comfortable circumstances as not necessarily permanent. 'It's [poverty is] scary, because it can happen to any one of us, and I know it. I've been there, and it's constantly in the back of my mind, that things can change overnight, and you really have no control.' Anyone is susceptible to poverty.

Less forgiving than Rina, eighteen civic leaders did blame poverty on the poor themselves, not attributing it to misfortune or to structural political or economic conditions. For them, a major cause of poverty was that society did not force the poor to take responsibility. Greg, who supported the 21.6 per cent cutbacks in welfare payments that had occurred in Ontario shortly before he was interviewed, thought that 'the more welfare is offered, the more welfare is used.'[22] He explained, 'there is self-perpetuating, generation-to-generation poverty ... [T]he more we look after ... the poor, the more poor there are. Which suggests that there is a component ... of the population who are all too willing to take advantage of whatever society will dish out.' Brian thought the poor simply lacked ambition, basing his opinions on his own experience of growing up poor in Hamilton. Characterizing the poor, he mentioned 'lack of drive, lack of ambition, more susceptible to get into substance abuse, less willingness to work, or just work to reach a certain amount, and then when you don't have to work, then don't work anymore.'

Twelve civic leaders agreed that the poor were partly to blame for their own social condition, but also blamed society as a whole. Yin attributed poverty to 'Half and half ... First, the individual must have the will to succeed, to progress; he must exert himself to work harder if he is in a disadvantaged position, but on the other hand ... I understand that once you are in a poverty condition that you just give up, because you are surrounded by people who are poor, you don't have the start in the first place, and so I think it's a vicious circle.' Elliott thought of responsibility for poverty as a 'two-way street.' Both the poor themselves, and society as a whole, have to accept responsibility for remedying poverty. 'I don't think,' said Elliott, 'the poor can look to society as being responsible for the problem, therefore totally responsible for the solution. At the same time, society cannot look at the poor and say, "It's your fault that you're poor, this is a land of opportunity and therefore you have to pull yourself up by your own bootstraps."'

For many of these civic leaders, then, 'the poor are always with us.' They acknowledged the multiplicity of factors, both social and personal, that might cause an individual to stay in poverty even when resources were available to her or him, but they did not have any solution to this problem. Therefore, the only thing to do was at least to make sure the poor could live reasonably secure lives. Some civic leaders considered welfare a reasonable price to pay in order to have an orderly society. George thought, 'If you have a number of people who don't have the wherewithal to live ... and you don't provide those people with their basic needs ... then these people are going to take it from you who have ... [F]or your own protection ... it is incumbent on you to provide the safety net.' A small number of the civic leaders thought that poverty in the mid-1990s had risen to such an extent that a social revolt might be anticipated, and they supported generous welfare payments in order to stave it off. Referring to the recent cuts in welfare, Muriel argued, 'I see it [the cuts] as being too much of a shock, too sudden, and I fear that the poor will rise up ... [I]t's going to be those people who just can't take it any longer ... [T]here's just going to be chaos.' For Muriel, then, it was better to support the poor than risk extreme social disorder. Even if the poor are responsible for their own fate, the self-interest of everyone else lies in making sure that they live at a minimum standard of comfort. Irresponsibility might explain why some people are poor, but it is not an excuse for the rest of society to ignore those people.

Irresponsibility was also at the heart of the discussion about what to do about young never-married mothers and their children.

Unwed Mothers

Having come to Canada as a teenager from South Asia, Nerinder found unwed motherhood to be a problem that reflected lack of family and community commitment. 'Coming to Canada was something very strange. You have young ladies ... having kids without getting married ... It was a cultural shock for me ... I think it is part of Canadian culture that the way society is now ... they are very much intolerant of each other ... That's why we as a culture have a lot more single mothers, and it does put a lot of stress on the community.'

Nerinder's remark about 'intolerance' is an observation about family breakdown. Instead of caring about each other and recognizing each others' foibles, it seemed to him, people such as young unmarried mothers removed themselves from the family unit. It seemed to many Hamilton civic leaders that families had become fractured and unstable. As Isaac, a retired teacher, put it, '[T]here's so little familial love; there's no ... concept of "somebody caring about me" ... And I think for some of the girls ... there's a great need that's not being met.' Not having received proper loving care from their own parents, Isaac believed, young girls chose to have babies to have someone to love, and by whom to be loved. The lack of family unity, the cavalier way some individuals seemed to treat their sacred commitments, was a social problem that many Hamilton civic leaders recognized, but could not explain or solve.

I did not specifically ask the civic leaders about family breakdown, which was Nerinder's chief concern, but I did ask them about the apparently rising number of young unwed mothers in Canada. These young women and their children are among the poorest citizens of the country. In 1995, 56.8 per cent of lone-parent female-headed families in Canada were estimated to be poor.[23] Children of these families are frequently locked in a cycle of poverty. They suffer from inadequate social support, inadequate social capital, and the inability to avail themselves of educational and other opportunities. These characteristics cause some people born into poverty to remain in that state all their lives.

Many civic leaders worried about these young, never-married mothers and their children. They attributed their problems in part to a breakdown in social mores in Canada in the preceding decades. Bruce, an older man, thought that the modern system of accepting unwed mothers and their children into the community was better than the older system where 'they were named as bastards ... and so that classified them immediately as being not as good as you or I if we came from a couple that was married.' Nevertheless, he worried that 'our morals have become looser, our understanding of each other has become less sensitive, we don't have the feeling of compassion ... We've become hardened.' In Bruce's view, underneath the social rules that used to control marriage and family relations was a compassion for human frailty and an understanding that such frailty required social control. Now, with less social control, people were free to go their own way and make their own mistakes, but also to suffer alone, without social support, the sometimes dire consequences of those mistakes.

In his youth, Leo had been by his own description a flower child, a hippie. Now, he believed the lax generation of the 1960s had caused 'the breakdown of a sense of morality and responsibility ... [T]here's no sense of shame ... there's very little to control human behaviour other than force. ... [T]here's very little to stop you from doing whatever you want.' Laurence used the same vocabulary as Leo. 'See, there's not that shame attached to stuff any more ... [A]lthough people don't like to see their children get pregnant, a lot of people would still support that.' Leo and Laurence pinpointed the decline in one of the key emotions that cause conformity to dominant social mores. Lack of a sense of shame and embarrassment in individuals who commit acts previously considered socially deviant, such as bearing children out of wedlock, results in a decline in the moral and social bond. Without shame, individuals are less likely to take responsibility for their own actions and for those actions' effects on the entire community.[24]

This was a common concern among the Hamilton civic leaders. Children do not create their own morality; older people are responsible for inculcating the morality they absorb. One problem was a school system that did not teach moral values, but simultaneously did not teach proper birth control methods. Kathleen argued that '[K]ids view sex as recreational now'; nevertheless, they still were uncomfortable with sex emotionally. 'And so they ... don't plan to have sex ... They're not going to use a condom because, my God, they'd have to buy it, and then they'd actually have to touch it, and then they'd have to actually put it on.' Despite the existence of sex education programs in the public schools, several individuals felt that the sex education children received was inadequate. Compounding this problem in Hamilton, as in all of Ontario, was the existence of a Catholic school system where education about birth control was severely constrained by religious authorities. 'You know, Roman Catholic schools won't even educate kids about birth control, 'cause it's immoral. So ... it's hard just to say it's the unwed mother's responsibility,' argued Lily. In Hamilton in 1998–9, as noted in chapter 6, 48 per cent of children attended Catholic schools; presumably, they were not receiving complete, medically valid education about contraception and abortion.[25]

Without emotional support and a strong sense of moral boundaries, children improperly raised by their parents often are at a loss for self-respect. Charlene, an Aboriginal civic leader, attributed the high number of young, unwed mothers to 'low self-esteem, because they probably feel, "What the heck, I may as well have a kid and go on family benefit" ... They can't get a job: "Well, I'll just have a kid."' Sylvia, also an Aboriginal civic leader, believed that young girls deliberately become pregnant in order to avoid the responsibilities of adulthood otherwise facing them. '[A] lot of the girls that I talk to ... they were really scared ... [T]hey're expected now that they're going to have to get a job, get a career direction, start making money ... so that they feel that the easy way out is to become pregnant and to have a baby.' In Sylvia's view, these were young girls who felt they did not have the resources to properly enter the adult world, yet they should have been given those resources by the adults around them, not only by their parents but also by their teachers and the wider society.

According to the Hamilton civic leaders, though, part of the difficulties parents encountered in raising teenagers lay in a peculiarity of the state welfare system, which had permitted children aged sixteen and seventeen to leave home and be supported by welfare. For some people, this policy undermined the authority of the family, as Catherine noted. 'In my day, if I'd had a baby that I chose to keep, it would have been my parents' money that would have kept me and that baby ... But now we're making it very easy for those mothers to get money ... [A]t sixteen you can walk out [of home] and have money the next day from the welfare office, and as a parent I can't stop that.' Partly in response to this type of concern, one of the reforms of the Progressive Conservative government was the requirement that parents aged sixteen and seventeen on welfare stay in school.[26]

Another aspect of what might be seen as a compassionate approach to young unwed mothers was the provision of childcare services in high schools. Whereas in previous generations, pregnant girls had been expelled from school, by the mid-1990s they were encouraged to continue their education. This makes economic sense: unwed mothers who graduate from high school have much better economic prospects than unwed mothers who do not; in consequence, so do their children.[27] Nevertheless, the provision of these social services seemed to reduce the need for self-control and postponement of parenthood until adulthood. As Nora noted, '[T]he way the whole thing is structured, where high schools have daycare centres ... it's not such a social stigma for a teenage girl to keep a baby.'

At the time many of the older Hamilton civic leaders had been teenagers themselves, young unwed mothers were severely stigmatized for having become pregnant and strongly pressured to give up their babies for adoption. Few civic leaders wanted to return to such social stigma. In response to my question whether young unwed mothers should be encouraged to give up their babies for adoption, only nineteen individuals agreed, and most agreed only in the sense that they thought the option of giving up a baby should be put before the young mother, leaving her to decide. They were aware that the child itself might be much better off adopted by a more prosperous, older, and married couple than living with its biological mother, as Anthony noted: '[T]he young child is less likely to start life as a poor person, and is likely to then have a much better chance of success.' Yet forty-two people argued that it was better for a young unwed mother to keep her child. Louise had been a single mother herself, like several other women among the civic leaders. 'I don't think anybody should be forced [to give up a child], it's like saying, "Should they be forced to have an abortion?" No, not at all.' Other civic leaders simply had a compassionate belief that to remove a child from its mother – even if the mother were a very young teenager – would be very cruel. Frances, a married mother of two children, said, 'Definitely not. No one should be forced to give up their children for adoption unless they absolutely ... abuse them terribly or neglect them terribly.'[28]

Belying the perception that Western society is composed entirely of 'me-first' individualists, many civic leaders argued that both the fathers of the newborn babies, and the grandparents, should take some responsibility for their welfare. '[I]t wasn't all her fault: it takes two to tango,' said Edith, referring to pregnant girls. 'Where is Daddy in this picture? They didn't become mothers all by themselves ... [B]oth parents are directly responsible for the care of the children,' said Colleen. In part, this type of response reflected the rising feminist consciousness in Canada over the previous three decades, and the feminist conviction that both parents are responsible for their children. In part, it reflected an older social world in which a boy who made a girl pregnant would be subject to some form of 'shot-gun marriage'; that is, strongly pressured by one or both sets of parents to marry her.

Several civic leaders argued that grandparents of children born of young unwed mothers should welcome those children into their families. Said Walter, 'We're not living forty years ago; we're supposedly to have progressed into the nineties ... If the mother is a child herself ... I would hope that the parents of that child would say, "We'll take your baby and we'll help you raise that baby" ... I mean, we're supposed to be a caring society.' Eugene wondered where the family had been in the first place. '[W]here were the parents of that child [the young mother] when she needed them? Were they at home to guide her and help her along? Or the parents of the young men, for that matter ...?' Both these responses alluded to the problem of the lack of an extended family structure, and of extended family commitment, in Canada.

Aware that in Canada the extended family is no longer a reality for most people, many civic leaders argued instead for a social system that helped young women care for their babies. Social supports such as childcare in high schools could help young mothers raise their own children. 'I've seen ... in my experience a lot of young single mothers who have worked very hard to be good loving mothers and who are continuing to work hard. And with appropriate supports, it can work,' said Lynn, who had worked in social services for many years. Here, the civic leaders argued for a collective social responsibility. Ricardo, a young man who had grown up in an era when young unmarried mothers were no longer shamed, wanted to make sure that Canadians not assume that 'a single parent is a bad parent.' Rather, 'society bears the responsibility for the fact that ... they [single mothers] can't work because they have kids ... I mean, society, in order to go on, has to have children, right? So whose responsibility is it?... [S]ociety needs to put resources into children.'

The belief that fathers, grandparents, or the society as a whole should care for the babies of young unwed mothers did not mean that the Hamilton civic leaders thought that there should be no constraints on mothers' behaviour. Many were willing to give the first-time young unwed mother a break. No one is perfect; everyone can make mistakes. The type of moral judgment that prevailed when the older civic leaders themselves were growing up struck many of them as cruel. As William put it, 'I don't agree that things [should be as they] used to be when I was a kid, that ... a single [mother] was "Oh, shame, shame" and, you know, people talk about you when you go down the street ... [M]istakes do happen, and I think it's very archaic to be a moral judge of people.' On the other hand, according to some civic leaders, even if it takes two to tango, a second pregnancy or an even later one is a sign of gross irresponsibility on the part of the young mother. Something should be done to penalize her. 'Okay, the first pregnancy I can understand ... And I'm quite willing to help pay for that,' said Margaret, herself a widowed mother, 'but when they get pregnant a second time, I don't want to have to pay for that.' Since the state pays for contraception, Margaret believed, there was no excuse for a young woman's repeated unplanned pregnancies.

This discussion of the social problem of young, never-married mothers points out, once again, the concern among Hamilton civic leaders to both insist on personal responsibility and to have a compassionate approach to those less fortunate in society. Problems of poverty in developed Western societies in one way seem absurd: in such wealthy, highly educated countries, why should anyone be poor? Yet humans are still fallible, and personal problems can be caused as much by emotional abuse or psychological difficulties as by structural inadequacies. There is no easy remedy to such problems, other than to remember to think about the poor with compassion.

The Work Ethic and the Welfare Trap

The question of personal responsibility versus social compassion was one that had been much on the public agenda in Ontario just prior to my interviews. The Progressive Conservative government, elected in 1995, had begun to cut welfare payments. It had also attempted to introduce a policy officially known as 'Ontario Works,' but more commonly referred to as 'workfare.' This policy required recipients of welfare to work for wages, to take training courses, or to perform voluntary work in the community.[29] The program was very difficult to implement.[30] Nevertheless, in its early stages it provoked a debate in Ontario about the meaning of work.

I asked the Hamilton civic leaders if they thought that the current welfare amounts in Ontario were too much, too little, or about right. Of sixty-five individuals who answered this question, thirty-nine thought the amounts were too little, fourteen thought they were too much, and twelve thought they were just right.

Jacob thought that welfare payments were so low that, in effect, people on welfare were treated like garbage. '[I]f I want to teach my children not to shout and to be responsible and to be loving, caring human beings I shouldn't be treating them like garbage. Why would I think it's any different for an adult?' he asked rhetorically. He believed that a better policy would be 'a guaranteed annual income that affords every Canadian the ability to live with dignity.' In this belief, he was joined by 41 per cent of Ontarians who in 1994 supported a guaranteed annual income.[31] Ruth, experienced in working with disadvantaged women, had real evidence of the effects of welfare cuts. '[U]p until a year ago ... a woman could have a reasonably comfortable existence [on welfare] ... the basic things were taken care of. It's gone below that now for many women. They are struggling ... they have to use food banks more.' For Ruth, as for quite a few other civic leaders, the increased use of food banks in Ontario in the mid-1990s was shocking. It eroded their image of Canada as a country that took care of its own.

For other civic leaders, however, that a woman had been able to live comfortably on welfare was part of the problem: such comfort was a disincentive to work. Zelda thought that too much money had been given in welfare, reducing the incentives for families to support themselves. 'I think sometimes it's too much. When I see the kinds of things that are available to ... young families that I think are quite able ... to find jobs out there ... [T]he welfare system is sometimes too much of a safety net.' Susan, who thought that the amount after welfare cuts was about right, said, '[I]t [welfare] was too generous ... [I]t didn't demand enough from a certain segment of the welfare society. I think you have to be more careful in identifying exactly who is needy and who isn't, and I think we weren't doing that.' Susan agreed with the new work-fare policy because 'it reinforces the idea that you have to work for what you can get.' Here Susan reflected the opinions of many of her fellow civic leaders, who thought that work was a social responsibility.

At least twenty-four Hamilton civic leaders had been raised in pov-erty themselves and some had lived on welfare or its predecessors, especially during the Depression of the 1930s. Others had lived in pov-erty at some stage of their lives, several as single mothers, sometimes unwed and sometimes abandoned by their husbands. For most of those who had experienced poverty, this was not what might be called 'hun-ger poverty,' but it was enough to give them a strong sense of what life was like for the poor. Graham's father had had to go on 'relief,' as it was then called, after an accident. Like Jacob, Graham believed in a guaran-teed annual income, but he also believed everyone should work. 'Yes, I believe in workfare. Because I think everybody should be working poor,' he said, meaning that none of the poor should be without work. '[I]f they're able-bodied and able to, yes, I think they should work.' Natalie had been raised on mother's allowance and had little tolerance for those who took welfare when they did not need it. 'If they are people who are committing welfare fraud, they should be forced to work ... It's the ones who are sponging off the system who should get a bit of a kick in the butt.' Thus there was some concern among the Hamilton civic leaders that the welfare system was subject to deliberate abuse by peo-ple who actually could obtain employment. Most of the civic leaders, however, thought that the numbers who abused welfare in this manner were too few to warrant an overhaul of the entire system. They feared that reducing eligibility in order to catch cheaters would result in exclu-sion of those who legitimately needed help.

Not only those who had been poor, but also those who had worked very hard all their lives, were likely to condemn the poor who abused the system. Eduardo was an immigrant who had worked most of his early life at labouring jobs. 'I like to help people, but I hate like hell to be abused, and that is the problem with the system right now ... I don't have a problem with the welfare system helping the poor ... but ... when there is an abuse of the tax dollars of the taxpayer, then I don't like it.' Nicky saw herself as a member of a hard-working family living a relatively frugal life; she had little patience for those who lived what she saw as an easy life, while she worked. '[T]here's that age-old thought that ... they're on welfare, and they're drinking, they're not working, and they have free education, they're not taking advantage of it ... There has to be accountability and responsibility from people ... I think ... in Canada we make it pretty easy to stay at home and have a lifestyle without working.'

This is not merely a question that pertains to Canada. Amartya Sen, the Nobel Prize–winning economist and philosopher, points out the need in all countries of the world to consider what he calls the efficiency-equity balance in the provision of public services.[32] It is undoubtedly equitable to make sure that everyone enjoys his or her basic economic rights via the provision of public services. Yet efficiency in production may require incentives. One incentive that forces people to be more efficient is the threat of poverty. If even on welfare one would live a life of dire poverty, so the argument goes, then one would have an incentive to go out and find a job instead. This was the thinking behind the Ontario government's attempt to introduce workfare. Living on taxpayers' funds should not be comfortable. Working for wages should be seen as a more attractive option than living on welfare.

The issue of workfare was very difficult for the Hamilton civic leaders. Thirty-two thought that in general it was a good idea. One reason for workfare was to cut down on the numbers of people who abused the welfare system. Henry wanted to reduce the number of what he called 'professional welfare people,' confining welfare to those, such as mothers and children, who really needed it. Twenty-two civic leaders mentioned the responsibility to support oneself, rather than living on taxpayers' money. '[I]f an able-bodied person ... is just lazy because he's grown up that way or he's figured this is an easy touch ... then I would say that he should be told ... you must go out and try to get work,' argued James. On the other hand, Kevin opposed workfare. For him, it was not welfare abusers but the rest of the population who exhibited moral failings. '[I]t's appealing to people's meanness, people's sense of being exploited; there are people out there abusing welfare, and workfare just appeals to sort of getting even with them.' For Kevin, a professional man with a philosophically liberal outlook on life, workfare was a form of social scapegoating.

Many other Hamilton civic leaders agreed with Kevin's concerns about scapegoating. Nevertheless, they also thought that there was some value for the individual welfare recipient in working. As Christopher, who was a social worker explained, 'Work ... is empowering, work is a key concept of ... self-image for most people and ... apart from family, it's the major core of your life.' For some civic leaders, work was essential to human dignity. Workfare was a good idea because any sort of job is better than no job. At the least, as several people said, a job gets you into the public world. As Michelle put it, 'From a practical point of view, if you allow people the opportunity to work, and they get remunerated for it, they develop a more positive ... attitude because they are actually getting up in the morning, they're physically doing something, they're starting to be part of an active population.'

Unemployment itself is a degradation, as Sen points out. '[U]nemployment is not merely a deficiency of income ... it is also a source of far-reaching debilitating effects on individual freedom, initiatives, and skills ... [U]nemployment contributes to the "social exclusion" of some groups, and it leads to losses of self-reliance, self-confidence and psychological and physical health.'[33] From this perspective, the civic leaders who stressed the dignity of work were quite right. To 'earn' one's public assistance was better than merely to receive it, if one were not disabled or encumbered by other responsibilities such as caring for young children.

Yet in the eyes of many of the Hamilton civic leaders, the workfare program devised by the Ontario government was not the way to ensure the dignity of their fellow citizens. The Ontario Works program prescribed that recipients must accept any type of work for which they were physically capable.[34] It was degrading to expect an individual who was down on his luck, perhaps because of having been laid off from his regular employment, to accept any kind of work available. Not only is poverty an indignity, so also are certain types of work. 'I don't think a person who is qualified, say, as an accountant should be made to work on road maintenance ... [I]f we could ... match work ... to the person's capabilities ... then I would feel a little bit better [about workfare],' said Barry. Gina agreed: 'I don't think anybody should be forced into [just] any kind of work. It's against any kind of human rights.' These civic leaders were particularly aware of the degradation of what Michael Walzer calls 'dirty work.'[35] To be forced through no fault of your own to do dirty work is to receive a message that you are yourself a piece of social dirt.[36]

Indeed, for some civic leaders workfare was close to being forced labour. Gerard believed '[I]t is very akin to forcing people to work, which is akin to some kind of slave labour ... [W]hat kinds of benefits,

rights, etc. would a person have in [a] workfare setting?' Linda, who
had grown up in quite severe poverty, was very angry about workfare.
'[T]hat's where you start losing rights, when someone says, "Excuse
me, but you have to work for this ... it's mandatory" ... And all you're
doing is humiliating a lot of people ... Again, this whole stigma around
being underprivileged. I just think that slavery ended long ago.' There
was also a concern among a few people that workfare would merely
result in taking away jobs from other people. As Kari put it, 'Suppos-
ing you're a street cleaner ... is that now going to be workfare? So, that
[workfare] just put[s] somebody else out of work.' In fact, Robert
Solow has argued that displacement of paid workers by workfare
recipients is indeed a consequence of workfare policies in the United
States.[37]

Thus, the Hamilton civic leaders were torn between stressing the
need for welfare recipients to take personal responsibility for their own
lives, and the need to respect their dignity by not forcing them to accept
degrading work. Sen argues that individual responsibility is necessary,
but is always dependent on circumstances. 'There is no substitute for
individual responsibility ... However, the substantive freedoms that we
respectively enjoy to exercise our responsibilities are extremely contin-
gent on personal, social, and environmental circumstances ... The argument for social support in expanding people's freedom can, therefore,
be seen as an argument *for* individual responsibility.'[38] This is a position
with which many of the Hamilton civic leaders agreed. They were
aware of the difficulties of simply 'pulling oneself up by one's bootstraps,' without a supportive social climate. Most spoke compassion-
ately about fellow citizens trapped in cycles of poverty, rather than
blaming them for lack of initiative. They wanted work to be a free
choice, even for recipients of welfare. Knowing that work is an integral
part of most people's identity, they did not want welfare recipients
forced to accept work that they might see as degrading.

This concern for human dignity on the part of Hamilton civic leaders
is not a mere luxury of late-twentieth-century capitalist society. In
international law, human dignity is considered fundamental to human
rights. The Preamble to the Universal Declaration of Human Rights
begins with the assertion that 'recognition of the inherent dignity and
of the equal and inalienable rights of all members of the human family
is the foundation of freedom, justice and peace in the world.'[39] The
right to work is also mentioned in the Universal Declaration (Article

23.1) as well as in the Covenant on Economic, Social and Cultural Rights (Article 6.1). Whether the state is obliged to actually provide work, as opposed to not preventing an individual from working (e.g., because of the individual's gender, ethnicity, or political opinions) is debated, but the principle that work is inherent to dignity finds broad support.

Short Bootstraps

The views of the Hamilton civic leaders on poverty give some indication of how far a society like Canada can go, either to reduce or to enhance collective obligations to the poor. Possessed of common sense and also of some experience with poverty themselves, the Hamilton civic leaders were aware that some poverty is personally avoidable. Some who live in poverty are irresponsible, not willing to assume the obligation to work that is natural to most Canadian adults. While anyone can be a victim of misfortune, in no society should there be a free ride for those who refuse their obligations not to be a burden on society. It would be better for society as a whole if more people felt a sense of shame at their lax sexual behaviour or their unwillingness to work.

On the other hand, anyone can make mistakes. Anyone can be a victim of misfortune. Through its economic arrangements, society imposes that misfortune on many. Society's economic arrangements should be structured to take care of the poor, as, for most of them, poverty is not their own fault. It is better to support a few malingerers through the welfare system than to humiliate large numbers of those who lack the resources to pull themselves out of poverty. The bootstraps are short, if not non-existent. The indignity of misfortune should be regarded with compassion, and further indignities, such as imposing degrading work on the involuntarily unemployed, should not be permitted.

On the whole, then, the civic leaders applied the same internal moral standards to their thoughts about the poor as they did to their thoughts about other less privileged categories of people. As the dignity of Aboriginal people, immigrants, or gays and lesbians must be upheld, so the dignity of the poor must also be upheld. Everyone should be treated with respect, even those who show by their personal actions that they probably do not deserve it. To these civic leaders, there is such a thing as community. The community must take care of its own poor, not abandon them to an individualized fate.

Nor was this merely a statement of principle. The majority of the civic leaders felt a personal obligation to the poor. Most often, they discharged that obligation via financial donations to the various charities they supported, or via their contributions to or participation in the work of their various faith communities or other voluntary groups. Typically, Karl remarked that 'my church works with the poor ... We have poor members of our congregation, we distribute food vouchers ... We provide assistance in finding jobs, and we direct people toward public counselling services.' Although himself unemployed at the time, Neil was very proud that a group of disadvantaged people to which he belonged had been able to donate money to a shelter for battered women. '[W]e had a bake sale ... And we were able to give them $225, and when we took that money to them ... they were in tears. They said, here we are, another organization of people of whom the majority ... are probably below the poverty line themselves, helping people who are in the same boat.' Neil's own bootstraps were very short; as a person with a severe lifelong disability, he had had to rely at various times in his life on public assistance. Yet he felt an obligation to help even less fortunate people. His philosophy reflected that of Mabel, an older immigrant woman, who said she felt personally responsible to understand why some people were poor. 'And understanding that it wasn't all their fault, that they were poor. I have friends who are in that situation. I feel responsible to help them get through, especially these hard times now ... I feel responsible as a neighbour, as a friend, as a Canadian.'

If a community is a group of people who feel a responsibility to each other, then the dominant attitude of the Hamilton civic leaders to the poor demonstrated a sense of community. As I have argued elsewhere, 'societal concern and respect require that all citizens enjoy minimum economic rights ... Concern for another's dignity is meaningless if it is confined to the legal and political spheres but excluded from the economic.'[40] Concern for economic well-being requires community commitment. 'Economic, social and cultural rights,' says the Dutch economist Bas de Gaay Fortman, 'presuppose not just free individuals but a community that accepts responsibility for the fulfilment of everybody's basic needs.'[41]

Although Canadian law is deficient regarding economic rights, most Hamilton civic leaders did not reflect that deficiency in their moral philosophy. They were not human rights minimalists, concerned only with civil and political rights, or, reflecting much Canadian academic discussion of the 1990s, concerned only with non-discrimination rights. Most of them retained an active and compassionate sense of obligation to the poor, whom they saw not as strangers – a species of 'Other' unable to keep up the common material decencies of life – but as members of their own social family.

Chapter Ten

A Comfortable Consensus: Responsibility to Strangers

We have the same level of responsibility [to strangers as to Canadians], but that includes the responsibility to maintain a healthy economy and a healthy environment within our own territory. ... And ... a number of thing[s] ... will flow from that, such as not having unlimited immigration.

Elliott

National versus International Obligations

The issues discussed in the preceding chapters had all been part of the Canadian public agenda for several years. They were familiar to the Hamilton civic leaders, even when they did not have a good sense of how to resolve them. This short chapter deals with a different kind of problem, which was evolving as an important international issue at the end of the twentieth century. The issue is, What is our responsibility to strangers outside the borders of Canada? Are Canadians, along with other Westerners, practising a form of apartheid in the international arena, by disregarding the needs of (mostly non-white) strangers?

After the United States and Canada ended segregation in the 1960s, South Africa was the only Western country to have legally sanctioned racism. This peculiarity, that racism was not only practice but also law, was what made South Africa an international pariah, and was what justified special international attention to its human rights abuses, even when many other states in Africa were also abusing human rights.[1] The defeat of apartheid in South Africa was, therefore, a major achievement for international human rights.[2]

Yet the very states that condemned South Africa throughout the period of apartheid all participate in what might be considered a different form of legalized segregation, namely, the perpetuation of the right of states to decide who shall, or shall not, be permitted to enter their territory and become part of their community. Control over immigration and citizenship by individual states means that the most important possession a citizen of Canada has is one that many Canadians never think about, namely, their actual citizenship rights. As Joseph Carens puts it, 'Citizenship in Western liberal democracies is ' the modern equivalent of feudal privilege.'[3] This privilege entitles people within Canada's borders to a standard of living far exceeding that of most people in the world. With a national per capita income of U.S. \$19,170 in 1998, Canada was the world's twenty-sixth richest country. Its national per capita income was 6.4 times that of the average middle-income country in 1998, and 36.8 times that of the average low-income country.[4]

This increasing problem of international inequality is one that President Thabo Mbeki of South Africa brought to the world's attention on 7 September 2000 when he spoke at the United Nations Millennium Summit about the rich-poor gap. Said Mbeki, 'Billions ... struggle to survive in conditions of poverty, deprivation and underdevelopment, as offensive to everything humane as anything we decry about the second millennium ... The question these billions ask is – what are you doing ... to end the deliberate and savage violence against us that, everyday, sentences many of us to a degrading and unnecessary death!'[5] Mbeki's is a powerful plea to remember that world economic and political arrangements immiserate many, even as others are lifted out of poverty.[6]

It is now common to speak of the turn-of-the-millennium era as one of globalization. Globalization as an economic phenomenon includes the internationalization of property, so that, increasingly, citizens of any country are permitted to buy property anywhere. It also includes the internationalization of capital, which flows within seconds from one country to another.[7] Yet, while these two factors of production are internationalized, the third factor, labour, lags far behind. Its flow is not free. Those who wish to leave their homelands to labour in richer parts of the world face heavy controls. Nevertheless, compared to the benefits of migration to richer parts of the world, the price of staying at home is so high that millions of people every year make arduous journeys to uncertain and legally dubious lives in the West.

International law protects the right of all countries to control their borders, deciding whom they wish to admit. This right is not absolute; countries that have signed the 1951 United Nations Convention on Refugees, as Canada did in 1969, do have legal obligations to admit those who arrive in their territory and are subsequently judged to be legitimate refugees.[8] Refugee status, however, can be claimed only for political reasons.[9] Economic hardship, no matter how dire, is not a legitimate ground for refugee status. Nor is there any international right to emigrate from one's own country to another. While, according to the United Nations Convention on Civil and Political Rights, Article 12, everyone has the right to enter and to leave his own country, no one has the right to enter another country at will, unless he is a refugee.[10]

Thus, a system of de facto global apartheid exists.[11] It is not strictly racially based; many of the richest countries, such as Canada, the United States, Britain, and the Netherlands, are now multiracial. This multiracialism is controlled, however, and in Canada has long favoured those from non-Western, non-white countries who arrive with money, skills, or entrepreneurial talent.[12] The masses of non-whites in Asia, Africa, and the Americas, as well as the impoverished masses of the former Soviet bloc, are required to stay in their countries of origin.

There is no easy solution to the severe problem of international inequality. In the medium to long term, growth within each part of the world is undoubtedly the best answer. Indeed, the medium term may not be very long, as the astounding growth in South Korea since 1950 has demonstrated.[13] Nor is capitalism the villain of the piece; much historical evidence shows that, over the long term, it is the hero, not only economically but also as a necessary condition for political democracy.[14] In the short run, though, people cannot wait. Billions live in dire poverty; hundreds of millions dream of migration.

What, then, are the obligations of Canadians to these people? That is the question that impels this chapter. I asked the Hamilton civic leaders what they thought Canada's responsibilities to strangers should be, if any. I defined strangers as new immigrants, refugees, and people living outside Canada. Strangers, then, included people not yet, or not likely ever to be, members of the Canadian community. I wanted to know if the civic leaders thought that they had a greater or lesser level of responsibility, or the same level, to strangers as they did to their fellow Canadians.[15] To pinpoint their views, I asked a series of questions about new immigrants and refugees, and I asked them about Canadian foreign aid.

Responsibility to Strangers

For the most part, the Hamilton civic leaders were people of goodwill, anxious to do the right thing and concerned for those worse off than themselves. Yet, when faced with the question of whether their level of responsibility to strangers outside Canada was equal to their responsibility to people within Canada, the majority said no.

I did not pose this question in every interview, and some people found it too difficult to answer. Of the fifty-two responses I did receive, twenty-nine gave priority to Canada, twenty-one argued for equal responsibility to Canadians and to strangers, and two were ambiguous. Among those suggesting that Canadians had equal responsibility to strangers and to outsiders, eleven, or about half, were immigrants, while among those arguing for Canada first, nine, or about 30 per cent, were immigrants. Put another way, among the immigrants, 45 per cent argued for Canada first. Among the Canadian-born who answered this question, twenty of thirty, or 66 per cent, opted for Canada first. This suggests a somewhat stronger commitment to, or familiarity with, the world outside Canada on the part of those Hamilton civic leaders who were immigrants than on the part of those born in Canada.

Among those arguing that Canada should come first, a standard response was that you should give priority to your own affairs. You need to 'put your house in shape first,' said Adnan, a South Asian immigrant. Edith, an 'old-stock' Canadian, agreed: 'We have to think of home first.' Many of these civic leaders were in the habit of giving money to charities engaged in overseas development work, and several had foster children 'adopted' overseas, through charities that encouraged monthly donations for a specific child. Nevertheless, they believed that their first responsibility was to Canada.

In explaining their 'Canada-first' reasoning, several people resorted to a logic of concentric circles of responsibility. Jacob, who was Canadian-born, argued, 'You first have an obligation to preserve the fabric of your society, and you start ... with yourself, with your family, with your town, with your province, with your country. And you go in that order ... Our first obligation is to our [own] citizens.' Anthony, an adult immigrant from Africa, shared this viewpoint. '[W]hen they're outside of the country ... I would say much less of a responsibility.'

For several individuals, the reason for the greater responsibility to Canada was obvious. Canada is not a perfect country: it has its own share of social problems. These civic leaders knew that the Canadian government often criticized other countries' human rights performance, yet they felt that Canada had no right to preach to them when it could not properly run its own affairs. Said Nicky, 'I mean, when we're having people in Toronto freeze to death ... last year with three deaths on the street ... we're sending money and foreign aid overseas and yet in our own backyard, people are not able to make ends meet.' Elaine, an Aboriginal civic leader, said, 'It just blows me away at times when you see our government going out there, spending millions of dollars helping a situation when you know facts about your own community ... Canada is supposed to be ... one of the wealthiest countries, and yet we have children that are starving ... not just ... Aboriginals, I mean our people overall ... We need to help our own first ... clean up the messes here first.' To these civic leaders, it seemed hypocritical to devote Canadian resources to foreigners when so many Canadians were still in dire need.

Several civic leaders were aware of the tension between the two sets of obligations, but reluctantly asserted that obligations at home must come first. Christopher said, 'Practically, I suppose we have a primary responsibility to citizens of the country, but you have to treat it as a tension or a dilemma always to be managed, that you have a strong, almost equal responsibility to people in need around the world.' Such responses showed the difficulties in thinking through this question. Aware of the interconnectedness of the modern world, some individuals argued for an equal ethical responsibility, no matter where people lived and how loose or non-existent their connections to Canada. Others experienced a feeling of unease in suggesting that Canadians could reduce their commitment to their own poor in order to take care of others.

Countering this feeling of unease was the feeling that since we are all human, no matter where we live, Canadians have equal responsibilities to everyone in the world. Karl, a devout Christian, argued, 'I think that God created us all as human beings. We're first human beings, then we're Canadians, Americans, Somalians. I think it's wrong to differentiate between groups.' Those who identified strongly with their various religions were somewhat more likely to argue for an international, rather than merely a national, sense of responsibility to others. The belief in a universal responsibility, however, was more general than religious commitment alone would suggest. Lynn, far less religious, agreed with Karl: 'It's all one world ... And whether I'm a street away from you, or an ocean away from you, we're all related, and we all have an obligation to look after one another.'

Some civic leaders referred to Canada's wealth, viewing it as a consequence of others' poverty. As Ruth put it, 'I sort of believe charity begins at home. But that doesn't mean to say I don't believe in the principle [of universal responsibility] ... We're benefiting from people in Mexico making lower wages, we're benefiting from people in Indonesia ... we're benefiting from some of the sweatshops that are happening over there.' Rina thought that since Canada has been such a fortunate country, Canadians have obligations to outsiders. 'We owe ... the rest of the world. We've been really lucky ... We have a moral obligation to the rest of the world.' There was also a pragmatic reason to act on this universal responsibility, as Laurence pointed out. 'If we don't show some responsibility to helping those people, they'll be breaking down the doors of Canada and every other nation that is rich.'

The above section focused on general principles of responsibility, about which the Hamilton civic leaders spoke mainly in ethical terms. The questions on refugees and immigrants, and on foreign aid, showed a more pragmatic approach to responsibility.

Refugees and Immigrants

I posed a series of questions to the Hamilton civic leaders about refugees and immigrants. Thinking of opinion polls that consistently suggested about 40 per cent of Canadians would like to see immigration reduced, I asked what they thought about both the number of immigrants and the number of refugees that Canada accepts every year.[16] I also asked if they thought immigrants and refugees were too demanding with regard to the benefits they might receive once they arrived in Canada. In particular, I mentioned their rights to health care, education, and welfare.

There was very little concern among the Hamilton civic leaders about refugees asking too much from Canada. 'I think they're very grateful for anything they get,' was Colleen's typical response. Canadians were responsible to make sure refugees were properly cared for once they arrived in the country. The civic leaders' attitude was 'If you're in, you're in.' Those who were permitted entry to Canada were as entitled to social benefits as any Canadian citizen. They were human beings, and it would be unconscionable to deny them the basic benefits that Canadians took for granted.

Nor was there much concern among Hamilton civic leaders about the number of refugees and immigrants coming into Canada. Most were not aware of the numbers in any case, and often they asked me for clarification. Their reaction to the numbers I gave them (between 125,000 and 250,000 immigrants a year, and about 25,000 to 50,000 refugees a year) was usually to suggest that such numbers were appropriate, or a little on the low side. Of the sixty-seven individuals who answered my question about the number of refugees, eight said they did not know enough to answer. Of the others, thirty-two said that the number seemed about right to them, depending on the circumstances determining refugee policy, twenty-two thought that the number was rather low, and only five found the number somewhat high, of whom only two disapproved of its being so high. Those who thought Canada should accept more refugees usually explained their opinions by reference to the refugees' need. Basil said, 'fifty-thousand is small. I'm thinking in terms of the millions of people who are displaced around the world ... Part of our responsibility has been to help those people out ... Bring in a couple of thousand more, a few thousand more.'

With regard to immigrants, the general response was similar. Of the sixty-two civic leaders who answered my question about numbers, only three thought that Canada was accepting too many immigrants. One of these was Sylvia, an indigenous person who thought that there was already too great an imbalance between the indigenous and the non-indigenous populations. 'That [number of immigrants] sounds like an awful lot. I mean, there aren't that many Aboriginal people left here ... There isn't a balance. It's way out of whack.' Twenty-one people thought the number of immigrants could be raised. Some of these thought that immigration should be based on the needs of the potential migrants. According to George, an adult immigrant, 'There is so much turmoil in this world ... There are a lot of people suffering, and to the extent that you can ... help some of these people who are suffering, I think ... it's only right.' Others believed that immigration improved the Canadian economy; thus, the more immigrants the better. As Emilio, himself a child immigrant, put it, 'Immigration of any sort is helping Canada. I don't believe that because we have an employment problem, refugees or other immigrants would cause even greater unemployment. I think that's how you get the economy going, you get more people working ... more shoes to provide and clothing and so on and housing, and therefore [the] economy gets going.'

Thirty-two civic leaders thought that the appropriate number of immigrants depended on the kind of circumstances that the government already took into account in deciding on immigration numbers every year. If we could afford it, most argued, it would be good to accept more people, but not if they could not be properly integrated into Canadian society. 'I don't think the numbers matter. I think that if the country ... can support [them] and they [immigrants] can do what they want to do when they come here, that matters,' said Dorothy, an infant immigrant from Britain. Such integration meant, especially, making sure that jobs were available for immigrants. It also meant making sure that they were eligible for all social benefits for which Canadian citizens were eligible. As Linda, a native-born black Canadian, put it, 'I'd rather have two [immigrants] come in and it be wonderful for them, and a wonderful experience and things go well, and the racism ends ... rather than to bring in thirty-thousand, and it's just chaos.'

While some civic leaders thought that Canada should accept more immigrants because of the potential immigrants' needs, more referred to Canada's own need for new citizens. Demographic changes were creating an aging society. Younger migrants with families might help to rectify this imbalance, especially as Canada had a fertility rate lower than the level needed to replace its population.[17] Kevin was a highly educated professional man who was aware of these social trends. He argued, 'We will not have the workforce to deal with the society that we are going to have twenty years from now. And unless everybody goes out there and starts making babies really fast, the only way we're going to do it is through immigration.' To many of the civic leaders, immigrants and refugees were hard-working people, as likely to have jobs as native-born Canadians, if not more so. 'Refugees in the long run end up contributing very much to Canadian society in the skills, abilities, culture, etc. that refugees and immigrants do bring to this country ... [I]n the long term refugees end up being very good citizens, and contribute to ... Canada's well-being,' thought Gerard, who had spent part of his career engaged in international development work.

Moreover, the civic leaders expressed few concerns about the types of immigrants chosen to come to Canada. My observation that some people thought there should be more immigrants coming from Europe, and proportionately fewer from non-European parts of the world, drew incredulous responses from the vast majority. Some argued that such a concern was outright racist; others argued that Europeans no longer wished to emigrate in large numbers as the European economy was very strong, as Eduardo contended. 'I doubt it very much if you could entice another wave of European immigrants ... because their standard of living has been raised.' The majority argued that immigrants should be accepted on the basis of their qualifications, with no concern given to their place of origin. In this, they reflected Canadian public opinion as a whole: in a 1993 survey, only 11 per cent of Canadians were adamant in their opinion that a higher percentage of immigrants should be white.[18]

Possibly as a consequence of media exposure, a few civic leaders were worried about crime, and did not want gang members from other countries entering Canada. There was also some concern about queue-jumping, especially people entering the country as refugees who would not be acceptable as immigrants. Barry, a black adult immigrant himself, complained that 'A lot of people are coming under the banner of being refugees, and they are nothing else but people trying to bilk the system.' The civic leaders also expressed a mild degree of concern over some of the criteria used to choose immigrants. The greatest concern was over immigrants who entered Canada as investors, demonstrating that they had a certain minimum amount of wealth available.[19] This was perceived by some civic leaders as buying their way into Canada. Some individuals thought it was unfair to give preference to prospective immigrants who could bring skills to Canada, or who already spoke the language. This was the case especially among those civic leaders whose own parents had come to Canada as unskilled immigrants speaking neither English nor French. As Eugene, who was from Italy, put it, 'When we came here [we] did not speak the language ... [M]y father did not have a formal education. If he had to apply under today's standard he probably would have failed, and not be allowed to come to this country.'

A few civic leaders objected to the definition of 'family' used by Citizenship and Immigration Canada, which they felt unduly restricted which categories of relatives could be sponsored to immigrate by Canadian citizens.[20] Some individuals also thought that although the number of immigrants and refugees was appropriate or could be increased, more measures should be taken to discourage them from concentrating in the three large cities of Montreal, Toronto, and Vancouver, as such concentration resulted in problems of absorption. Finally, several expressed concern that immigrant professionals were not able to requalify in Canada, their potential to contribute to Canadian society thus being wasted. As Kathleen, a native-born white Canadian, put it,

'A lot of the people who come to this country ... were doctors and law-yers and ... they're coming here now and working in McDonald's.'

The predominant attitude among the civic leaders, that immigrants and refugees should be properly integrated into Canada on an equal basis with Canadian citizens, demonstrates a sense of generosity to strangers. Nevertheless, it equally demonstrates that Canadians agree with their government that the numbers taken in should be deter-mined by Canada's capacity to absorb them. Those civic leaders who suggested accepting more immigrants or refugees generally proposed only small increases, consistent with Canada's absorptive capacity. If the costs of absorption became too high, for example, in paying for education or language training, then the numbers of refugees and immigrants should be limited accordingly.

In this respect, the civic leaders agreed with Canadian policy as it existed at the time they were interviewed. To most of them, no one's responsibility went so far as to undermine his own standard of living. Canada's first responsibility was to its own citizens, not to outsiders. As Dan argued. 'We have to be careful that we don't overextend, and cause people who are already [here] to be at a disadvantage.'

Foreign Aid

Despite the hope expressed by many of the Hamilton civic leaders that Canadians would treat all people in the world equally, when it came to practical questions about distribution of Canadian resources, most made a clear distinction between Canadians and strangers outside Canada's borders. Anyone admitted to Canada was entitled to the social programs and benefits that were available to any eligible citizen of Canada. Foreign aid, however, should be given sparingly, taking into account the need first to reduce Canadian debt and to keep the Canadian economy going. These distinctions were made by those who argued for universal responsibility as well as those who took the posi-tion of 'Canada first.'

I asked the civic leaders whether Canada should raise its aid contri-butions to meet its then target of 0.7 per cent of gross national product per year, a target proposed by the United Nations for wealthy coun-tries.[21] Of the fifty-six civic leaders who directly answered this question, forty-five said that it should be increased, six that it should be main-tained as it was, three that it should be reduced, and two that the amount depended on other factors. The answer given by Jacqueline, a black immigrant from the Caribbean, was typical. 'I think we should try to meet the UN target, especially since Canada is supposed to be one of the richest countries in the world.' In the eyes of these civic leaders, Canada had a duty to help other countries, and that Canada did not at least meet UN targets struck them as rather mean-spirited. As Bruce, a white adult immigrant, said, 'Why not [give more], because we've got so much. Gosh, we're so rich, and nobody knows it in this country.'

Those who said Canada's aid budget should be increased, however, may not have been aware of what attaining this target might have meant in absolute terms. By way of illustration, Canada's contribution to official development assistance (foreign aid) in 1998 was only 0.29 per cent of its gross national product.[22] To raise its contribution to 0.7 per cent would have meant an increase of 0.41 per cent of its gross national product, or U.S.$2.38 billion.[23] To attain the target of 0.7 per cent of gross national product seemed reasonable to the civic leaders, but one cannot conclude that they would have responded the same way if I had proposed the actual amount involved to them.

Despite the majority's generous views about the amount of foreign aid, the civic leaders did believe that it should be given with careful consideration for its possible efficacy. Many were aware of the debates about the problems involved in giving foreign aid.[24] Thus, even if they expressed willingness to increase the amount of money Canada donated, they tempered their willingness by reference to some of the difficulties encountered in disbursing it. Some referred to what they perceived as costly or inefficient administration. Naimah felt that 'with a better management Canada will be able to give more ... foreign aid, but with the existing structure I don't think anyone [is] willing to pay, especially businesspeople.' Others referred to the likelihood that corruption in the recipient country would divert aid from its intended recipients. As Matthew said, 'There is a perception that the stuff [aid] goes into a lot of deep pockets, and it doesn't see the light of day where it's required.'

Nineteen people felt that the aid being given was technologically inappropriate. Several cited some variant of the adage 'Give a man a fish, and he will eat for one day; teach him to fish, and he will eat for life' to indicate their belief that aid was not being disbursed in a manner that would result in long-term benefits. Finally, a few were aware of the problem of tied aid, that is, aid distributed on condition that it buy Canadian goods and services. Greg brought both these points together. 'A significant part of our foreign aid is misdirected ... or is technically poor ... [It is] North American technology, jammed down the throats of people who know better themselves, traditionally, with their own medicines and their own ways, and with strings attached like "Well, yes, we'll help you build the houses in your village, and you've got to buy the concrete block from Canada."'

This awareness of the difficulties entailed in actually designing effective foreign aid tempered the endorsements many civic leaders gave to increasing the amount Canada donated. They reasoned that the solutions to poverty elsewhere were not in Canada's hands. Whether equal to or less than their sense of obligation to Canadians, their sense of obligation to strangers did not require a waste of resources. It made sense to many civic leaders to at least realize the UN's aid target level; this would be, in part, a signal that Canada is a responsible member of the international community. It did not make sense to give money that would be unwisely used. Nor would it make sense to reduce Canadians' own standard of living in order to help people living in other countries. As Yin argued, 'The country [Canada] is in a very serious debt at the moment. Until we have resolved it, we shouldn't increase [aid] any more.'[25]

Goodwill and Legitimate Self-Interest

Unlike the opinions discussed in some other sections of this book, the opinions of the Hamilton civic leaders regarding refugees and immigrants did not reflect the opinions of the Canadian population as a whole. As noted above, in the 1990s about 40 per cent of the Canadian population thought that too many immigrants were being allowed into the country. The more liberal attitude of the Hamilton civic leaders may reflect the fact that a disproportionate number of them, 46 per cent, were themselves immigrants. Alternately, it may reflect that fact that they were a highly educated group, and individuals with higher education are more like to be tolerant of a multicultural Canada.[26]

Like other Canadians, however, the Hamilton civic leaders were concerned about the types of refugees and immigrants who arrived, and about the social burdens they might impose. To the civic leaders, preservation of the fabric of Canadian society was a legitimate national goal. They valued social order. The immigrant who upset that order was unwelcome, while the immigrant who conformed to Canadian social norms was quickly accepted. As Betty, a native-born white, argued when discussing whether there should be more immigrants from Europe, 'I can accept a person ... more on their values than their colour. If they are hard-working people and they're kind, and they're good neighbours, and they cut their grass and keep their house looking tidy, that's fine, you can be my neighbour. But if ... you're a white person, and you never cut your grass and your kids run wild and you break my windows, I don't want you as a neighbour.' This, one could argue, is part of what it means to live in a community. Canadians, according to the Hamilton civic leaders, have the right to control their community. They have the right to manage immigration and refugee policy so that if social change does occur, it does so slowly, and without stress on the people already in the country.

If preservation of the fabric of one's own society, a goal noted by Jacob earlier in this chapter, means keeping out those who wish to enter it, is such preservation morally legitimate? Maya, the daughter of northern European immigrants, believed it was not: 'I just can't see saying that this [Canadian] border makes it possible for me to live this way, and not for you.' Most of the civic leaders, however, agreed with Jacob. The Canadian society they lived in was a good one. Unmanaged immigration, or too much devotion of resources to foreign aid, could upset the system that kept most Canadians comfortable in their own country. The Hamilton civic leaders were a group of people possessed of goodwill toward strangers, but that goodwill was limited.

That the issue of responsibility to strangers is still discussed in Canada in terms of who gets in versus who stays out reflects a comfortable consensus in the Western world as a whole that may not last long into the twenty-first century. This consensus was shared, for the most part, by native-born and immigrant Hamilton civic leaders, by whites and members of visible minorities. They believed that Canadians were responsible for the well-being of those within the country's borders, even if they had arrived only yesterday. Canada should not deny any rights to those legitimately in the country. These civic leaders would devote tax money to make sure that immigrants and refugees settled well, that they and their children were well cared for, and that they became productive citizens. Nevertheless, Canada retained the right to control who arrived. Aside from a few adjustments needed here and there, the civic leaders believed the government was doing a good job of maintaining those controls. Moreover, the obligations Canadians had to potential immigrants, refugees, and others outside Canada's borders did not imply that Canadians must lower their own standard of living to help others.

Perhaps more important, the comfortable consensus that allowed these Canadians to express goodwill toward strangers did not compel them to be aware of conditions beyond their own borders. Nega Mezlekia, an Ethiopian who entered Canada as a refugee in 1985, comments on Canadians' kindness to strangers in their own country, in contrast to their lack of understanding of or interest in the events that cause those very strangers to seek succour in Canada. 'Canada has been good to me from my earliest days here as a political refugee ... I have nothing but good things to say about the Canadian people. I have only wished that they, like much of the Western world, could be more considerate of the welfare of those who live in distant places.'[27] Mezlekia contrasts Canada's willingness to accept him as a political refugee with Canada's aid to the very brutal Marxist regime that forced him to flee Ethiopia in the first place.[28] Only a few of the Hamilton civic leaders concerned themselves with the international issues of war, conflict, and underdevelopment, which produced large refugee flows in the first place.

At the moment, there is little need for Canadians to step outside this comfortable consensus of preserving the Canadian way of life before paying attention to others. International law does not confer upon individual human beings the right to enter countries not their own, unless they can show that they are legally Convention refugees. Nor does international law compel wealthy countries to share their wealth with poorer countries.[29] Development aid is a matter of public policy choice in the country that proffers that aid; it is not a right that other countries can demand. While, according to the United Nations, everyone has a right to development, no one has a right to claim other people's resources in order to enjoy that development.

Perhaps this is as it should be. There is, after all, considerable evidence that development is primarily an internal matter, depending on how each society organizes and administers its own resources.[30] Such evidence, however, is small comfort to the millions of economic refugees, as they might well be called, already infiltrating illegally into Canada, the United States, and Western Europe. Globalization theory tells us that the borders of nation states are eroding, and that sovereignty is being loosened.[31] Nevertheless, the sovereign power to control who is allowed within a country's borders is still one of the most secure prerogatives of every state. It is this power that permits Canadians to have such a comfortable consensus as this book demonstrates on so many human rights issues.

The rights Canadians enjoy are distributed to a very small number of people. That small number can afford, imperfectly, to accommodate itself to diversity and difference. If and when the floodgates of international migration are opened, however, and Canada is no longer permitted to decide who shall, and who shall not, join its exclusive club of Canadian citizens, the rest of Canadians' human rights may easily be eroded.

Chapter Eleven

Compassionate Canadians

Compassion and Empathy

This book has shown how some Canadians think through questions of individual and group rights, social obligation, and community. It demonstrates the importance of citizens' use of philosophical agency to develop empathic attitudes to people often different from themselves, and to support their claims for human rights. The Hamilton civic leaders' support for human rights was grounded in their ability to empathize with others, not only with people who might be considered their 'own kind,' but also with people ostensibly very different from themselves.

Overall, the Hamilton civic leaders were a very compassionate group. Martha Nussbaum defines compassion as 'a central bridge between the individual and the community ... our species' way of hooking the interests of others to our own personal goods.'[1] The civic leaders illustrated this definition. Through compassion, they hooked the good of others in the community to their own personal good. Their capacity for empathy and compassion provided the feelings and beliefs that must accompany the law, if a society that protects human rights is to survive. Indeed, one might paraphrase the famous statement by the American judge Learned Hand, pointing out the need for social support for law. 'I often wonder whether we do not rest our hopes too much upon constitutions, upon laws and upon courts. These are false hopes ... Liberty [human rights] lies in the hearts of men and women.'[2] The Hamilton civic leaders were a group of women and men who, for the most part, accepted in their hearts the fundamental principles of human rights.

It might be considered that the civic leaders' acceptance of these principles was merely a consequence of their political socialization. Sniderman et al. discuss the question of whether the Canadian Charter of Rights and Freedoms acts as a 'springboard' in Canada, that is, 'whether citizens and decision makers are more likely to accept a right as legitimate because the Charter of Rights declares it to be a right.'[3] The Hamilton civic leaders often referred to the Charter and expressed a feeling of duty to uphold it. This supports the social-learning theory of democracy, summarized by Sniderman et al. as the view that 'support for democratic rights is a function of the extent to which citizens have been exposed to the norms of the culture, understand them, and are motivated to accept them.'[4]

With an average age in 1996–7 of fifty, however, most of the civic leaders had grown up before the Charter became part of the Canadian Constitution in 1982. They had also grown up before Canadian schools began to devote attention to the principles of anti-racism, multiculturalism, respect for women's rights, and, latterly, even respect for the rights of gays and lesbians.[5] Moreover, the nineteen adult immigrants had grown up elsewhere, and some of the child immigrants had had their early schooling elsewhere. Their views stemmed at least in part, therefore, from their own philosophical agency. As human rights laws and values changed in Canada, so those who had spent all or most of their lives in the country had to think through their own beliefs, as chapter 5, on gay and lesbian rights shows most clearly. These civic leaders were not mere passive recipients of human rights norms passed down from above; they were active participants in the creation and internalization of these norms among the Canadian population.

It is notable here that a significant proportion of the Hamilton civic leaders referred in passing to their religious beliefs when explaining their commitments to civic well-being and their attitudes toward human rights questions. The legal scholar Abdullahi A. An-Na'im has commented on the importance both of human agency and of religious principles in grounding human rights norms among the population at large. He wants to reconcile the secular origins of human rights principles with the religious beliefs still held by the vast majority of the world's population. 'The approach I propose for achieving this reconciliation is premised on a belief in the ability of *human agency* to promote understandings of religion that are conducive to meaningful inter-dependence of human rights, religion and secularism.'[6] The Dutch human rights scholar Bas de Gaay Fortman takes a similar approach to An-Na'im's. '[T]he global project for universal responsibility of people for one another's freedom and welfare cannot do without constant moral injection. It is primarily in their transcendental [religious] orientation that human beings learn to rise above their immediate patterns of needs.'[7]

Although strong conclusions cannot be reached from the evidence I present in this book, especially since I did not originally design my interviews to investigate the strength of the Hamilton civic leaders' religious beliefs, their frequent references to religion suggest that An-Na'im and de Gaay Fortman may be right. The civic leaders used their capacity for philosophical agency to apply, or sometimes to rethink, their religiously based ethical beliefs. Religion to many of them was a serious matter that did indeed motivate their commitments to civic welfare. Among the Hamilton civic leaders, human agency in the contemplation of both religious and secular normative principles resulted in a strong commitment to human rights based above all on the principle of respect.

Not all the civic leaders referred to their religious beliefs in explaining their reasoning, however. Some were quite secular in their approach to human rights. Both groups may also have been expressing what some theorists call postmodern values. Inglehart, Nevitte, and Basanez explain the emergence of these values. '[I]n postindustrial society, historically unprecedented levels of wealth and the emergence of the welfare states have given rise to a shift from scarcity norms, which emphasize hard work and self-denial, to postmodern values, which emphasize the quality of life, emancipation of women and sexual minorities, and related postmaterialist priorities such as emphasis on self-expression.'[8] As mentioned earlier in this book, nineteen of the civic leaders volunteered that they had grown up in poverty. Others may also have done so, and many were familiar with poverty through their professional or voluntary work, both in Canada and abroad. This was not a group, then, that unthinkingly disregarded the continued problems of material scarcity. They were, however, also aware of social and psychological needs of a non-material kind, which human rights could help to fulfil. Among these were the needs for equality, for respect, and for recognition of one's particular identity, whether it be as an individual with an unusual (in Canada) religion or culture, a homosexual, or an Aboriginal person.

The civic leaders also illustrated a particular cultural syndrome identified by Inglehart, Nevitte, and Basanez. This is a set of cultural values strongly correlated to political democracy: 'a culture of trust, tolerance, subjective well-being, and postmaterialist values.'[9] On the whole, the Hamilton civic leaders were a self-confident group. They trusted themselves, their fellow citizens, and their government, although such trust did not prevent them from being critical. They were able to tolerate those different from themselves because they were able to view all people as individuals, with individual wants and needs for respect, equality, and dignity. They also understood that such wants and needs often entailed expression in group contexts. These postmodern values could be realized in a Canada in which most individuals enjoyed at least minimal economic security, and they could be promoted by citizens, such as the Hamilton civic leaders, who for the most part enjoyed both material and subjective well-being themselves.

The Hamilton civic leaders' value systems also provided evidence of the existence of ethical individualism, as a moral principle to which many citizens in post-industrial societies adhere. The prominent Canadian philosopher C.B. Macpherson argued that possessive individualism characterized capitalist (Western) societies. This individualism's possessiveness was found 'in its conception of the individual as essentially the proprietor of his own person or capacities, owing nothing to society for them.'[10] His argument posited a society of each for himself, seeking material wealth and unconcerned with others. Yet this is not the type of society Canada is. In Hamilton in 1993, for example, out of a then population of 317,000, there were estimated to be about 91,000 volunteers, that is, people who voluntarily helped others without pay.[11] These volunteers, like the seventy-eight civic leaders whose opinions shaped this book, practised a form of what philosopher Guy Haarscher calls 'ethical-universalistic individualism.' Ethical-universalistic individualism means that 'every individual has to be respected as a person ... this is a duty, a categorical imperative, an unconditioned value.'[12] Far from believing they owed nothing to society, the civic leaders, whether motivated by religious or secular beliefs, were of the opinion that they owed society a great deal. They had strong ethical commitments, grounded both in their sense of individual rights and in their understanding that individuals also sometimes need group rights. To most of them, the duty to respect every individual as a person was indeed a categorical imperative.

This understanding of the motives of the Hamilton civic leaders suggests that there is more to human life than self-interest. Given the right conditions, such as exist in a post-materialist Canada, many individuals want to help others. Amartya Sen argues that human beings are not interested only in their selves, either their selves as individuals or their selves as members of groups. Individuals, says Sen, do have a sense of social justice. '[W]e ... see actions – day in and day out – that reflect values which have clear social components that take us well beyond the narrow confines of purely selfish behaviour.' Individuals are capable of 'socially responsible reasoning,' and 'have the ability to contemplate the lives of others.'[13] Applying their reason to observation of the lives, suffering, and needs of others – the compassionate reasoning about which Nussbaum writes[14] – the Hamilton civic leaders were frequently able to transcend their purely personal interests in considering human rights dilemmas in Canada.

Elsewhere, in a discussion of the capacity of citizens of the so-called Third World to contemplate human rights norms, I argued that they were capable of 'consider[ing] transcendent ethical norms which, if implemented in their own societies, might well result in the betterment of their own lives.'[15] In that case, I was considering citizens' own direct interest in the protections that human rights offer. Among the Hamilton civic leaders, some of the concern for human rights stemmed from direct interest. The Aboriginal leaders and the gay and lesbian leaders were still engaged in the struggle for rights, and some of the non-whites and non-Christians still experienced prejudice despite formal human rights protection. By contrast, most of the other civic leaders already enjoyed the full range of human rights. Nevertheless, almost all had both a direct and an altruistic interest in protecting the human rights of others in their society. Aboriginal leaders worried about gays and lesbians, for example, and gays and lesbians worried about Aboriginals.

Altruism may be defined as 'voluntary behavior directed toward increasing another's welfare without the expectation of external reward.'[16] Altruism is a complex entity: it is part emotion and part moral value.[17] It impels some individuals to take actions that directly contradict their perceived immediate self-interest, as in the case of Holocaust rescuers.[18] More commonly, many individuals derive pleasure from helping others in political conditions that, unlike the Holocaust, do not punish people for assisting the less fortunate. Social commitment based on reason is supplemented by an active emotional commitment based on one's connection to one's fellow human beings. The Hamilton civic leaders revealed that their interests were often in protecting others' human rights. Nor was this mere self-interest. For most of the civic leaders, their capacity for philosophical agency resulted in an active empathic commitment to the community at large.

The civic leaders' opinions cannot be completely removed from their own personal identities and experiences, as if they were absolutely autonomous philosophical agents floating in an abstracted ether unconnected to their own lives. As I discussed in chapter 1, for some the primary locus of their community involvement was within organizations devoted to the advancement of their own particular social group. For most of the Hamilton civic leaders, however, their membership in collective identity groups was not the overriding aspect of their being. They often had multiple identities. They also had multiple roles and multiple interests, as well as personal experiences and idiosyncratic ideas.

Empathy toward people who are different from oneself is possible.[19] Empathy is the capacity to imagine oneself in another's shoes, to recognize a stranger's humanity. Instead of viewing a stranger as so different from oneself as to be unworthy of one's regard, one views the stranger as having an equal claim to humanity and respect, regardless of his or her race, ethnicity, gender, sexual orientation, or social position. The personal identities of citizens may be less important than their sense of common humanity, or their capacity to view each other with compassion and understanding. The Hamilton civic leaders showed this empathy, compassion, and understanding in their discussions of the rights of gays and lesbians, of religious and ethnic minorities, of indigenous peoples, and of the poor.

Empathy is possible in part because individuals are capable of philosophical agency. The Hamilton civic leaders demonstrated this in their differing and somewhat unexpected views on hate crime sentencing. Philosophical agency implies that the individual can 'think' herself beyond her personal identity, experience, and interest. Thus, the non-white civic leaders who thought that assaults on white people should be taken just as seriously as assaults on black people were able to think themselves into the feelings and suffering of white victims of assault. They could think themselves into the position of whites because they recognized that white people were individuals with the same needs for personal security as they had. The whites who supported differential punishments for hate crimes were also thinking themselves into the position of others, imagining what it might be like to be assaulted because of one's skin colour.

Helen Fein has found that, in general, altruistic people view those they help as individuals, not as members of a strange group, and that they define those individuals as members of their own universe of obligation. For the altruistic person, says Fein, there is no 'Other': '[I]dentification with the other as other tends to be a self-annulling motive in an altruistic transaction ... for as one begins to identify ... and internalizes the role of the other(s), he or she is no longer perceived as the other but simply as a fellow human.'[20] Psychological studies show that 'a crucial aspect of our capacities as social creatures is that we can empathize with others,' by taking the role of the other or by imaginative inner imitation. Empathy means being able to 'envisag[e] ... others in their local circumstances.'[21] It may be more difficult to envisage others in their local circumstances when those circumstances are markedly different from one's own, and when there is no immediate basis of common understanding. Yet, it is not impossible.

In the case of the Hamilton civic leaders, their identification with Canada as a nation, as discussed in chapter 2, made it easier to accept that members of all the groups about whom I asked them questions were fellow citizens. As such, they were members of the Canadian community, to whom the civic leaders had obligations. The concentric circle theory, to which many referred in chapter 10 in their discussion of obligations to strangers outside Canada, suggested that, for some, lack of closeness hampered identification with others. Nevertheless, the reaction of those civic leaders who thought they had just as much obligation to strangers outside Canada as to fellow citizens suggests that, even with very little basis for common understanding, the empathic imagining of oneself in others' shoes is possible.

When engaged in the sort of moral reasoning exemplified by the Hamilton civic leaders, many people are capable of stepping outside their own personal experience. Their 'universe of obligation,' to use Helen Fein's trenchant phrase, is not confined to the 'Us,' as opposed to the 'Them.'[22] I found Canadians of all origins, European and non-European background, white and non-white, heterosexual and homosexual, capable of adopting empathic attitudes to those who might seem very different from themselves. The Hamilton civic leaders did not box each other into categories: white or non-white, Christian and other, gay or straight, Aboriginal or settler. Instead, they tried to consider their mutual interest in a normative order based on human rights. They based their assumptions upon a universal human nature, a universal need for respect and dignity. This suggests an empathic capacity among the larger Canadian population as well.

Thus, the Canadians studied in this project were capable of resolving human rights dilemmas in two senses. First, through empathic imagination, they were capable of considering the human rights interests of those who seemed at first glance to be radically different from them. Second, they were capable of resolving dilemmas about competing human rights principles, usually in favour of accommodating groups that they considered to occupy a vulnerable position in Canadian society.

A Group Rights Consciousness

As I explained in chapter 8, on Aboriginal rights, I do not accept the proposition that all numerical aggregates of individuals who share human rights needs or interests constitute distinct groups, for purposes of claiming human rights. I do accept that there are some collectivities that need specific rights – most clearly, in Canada, Aboriginal peoples – so that they may maintain themselves as collectivities and so that the individuals within those collectivities can assert their cultural identities along with others in the same group. Whether these collective rights ought to be considered human rights, or whether they ought better to be considered a distinct category of legal rights, is a complex question that I cannot answer here.

By contrast, the Hamilton civic leaders were much more comfortable with the idea of group rights than I am. They thought easily in terms of groups. Groups – social categories – are easily identifiable. Which groups are, or are not, subject to human rights violations, especially violation of the principle of non-discrimination, is fairly easy to sort out. Individual civil and political rights, on the other hand, do not seem to be violated in Canada. The civic leaders tended to take for granted the basic civil and political liberties, perhaps unaware of how hard won they had been in Canadian history.

When I began this research project, I was worried that Canadian public discourse was going too far in the direction of group rights, and that such group rights might undermine the individual civil and political rights that, I believe, are fundamental to the liberal-democratic order.[23] I am now less worried by this possibility, but I still believe that Canadians are not as careful to defend individual civil and political rights as they should be. The potential difficulties in resolving conflicts between group and individual rights are most clearly seen in the matter of hate speech. I believe that Canada should have hate speech laws; this accords with international law, as I explained in chapter 3, and it protects extremely vulnerable groups against real threats to their lives, property, and dignity. Nevertheless, in the attempt to protect the dignity of vulnerable groups and to make sure that they are never offended, perhaps sometimes the Canadian public, if not Canadian law, goes too far.

Most of the examples discussed in chapter 3 were of 'old' free speech issues such as anti-Semitism, or racism against persons of African descent. In each of these cases, majority Canadians (Christians, whites) were accused of hate speech against minority Canadians (Jews, blacks). As Canada's demographic composition changes, however, new issues are likely to arrive on the agenda of freedom of speech; indeed, some have arrived already. In these cases, members of one vulnerable group attack the free speech rights of members of another vulnerable group. It is going to be difficult to sort through freedom-of-speech issues when those accused of offensive speech are not members of the white, male, Christian, or heterosexual majority, but rather members of the very racial, gender, religious, or other groups that freedom of speech is meant not to offend.

One such incident occurred in a university setting in 1993. Matin Yaqzan, a professor of mathematics at the University of New Brunswick, wrote an editorial in a student newspaper suggesting that in this age of sexual promiscuity, date rape was not a serious offence. Therefore, he argued, the appropriate response to it should be monetary compensation, not criminal prosecution. These views evoked a storm of feminist protest by students and others, culminating in Yaqzan's being banned from campus for a week and eventually persuaded to take early retirement. The administration of the university sided with the protestors and did not defend Yaqzan's right either to academic freedom or to freedom of speech in general. Yet Yaqzan was an immigrant from a non-Western society. Immigrants from such societies frequently hold views on questions of personal morality that do not conform to the accepted Canadian feminist discourse.[24]

Another incident, which did not provoke the national press discussion occasioned by the Yaqzan affair, concerned public criticism of Jews by the editor of a black newspaper. The issue at hand was a presentation in North York, Ontario, in 1993 of the musical *Showboat*, set in the late-nineteenth-century U.S. South. *Showboat* had drawn much public protest by some activist African-Canadians, who argued that it was a racist play. Arnold A. Auguste, the editor of the African-Canadian newspaper *Share*, pointed out that *Showboat* had been written by a Jew and was being produced by a Jew, and that the person slated to preside over its opening ceremonies was a Jew. Moreover, in a letter to the Canadian Civil Liberties Association Auguste professed his distress that other Jews in the community had not dissociated themselves from the activities of these particular Jews, thus implying that Jews as a people bore a collective responsibility for those activities of some Jews that offended some blacks.[25] That Auguste's views did not occasion public discussion and censure suggests that there is a hierarchy of vulnerability in the mind of the Canadian public. Jews still suffer racist attacks in Canada, but their economic situation is much better than that of blacks.[26] Therefore, blacks – or, at least, the editor of a black newspaper – seem to be permitted to criticize Jews in a manner that would be impermissible if the two groups were reversed.

Attempts to curb offensive speech clash as well with gay and lesbian rights. In discussing hate speech, two or three of the Hamilton civic leaders defended lesbian pornography on the grounds that 'one woman's poison is another woman's pleasure'; that is, that what they personally might consider pornographic might be pleasurable to lesbian women. As Lynn put it, '[T]here are women who I have met who have told me that this is what they choose to do with their lives, and who am I to decide that it is not their right?' According to Lynn, non-discrimination against lesbians required the right to produce and possess pornography. Yet others in Canada are so upset by representations of the degradation of women in heterosexual pornography that they advocate its restriction. It would seem inconsistent to permit lesbian and gay pornography – including degrading and violent pornography – on the grounds that one does not want to further oppress already suffering minorities, yet censor heterosexual pornography on the grounds that it perpetuates sexist stereotypes and (may) result in actual harmful acts by men against women.[27]

Thus, the question becomes, should any particular groups have more rights than others, because they are more vulnerable? This question suggests that perhaps protection of the individual right to freedom of speech is, after all, the best remedy to ensure that all voices in a multicultural liberal democracy are heard. The alternative might be a legislated hierarchy of vulnerability, limiting the free speech rights of some groups but not of others, according to how much power each group is seen to have in the society as a whole.

I do not wish to belabour this point. Aside from these small incidents of violations of freedom of speech, attempts to accommodate the rights of vulnerable groups in Canada do not appear to threaten the civil and political rights of individuals. In large part, this is because the rights that most vulnerable groups in Canada need – to non-discrimination, to religious freedom, to equal rights regardless of sexual orientation – are adequately covered (or, in the case of gays and lesbians, almost adequately covered) by the individual rights already in place. One does not need to demonstrate one's identity as a member of a group in order to assert one's claim to these rights. The one clearly distinct collectivity, Aboriginal people, has both legal rights and constitutionally entrenched special human rights, however far from realization in practice these rights still are.[28]

In my view, it would be unwise to push a legal assertion of group rights beyond the protections already in existence for Aboriginal peoples. The guarantees provided by both the Charter of Rights and Freedoms and the Canadian Multiculturalism Act are sufficient to accommodate members of new minorities resident in Canada. They provide not only for minorities' rights to speak their own language, practise their own religion, and engage in their own cultural practices (as long as these do not violate other human rights, as in the case of female genital mutilation), but also for some state involvement to preserve and promote their cultures on Canadian territory. Moreover, Section 27 of the Charter of Rights and Freedoms provides explicitly that the Charter 'shall be interpreted in a manner consistent with the preservation and enhancement of the multicultural heritage of Canadians.'[29] This asserts a legal social value that would protect minority cultural groups, should any laws to abrogate the rights they now enjoy be suggested.

In chapter 6, we saw that most Hamilton civic leaders did not believe that the need to respect minority cultures should be permitted to undermine the basic human rights of either women or gays and lesbians. That is, in my view, an appropriate response to the current round of social, demographic, and cultural change in Canada. The basic liberal principles of human rights and democratic order must not be undermined. Moreover, it is precisely to enjoy these basic principles that many immigrants come to Canada in the first place. A Sudanese homosexual immigrant, for example, expects that he will enjoy all the rights currently available to gays and lesbians. He does not immigrate in the expectation that such rights will be modified to suit the belief system of other Sudanese immigrants, who may dislike homosexuals and think that they should be cast into prison or worse.

Another public issue seeming to pit the rights of individuals in

Canada against the rights of groups is employment equity. As shown in chapter 7, employment equity programs offend many citizens' views of fairness. They seem to privilege some groups above others, and deny individuals the right to compete for employment without any group characteristics being taken into account. Properly designed employment equity programs, addressing real, not perceived, disadvantages, might help to defuse such a sense of offense.

International law permitting affirmative action programs is more restrictive than Canadian law. Article 1 of the International Convention on the Elimination of All Forms of Racial Discrimination permits 'special measures ... for ... securing adequate advancement of certain racial or ethnic groups,' but specifies that 'such measures do [must] not, as a consequence, lead to the maintenance of separate rights for different racial groups.' It also specifies that such special measures must 'not be continued after the objectives for which they were taken have been achieved.'[30] Canada ratified this Convention on 14 October 1970. In so far as employment equity programs in Canada or Ontario propose remedying social ills that do not actually exist, such as favouring for employment members of racial groups that already enjoy high educational and income standards, they might be seen to violate this Convention. These groups appear to be enjoying special measures that they do not need. More narrowly defined employment equity programs, addressing the most severely disadvantaged racial groups, namely, Aboriginals and blacks, might defuse some of the resentment against these programs.

Finally, 'group' rights, as such, would not help the poor. The poor are not a fixed body of Canadian citizens. While some individuals or families are trapped in a multigenerational cycle of poverty, others enter or leave poverty depending on circumstances such as single motherhood or unemployment. The economic rights that these individuals need are not group rights. They are individual rights, which should be claimable by individuals. That they are not constitutionally protected is certainly a major failure of the Canadian human rights regime. It is not, however, a failure that needs a new definition of 'groups' in order to be remedied.

Thus, the easy categorization of their fellow citizens into groups by the Hamilton civic leaders does not imply a need for a new category of human rights laws in Canada. The discourse of groups is overdone; aggregate quantifiable categories are not always social groups requiring special rights. Even the rights that women need are normally rights that men need too. Men as well as women need protections of their reproductive rights (though not, obviously, the right to abortion), protections against sexual assault, and special measures to assist single parents. That these rights were first claimed by the feminist movement on behalf of women does not belie their pertinence to men, even if in much smaller numbers.[31]

The Hamilton civic leaders thought in terms of groups, but their thinking did not extend so far as to differentiate the legal principles beneath individual and group rights. They were more concerned with the principle of inclusivity; that is, making sure that everyone physically in Hamilton, or in Canada, was also socially included. What they perceived was in large part the social reality, that some social aggregates – blacks, gays and lesbians, Muslims, Aboriginal people – were likely to be excluded as 'Others.' The civic leaders' thinking was essentially communitarian: they wished to ensure that everyone, and every group, was perceived to be part of the community.

Human Rights and the Sense of Community

I began this research project in 1996 in part as an empirical inquiry into theoretical conclusions I had reached in an earlier book, *Human Rights and the Search for Community*, to which I have made occasional reference earlier in these pages. My other motive was an interest in the viewpoints of civic leaders whom I had met during my own membership, from 1991 through 1996, on a Hamilton city committee devoted to a human rights issue. The people I met on that committee, some of whom are quoted in this book, were very thoughtful individuals, often dealing on a day-to-day basis with human rights problems that I dealt with only as abstract academic questions.

My earlier book was in large part a reply to the position put forward in much international debate on human rights, that Western society is overly individualistic, materialistic, and unconcerned with obligations to the family and to society as a whole. Many commentators in the international debate think that the liberal human rights-based individualism of the West has undermined community. Against this position, I argued that it is possible to have a sense of community in modern society. This is, however, a 'thin' community, not rooted in real or even fictive kinship, and in immigrant societies such as Canada not binding together people who have a historically common heritage. Community in Western societies is based on common interests as much as, or even more than, common identity. It is based on a philosophical, religious, and ethical sense of commitment to the relative strangers among whom one lives, rather than on a feeling that the strangers are, in some sense, a part of one's own family.

In my earlier book, I defined a community as a group of people who have a sense of obligation to one another.[32] This is not a standard definition of community, which is often regarded as persons sharing language, religion, heritage, even physical kinship. Nevertheless, it is a definition that fits the modern, highly mobile immigrant society that is Canada. It is difficult to create a sense of community in such a society; it is more difficult to feel a sense of obligation or duty to relative strangers than to family or personal friends. It can, nevertheless, be done.

Amitai Etzioni defines a community as having two elements: 'A web of affect-laden relationships among a group of individuals, relationships that often crisscross and reinforce one another ... [and a] measure of commitment to a set of shared values, norms and meanings, and a shared history and identity – in short, to a particular culture.'[33] Hamilton is not a city in which it is possible for all residents to have the 'thick' affective bonds that might exist in a small, close, intermarried village, although such bonds do exist among people whose families are from Hamilton and who have lived all their lives in the city. It is, however, a city in which among many residents there is a common set of values, norms and meanings. Without common history and religious or ethnic identity, these attributes constitute the culture of respect and commitment to others that informed the world views of most of the civic leaders I interviewed. Sharing this normative culture, the civic leaders were able to engage in 'moral dialogue[s],' 'intensive discussions in which their normative commitments ... [were] engaged.'[34] These dialogues permitted them to consider human rights laws and to consider their own responsibilities to uphold the human rights of others.

The Hamilton civic leaders often acknowledged their sense of responsibility to others. The duty to respect others was the responsibility that they most frequently articulated. Respect meant knowledge, understanding, and a willingness to be open to new sorts of human rights claims. Respect meant overcoming one's prejudices against gays and lesbians, thinking about possible changes in hate speech and hate crimes principles, and thinking about how to reconcile fundamental principles such as women's rights with the religious and cultural beliefs of new immigrant minorities. It meant, above all, learning about and understanding Aboriginal peoples. There were also direct duties, such as to give money to local and international charities, and to take part in civic affairs.

Since about 1990, in part as a response to the non-Western criticisms of the West that I mentioned above, the international debate on human rights has included some discussion of a potential set of universal duties, as well as a set of universal rights. Duties made instinctive sense to the Hamilton civic leaders, whose general approach to life was far less individualistic and materialistic than stereotyped criticisms of 'the West' would suggest. In a city and a country filled with human rights violations – if very minor compared to the types of violations one would find in less wealthy and less democratic societies – many of the civic leaders had had lifetime careers of community service. To them, the community of obligation was to all Canadians, with whom they had a sense of 'common identification and ... mutuality.'[35]

Nevertheless, this common identification did not mean that all assertions of human rights claims met with universal approbation by all the civic leaders. In particular, rights claims that hit the pocketbook were far less easily accepted than those that simply asserted the need for equal treatment and personal respect. In chapter 7 I showed how only on the issue of employment equity was there anything resembling a perceivable split between the white and the non-white civic leaders. Some whites regarded employment equity as implying a real cost to them or to younger members of their families, while some non-whites thought that the absence of employment equity programs constituted a real personal economic cost. In chapter 8, I cautioned that the principled respect that most of the civic leaders showed for the rights of Aboriginal peoples might be modified were their own property or privileges to be challenged by Aboriginal claims, as has happened in other parts of Canada. Chapter 10 showed that most of the civic leaders were willing to support immigrants and refugees on Canadian soil with all the resources ordinarily available to Canadian citizens. Their sense of responsibility to strangers outside Canada, however, did not extend to an increase in national costs that might undermine their current standard of living.

While the civic leaders acknowledged responsibility to others, they also stressed others' responsibility to them. Community included everyone's taking his or her share of responsibility. This was particularly evident in chapter 9, on poverty. The civic leaders were quite willing to allow people to make mistakes, and quite concerned to make sure that everyone lived at a reasonable standard and was not humiliated or degraded by social policies such as workfare. Nevertheless, they also insisted that young people and the poor should take as much responsibility as they could for their own lives. Not to take such responsibility was to demonstrate disrespect for the vast majority of Canadians, who worked hard and were not a charge on the public purse. The civic leaders believed that given a fair and just set of social rules, everyone ought to be as responsible as possible for his or her own fate.

The fairness and justness of social rules was an important aspect of the civic leaders' commitment to Canada as a whole, and what made them feel that Canada was a worthwhile place to live. In this respect, violations of the implicit social bargain that I discussed in chapter 7 struck them hard. They wanted to ensure that the basic liberal principle of equal opportunity in a competitive society was protected, although some thought employment equity would constitute such protection, while others thought it would violate it. Their right to fair and just social rules also guided the civic leaders' views on other issues. They did not like the idea of being taken advantage of by the poor; nor did some of them like the fact that wealthy immigrants could, as they saw it, buy their way into Canada. A few civic leaders also thought that Aboriginal people were relying too much on their specific legal rights such as certain tax exemptions, and not doing enough to support themselves in the manner incumbent on all other Canadians. These were all symbolic insults to the civic leaders' own identities as sober, hard-working people.

For some civic leaders, differential punishments for hate crimes were also a type of symbolic insult. Such punishments suggested that violations of some peoples' right to live peaceably in their own communities were more socially upsetting than violations of the same right of other people. If equality is a fundamental principle of the Canadian liberal-democratic order, some of the Hamilton civic leaders felt, then it should be enforced in such an important matter as protection of citizens' physical integrity.

Finally, the civic leaders expected some sense of social decorum in the community as a whole. For some of them, the limit of gay and lesbian rights was the flaunting of their sexuality in public. Private sexual relationships should be kept private, even if the right to make private sexual choices was protected by the wider citizenry. A community has implicit social rules about how to behave; these rules are known, even if not explicitly taught, and should be respected. Those living conservative lives considerate of others should not be mocked, as it were, in public places.

These small cautions about the overall commitment to human rights of the majority of the Hamilton civic leaders show that their social commitment to others can be undermined if those others break the implied rules of community life. The 'thin' community that exists in Canada, as in other Western societies, requires constant injections of social commitment from its citizens to keep it in existence. Civil society depends on voluntary activity; it depends on myriad individuals deciding to devote their time to the collective good rather than to their own individual self-interest. The collective good, moreover, is one that increasingly pertains to strangers; that is, to persons who at first glance seem radically different from oneself. The Hamilton civic leaders had been able to overcome much of this sense of strangeness by contemplation of the legitimate need for respect for various new, or newly emerging, social groups in Canada. Both in their articulations of principle and in their actual careers as civic activists, they tried to support the rights claims of those to whom a theory of 'thick' community would suggest that they might feel no obligations, not being related to those others by kinship or culture. They expected, in return, personal responsibility, social decorum, and respect for their own way of life.

Compassionate Canadians?

The title of this book, *Compassionate Canadians*, might seem overly congratulatory. The Hamilton civic leaders I interviewed were presumably on their best behaviour when I spoke to them; indeed, only a few ventured any opinions that would be considered illegitimate in polite Canadian liberal discourse. Moreover, they were a select group of older, educated civic leaders, not statistically representative of the entire Canadian population.

Yet on the whole, the Hamilton civic leaders were strikingly compassionate people. Their opinions were thoughtful and considerate, drawing on their own experiences of life, their religious and other beliefs, and stories others had told them, as well as on both their paid and their voluntary work. This book was not meant to suggest that their views were representative of Canada as a whole. It was, rather, an investigation into the way that the Hamilton group – possibly typical of civic leaders across Canada – thought through human rights dilemmas. As opinion leaders, identifiers of civic needs, and mobilizers of public resources to fulfil those needs, the individuals I interviewed had some influence on local affairs, on the official positions of the various community groups to which they belonged, and on public opinion more broadly. Thus, they were integrated into the broader Canadian discussion of human rights, and active participants in establishing and consolidating the normative underpinnings of human rights law.

Yet, a nagging question remains. The Hamilton civic leaders exemplify a consensus on the need to respect all Canadians, however novel certain human rights claims might be. Can this consensus survive the current long period of relative prosperity and security in Canada, lasting since the Second World War? Or could a political, social, or economic crisis put the lie to the belief that human rights were far more deeply entrenched in Canadian society in 1996 than they had been fifty years earlier? The Canada of fifty years earlier was a very different society than the one the civic leaders knew when they were interviewed. It was racist, anti-Semitic, sexist, and homophobic, and it was deeply abusive of the dignity and rights of Aboriginal peoples. A long period of establishment of human rights law, entrenchment of constitutional protections of human rights in the Charter of Rights and Freedoms, and much human rights socialization in the educational system and in the mass media has changed these practices. One hopes that it has also created a deep normative commitment to human rights in the Canadian population as a whole, but one cannot be sure of that.

Some standard threats to any modern society's normative order can be identified. One is deep economic crisis, such as the Depression of the 1930s. We cannot predict whether Canada is likely in the foreseeable future to undergo economic crisis of this kind, nor what its consequences might be. Another standard threat is political uncertainty or chaos; here, the immediate threat in Canada is Quebec secession. Finally, there is social chaos, such as might occur if huge numbers of immigrants and refugees suddenly obtained the right to enter Canada. Economic, political, and social chaos often results in a battening down of the social hatches, an exclusion both of real strangers and of citizens suddenly deemed to have been strangers all along.

A standard referent for considering the consequences of these kinds of threats is Nazi Germany, with post–Soviet Russia constituting another, more contemporary reference point. In both societies, deep economic crisis combined with political uncertainty created much social chaos. In Germany, fascism took over: in Russia, fascism remains a threat. However, neither country had had a history of political democracy (with the exception of Germany's fifteen years of Allied-imposed Weimar democracy, 1918–33). Canada is a stable democracy of over 135 years' standing. Democratic discourse and practice provide a more coherent and deeper basis for human rights than mere law, imposed from above. Yet, should Canada become less wealthy and its citizens less competitive in the global economy; should it be riven and torn by the nationalist movement in Quebec; or should it be over-whelmed with immigrants and refugees, public reaction might become ungenerous and uncharitable. However empathic the relatively pros-perous, highly educated Canadians discussed here were, such empa-thy might not survive severe crisis.

Academics are constantly warned not to make prospective judg-ments; better, it is thought, to leave such judgments to policy-makers. Indeed, I cannot do more in this brief conclusion than raise the ques-tion of whether the empathic, compassionate people I interviewed for this study are typical of Canadians, and whether their attitudes would change under significant social, economic, or political strain. This is a question that Canadian policy-makers have to wrestle with when they introduce new human rights laws, when they make decisions on the numbers of refugees and immigrants to accept, when they decide who should receive more – and who perhaps should receive less – social support.

Nevertheless, my tentative answer to the question I have posed above is the following: Basic liberal rights to non-discrimination would probably survive severe social strain. This includes rights for women, which were unproblematic for the Hamilton civic leaders. The social value of non-discrimination has been deeply embedded in Canadians for two generations. New claimants for non-discrimination rights might, however, be scapegoated in a society in crisis. In this connec-tion, gays and lesbians seem the most likely candidate, as their claims for rights most fundamentally undermine the basic social morality of the duty to enter into heterosexual marriage and have a family.[36] Gen-erosity to strangers from outside Canada's borders is also unlikely to survive crisis, both because of the economic costs, and because fear of strangers tends to heighten in times of crisis. Finally, there may come a point at which settler Canadians, all those people not of Aboriginal descent, decide they have had enough of Aboriginal claims to collec-tive rights. The Aboriginal peoples of Canada, it is sad to say, rely heavily on the goodwill of the majority population. The economic resources and self-governing administrations they currently command could easily be removed from them, should the wider society decide to do so. They are in a uniquely vulnerable position.

Non-white, and non-Christian, immigrants from the various parts of the non-Western world might also be especially vulnerable in a Canada in crisis. Immigrants from the non-white 'Rest' can fit nicely into Western societies that operate on principles of non-racialism, as long as they are carefully selected for education, income, and professional status. More and more white Canadians have internalized these principles of non-racialism, especially as their own families become more complex. Among the Hamilton civic leaders, for example, one fairly conservative white woman had become used to having a black brother-in-law, and another had become quite fond of a West Indian daughter-in-law. Such tolerance, however, seems to depend in large part on immigrants' not being associated with pockets of poverty or social disorder. It also seems to depend on their adopting 'Canadian' social norms, relegating particular aspects of their identities to the private realm. If immigrants insist on publicly maintaining unusual aspects of their identity, the dominant Canadian population might not be so tolerant. In this respect, given the social visibility of some of their female members who wear traditional dress, and given the current world geopolitical situation, Muslim Canadians seem especially vulnerable to scapegoating.[37]

Finally, there remains the problem that although Canada is a liberal democracy, it is also a class society. The Canadian poor, those who are 'always with us,' have strong entitlements in law to a variety of financial and social supports, but these are still not seen as human rights. The sense of obligation their fellow citizens have to them rests still, to a large extent, on a sense of charity.[38] The poor are therefore always at risk of increased social exclusion, if the cost of their support seems too high, or if they are perceived to be personally irresponsible.

In Canada, poverty is the deepest and most profound social degradation. All other types of exclusion can fall by the wayside in a liberal and democratic society that believes in equal opportunity and the necessity of universal social respect. Class prejudice remains, along with resentment of the real material costs necessary to ameliorate the suffering of the excluded poor. The generosity of spirit exemplified by the compassionate Canadians about whom I have written in this book is not reflected by all of their fellow citizens. Compassion is often a luxury of the comfortable.

Appendix
Interview Schedule

Note: As discussed in chapter 1, this interview schedule served only as a rough guide to the Hamilton civic leaders' interviews, which were semi-structured.

Personal Data

Place of birth

(If immigrant) year came to Canada and why

Marital status

Number of children
– age, sex, and occupation of children

Ethnic/racial identification

Church/religion
– any changes in religions/churches and why

Level and place of education
– type of school

Current occupation
– jobs held in the past
– jobs held before coming to Canada (if relevant)

Occupational ambitions

Age

Activism History

What civic office/organizational memberships (if any) do you hold?

What organizations are you active in?
– offices held?

What organizations do you belong to but are inactive in?
– offices held?

What organizations have you belonged to in the past?
– offices held?

What got you involved in office/organization?

Have you been able to accomplish what you hoped to?

Are there other organizations you would like to join or establish?
– why?

Are there any other activities/interests you hold that I should know about?

Women

What does feminism mean to you?

Do you consider yourself a feminist?
– why?

Do you support feminism?

Do women in Canada have enough rights nowadays; or are there rights that women still need?

Some people think that feminists are asking for too many rights nowadays; what is your view?

   Are women's rights undermining the family?
   Do feminists neglect housewives?
   Are feminists too biased against men?

Aside from the obvious biological differences, are women the 'same' as men, or are there differences?

Is abortion wrong?

Canada currently has no law on abortion; it's a matter between a woman and her doctor. Do you think there should be changes in this policy?

Should all ethnic and/or religious groups have to support women's rights, even if it is not part of their tradition or religious beliefs?

Do you have any other opinions about women's rights?

Gays and Lesbians

What do you think the gay rights movement is all about?

Do you support the gay rights movement?

Have gays and lesbians achieved enough rights in Canada now, or do they need more rights than they have today?

Do you agree with legalizing gay marriages?

Do you agree with letting gays and lesbians adopt children?

Do you agree with teaching children about the gay lifestyle in school?

Should they be taught that the gay and straight lifestyles are equally valid?

In your personal opinion, is what gays and lesbians do (in bed) wrong?

Are we going too far with gay rights?

Should all ethnic and/or religious groups have to support gay rights, even if it is not part of their tradition or religious beliefs?

Have your own opinions on gays and gay rights changed over the years?

Do you have any other opinions about gay rights?

Freedom of Speech

Should people be allowed to say or print anything they want?

If not, what kinds of speech (if any) should not be allowed?
- racism?
- sexism?
- insulting another ethnic group?
- insulting gays?
- blasphemy?
- adult's access to pornography (assuming adequate controls on child pornography and children's access to pornography)?

Should a teacher be allowed to give any opinions he or she believes in an elementary or high-school classroom?

Should public officials be punished or removed if they make insulting comments about a group?
– if so, by the electorate?
– by other officials (e.g., by employers, by party officials?)

Should people be allowed to have demonstrations to promote hateful views (e.g., white-supremacist groups such as the Ku Klux Klan)?

Should crimes motivated by hatred be punished more severely than other crimes (e.g., a racist assault, or gay-bashing?)

If you respond violently to a racist or homophobic insult, should that be taken into account in assessing a punishment against you? (E.g., if you are young black man, and someone makes a racist remark to you?)

Should we get rid of all hate speech laws, or should we keep them?

Do you have any other opinions about freedom of speech?

Multiculturalism

What do you think the Canadian policy of multiculturalism means?

Do you agree with multiculturalism?

Do you feel more/less able to express your own ethnic identity (or no difference) since we got multiculturalism?

Do you feel more/less 'Canadian' (or no difference) since we got multiculturalism?

Do white people in Canada have too much power or privilege compared to other people?

Are new immigrant groups (especially non-whites) making too many demands on the rest of Canadians?

Does multiculturalism give too much attention/power/privilege to non-whites?

What does employment equity/affirmative action mean to you?

Do you agree with employment equity/affirmative action policies?
– why?

Should employment equity/affirmative action include gays?

Do you think employment equity and affirmative action policies are upsetting white males?
– even if they are upsetting white males, does it matter?

Do you have any other opinions about multiculturalism?

Aboriginals

What (if anything) does everyone else in Canada owe to Aboriginals?

Do you feel that you have a personal responsibility to Aboriginal people?

Is there any similarity between Aboriginals and other minorities in Canada (same problems, similar status, same causes of problems)?

Could Aboriginals get ahead better if they just integrated into the Canadian mainstream like everybody else?

What do you think Aboriginal activists mean by sovereignty/self-determination/self-government?

Should Canada grant sovereignty/self-determination/self-government to Aboriginal peoples?

If Canada were to grant sovereignty or self-determination to Aboriginal peoples, should it first demand that they accept 'Canadian' human rights values such as
– women's rights?
– gay rights?
– freedom of speech?

Do you have any other opinions about Aboriginal rights?

Poverty

Who is responsible for poverty, the poor themselves or the whole society?

Do you yourself feel personally responsible to help the poor?

Looking at Ontario now, in 1996–7, do we have too much or too little of a welfare safety net, or is it about right?

Should able-bodied people on welfare be made to work?

Are single mothers responsible for their own problems?

Should young single mothers be (strongly) encouraged to give up their children for adoption?

Are visible minorities more likely to be poor than others in Canada?
– what about blacks specifically?

Are immigrants more likely to be poor than others in Canada?

Are Aboriginal people more likely to be poor than others in Canada?

Do you have any other opinions about poverty?

Responsibility to Strangers

Do we have the same level of responsibility to strangers as we do to people in Canada?

At present we accept about twenty-five-thousand refugees a year in Canada. Should we allow more refugees into the country, or fewer?

Do we give too much to refugees (health services, schools, welfare)?

Do refugees expect too much from Canadians?

We usually accept between 150,000 and 225,000 immigrants every year to Canada. Is this about the right number?

How should immigrants be chosen? (family status, language, occupation/education, wealth)?

Should more immigrants come from Europe? (In recent years, about two thirds of our immigrants have come from other places.)

At present we give less than half of one per cent of our GNP to foreign aid. Should we give more or less than that amount?

Are you willing to devote more tax dollars to help poor countries?

Are you involved in a refugee or immigrant aid group, or any group that helps people in underdeveloped countries?
– why?

Do you think you personally should do more to help them?

If so, what kinds of things do you think you could do that would help them?

Do you have any other opinions about our responsibility to strangers?

To Be a Canadian

Finally, I'm trying to get a sense of what it means to you to be a Canadian.

Do you yourself feel Canadian?
– why or why not?

Off the top of your head, could you tell me what being Canadian means to you, if anything?

When you think of a typical Canadian, do you think of any particular
– racial/ethnic group?
– language group?
– religion?

Can you think of how a typical Canadian might behave?

Can you think of any 'un-Canadian' behaviours, or attitudes or beliefs?

Are there attitudes of ways of life that immigrants should adopt to be more Canadian?

(If an immigrant) at what point did you start to feel Canadian? Or if you don't feel Canadian, why not?

If you don't feel Canadian, what could be changed about Canadian society to make you feel more Canadian?

Does it matter if people living in Canada 'feel' Canadian or not?

Do you have any other opinions about being Canadian?

Comments on this Interview

Are there any other matters you would like to talk about in this interview, that I might have neglected?

Did you find this interview tiring?
– difficult?

Can you recommend anyone else I should interview or organizations I should contact?

Notes

Chapter 1

1 Michael Ignatieff, speech to the Nexus Instituut, Catholic University of Tilburg, The Netherlands, 24 October 2000.

2 Rhoda E. Howard, *Human Rights and the Search for Community* (Boulder: Westview, 1995), 222.

3 Emile Durkheim, *The Division of Labor in Society* (New York: The Free Press, 1933 [1st ed. 1893]), 79.

4 Paul Bohannan, '*Conscience Collective* and Culture,' in *Essays on Sociology and Philosophy by Emile Durkheim et al.*, ed. Kurt H. Wolff (New York: Harper Torchbooks, 1960), 82.

5 Statistics Canada, 'Statistical Profile: Income and Work Statistics for Hamilton (Census Metropolitan Area), Ontario,' accessed 14 January 2000, available through http://ceps.statcan.ca/english/Profil/PlaceSearchForm1.cfm.

6 Calculated from Statistics Canada, 'Statistical Profile ... Hamilton.'

7 Calculated from Statistics Canada, *Profile of Census Tracts of Hamilton*, Catalogue no. 95-202-XPB (Ottawa: Minister of Industry, 1999), 10.

8 Statistics Canada, 'Statistical Profile ... Hamilton.'

9 Statistics Canada, *Profile of Census Tracts of Hamilton*, 6.

10 Robert D. Putnam, 'Bowling Alone: America's Declining Social Capital,' *Journal of Democracy* 6, no. 1 (1995): 65–78. See also Lawrence M. Friedman, 'The Way We Live Now,' in his *The Horizontal Society* (New Haven: Yale University Press, 1999), 16–52.

11 Charles C. Ragin, *Constructing Social Research: The Unity and Diversity of Method* (Thousand Oaks, CA: Pine Forge Press, 1994), 92.

12 Michael Quinn Patton, *Qualitative Evaluation and Research Methods*, 2d ed. (Newbury Park, CA: Sage Publications, 1990), 177.

13 Patton, *Qualitative Evaluation*, 169.

14 Patton, *Qualitative Evaluation*, 165.

15 Patton, *Qualitative Evaluation*, 184.

16 W. Paul Vogt, *Dictionary of Statistics and Methodology*, 2d ed. (London: Sage, 1999), 268.

17 Statistics Canada, *Profile of Census Tracts in Hamilton*, table 1.

18 Statistics Canada, *Profile of Census Tracts in Hamilton*, and Statistics Canada, *Statistics Canada Daily*, 4 November 1997, as reported in http://www.acs.calgary.ca/~ponting/SocialFacts.html;#Demography.

19 Statistics Canada, *Profile of Census Tracts in Hamilton*.

20 All national figures for 1991 from Statistics Canada, *Religions in Canada*, 1991 Census of Canada, Catalogue no. 93–319 (Ottawa: Industry, Science and Technology Canada, 1993).

21 Reginald W. Bibby, *Unknown Gods: The Ongoing Story of Religion in Canada* (Toronto: Stoddart, 1993), 22–7.

22 Alan Wolfe, *One Nation, After All* (New York: Viking, 1998), 18.

23 On the formation of public policy in Canada, see Stephen Brooks, *Public Policy in Canada: An Introduction* (Toronto: Oxford University Press, 1998).

24 Jurgen Habermas, 'Struggles for Recognition in the Democratic Constitutional State,' in Charles Taylor, with Respondents, *Multiculturalism* (Princeton, NJ: Princeton University Press, 1994), 125.

25 James Q. Wilson, *The Moral Sense* (New York: The Free Press, 1993), vii.

26 In a search of human rights journals until 2000, I did not locate any other study of ordinary citizens' views on human rights questions. There is an important and wide-ranging book on human rights questions in Canada, based on quantitative survey research, which was published just as I began my research; namely, Paul M. Sniderman, Joseph F. Fletcher, Peter H. Russell, and Philip E. Tetlock, *The Clash of Rights: Liberty, Equality, and Legitimacy in a Pluralist Democracy* (New Haven: Yale University Press, 1996).

27 Sniderman et al., *The Clash of Rights*, 8.

28 See, for example, Will Kymlicka, *Multicultural Citizenship* (Oxford: Clarendon Press, 1995); Charles Taylor, with Respondents, *Multiculturalism*; and Joseph H. Carens, *Culture, Citizenship, and Community: A Contextual Exploration of Justice as Evenhandedness* (Toronto: Oxford University Press, 2000).

29 Amitai Etzioni, 'Social Norms: Internalization, Persuasion, and History,' *Law and Society Review* 34, no. 1 (2000): 159, 177.

30 Robert R. Alford and R. Friedland, *Powers of Theory: Capitalism, the State, and Democracy* (New York: Cambridge University Press, 1985), 62.

31 On reflexivity as a condition of modern life, see Anthony Giddens, *The Consequences of Modernity* (Stanford: Stanford University Press, 1990), 149.

32 On Canada, see Judith Baker, ed., *Group Rights* (Toronto: University of Toronto Press, 1994). On the more general debate, see Marlies Galenkamp, *Individualism versus Collectivism: The Concept of Collective Rights* (Rotterdam: Erasmus University, 1993).

33 Putnam, 'Bowling Alone,' 67.

34 Alan Ryan, 'My Way,' *New York Review of Books* 47, no. 13 (2000): 48.

35 Bibby, *Unknown Gods*, 4.

36 Michael Hall et al., *Caring Canadians, Involved Canadians: Highlights from the 1997 National Survey of Giving, Volunteering and Participating*, Catalogue no. 71-542-XIE (Ottawa: Minister of Industry, 1998), 32.

37 On this perspective, see also Abdullahi A. An-Na'im, who agrees that the Golden Rule, 'shared by all the major religious traditions of the world,' is a good basis for human rights. An-Na'im, *Toward an Islamic Reformation: Civil Liberties, Human Rights, and International Law* (Syracuse, NY: Syracuse University Press, 1990), 162–3.

38 Robert Allan McChesney, 'Canada,' in *International Handbook of Human Rights*, ed. Jack Donnelly and Rhoda E. Howard (Westport, CT: Greenwood Press, 1987), 30.

39 Irving Abella and Harold Troper, *None Is Too Many: Canada and the Jews of Europe 1933–1948* (Toronto: Lester and Orpen Dennys, 1986), 34.

40 Ellen Baar, 'Issei, Nisei and Sansei,' in *Modernization and the Canadian State*, ed. Daniel Glenday, Hubert Guindon, and Allan Turowetz (Toronto: Macmillan, 1978), 335–55.

41 Robin W. Winks, *The Blacks in Canada: A History*, 2d ed. (Montreal and Kingston: McGill-Queen's University Press, 1997), 362–89.

42 On Nova Scotia African-Canadians in the 1960s, see Frances Henry, *Forgotten Canadians: The Blacks of Nova Scotia* (Don Mills, ON: Longman Canada, 1973).

43 E.B. Wickberg, 'Chinese,' in *The Canadian Encyclopedia*, vol. 1 (Edmonton: Hurtig, 1985), 336.

44 Hugh Johnston, 'Komagata Maru,' in *The Canadian Encyclopedia*, vol. 2 (Edmonton: Hurtig, 1985), 948.

45 Jean Leonard Elliott and Augie Fleras, *Unequal Relations: An Introduction to Race and Ethnic Dynamics in Canada* (Scarborough, ON: Prentice-Hall Canada, 1992), 239.

46 Ronald Manzer, *Public Policy and Political Development in Canada* (Toronto: University of Toronto Press, 1985), 153.

47 Thomas R. Berger, *Fragile Freedoms: Human Rights and Dissent in Canada*

(Toronto: Clarke, Irwin and Company, 1981), 235. See also Geoffrey York, *The Dispossessed: Life and Death in Native Canada* (Toronto: Lester and Orpen Dennys, 1989).

48 Angus McLaren, *Our Own Master Race: Eugenics in Canada, 1885–1945* (Toronto: McClelland and Stewart, 1990).

49 Berger, *Fragile Freedoms*, 127–62.

50 Manzer, *Public Policy and Political Development in Canada*, 165.

51 R. Brian Howe and David Johnson, *Restraining Equality: Human Rights Commissions in Canada* (Toronto: University of Toronto Press, 2000), 5.

52 Manzer, *Public Policy and Political Development in Canada*, 166.

53 Manzer, *Public Policy and Political Development in Canada*, 167.

54 Howe and Johnson, *Restraining Equality*, 8.

55 Manzer, *Public Policy and Political Development in Canada*, 168.

56 Howe and Johnson, *Restraining Equality*, 14.

57 McChesney, 'Canada,' 33, and Manzer, *Public Policy and Political Development in Canada*, 154. See also Walter Tarnopolsky, *The Canadian Bill of Rights*, 2d ed. (Toronto: McClelland and Stewart, 1975).

58 The Charter can be found in Berger, *Fragile Freedoms*, 278–84, as well as in many other books and on many web sites.

59 Commenting on the notwithstanding clause, L.C. Green noted in 1982, 'Herein is the route for any legislature ... to ensure by a series of such declarations that all or some of the substantive clauses of the Charter of Rights are in fact nullified for all time.' He goes on to quote Oliver Cromwell: 'Of what assurance is a *Law* ... if it lie in the same Legislature to *un*law it again?' L.C. Green, 'The Canadian Charter of Rights and International Law,' *Canadian Yearbook of International Law* 20 (1982): 18–19.

60 For example, Joseph Carens asserts that the notwithstanding clause poses no threat to Canadians, although he states that he would not permit any other liberal-democratic state to override freedom of opinion or expression. Carens, *Culture, Citizenship, and Community*, 31, 45.

61 A deficiency noted some time ago by John Humphrey, the Canadian human rights scholar and activist who helped to draft the United Nations' Universal Declaration of Human Rights. John Humphrey, *No Distant Millennium: The International Law of Human Rights* (Paris: United Nations Educational, Scientific and Cultural Organization, 1989), 21.

62 F.L. Morton and Rainer Knopff, *The Charter Revolution and the Court Party* (Peterborough, ON: Broadview Press, 2000).

63 For further discussion of these collective rights, see Green, 'The Canadian Charter of Rights and International Law,' 8–11.

64 Michael Ignatieff, *The Rights Revolution* (Toronto: Anansi, 2000), 57 and 18.

65 For an extended philosophical exploration on how to reconcile liberal individualism with the rights of minorities, see Kymlicka, *Multicultural Citizenship*.

66 David J. Elkins, 'Facing Our Destiny: Rights and Canadian Distinctiveness,' *Canadian Journal of Political Science* 22, no. 4 (1989): 706.

67 Walter S. Tarnopolsky, 'The New Canadian Charter of Rights and Freedoms as Compared and Contrasted with the American Bill of Rights,' *Human Rights Quarterly* 5, no. 3 (1983): 227–74.

68 John Hucker, 'Antidiscrimination Laws in Canada: Human Rights Commissions and the Search for Equality,' *Human Rights Quarterly* 19, no. 3 (1997): 547–71.

69 House of Commons, Bill C-23, 'The Modernizing Benefits and Obligations Act,' 2d Sess., 36th Parliament, 48–49 Elizabeth II, 1999–2000.

70 This finding is confirmed by Joseph F. Fletcher and Marie-Christine Chalmers, 'Attitudes of Canadians toward Affirmative Action: Opposition, Value Pluralism, and Nonattitudes,' *Political Behavior* 13, no. 1 (1991): 78. In their national survey of Canadians conducted in 1987, 72 per cent of anglophone respondents said equality between men and women was very important, with another 23 per cent saying it was somewhat important.

71 On such punishments in the mid-1990s, see Laura Bruni, 'Index Amorum Prohibitorum [Index of Prohibited Love],' *Index on Censorship* 24, no. 1 (1995): 195–204.

Chapter 2

This chapter is a revised version of Rhoda E. Howard, 'Being Canadian: Citizenship in Canada,' *Citizenship Studies* 2, no. 1 (1998): 133–52.

1 See Angus Reid Group, *Multiculturalism and Canadians: Attitude Study 1991– National Survey Report* (Ottawa: Multiculturalism and Citizenship Canada, August 1991); Monica Boyd et al., *Ascription and Achievement: Studies in Mobility and Status Attainment in Canada* (Ottawa: Carleton University Press, 1985), 357–9; Marlene Mackie and Merlin B. Brinkerhoff, 'Measuring Ethnic Salience,' *Canadian Ethnic Studies* 16, no. 1 (1984): 114–31; and Edward T. Pryor, Gustave J. Goldmann, Michael J. Sheridan and Pamela M. White, 'Measuring Ethnicity: Is "Canadian" an Evolving Indigenous Category?' *Ethnic and Racial Studies* 15, no. 2 (1992): 214–35.

2 This belief that one cannot describe oneself as an ethnic Canadian is in part an artifact of Canadian public policy and the lack, until 1996, of an ethnic category called 'Canadian' on the national census form. For a debate on

whether public policy should recognize 'Canadian' as an ethnic category, see my '"Canadian" as an Ethnic Category: Implications for Multicultural-ism and National Unity,' *Canadian Public Policy* 25, no. 4 (1999): 523–37; Yas-meen Abu-Laban and Daiva Stasiulis, 'Constructing "Ethnic Canadians": The Implications for Public Policy and Inclusive Citizenship: Rejoinder to Rhoda Howard-Hassmann,' *Canadian Public Policy* 26, no. 4 (2000): 477–87, and my 'Rebuttal to Abu-Laban and Stasiulis,' *Canadian Public Policy* 26, no. 4 (2000): 489–93. My argument for 'Canadian' as an ethnic category is too complex to recapitulate here, but rests on the premise that ethnicity is the result of social practice, not biological ancestry. On this discussion, see also Monica Boyd, 'Canadian, eh? Ethnic Origin Shifts in the Canadian Census,' *Canadian Ethnic Studies* 31, no. 3 (1999): 1–19; Madeline A. Kalbach and Warren E. Kalbach, 'Becoming Canadian: Problems of an Emerging Ident-ity,' *Canadian Ethnic Studies* 31, no. 2 (1999): 1–16; and Ravi Pendakur and Fernando Mata, 'Patterns of Ethnic Identification and the "Canadian" Response,' *Canadian Ethnic Studies* 30, no. 2 (1998): 125–37.

3 Raymond Breton, 'Multiculturalism and Canadian Nation-Building,' in *The Politics of Gender, Ethnicity and Language in Canada*, ed. Alan Cairns and Cynthia Williams (Toronto: University of Toronto Press, 1986), 55, emphasis in original.

4 The phrase 'small differences' is from Max Weber, *Economy and Society*, ed. Guenther Roth and Claus Wittich (Los Angeles: University of California Press, 1978), 388.

5 On Canadian self-image, see also Keith Spicer, 'Chairman's Forward,' in *Citizens' Forum on Canada's Future: Report to the People and Government of Canada, 1991* (Ottawa: Supply and Services Canada, 1991), 1–11; and Anthony Wilson-Smith, 'Canada and the World,' *Maclean's* 110, no. 15 (1997): 12–15.

6 Robert D. Putnam, *Making Democracy Work: Civic Traditions in Modern Italy* (Princeton, NJ: Princeton University Press, 1993), 163–85; Thomas Janoski, *Citizenship and Civil Society: A Framework of Rights and Obligations in Liberal, Traditional, and Social Democratic Regimes* (New York: Cambridge University Press, 1998), 75–103.

7 Breton, 'Multiculturalism and Canadian Nation-Building,' 29, 28, quoting Orrin E. Klapp, *Collective Search for Identity* (New York: Rinehart and Win-ston, 1969), 317.

8 On the importance of sport in unifying a nation, see Eric Hobsbawm, *Nations and Nationalism since 1780: Programme, Myth, Reality* (New York: Cambridge University Press, 1990), 142–3.

9 Desmond Morton, 'Divided Loyalties? Divided Country?' in *Belonging: The*

Meaning and Future of Canadian Citizenship, ed. William Kaplan (Montreal and Kingston: McGill-Queen's University Press, 1993), 60.

10 On the history of anti-Semitism in Ontario, see Stephen Speisman, 'Anti-semitism in Ontario: The Twentieth Century,' in *Antisemitism in Canada: History and Interpretation*, ed. Allan T. Davies (Waterloo, ON: Wilfrid Laurier University Press, 1992), 113–33.

11 Darlene Johnston, 'First Nations and Canadian Citizenship,' in *Belonging*, ed. Kaplan, 363. On the compulsory citizenship of Aboriginals in Canada, see also Joseph H. Carens, *Culture, Citizenship, and Community: A Contextual Exploration of Justice as Evenhandedness* (Toronto: Oxford University Press, 2000), 185–8.

12 Subhas Ramcharan, 'The Economic Adaptation of West Indians in Toronto, Canada,' *Canadian Review of Sociology and Anthropology* 13, no. 3 (1976): 295–304.

13 Frances Henry, *The Caribbean Diaspora in Toronto: Learning to Live with Racism* (Toronto: University of Toronto Press, 1994), 44 and 51. Immigrants of colour who do not enjoy professional status may well not feel as comfortable in Canada as those who do. See, e.g., Patricia Daenzer, *Regulating Class Privilege: Immigrant Servants in Canada, 1940s-1990s* (Toronto: Canadian Scholars' Press, 1993), and Makeda Silvera, *Silenced: Talks with Working Class Caribbean Women about Their Lives and Struggles as Domestic Workers in Canada*, 2d ed. (Toronto: Sister Vision, 1995). In addition, personal and anecdotal accounts by minority Canadians will lay various amounts of stress on feelings of alienation and marginalization caused by racism. See, e.g., Carl E. James, *Seeing Ourselves: Exploring Race, Ethnicity and Culture*, 2d ed. (Toronto: Thompson Educational Publishing, 1999), based on written accounts by James's students, and Cecil Foster, *A Place Called Heaven: The Meaning of Being Black in Canada* (Toronto: HarperCollins, 1996), an anecdotal account by a professional journalist.

14 Glenda P. Simms, 'Racism as a Barrier to Canadian Citizenship,' in *Belonging*, ed. Kaplan, 334.

15 Howard-Hassmann, '"Canadian" as an Ethnic Category.'

16 Jeff Spinner, *The Boundaries of Citizenship: Race, Ethnicity, and Nationality in the Liberal State* (Baltimore: Johns Hopkins University Press, 1994), 67, speaks of 'weak ethnic attachments.'

17 Herbert J. Gans, 'Symbolic Ethnicity: The Future of Ethnic Groups and Cultures in America,' *Ethnic and Racial Studies* 2, no. 1 (1979): 1–20.

18 Lance W. Roberts and Rodney A. Clifton, 'Exploring the Ideology of Canadian Multiculturalism,' *Canadian Public Policy* 8, no. 1 (1982): 88–94.

19 Gans, 'Symbolic Ethnicity,' 13.

20 Spinner, *The Boundaries of Citizenship*, 173.
21 Spinner, *The Boundaries of Citizenship*, 6.
22 Spinner, *The Boundaries of Citizenship*, 39.
23 William Kaplan, 'Introduction,' in *Belonging*, ed. Kaplan, 10.
24 On the use of myths, museums, etc. to create a sense of nationhood, see Benedict Anderson, *Imagined Communities: Reflections on the Origin and Spread of Nationalism* (New York: Verso, 1991). On the creation of one important Canadian symbol, the flag, see Henry S. Albinski, 'Politics and Biculturalism in Canada: The Flag Debate,' *Australian Journal of Politics and History* 13 (1967): 169–88.
25 Alan C. Cairns, 'The Fragmentation of Canadian Citizenship,' in *Belonging*, ed. Kaplan, 182.
26 Morton, 'Divided Loyalties? Divided Country?' 51.
27 Paul Martin, House of Commons, *Debates*, 20 March 1946, 131, quoted in Martin, 'Citizenship and the People's World,' in *Belonging*, ed. Kaplan, 73.
28 Kaplan, 'Introduction,' 16–17.
29 The phrase is from Alisdair MacIntyre, 'Is Patriotism a Virtue?' in *Theorizing Citizenship*, ed. Ronald Beiner (Albany: State University of New York Press, 1995), 221.
30 Mavis Gallant, *Home Truths* (Toronto: Macmillan, 1981), xiii, quoted in Ramsay Cook, 'Nation, Identity, Rights: Reflections on W.L. Morton's *Canadian Identity*,' *Journal of Canadian Studies* 29, no. 2 (1994): 5–18.

Chapter 3

This chapter is a revised version of Rhoda E. Howard-Hassmann, 'Canadians Discuss Freedom of Speech: Individual Rights Versus Group Protection,' *International Journal on Minority and Group Rights* 7, no. 2 (2000): 109–38.

1 The Klan itself maintains that it is not a hate group, merely a group that believes 'that the United States of America was founded as a white Christian nation.' Official web site for the Knights of the Ku Klux Klan, 'Frequently Asked Questions,' 1998, http://www.kukluxklan.org/faq.htm, accessed 21 January 2000. The Klan has existed in Canada since the 1920s, and possibly earlier. Stanley R. Barrett, *Is God a Racist? The Right Wing in Canada* (Toronto: University of Toronto Press, 1987), 20–2, 120–55.
2 On the university debate, see See Peter C. Emberley, *Zero Tolerance: Hot Button Politics in Canada's Universities* (Toronto: Penguin Books, 1996); John Fekete, *Moral Panic: Biopolitics Rising* (Montreal-Toronto: Robert Davies Publishing, 1994); and M. Patricia Marchak, *Racism, Sexism, and the Univer-*

sity: The Political Science Affair at the University of British Columbia (Montreal and Kingston: McGill-Queen's University Press, 1996). For my own views on this debate, see Rhoda E. Howard, 'Academic Freedom and Inclusivity in Canadian Universities,' in *Mistaken Identities: The Second Wave of Controversy over 'Political Correctness,'* ed. Cyril Levitt, Scott Davies, and Neil McLaughlin (New York: Peter Lang, 1999), 172–86.

3 Stanley Fish, *There's No Such Thing as Free Speech ... and It's a Good Thing Too* (New York: Oxford University Press, 1994), 106.

4 Gouzenko was the pseudonym of a Soviet spy who defected to Canada in the late 1940s, naming many Canadians as collaborators with the Soviet Union. For a general description of the Gouzenko affair, see Robert Bothwell and J.L. Granatstein, eds., 'Introduction,' in *The Gouzenko Transcripts*, 3–22 (Ottawa: Deneau Publishers, 1982).

5 Thomas R. Berger, *Fragile Freedoms: Human Rights and Dissent in Canada* (Toronto: Clarke, Irwin and Company, 1981), 163–89.

6 Berger, *Fragile Freedoms*, 202.

7 Michiel Horn, *Academic Freedom in Canada: A History* (Toronto: University of Toronto Press, 1999).

8 Robert Allan McChesney, 'Canada,' in *International Handbook of Human Rights*, ed. Jack Donnelly and Rhoda E. Howard (Westport, CT: Greenwood Press, 1987), 29.

9 *Martin's Annual Criminal Code 1999* (Aurora, ON: Canada Law Book Inc., 1998), S. 318 and 319.

10 For a general article on hate speech legislation in Canada, see Jeffrey Ian Ross, 'Hate Crime in Canada: Growing Pains with New Legislation,' in *Hate Crime: International Perspectives on Causes and Control*, ed. Mark S. Hamm (Cincinnati: Anderson Publishing, 1994), 151–72. For a detailed comparative discussion of hate speech laws, see Thomas David Jones, *Human Rights: Group Defamation, Freedom of Expression and the Law of Nations* (Boston: Martinus Nijhoff, 1998), including 205–11 on Canada. See also Johannes Morsink, *The Universal Declaration of Human Rights: Origins, Drafting and Intent* (Philadelphia: University of Pennsylvania Press, 1999), 65–72, for early international discussions of free speech and hate speech.

11 Paul M. Sniderman, Joseph H. Fletcher, Peter H. Russell, and Philip E. Tetlock, *The Clash of Rights: Liberty, Equality, and Legitimacy in a Pluralist Democracy* (New Haven: Yale University Press, 1996), 10, fn. 13.

12 Paul Tuns, 'Three Pro-Lifers Arrested in Toronto Bubble-Zone,' *The Interim: Canada's Pro-Life, Pro-Family Newspaper* XVII, no. 5 (1999): 1–2. On this law, see also A. Alan Borovoy, *The New Anti-Liberals* (Toronto: Canadian Scholars' Press, 1999), 139–43.

13 On restrictions on Aboriginal speech and political activism from the 1920s to the 1950s, see Geoffrey York, *The Dispossessed: Life and Death in Native Canada* (Toronto: Lester and Orpen Dennys, 1989), 246–50.

14 House of Commons, Bill C-93, 'An Act for the Preservation and Enhancement of Multiculturalism in Canada,' 2d Sess., 33rd Parliament, 12 July 1988, Article 3 (1) (b).

15 Citizenship and Immigration Canada, *A Look at Canada* (Ottawa: Minister of Public Works and Government Services Canada, 1999), 5.

16 Quoted in Evelyn Kallen, 'Never Again: Target Group Responses to the Debate Concerning Anti-Hate Propaganda Legislation,' *Windsor Yearbook of Access to Justice, 1991* (Windsor: University of Windsor Press, 1992), 68.

17 For a brief history of racism in Canadian immigration policy, see Jean Leonard Elliott and Augie Fleras, *Unequal Relations: An Introduction to Race and Ethnic Dynamics in Canada* (Scarborough, ON: Prentice-Hall Canada, 1992), 237–44.

18 See, e.g., Judith Baker, ed., *Group Rights* (Toronto: University of Toronto Press, 1994), and Nathan Glazer, 'Individual Rights against Group Rights,' in *Human Rights*, ed. Eugene Kamenka and Alice Erh-Soon Tay (New York: St Martin's Press, 1985), 87–103.

19 Alan Davies, 'The Keegstra Affair,' in *Antisemitism in Canada: History and Interpretation*, ed. Alan T. Davies (Waterloo, ON: Wilfrid Laurier University Press, 1992), 227–47; Bruce P. Elman, '*Her Majesty The Queen v. James Keegstra*: The Control of Racism in Canada, A Case Study,' in *Under the Shadow of Weimar: Democracy, Law, and Racial Incitement in Six Countries*, ed. Louis Greenspan and Cyril Levitt (Westport, CT: Praeger, 1993), 149–76.

20 Canadian Press Newswire, 'Supreme Court of Canada Rules Author of Anti-Semitic Books Can't Teach Children,' 3 April 1996; and 'Ross Ruling Gives Jews Extra Reason to Celebrate,' *Canadian Jewish News* 36, no. 49 (1996): 3.

21 I cannot explain why this was the case, except to speculate that teachers have a high commitment to the social good and are likely therefore to become civic leaders; or, alternately, that their flexible schedule allows them to participate in public activities. Also, teaching was a very common occupation for women graduating from Canadian universities until the 1970s, given the discrimination against them in other occupations; several female civic leaders had started life as teachers and moved to other occupations as discrimination lessened. I did not screen the civic leaders by occupation prior to interviewing them.

22 The province of Ontario has a publicly funded Catholic school system, the result of the historic compromise between English Protestants and French

Catholics that resulted in the formation of Canada in 1867. In May 1999, 48 per cent of the children in the Hamilton-Wentworth (city and surrounding township) region attended Catholic schools. Information provided to Rina Rodak by Hamilton-Wentworth School Board, May 1999.

23 Anne McIlroy and Susan Delacourt, 'Chretien on Attack over Rights for Gays: Reform MP Draws Stinging Rebuke,' *Globe and Mail*, 1 May 1996, Toronto edition, A1 and A9. According to the authors of this article, the quotation originally appeared in the *Vancouver Sun*, 30 April 1996. On the Ringma affair, see also Sheridan Hay, 'Blacks in Canada: The Invisible Minority,' *Canadian Dimension*, November–December 1996, 14–17.

24 In fact, Ringma had not used the word *nigger*. Nor was he a member of the government: he was a member of an opposition party.

25 Philippa Strum, *When the Nazis Came to Skokie: Freedom for Speech We Hate* (Lawrence, KS: University Press of Kansas, 1999).

26 Sniderman et al., *The Clash of Rights*, 22.

27 Strum, *When the Nazis Came to Skokie*, 115.

28 Salman Rushdie, *The Satanic Verses* (New York: Viking Penguin, 1989). For a discussion of the Islamic legality of this declaration, see Abdullahi Ahmed An-Na'im, *Toward an Islamic Reformation: Civil Liberties, Human Rights, and International Law* (Syracuse, NY: Syracuse University Press, 1990), 182–7.

29 A. Alan Borovoy, *Uncivil Obedience: The Tactics and Tales of a Democratic Agitator* (Toronto: Lester Publishing, 1991), 126. For a plea by a (presumed) Muslim for Canadians to understand that Rushdie's book was hate speech, see Hesham Sabry, 'Freedom of Speech: David Irving versus Salman Rushdi [*sic*],' *Cross Cultures* Magazine 7 (December 1992–January 1993): 6–7.

30 There is a law in Canada against 'blasphemous libel' (Criminal Code of Canada, Section 296), but the law clarifies that 'no person shall be convicted of an offence under this section for expressing in good faith and in decent language, or attempting to establish by argument used in good faith and conveyed in decent language, an opinion upon a religious subject.'

31 R. v. Butler, *Canada Supreme Court Reports*, part 3, vol. 1, 1999, 455. For an article supporting what later was the Supreme Court's stance, see Kathleen Mahoney, 'The Canadian Constitutional Approach to Freedom of Expression in Hate Propaganda and Pornography,' *Law and Contemporary Problems* 55, no. 1 (1992): 77–105. On the consequences of the Butler decision, see Jeffrey Toobin, 'X-Rated,' *New Yorker* 70, no. 3 (1994): 70–8.

32 Sniderman et al., *The Clash of Rights*, 76.

33 Strum, *When the Nazis Came to Skokie*, 123.

34 Fish, *There's No Such Thing as Free Speech*.

35 R. Smolla, *Free Speech in an Open Society,* cited in Stanley Fish, handout for lecture at McMaster University, Hamilton, Ontario, 22 January 1999.
36 Strum, *When the Nazis Came to Skokie,* 31.
37 Sniderman et al., *The Clash of Rights,* 59–60.
38 Laura Leets and Howard Giles, 'Words as Weapons – When Do They Wound? Investigations of Harmful Speech,' *Human Communication Research* 24, no. 2 (1997): 275.
39 Sniderman et al., *The Clash of Rights,* 41.
40 For Zundel's own views, see Ernst Zundel, 'Holocaust 101,' http://www.lebensraum.org, accessed 28 May 2001. On Zundel's trial and acquittal on the charge of spreading false news, see Manuel Prutschi, 'The Zundel Affair,' in *Antisemitism in Canada,* ed. Davies, 249–77.
41 Fish, *There's No Such Thing as Free Speech,* 109. On this issue, see also Maxwell Yalden, 'Collective Claims on the Human Rights Landscape: A Canadian View,' *International Journal on Group Rights* 1 (1993): 24.
42 Ronald Dworkin, *Taking Rights Seriously* (Cambridge, MA: Harvard University Press, 1978), 273.
43 Ronald Dworkin, 'The Coming Battles over Free Speech,' *New York Review of Books* 39, no. 11 (1992): 55–64. In this article Dworkin criticizes the Canadian Supreme Court's Butler decision (p. 61). For an argument about the right of American minorities to equal concern and respect, and the consequent need for hate speech laws in the United States, see Jones, *Human Rights,* 243–58.
44 Kallen, 'Never Again.'
45 Canada, *Shaping Canada's Future Together, Proposals* (Ottawa: Government of Canada, 1991), 3, quoted in Will Kymlicka, 'Individual and Community Rights,' in *Group Rights,* ed. Baker, 24.
46 Sniderman et al., *The Clash of Rights,* 16.

Chapter 4

Epigraph source: Elwin Hermanson, MP for Kindersley-Lloydminster, Reform, House of Commons, *Debates,* 13 June 1995, 13791.

1 Mark S. Hamm, ed., *Hate Crime: International Perspectives on Causes and Control* (Cincinnati: Anderson Publishing, 1994).
2 House of Commons, Bill C-41, 'An Act to Amend the Criminal Code (Sentencing) and Other Acts in Consequence Thereof,' 1st Session, 35th Parliament, 42-43-44 Elizabeth II, 1994–5, 15 June 1995, 8–9.
3 Peter Rosenthal, 'The Criminality of Racial Harassment,' *Canadian Human*

Rights Yearbook 1989–90 (Ottawa: Human Rights Research and Education Centre, University of Ottawa, 1990), 150–1. The case in question is *Smithers v. The Queen*.

4 EGALE (Equality for Gays and Lesbians Everywhere), 'EGALE Condemns Attempts to Water Down Hate Crimes Bill,' 14 June 1995, http://www.egale.ca/pressrel/950614.htm, and CJN Staff, 'Jewish Groups Back Bill's Protection of Gays,' *Canadian Jewish News*, 1 December 1994, 4.

5 Jacquelyn Nelson and George Kiefl, *Technical Report: Survey of Hate-Motivated Activity*, TR 1995-4e (Ottawa: Department of Justice Canada, 1995), 10.

6 This diversity in opinion is also reflected by the Coalition of Concerned Canadians, reported to have been formed by members of various ethnic and religious minority groups who were concerned about the protections of gays and lesbians under Bill C-41. Some also opposed other protective measures such as employment equity, which they viewed as imposing precisely the kind of racial classifications they had come to Canada to avoid. Catherine Dalzell, 'New Canadians in Search of the Old: Ethnic and Religious Minorities Unite Against "Tolerance",' *Alberta Report*, 15 May 1995, 11.

7 The amendment stated, 'For greater certainty, conduct that constituted an offence under the Criminal Code before the date on which this section comes into force constitutes the same offence after that date.' Don Boudria, MP for Glengarry-Prescott-Russell (Liberal), House of Commons, *Debates*, 14 June 1995, 13826.

8 See, e.g., Davis Sheremata, '[Allan] Rock's Agenda on the Rocks: Opposition to Ottawa's Progressive Justice Minister Grows,' *Alberta Report*, 10 April 1995, 6–7; Peter Verburg, 'A Paper Crime Wave: Rock's Criminologist Speculates Hate Crime is Rampant,' *Alberta Report*, 4 March 1996, 26–7; Joe Woodard, 'Victims at Last: The Prime Minister Promises Special Rights for Homosexuals,' *B.C. Report*, 19 June 1995, 16–19; and Robert Eady, 'Homosexuals Battering the Family (Bill C-41 and "sexual orientation"),' *Catholic Insight* 3, no. 1 (1995): 14–15.

9 House of Commons, *Debates*, 20 September 1994, 5871.

10 House of Commons, *Debates*, 13 June 1995, 13795.

11 House of Commons, *Debates*, 14 June 1995, 13818.

12 House of Commons, *Debates*, 20 September 1994, 5910.

13 Valerie Jenness and Kendal Broad, *Hate Crimes: New Social Movements and the Politics of Violence* (New York: Aldine de Gruyter, 1997), 172.

14 Cliff Breitkreuz, MP for Yellowhead (Reform), House of Commons, *Debates*, 20 September 1994, 5920.

15 Chuck Strahl, MP for Fraser Valley East (Reform), House of Commons, *Debates*, 13 June 1995, 13786.

16 *R. v. Lelas* (1990), 74 O.R. (2d) 552 (C.A.), quoted in Cynthia Petersen, 'A Queer Response to Bashing: Legislating against Hate,' *Queen's Law Journal* 16, no. 2 (1991): 259, n. 90.

17 Martha Shaffer, 'Criminal Responses to Hate-Motivated Violence: Is Bill C-41 Tough Enough?' *McGill Law Journal* 41 (1995): 210.

18 Shaffer, 'Criminal Responses,' 209. The case is cited by Shaffer (p. 209, n. 41) as (1977) 35 C.C.C.(2d) 376 (Ont. C.A.), *Ingram*.

19 House of Commons, *Debates*, 14 June 1995, 13825–6.

20 Shaffer, 'Criminal Responses,' 216–20, argues that hate crimes legislation does not undermine freedom of speech.

21 One exception is Rachel Giese, 'Hating the Hate-Crimes Bill,' *This* Magazine, November 1995, 7–9.

22 Julian V. Roberts, *Disproportionate Harm: Hate Crime in Canada*, WD1995–11c (Ottawa: Department of Justice Canada, Research, Statistics and Evaluation Directorate, 1995), 23, 50.

23 Petersen, 'A Queer Response to Bashing,' 248.

24 Shaffer, 'Criminal Responses,' 203.

25 I agree with Roberts that 'Hate or bias crimes carry an added dimension of crime seriousness. This dimension includes elements such as the threat to other members of [the] group victimized.' I am not as sure as Roberts that such crimes also constitute an 'affront to the general community,' although I hope that they would. Both quotations from Roberts, *Disproportionate Harm*, 36.

26 Mark S. Hamm, 'Conceptualizing Hate Crime in a Global Context,' in *Hate Crime*, ed. Hamm, 178. I have characterized rapes and lynchings (of women and blacks) in North America as social terrorism in Rhoda E. Howard, *Human Rights and the Search for Community* (Boulder: Westview, 1995), 150–6.

27 Shaffer, 'Criminal Responses,' 232.

Chapter 5

This chapter is a revised version of Rhoda E. Howard-Hassmann, 'The Gay Cousin: Learning to Accept Gay Rights,' *Journal of Homosexuality* 42, no. 1 (2001): 127–49.

1 In using the terms gays/lesbians, or homosexuals, throughout, I recognize that there are other sexual minorities also seeking rights, including bisexuals and transsexuals.

2 'Universal Declaration of Human Rights,' Article 2, in *United Nations: The*

International Bill of Human Rights (New York: United Nations, 1978) emphasis mine.

3 For a history of the gay and lesbian movement for human rights, see Miriam Smith, *Lesbian and Gay Rights in Canada: Social Movements and Equality Seeking, 1971–95* (Toronto: University of Toronto Press, 1999).

4 Angus Reid/Southam News Poll, *Public Attitudes on Specific Gay Rights Issues*, 7 June 1996, http://www.angusreid.com/pressrel/gayrights.html; and Lorne Bozinoff and Peter MacIntosh, 'Majority Oppose Same Sex Marriage,' *The Gallup Report*, 21 May 1992.

5 EGALE (Equality for Gays and Lesbians Everywhere), 'Canada Watch: Who's Doing What,' 27 December 1998, http://www.egale.ca/features/watch.htm.

6 Aaron Belkin and Jason McNichol, 'Homosexual Personnel Policy in the Canadian Forces: Did Lifting the Gay Ban Undermine Military Performance?' *International Journal* 56, no. 1 (2000–1): 77.

7 House of Commons, Bill C-23, 'The Modernizing Benefits and Obligations Act,' 2d Sess., 36th Parliament, 48–49 Elizabeth II, 1999–2000.

8 EGALE, 'Canada Watch.'

9 Edward O. Laumann, John H. Gagnon, Robert T. Michael, and Stuart Michaels, *The Social Organization of Sexuality: Sexual Practices in the United States* (Chicago: University of Chicago Press, 1994), 107.

10 On flaunting, see also William N. Eskridge, Jr, *The Case for Same-Sex Marriage: From Sexual Liberty to Civilized Commitment* (New York: The Free Press, 1996), 183–91.

11 See Deborah P. Amory, '"Homosexuality" in Africa: Issues and Debates,' *Issue: A Journal of Opinion* 25, no. 1 (1997): 5–10; Chris Dunton and Mai Palmberg, 'Human Rights and Homosexuality in Southern Africa,' in *Current African Issues* 19 (Uppsala, Sweden: Nordiska Afrikainstituet, June 1996); Gilbert Herdt, *Same Sex, Different Cultures: Exploring Gay and Lesbian Lives* (Boulder: Westview, 1997); and Arlene Swidler, ed., *Homosexuality and World Religions* (Valley Forge, PA: Trinity Press International, 1993).

12 Studies, however, indicate that 'no evidence exists that having a gay parent or role model is harmful to the child.' Gregory M. Herek, 'Myths about Sexual Orientation: A Lawyers' Guide to Social Science Research,' *Law and Sexuality* 1 (1991): 157.

13 For confirmation that exposure to gays results in more liberal attitudes, see Gregory M. Herek, 'Heterosexuals' Attitudes to Lesbians and Gay Men: Correlates and Gender Differences,' *Journal of Sex Research* 25, no. 4 (1988): 451–77; Larry M. Lance, 'The Effects of Interaction with Gay Persons on Attitudes toward Homosexuality,' *Human Relations* 40, no. 6 (1987): 329–36;

and William Schneider and I.A. Lewis, 'The Straight Story on Homosexuality and Gay Rights,' *Public Opinion* 7 (February/March 1984): 16–20 and 59–60.

14 On this, see also Herek, 'Heterosexuals' Attitudes.'

15 Statistics Canada, *Religions in Canada*, 1991 Census of Canada, Catalogue no. 93–319 (Ottawa: Industry, Science and Technology Canada, 1993), Table 1, 12.

16 United Church of Canada, *Gift, Dilemma and Promise: A Report and Affirmations on Human Sexuality* (Toronto: United Church of Canada, 1984).

17 United Church of Canada, *Gift, Dilemma and Promise*, 71. For a description of the evolution of Christian and Jewish thought regarding homosexuals in the United States that confirms my analysis here, see Robert Nugent and Jeannine Gramick, 'Homosexuality: Protestant, Catholic, and Jewish Issues; a Fishbone Tale,' *Journal of Homosexuality* 18, no. 3/4 (1989): 46.

18 Wolfgang Lienemann, 'Churches and Homosexuality: An Overview of Recent Official Church Statements on Sexual Orientation,' *The Ecumenical Review* 50, no. 1 (1998): 7–21.

19 Ralph Heynen et al. (Homosexuality Committee), 'Homosexual Behavior and the Church: A Christian Reformed View, Looking at the Scriptures,' in *A Crisis of Understanding: Homosexuality and the Canadian Church*, ed. Denyse O'Leary (Burlington, ON: Welch Publishing Company, 1988), 68.

20 This is despite the fact that evidence of 'biological' causes of homosexuality is still in its infancy. See Chandler Burr, 'Homosexuality and Biology,' *Atlantic Monthly* 271, no. 3 (1993): 47–65; William Byne, 'Why We Cannot Conclude That Sexual Orientation Is Primarily a Biological Phenomenon,' *Journal of Homosexuality* 34, no. 1 (1997): 73–80; and John P. DeCecco and David Allen Parker, 'The Biology of Homosexuality: Sexual Orientation or Sexual Preference?' *Journal of Homosexuality* 28, no. 1/2 (1995): 1–27.

21 For additional evidence that those who believe homosexuals are 'born that way' have more positive attitudes to them, see Kurt E. Ernulf, Sune M. Innala, and Frederick L. Whitam, 'Biological Explanation, Psychological Explanation, and Tolerance of Homosexuals: A Cross-National Analysis of Beliefs and Attitudes,' *Psychological Reports* 65 (1989): 1003–10.

22 Bill 167, 3rd Sess., 35th Legislature, Ontario, 43 Elizabeth II (1994).

23 Hon. Marion Boyd, Attorney-General, in Ontario, Legislative Assembly of Ontario, *Official Reports of Debates*, 19 May 1994, 6454, and 1 June 1994, 6573.

24 Mrs Joan M. Fawcett, Liberal MPP for Northumberland, in Ontario, Legislative Assembly of Ontario, *Official Reports of Debates*, 2 June 1994, 6626.

25 George Radwanski, *Trudeau* (Toronto: Macmillan, 1978), 90–7.

Chapter 6

This chapter is a revised version of Rhoda E. Howard-Hassmann, 'Multiculturalism, Human Rights, and Cultural Relativism: Canadian Civic Leaders Discuss Women's Rights and Gay and Lesbian Rights,' *Netherlands Quarterly of
Human Rights* 18, no. 4 (2000): 493–514.

1 For my own contribution to the debate, see Rhoda E. Howard, 'Cultural
Absolutism and the Nostalgia for Community,' *Human Rights Quarterly* 15,
no. 2 (1993): 315–38.
2 For fears about the fraying of Canadian society, see Reginald W. Bibby,
Mosaic Madness: Pluralism without a Cause (Toronto: Stoddart, 1990), and
Neil Bissoondath, *Selling Illusions: The Cult of Multiculturalism in Canada*
(Toronto: Penguin Books, 1994).
3 In 1990 there was a prolonged public debate in Canada over whether male
Sikh members of the Royal Canadian Mounted Police should be allowed
to wear turbans; eventually, they were permitted to do so. In 1999 controversy arose in Toronto when a bus driver refused to accept the bus pass
of a veiled woman originally from Somalia, since he could not see her
face. Michael Valpy, 'Veil of Tears: Muslim Woman Back on Bus,' *Globe and
Mail*, 1 September 1999, Toronto edition.
4 Arati Rao, 'The Politics of Gender and Culture in International Human
Rights Discourse,' in *Women's Rights, Human Rights: International Feminist
Perspectives*, ed. Julie Peters and Andrea Wolper (New York: Routledge,
1995), 169.
5 Susan Moller Okin, with Respondents, *Is Multiculturalism Bad for Women?*
(Princeton, NJ: Princeton University Press, 1999), 9.
6 Jack Donnelly, *Universal Human Rights in Theory and Practice* (Ithaca, NY:
Cornell University Press, 1989), 110.
7 Gross human rights violations are usually assumed to be those that cause
death or violate bodily integrity. Alex P. Schmid, *Research on Gross Human
Rights Violations* (Leiden: University of Leiden, Center for the Study of
Social Conflicts, Publication #30, 1989). Female genital mutilation consists
of 'operations,' usually without anaesthetic and in unhygienic conditions,
performed in some African, Middle Eastern, and other cultures on girls and
women to remove parts of the outer genitalia. These operations can have
very severe, long-term medical side effects. Nahid Toubia, 'Female Genital
Mutilation,' in *Women's Rights, Human Rights*, ed. Peters and Wolpers,
224–37.
8 Quotation from Allan Thompson, 'Most Think Immigrants Must Adapt,

Survey Says,' *Toronto Star*, 14 December 1993, A2. Results of this poll, conducted by Decima Research, were also reported in Brian Bergman, 'A
Nation of Polite Bigots,' *Maclean's*, 27 December 1993, 42–3. I was unable to
obtain access to the original poll.

9 Paul M. Sniderman, Joseph F. Fletcher, Peter H. Russell, and Philip E. Tetlock, *The Clash of Rights: Liberty, Equality, and Legitimacy in Pluralist Democracy* (New Haven: Yale University Press, 1996), 113.

10 Sniderman et al., *The Clash of Rights*, 111.

11 Sniderman et al., *The Clash of Rights*, 110.

12 John C. Harles also found Laotian immigrants in Ontario who believed
strongly that immigrants should adapt to Canadian norms. See his 'Integration *before* Assimilation: Immigration, Multiculturalism, and the Canadian
Polity,' *Canadian Journal of Political Science* 30, no. 4 (1997): 732, emphasis in
original title.

13 Thompson, 'Most Think Immigrants Must Adapt,' A2.

14 Carol's statement about Saudi Arabia is correct. In public, women are
expected to wear an *abaya*, a black garment covering head and face as well
as the entire body; Western women are also expected to follow this dress
code. U.S. Department of State, *1999 Country Reports on Human Rights
Practices: Saudi Arabia*, Bureau of Democracy, Human Rights, and Labor,
25 February 2000, http://www.state.gov/www/global/human_rights/
1999_hrp_report/saudiara.html.

15 House of Commons, Bill C-27, 'An Act to Amend the Criminal Code (child
prostitution, child sex tourism, criminal harassment and female genital
mutilation),' 2d Sess., 35th Parliament, 45 Elizabeth II, 1996, Article 5.

16 Martin is in error attributing female genital mutilation to the Middle East.
Not all Middle Eastern cultures practise this custom. And many non-Mid-
dle Eastern cultures, for example in Africa, do. Although there is not yet
any authoritative list of cultures practising female genital mutilation, a
good summary of existing information can be found at FGMNetwork,
Female Genital Mutilation around the World: Population Groups, http://
www.fgmnetwork.org/intro/world.html.

17 On the Taliban's treatment of women, see Zohra Rasekh et al., 'Women's
Health and Human Rights in Afghanistan,' *Journal of the American Medical
Association* 280, no. 5 (1998): 449–55.

18 On dowry, see Linda Stone and Caroline James, 'Dowry, Bride-Burning,
and Female Power in India,' *Women's Studies International Forum* 18, no. 2
(1995): 125–34.

19 Lawyers Committee for Human Rights, *Beset by Contradictions: Islamization,*

Legal Reform and Human Rights in Sudan (New York: Lawyers Committee for Human Rights, 1996), 63.

20 Laura Bruni, 'Index Amorum Prohibitorum [Index of Prohibited Love],' *Index on Censorship* 24, no. 1 (1995): 195–204.

21 A 1992 poll found that 60 per cent of Canadians answered 'yes' to the question 'Do you support the goals of the feminist movement or not?' Lorne Bozinoff and Peter MacIntosh, 'Feminist Movement Strongly Supported by Canadian Public,' *The Gallup Report*, 25 June 1992.

22 Ruth is correct. India outlawed the dowry in 1961. Kristin Olsen, *Chronology of Women's History* (Westport, CT: Greenwood Press, 1994), 295. See also Prabhati Mukerjee, 'Dowry,' in *Women's Studies Encyclopedia: Revised and Expanded Edition, A–F*, ed. Helen Tierney (Westport, CT: Greenwood Press, 1999), 387–90. Bride burning also is a crime in India.

23 Kogila Moodley, 'Canadian Multiculturalism as Ideology,' *Ethnic and Racial Studies* 6, no. 3 (1983): 320–31.

24 Michael Walzer, 'Comment,' in Charles Taylor, with Respondents, *Multiculturalism* (Princeton, NJ: Princeton University Press, 1994), 103.

25 Such views are described in Evelyn Kallen, *Ethnicity and Human Rights in Canada*, 2d ed. (Toronto: Oxford University Press, 1995), 173–5, passim.

26 Will Kymlicka, *Multicultural Citizenship* (Oxford: Clarendon Press, 1995), 152.

27 Kymlicka, *Multicultural Citizenship*, 170.

28 Jeff Spinner, *The Boundaries of Citizenship: Race, Ethnicity, and Nationality in the Liberal State* (Baltimore: Johns Hopkins University Press, 1994), 72.

29 On this debate, see Rhoda E. Howard, 'Human Rights and the Culture Wars,' *International Journal* 53, no. 1 (1997–8): 94–112.

30 The phrase is from Leslie Green, 'Internal Minorities and Their Rights,' in *Group Rights*, ed. Judith Baker (Toronto: University of Toronto Press, 1994), 116.

31 William H. Meyer, 'Toward a Global Culture: Human Rights, Group Rights and Cultural Relativism,' *International Journal on Group Rights* 3, no. 3 (1996): 192.

32 Rhoda E. Howard-Hassmann, 'Identity, Empathy and International Relations,' McMaster University, Institute on Globalization and the Human Condition, Working Paper Series, April 2000, http://www.humanities.mcmaster.ca/~global/global.htm.

33 Eva Brems, 'Enemies or Allies? Feminism and Cultural Relativism as Dissident Voices in Human Rights Discourse,' *Human Rights Quarterly* 19, no. 1 (1997): 162–3.

Chapter 7

1 For a history of early employment equity programs in Canada, see Morton
  Weinfeld, 'The Development of Affirmative Action in Canada,' *Canadian
  Ethnic Studies* 13, no. 2 (1981): 23–39. For later developments, see John
  Hucker, 'Affirmative Action Canadian Style: Reflections on Canada's
  Employment Equity Law,' in *Non-Discrimination Law: Comparative Perspec-
  tives*, ed. Titia Loenen and Peter R. Rodrigues (Boston: Martinus Nijhoff,
  1999), 265–77; Caterina Ventura, 'Racial Discrimination and Affirmative
  Actions: Canada's Experience with Anti-Discrimination Legislation,' in
  Combating Racial Discriminations: Affirmative Action as a Model for Europe, ed.
  Erna Appelt and Monika Jarosch (Oxford: Berg, 2000), 125–35; and Beatrice
  Vizkelety, 'Adverse Effect Discrimination in Canada: Crossing the Rubicon
  from Formal to Substantive Equality,' in *Non-Discrimination Law*, ed. Loenen
  and Rodrigues, 223–36.
2 Acts of the Parliament of Canada, 'An Act Respecting Employment Equity,'
  42-43-44 Elizabeth II, assented to 15 December 1995, Article 2.
3 Rainer Knopff, with Thomas Flanagan, *Human Rights and Social Technology:
  The New War on Discrimination* (Ottawa: Carleton University Press, 1989).
4 For an early and a recent criticism of employment equity/affirmative
  action, see Lance W. Roberts, 'Understanding Affirmative Action,' in *Discrimination, Affirmative Action, and Equal Opportunity: An Economic and Social
  Perspective*, ed. W.E. Block and M.A. Walker (Vancouver: The Fraser Institute, 1981), 147–82, and Martin Loney, *The Pursuit of Division: Race, Gender,
  and Preferential Hiring in Canada* (Montreal and Kingston: McGill-Queen's
  University Press, 1998).
5 'An Act Respecting Employment Equity,' Article 5, b, mandating that the
  degree of representation in the employer's workforce can reflect '(i) the
  Canadian workforce, or (ii) those segments of the Canadian workforce that
  are identifiable by qualification, eligibility or geography.'
6 Paul M. Sniderman, Joseph F. Fletcher, Peter H. Russell, and Philip E. Tetlock, *The Clash of Rights: Liberty, Equality, and Legitimacy in Pluralist Democracy* (New Haven: Yale University Press, 1996), 149.
7 Legislative Assembly of Ontario, Bill 79, 'An Act to Provide for Employment Equity for Aboriginal People, People with Disabilities, Members of
  Racial Minorities and Women,' 3rd Session, 35th Legislature, 42 Elizabeth
  II, 1993. On this, and other, NDP policies towards women and minorities,
  see Loney, *The Pursuit of Division*, 244–87.
8 Gallup Canada, '74% [of all Canadians] Oppose Employment Equity Programs,' *The Gallup Poll*, 23 December 1993. The precise question was, 'As

you know, women and minority groups are often under-represented at the management level of government and the broader public service. Do you believe governments should actively attempt to hire more women and minority group members for management positions, or should governments take no action whatsoever and hire new employees based solely on their qualifications?' Among the 21 per cent of the respondents who responded that governments should actively hire women and members of minorities, 96 per cent agreed that governments should encourage these categories of people to apply for jobs, but only 65 per cent agreed that general quotas should be set for them, and only 22 per cent agreed that certain jobs should be limited to women or minority-group applicants. This poll, however, was taken at what was probably the nadir of support for employment equity, shortly after a media scandal caused when the Ontario government advertised a job but said it was open only to members of the four categories legislated by the Employment Equity Act. In other words, 'Able-bodied white males need not apply' (Loney, *The Pursuit of Division*, 268–9).

9 Joseph F. Fletcher and Marie-Christine Chalmers, 'Attitudes of Canadians toward Affirmative Action: Opposition, Value Pluralism, and Nonattitudes,' *Political Behavior* 13, no. 1 (1991): 72. In April 2002 I presented this chapter at a special conference in Ottawa to celebrate the twentieth anniversary of the Canadian Charter of Rights and Freedoms, sponsored by the Association for Canadian Studies. In the audience was an Ontario civil servant who had taken part in the drafting of Bill 79. She told me her opinion that the NDP had seriously misjudged the public mood, realizing its mistake especially when women, supposed to be beneficiaries of the act, started complaining that their sons' job chances would be hurt by it.

10 Legislative Assembly of Ontario, 'An Act to repeal job quotas and to restore merit-based employment practices in Ontario,' 1st Sess., 36th Legislature, 44 Elizabeth II, 1995.

11 Barrington Moore, Jr, *Injustice: The Social Bases of Obedience and Revolt* (White Plains, NY: M.E. Sharpe, 1978), 35.

12 Jack Donnelly and Rhoda E. Howard, 'Assessing National Human Rights Performance: A Theoretical Framework,' *Human Rights Quarterly* 10, no. 2 (1988): 246–7.

13 In several studies of different population groups (students, housewives, workers), Tougas and Veilleux found that both women and men preferred the elimination of barriers to equal opportunity to preferential hiring policies for women. However, women were more likely than men to accept preferential policies if they thought the elimination of barriers to equal opportunity had been unsuccessful. Tougas and Veilleux do not mention

the racial or ethnic backgrounds of the individuals in their samples. Results reported in Francine Tougas and France Veilleux, 'Quelques Déterminants des Réactions des Hommes et des Femmes a l'Action Positive,' *Revue québecoise de psychologie* 13, no. 1 (1992): 128–39.

14 Glenn C. Loury, the distinguished African-American commentator on affirmative action, also worries about the effects of tokenism. *'The use of racial or sexual employment goals is … likely to alter the way in which minority or women managers are viewed by their white male subordinates and superiors.'* (Entire quotation in italics in original.) See his 'Why Should We Care about Group Inequality?' *Social Philosophy and Policy* 5, no. 1 (1987): 267.

15 Some such cases are mentioned in Neil Bissoondath, *Selling Illusions: The Cult of Multiculturalism in Canada* (Toronto: Penguin, 1994).

16 Henry Hess, 'Firefighters Face Rights Complaint: Union "Poisoned" Work Environment for Women, Minorities, Commission Says,' *Globe and Mail*, 17 December 1997, Toronto edition, A1; and Chris Champion, 'In Quest of the Perfectly Modern Mountie: The RCMP Announces This Year's Racial and Female Quotas,' *Western Report*, 2 September 1996, 28.

17 Loney, *The Pursuit of Division*, 361, n. 16. This decision appears to be a variant of what Melissa Williams calls the 'minimum threshold of qualification rule,' in which the employer decides to 'hire the woman or minority candidate over the male or the white candidate, even if the latter has significantly better qualifications.' Williams, 'In Defence of Affirmative Action: North American Discourses for the European Context?' in *Combating Racial Discrimination*, ed. Appelt and Jarosch, 73.

18 The youth (age fifteen to twenty-four) employment rate in Canada in 1996 was 51.1 per cent, down more than eleven percentage points from 1989. Canadian Centre for Adolescent Research, *Job Statistics*, http://ccar.brier-crest.ca/stats/jobs.shtml, accessed 22 June 2001. In Ontario between 1989 and 1997, the youth employment rate dropped by 15.4 per cent. Geoff Bowlby and Philip Jennings, 'Youth Employment: A Lesson on Its Decline,' in Statistics Canada, *Education Quarterly Review* 5, no. 3 (1999): 40.

19 For example, despite such affirmative policies at McMaster University, where I taught until 2003, only 20.5 per cent of undergraduate engineering students in 1998 were women. NSERC/Nortel Joint-Chair for Women in Science and Engineering in Ontario, http://www.carleton.ca/cwse-on/statistics.htm, accessed 31 January 2001.

20 In the 1980s and 1990s about three-quarters of Canada's immigrants and refugees came from regions other than Europe. Carol Agocs and Monica Boyd, 'The Canadian Ethnic Mosaic Recast for the 1990s,' in *Social Inequality in Canada: Patterns, Problems, Policies*, 2d ed., ed. James Curtis, Edward

Grabb, and Neil Guppy (Scarborough, ON: Prentice-Hall Canada, 1993), 331. Among these immigrants there were many groups not previously found in Canada, such as Sri Lankans and Somalis.

21 In fact, compensation for past discrimination is not the intent of government policy, as made clear by former chief justice of the Supreme Court of Canada Brian Dickson: 'the goal is not to compensate past victims ... Rather, an employment equity program is an attempt to ensure that future applicants and workers from the affected group will not face the same insidious barriers that blocked their forbears.' Cited in Ventura, 'Racial Discrimination and Affirmative Actions,' 128. Not only were Hamilton civic leaders unaware of this distinction, even learned commentators sometimes misunderstand it. See, e.g., Hucker, 'Affirmative Action Canadian Style,' 275, who refers to the 'historical wrongs' that employment equity policies were 'intended to correct.'

22 Brian Lee Crowley, 'Does Counting Bodies Add Up to Fairness?' *Canadian Business* 66 (November 1993): 71–8, points out that factors such as average age of an ethnic or racial group, average educational qualifications, traditional skill sets, and (in the case of women) choices between full-time parenthood and work outside the home can affect group members' occupational and income outcomes, absent any discrimination by employers. See also Agocs and Boyd, 'The Canadian Ethnic Mosaic,' and Monica Boyd, 'Gender, Visible Minority, and Immigrant Earnings Inequality: Reassessing an Employment Equity Premise,' in *Deconstructing a Nation: Immigration, Multiculturalism and Racism in '90s Canada*, ed. Vic Satzewich (Halifax: Fernwood Publishing, 1992), 279–321.

23 Aggregate statistical data bear out this perception, showing that 'the entry difference [of immigrants to the Canadian labour market] is eliminated within 25 years.' Derek Hum and Wayne Simpson, 'Wage Opportunities for Visible Minorities in Canada,' *Canadian Public Policy* 25, no. 3 (1999): 386.

24 Statistics Canada, 'Population 15 Years and Over by Sex, Visible Minority Population, Immigrant Status and Total Income Groups,' 1996 Census, 94F0009XDB96057. For a study based on the 1981 census showing that members of some visible minorities actually earned more than members of some white Canadian ethnic groups, see Conrad Winn, 'Affirmative Action and Visible Minorities: Eight Premises in Quest of Evidence,' *Canadian Public Policy* 11, no. 4 (1985): 684–700.

25 Hum and Simpson, 'Wage Opportunities,' 392.

26 Hum and Simpson, 'Wage Opportunities,' 390. For other studies also showing the wage and employment disadvantages of blacks in Canada, see J.G. Reitz, 'Statistics on Racial Discrimination in Canada,' *Policy Options* 14, no.

2 (1993): 32–6; and Frances Henry and Effie Ginzberg, 'Racial Discrimination in Employment,' in *Social Inequality in Canada*, ed. Curtis et al., 353–60.
27 Hum and Simpson, 'Wage Opportunities,' 392.
28 On the question of black youths and educational motivation, see Okey
   Chigbo, 'Reading, Writing and Racism: Black Ideology Is the Black Child's
   Most Debilitating Burden,' *The Next City* 2, no. 3 (1997): 33–53. Chigbo
   believes that 'while racism does indeed exist ... reasons for black educational underachievement can be found in the black community, the black
   family and the troubling subculture of black youth,' 34.
29 Robert Allan McChesney, 'Canada,' in *International Handbook of Human
   Rights*, ed. Jack Donnelly and Rhoda E. Howard (Westport, CT: Greenwood,
   1987), 29–47.
30 On Japanese-Canadians, see Ellen Baar, 'Issei, Nisei, and Sansei,' in *Modernization and the Canadian State*, ed. Daniel Glenday, Hubert Guindon, and
   Allan Turowetz (Toronto: Macmillan, 1978), 340. On segregated schools, see
   Robin W. Winks, *The Blacks in Canada: A History*, 2d ed. (Montreal and Kingston: McGill-Queen's University Press, 1997), 362–89.
31 Loury, 'Why Should We Care about Group Inequality?' 254.
32 Robert D. Putnam, *Making Democracy Work: Civic Traditions in Modern Italy*
   (Princeton, NJ: Princeton University Press, 1993), 167.
33 Sniderman et al., *The Clash of Rights*, 148.

Chapter 8

1 For some scholars, any identifiable category of people can be considered a
   group, and that category's search for rights can therefore be considered a
   search for group rights, e.g., William F. Felice, *Taking Suffering Seriously: The
   Importance of Collective Human Rights* (Albany: State University of New York
   Press, 1996), who considers both women's and gay rights to be collective
   (group) rights. Other scholars maintain that only individual rights are
   human rights; other categories of rights may be legal, but they cannot be
   human. Jack Donnelly, *Universal Human Rights in Theory and Practice* (Ithaca,
   NY: Cornell University Press, 1989), 143–60.
2 Rodolfo Stavenhagen, 'Ethnic Conflicts and Their Impact on International
   Society,' *International Social Science Journal* 127 (1991): 118.
3 S. James Anaya, *Indigenous Peoples in International Law* (New York: Oxford
   University Press, 1996), 101.
4 Matthew Coon Come, National Chief, Assembly of First Nations (Canada),
   'Address to the National Congress of American Indians, Speaking Notes,'
   56th Session, St Paul, Minnesota, 14 November 2000, http://www.afn.ca/

Press%20Realeses%20&%20Speeches/address_to_the_ national_
congress.htm.

5 J. Rick Ponting reports on studies conducted in 1976 and 1986 which
showed that 'levels of knowledge and awareness of aboriginal issues were
found to be generally low.' 'Public Opinion on Aboriginal Peoples' Issues in
Canada,' in Statistics Canada, *Canadian Social Trends* (Winter 1988): 9.

6 All figures from Department of Indian Affairs and Northern Development,
*Comparison of Social Conditions, 1991 and 1996: Registered Indians, Registered
Indians Living on Reserve and the Total Population of Canada* (Ottawa: Minister of Public Works and Government Services Canada, 2000), http://
www.ainc-inac.gc.ca/pr/sts/hac/socl_e.pdf, accessed 31 January 2001. For
figures showing improvement between 1986 and 1991, see Department of
Indian Affairs and Northern Development, *Highlights of Aboriginal Conditions 1991, 1986: Demographic, Social and Economic Characteristics*, Catalogue
no. R32-154/1-1986 (Ottawa: Information Quality and Research Directorate, October 1995), http://www.ainc-inac.gc.ca/pr/sts/hac/hilts_e.pdf.
For academic background on the situation of Canadian indigenous people,
see James S. Frideres with Lilianne Ernestine Krosenbrink-Gelissen, *Native
Peoples in Canada: Contemporary Conflicts*, 4th ed. (Scarborough, ON: Prentice-Hall, 1993); and Vic Satzewich and Terry Wotherspoon, *First Nations:
Race, Class, and Gender Relations* (Scarborough, ON: Nelson Canada, 1993).
For a more journalistic account, see Geoffrey York, *The Dispossessed: Life and
Death in Native Canada* (Toronto: Lester and Orpen Dennys, 1989).

7 A.C. Hamilton and C.M. Sinclair, *The Justice System and Aboriginal People*,
vol. 1 of *Report of the Aboriginal Justice Inquiry of Manitoba* (Winnipeg:
Queen's Printer, 1991), 87. On Aboriginal crime, see Julian V. Roberts and
Anthony N. Doob, 'Race, Ethnicity and Criminal Justice in Canada,' in *Ethnicity, Crime and Immigration: Comparative and Cross-National Perspectives*,
vol. 21, ed. Michael Tonry (Chicago: University of Chicago Press, 1997),
469–522.

8 Nancy Miller Chenier, 'Suicide among Aboriginal People: Royal Commission Report,' Library of Parliament, Parliamentary Research Branch, MR-
131E, 23 February 1995, http://www.parl.gc.ca/information/library/PRB-
pubs/mr131_e.htm. For an analysis of these high suicide rates, see Antoon
A. Leenaars et al., 'Genocide and Suicide among Indigenous People: The
North Meets the South,' *Canadian Journal of Native Studies* 19, no. 2 (1999):
337–63.

9 The idea of individual integration as the best path to rights for native peoples died an ignominious death in 1969 when then justice minister and later
Prime Minister Jean Chrétien advanced an unfortunately named and soon

shelved 'White Paper' advocating individual integration into Canadian society. Indian and Northern Affairs, *White Paper on Indian Policy* (Ottawa: Queen's Printer for Canada, 1969).

10 For one account of the decline of an Aboriginal community that supports this line of thinking, see Anastasia M. Shkilnyk, *A Poison Stronger than Love: The Destruction of an Ojibwa Community* (New Haven: Yale University Press, 1985).

11 There is evidence that this perception is correct: on-reserve registered Indians lag behind off-reserve Aboriginals, as well as behind non-Aboriginal Canadians, in labour force participation rates and levels of employment. Canada, Department of Indian Affairs and Northern Development, *Highlights of Aboriginal Conditions*, xi.

12 The term 'United Empire Loyalists' refers to the forty to fifty thousand people from the United States who were loyal to the British Crown, and fled the United States for Canada after the American Revolution. Bruce G. Wilson, 'Loyalists,' in *The Canadian Encyclopedia* (Edmonton: Hurtig, 1985), 1041–2.

13 The personal property of a status Indian or a band living on a reserve – including both goods and income – is tax exempt. Indian and Northern Affairs, 'Status Indians and Taxes,' December 1997, http://www.ainc-inac.gc.ca/pr/info/info113_e.html.

14 On residential schools and attendant sexual abuse, see Royal Commission on Aboriginal Peoples, *Looking Forward, Looking Back*, vol. 1 of *Report of the Royal Commission on Aboriginal Peoples* (Ottawa: Minister of Supply and Services Canada, 1996), 365–82. See also Celia Haig-Brown, *Resistance and Renewal: Surviving the Indian Residential School* (Vancouver: Tillacum Library, 1989).

15 W. Ofuatey-Kodjoe, 'Self-Determination,' in *United Nations Legal Order*, vol. 1, ed. Oscar Schachter and Christopher C. Joyner (Cambridge: Cambridge University Press, 1995), 349–89.

16 Anaya, *Indigenous Peoples in International Law*, 97–125, and Hurst Hannum, *Autonomy, Sovereignty, and Self-Determination: The Accommodation of Conflicting Rights* (Philadelphia: University of Pennsylvania Press, 1990), 74–103.

17 United Nations, 'Discrimination against Indigenous Peoples: Technical Review of the United Nations Draft Declaration on the Rights of Indigenous Peoples,' Commission on Human Rights, Sub-Commission on Prevention of Discrimination and Protection of Minorities, 46th Sess., E/CN.4/Sub.2/1994/2/Add.1, 20 April 1994.

18 Nunavut Planning Commission, 'General Information about Nunavut,' http://npc.nunavut.ca/eng/nunavut/general.html.

19 Anaya, *Indigenous Peoples in International Law*, 80.
20 Statement by the government of Canada at the UN Working Group on the Draft Declaration on the Rights of Indigenous Peoples, 31 October 1996. Obtained privately from the Department of Indian and Northern Affairs.
21 The interviews were conducted in 1996–7. On 30 October 1995, there was a referendum on sovereignty in Quebec. The proposal for sovereignty was very narrowly defeated, by a vote of 50.6 to 49.4 per cent.
22 In this, they agreed with the Royal Commission on Aboriginal Peoples, which concluded that 'Aboriginal peoples are entitled to negotiate freely the terms of their relationship with Canada and to establish governmental structures that they consider appropriate for their needs.' Royal Commission on Aboriginal Peoples, 'Conclusions,' in *Restructuring the Relationship*, vol. 2 of *Royal Commission on Aboriginal Peoples*, chapter 3, section 2.2, http://www.indigenous.bc.ca/v2/Vol2Ch3s2tos2.2.asp.
23 'Youths Banished,' *Windspeaker* 12, no. 21 (1995).
24 In fact, there are still many difficulties in setting up fair sentencing circles that accurately reflect Aboriginal traditions. See Mary Crnkovich, 'A Sentencing Circle,' *Journal of Legal Pluralism and Unofficial Law* 36 (1996): 159–81. On native healing circles, see Russel Lawrence Barsh and Chantelle Marlor, 'Alternative Paradigms: Law as Power, Law as Process,' in *Law in Society: Canadian Readings*, ed. Nick Larsen and Brian Burtch (Toronto: Harcourt Brace, 1999), 142–48.
25 Dates from Indian and Northern Affairs, 'Indian Residential Schools,' Information Sheet no. 46, April 1993.
26 Royal Commission on Aboriginal Peoples, *Looking Forward, Looking Back*, 1: 379. See also N. Rosalyn Ing, 'The Effects of Residential Schools on Native Child-Rearing Practices,' *Canadian Journal of Native Education* 18 (1990): 65–118.
27 E.g., Mary Ellen Turpel, 'Aboriginal Peoples and the Canadian *Charter*: Interpretive Monopolies, Cultural Differences,' in *Canadian Human Rights Yearbook 1989–90* (Ottawa: University of Ottawa Press, 1991), 3–45. See also Darlene M. Johnston, 'Native Rights as Collective Rights: A Question of Group Self-Preservation,' in *The Rights of Minority Cultures*, ed. Will Kymlicka (New York: Oxford University Press, 1995), 179–201, and, for a discussion of this issue by a non-Aboriginal scholar, Claude Denis, *We Are Not You: First Nations and Canadian Modernity* (Peterborough, ON: Broadview Press, 1997).
28 On this debate, see Radha Jhappan, 'Inherency, Three Nations and Collective Rights: The Evolution of Aboriginal Constitutional Discourse from

1982 to the Charlottetown Accord,' *International Journal of Canadian Studies* 7–8 (1993): 225–59.

29 Sally Weaver, 'First Nations Women and Government Policy, 1970–92: Discrimination and Conflict,' in *Changing Patterns: Women in Canada*, 2d ed., ed. Sandra Burt, Lorraine Code, and Lindsay Dorney (Toronto: McClelland and Stewart, 1993), 122.

30 Canada, *Consensus Report on the Constitution: Final Text* (Charlottetown, 28 August, 1992), chapter IV, articles 41 and 43.

31 Native Women's Association of Canada, 'Aboriginal Women and the Constitutional Debates: Continuing Discrimination,' *Canadian Woman Studies* 12, no. 3 (1992): 14–17. See also Jhappan, 'Inherency, Three Nations and Collective Rights,' 242–54, and for background on discrimination against Aboriginal women, Weaver, 'First Nations Women and Government Policy.'

32 For an early academic discussion of matriarchal rule in Iroquois society, see Judith K. Brown, 'Iroquois Women: An Ethnohistoric Note,' in *Toward an Anthropology of Women*, ed. Rayna R. Reiter (New York: Monthly Review Press, 1975), 235–51. Many non-academic observers confuse matrilineage (descent traced through the female line only) with matriarchy (a system of rule by women or clan mothers). According to Weaver, 'First Nations Women and Government Policy,' 96, pre-conquest Aboriginal societies were most likely to be bilineal in their descent rules, less likely to be matrilineal, and least likely to be patrilineal.

33 This assumes, of course, that the idea of a 'nation' can be stretched backwards into history to the period before nations were invented. On this, see Eric Hobsbawm, *Nations and Nationalism since 1780: Programme, Myth, Reality* (New York: Cambridge University Press, 1990), as well as Benedict Anderson, *Imagined Communities: Reflections on the Origin and Spread of Nationalism* (New York: Verso, 1991).

34 This accords with evidence from national surveys done in 1976 and 1986 that revealed that 'Canadians seem to recognize Natives' special relationship with the land' even when they otherwise felt that Natives were being granted special privileges. Ponting, 'Public Opinion,' 9.

35 Covering 1.9 million square kilometres, Nunavut comprises 19 per cent of Canada's total land mass. 'General Information about Nunavut.'

36 For information on some such disputes, see, e.g., Patricia Begin, Wendy Moss, and Peter Niemczak, 'The Land Claim Dispute at Oka,' Library of Parliament Research Branch, Background Paper BP-235E (Ottawa: Minister of Supply and Services Canada, 1992); Erin Anderssen, 'Ottawa to Return Ipperwash Land: Deal with Natives Ends 50–Year Feud,' *Globe and Mail*,

18 June 1998, Toronto edition; and John DeMont, 'Beyond Burnt Church: The Lobster War Escalates into a National Debate over Native Traditions and Special Rights,' *Maclean's* 112, no. 42 (1999): 34–5.

37 Denis, *We Are Not You*, 33.

Chapter 9

1 United Nations, International Covenant on Economic, Social and Cultural Rights, entered into force January 1976. See article 9 (social security), 11.1 (food, clothing, and housing), 12.1 (health), 13 (education), and 6.1 (work). In Center for the Study of Human Rights, *Twenty-Four Human Rights Documents* (New York: Columbia University, 1992), 6–9.

2 National Anti-Poverty Organization, 'NAPO Facts: More Facts about Child Poverty,' June 1996, http://www.napo-onap.ca/nf-child.htm. This figure may be rather high, however. As of January 1999, there were no good national data on homelessness; one figure from Toronto suggested that 'just under 26,000 people had used the shelter network ... in 1996.' Lyne Casavant, 'Counting the Homeless,' Government of Canada, Parliamentary Research Branch, Political and Social Affairs Division, PRB 99-1E, January 1999, http://dsp-psd.pwgsc.gc.ca/dsp-psd/Pilot/LoPBdP/modules/prb99-1-homelessness/counting-e.htm. For a report on the causes of homelessness, see Canadian Broadcasting Corporation, 'Homelessness: Canada's Mean Streets,' http://cbc.ca/insidecbc/newsinreview/dec98/homeless/why.htm.

3 Beth Wilson and Carly Steinman, *HungerCount 2000: A Surplus of Hunger*, prepared for Canadian Association of Food Banks, October 2000, http://www.icomm.ca/cafb/hc-2000.pdf.

4 Rhoda E. Howard, *Human Rights and the Search for Community* (Boulder, CO: Westview, 1995), 211.

5 Victor Dankwa, Cees Flinterman, and Scott Leckie, 'Commentary to the Maastricht Guidelines on Violations of Economic, Social and Cultural Rights,' *Human Rights Quarterly* 20, no. 3 (1998): 725–6.

6 James W. Nickel, *Making Sense of Human Rights: Philosophical Reflections on the Universal Declaration of Human Rights* (Berkeley, CA: University of California Press, 1987), 160–70.

7 National Anti-Poverty Organization, 'Poverty Statistics at a Glance,' April 1999, http://www.napo-onap.ca/glance.htm.

8 National Anti-Poverty Organization, 'Poverty Statistics at a Glance.'

9 Campaign 2000, 'Child Poverty in Ontario: Report Card 2000,' 5, http://www.campaign2000.ca.

10 Andrew Jackson, 'Social Inclusion/Exclusion of Canadian Children,' *Horizons: Policy Research Initiative* 4, no. 1 (2001): 4–5; see also Howard, *Human Rights and the Search for Community*, 165–93.

11 Henry Shue, *Basic Rights: Subsistence, Affluence and U.S. Foreign Policy* (Princeton, NJ: Princeton University Press, 1980), 69. For a widely cited argument against economic rights, see Maurice Cranston, 'What Are Human Rights?' in *The Human Rights Reader*, ed. Walter Laqueur and Barry Rubin (New York: New American Library, 1989), 17–25.

12 Ken Platt, 'Volunteering too Costly for the Disabled,' *Hamilton Spectator*, 18 June 2001, A10.

13 Lee Simpson, 'Perception of a Problem: Report on Hunger,' Totum Research Inc., August 2000, http://www.cafb-acba.ca/pdfs/other_documents/totum_e.pdf.

14 World Bank, *Entering the 21st Century: World Development Report 1999/2000* (New York: Oxford University Press, 2000), table 1.1, 'Size of the Economy.'

15 Rhoda E. Howard, 'Human Rights and the Culture Wars,' *International Journal* 53, no. 1 (1997–8): 94–112.

16 See, for example, Michael Sandel's critique of extreme individualism, 'The Procedural Republic and the Unencumbered Self,' *Political Theory* 12, no. 1 (1984): 81–96.

17 Hon. Henry N.R. Jackman (Lieutenant-Governor), Speech from the Throne, Legislative Assembly of Ontario, 1st Sess., 36th Parliament, *Official Reports of Debates*, 27 September 1995, 6.

18 Gallup Canada, '86% Favour Making Welfare Recipients Go To Work,' *The Gallup Poll*, 31 March 1994. The figure of 86 per cent refers to national results.

19 Simpson, 'Perception of a Problem.'

20 David Lewis, *Louder Voices: The Corporate Welfare Bums* (Toronto: James Lewis and Samuel, 1972).

21 Simpson, 'Perception of a Problem.'

22 The figure of 21.6 per cent cutbacks in Ontario welfare is widely cited. See, e.g., Campaign 2000, 'Child Poverty in Ontario,' 10.

23 Canadian Council on Social Development, 'Poverty Rates for Selected Non-elderly Family Types, 1980–1995,' prepared by the Centre for International Statistics www.ccsd.ca/fs_pov95.htm.

24 For a sociology of shame that sees it primarily as a negative personal emotion, rather than a positive emotion contributing to the social order, see Thomas J. Scheff, 'Shame and the Social Bond: A Sociological Theory,' *Sociological Theory* 18, no. 1 (2000): 84–99. See also Howard, *Human Rights and the Search for Community*, 135–64.

25 The 'Family Life Education' program for Hamilton-Wentworth elementary Catholic schools in 2001 contained no modules about birth control or abortion. Hamilton-Wentworth Catholic District School Board, 'Policy Statement: Family Life Education (Elementary Schools),' obtained by fax, 5 February 2001.

26 Ministry of Community and Social Services, 'Education Key to Getting Teen Parents Off Welfare: Baird Launches First Leap Program in Ontario,' 27 September 1999, http://www.gov.on.ca:80/CSS/page/news/nr98-99/sep2799.html.

27 Canadian Fact Book on Poverty, 'The Changing Face of Poverty: Statistics Canada Definition,' table 5.5, 'Comparison of Poor and Nonpoor Lone-Parent Mothers, 1991 Statistics Canada Definition,' http://www.cfc-efc.ca/docs/00000326.htm, accessed 01/04/2001.

28 On some of the psychological consequences of separation of children given up for adoption from their biological mothers, see Karen March, *The Stranger Who Bore Me: Adoptee-Birth Mother Relationships* (Toronto: University of Toronto Press, 1995).

29 Ministry of Community and Social Services, 'Ontario Works: Information for Participants,' http://www.gov.on.ca/CSS/page/brochure/owia.html.

30 Paul Weinberg, 'Poor Relations: Ontario Workfare Is Not Working,' *Our Times* 18, no. 3 (1999): 37–41; Canadian Press Newswire, 'Ontario Workfare Placements Finally up to Snuff: Baird,' 5 June 2000; and Christine Cox, 'Hamilton Finishes Last in Workfare Placements,' *Hamilton Spectator*, 19 June 2001, A1, A8.

31 Gallup Canada, '86% Favour Making Welfare Recipients Go To Work.' A variant of a guaranteed annual income is a negative income tax, designed to ensure everyone a minimum annual income. This was proposed by Milton Friedman, generally considered to be representative of a very conservative school of economics, in 1962. Milton Friedman, *Capitalism and Freedom* (Chicago: University of Chicago Press, 1962), 190–5.

32 Amartya Sen, *Development as Freedom* (New York: Alfred A. Knopf, 1999), 130.

33 Sen, *Development as Freedom*, 21.

34 Ministry of Community and Social Services, 'Ontario Works.'

35 Michael Walzer, *Spheres of Justice: A Defense of Pluralism and Equality* (New York: Basic Books, 1983), 174.

36 Howard, *Human Rights and the Search for Community*, 140.

37 Robert M. Solow, 'Guess Who Pays for Workfare?' *New York Review of Books* 45, no. 17 (1998): 27–8, 36–7.

38 Sen, *Development as Freedom*, 283–4, emphasis in original.

39 Center for the Study of Human Rights, *Twenty-Four Human Rights Documents*, 6.
40 Howard, *Human Rights and the Search for Community*, 17.
41 Bas de Gaay Fortman, 'Religion and Human Rights: Mutually Exclusive or Supportive?' *Studies in Interreligious Dialogue* 6, no. 1 (1996): 104.

Chapter 10

1 Rhoda E. Howard, 'Human Rights in South Africa versus Human Rights in Black Africa: An Illegitimate Comparison,' *Transafrica Forum* 5, no. 1 (1987): 39–56.
2 On Canada's relationship with South Africa during the period of apartheid, see Rhoda E. Howard, 'Black Africa and South Africa,' in *Human Rights in Canadian Foreign Policy*, ed. Robert O. Matthews and Cranford Pratt (Montreal and Kingston: McGill-Queen's University Press, 1988), 265–84, and sources cited therein. See also Renate Pratt, *In Good Faith: Canadian Churches against Apartheid* (Waterloo, ON: Wilfrid Laurier University Press, 1997).
3 Joseph H. Carens, 'Aliens and Citizens: The Case for Open Borders,' in *The Rights of Minority Cultures*, ed. Will Kymlicka (Oxford: Oxford University Press, 1995), 332.
4 All figures taken or calculated from International Bank, *World Development Indicators*, 2000, table 1.1., 'Size of the Economy.'
5 Thabo Mbeki, 'Statement at the UN Millenium Summit,' New York, 7 September 2000, http://www.anc.org.za/ancdocs/history/mbeki/2000/tm0907.html.
6 On the contradictory aspects world economic arrangements, see Anthony Giddens, *The Third Way and Its Critics* (Cambridge, UK: Polity Press, 2000), 122–62.
7 On globalization, see Malcolm Waters, *Globalization* (New York: Routledge, 1995), and Richard Falk, *Predatory Globalization: A Critique* (Cambridge, UK: Polity Press, 1999).
8 Rhoda Howard, 'Contemporary Canadian Refugee Policy: A Critical Assessment,' *Canadian Public Policy* 6, no. 2 (1980): 363–4.
9 Legally, a refugee is a person who 'owing to a well-founded fear of being persecuted for reasons of race, religion, nationality, membership of a particular social group or political opinion, is outside the country of his nationality, and is unable or, owing to such fear, is unwilling to avail himself of the protection of that country.' United Nations, *Convention Relating to the Status of Refugees*, 1951.

10 United Nations, 'International Convention on Civil and Political Rights,' General Assembly Resolution 2200A (XXI), 16 December 1966. Article 12, 2 'Everyone shall be free to leave any country, including his own,' but article 12, 4, 'No one shall be arbitrarily deprived of the right to enter *his own* country,' emphasis mine.

11 The term 'global apartheid' is from Anthony H. Richmond, *Global Apartheid: Refugees, Racism and the New World Order* (Toronto: Oxford, 1994), especially 206–17.

12 For example, the 1998 Canadian immigration plan proposed that of the total of 175,900 to 192,700 projected immigrants, 66 per cent would belong to the classes of skilled workers and business immigrants. Calculated from Citizenship and Immigration Canada, 'A Stronger Canada: 1998 Annual Immigration Plan,' tabled 23 October 1997, http://www.cic.gc.ca/english/pub/anrep98e.html.

13 International Bank, *World Development Indicators*, 2000, table 1.4, 'Trends in Long-Term Economic Development.'

14 See, e.g., Gary B. Madison, *The Political Economy of Civil Society and Human Rights* (New York: Routledge, 1998); William H. Meyer, *Human Rights and International Political Economy in Third World Nations* (Westport, CT: Praeger, 1998); and Dietrich Rueschemeyer, Evelyne Huber Stephens, and John D. Stephens, *Capitalist Development and Democracy* (Chicago: University of Chicago Press, 1992).

15 This is an extremely difficult question that confounds philosophers as much as it does ordinary citizens. See the discussion in Henry Shue, *Basic Rights: Subsistence, Affluence, and U.S. Foreign Policy* (Princeton, NJ: Princeton University Press, 1980), 131–52.

16 Gary Edwards and Josephine Mazzuca, 'Canadians Favour Decreased Immigration,' *The Gallup Poll* 58, no. 59 (1998): 'As has been the case since 1991, approximately four in ten Canadians would favour decreased immigration into Canada.'

17 Canada's total fertility rate in 1998 was 1.6; that is, women in their childbearing years bore on average 1.6 children. Canada's population of people aged 65 and over was projected to grow by 2.1 per cent annually between 1998 and 2015, while its population between the ages of 0 and 14 was projected to decline by 0.6 per cent annually during the same period. International Bank, *World Development Indicators*, 2000, table 2.16, 'Reproductive Health,' and 2.2., 'Population Dynamics.'

18 Angus Reid Group, 'The National Angus Reid Poll: Tolerance and the Canadian Ethnocultural Mosaic,' February/March 1993, 5.

19 The 1998 immigration plan was that 11 per cent of immigrants would enter

under the 'business' category, some of these, presumably, as investors. Calculated from Citizenship and Immigration Canada, 'A Stronger Canada.'

20 In the 1998 plan, family members were limited to spouses, fiancé(e)s, children, parents, and grandparents. Citizenship and Immigration Canada, 'A Stronger Canada.'

21 Department of Finance, 'International Monetary Fund, 2000 Article IV Consultation with Canada, Statement of the IMF Mission,' News Release 99–097, 16 November 1999, http://www.fin.gc.ca/newse99/data/99-097_1e.html.

22 Department of Finance, 'Internation Monetary Fund.'

23 Figure calculated from Canada's 1998 gross national product of U.S.$580.9 billion. International Bank, *World Development Indicators*, table 1.1.

24 An excellent compilation of articles about Canadian foreign aid published shortly before these interviews were conducted is Cranford Pratt, ed., *Canadian International Development Assistance Policies: An Appraisal* (Montreal and Kingston: McGill-Queen's University Press, 1994).

25 Reduction of the national debt became a serious issue in Canada in the 1980s, and resulted in reduction of aid monies. Cranford Pratt, 'Humane Internationalism and Canadian Development Assistance Policies,' in *Canadian International Development Assistance Policies*, ed. Pratt, 343–57.

26 Angus Reid Group, 'Tolerance and the Canadian Ethnocultural Mosaic,' 10.

27 Nega Mezlekia, *Notes from the Hyena's Belly: Memories of My Ethiopian Boyhood* (Toronto: Penguin, 2000), 250.

28 From the fiscal year 1975/6 to the fiscal year 1989/90, roughly the period of the Marxist regime of Mengistu Haile Mariam, Canada gave $302,699,000 to Ethiopia. Canadian International Development Agency, 'Country-to-Country ODA by Country, by Delivery Channel,' 10 March 2000, 10.

29 Article 3.3 of the Declaration on the Right to Development (United Nations General Assembly, Resolution 41/128, 4 December 1986) speaks of states' 'duty to cooperate with each other in ensuring development and eliminating obstacles to development,' but there is no duty to share wealth. The Declaration may be found in Micheline R. Ishay, ed., *The Human Rights Reader: Major Political Essays, Speeches, and Documents from the Bible to the Present* (New York: Routledge, 1997), 469–73.

30 See Rhoda E. Howard, 'Human Rights, Development and Foreign Policy,' in *Human Rights and Development: International Views*, ed. David P. Forsythe (London: Macmillan, 1989), 217–21, and sources cited therein.

31 Waters, *Globalization*, 97–123.

Chapter 11

1 Martha Nussbaum, 'Compassion: The Basic Social Emotion,' *Social Philosophy and Policy* 13, no. 1 (1996): 28.

2 Irving Dillard, ed., *The Spirit of Liberty: Papers and Addresses of Learned Hand* (London: Hamish Hamilton, 1954), 189–90.

3 Paul M. Sniderman, Joseph H. Fletcher, Peter H. Russell, and Philip E. Tetlock, *The Clash of Rights: Liberty, Equality, and Legitimacy in a Pluralist Democracy* (New Haven: Yale University Press, 1996), 134.

4 Sniderman et al., *The Clash of Rights*, 237.

5 On multicultural and anti-racist education, see Keith A. McLeod, 'Multiculturalism and Multicultural Education in Canada: Human Rights and Human Rights Education,' in *Beyond Multicultural Education: International Perspectives*, ed. Kogila A. Moodley (Calgary: Detselig Enterprises, 1992), 215–42, and Kogila A. Moodley, 'Multicultural Education in Canada: Historical Development and Current Status,' in *Handbook of Research on Multicultural Education*, ed. James A. Banks and Cherry A. McGee Banks (New York: Macmillan, 1995), 801–20.

6 Abdullahi A. An-Na'im, 'The Synergy and Interdependence of Human Rights, Religion and Secularism,' unpublished manuscript, 2001, emphasis in original. In disagreement with An-Na'im, I have myself asserted the primacy of secularism in the evolution of human rights norms in Rhoda E. Howard, *Human Rights and the Search for Community* (Boulder, CO: Westview, 1995), 12–13.

7 Bas de Gaay Fortman, 'Religion and Human Rights: Mutually Exclusive or Supportive?' *Studies in Interreligious Dialogue* 6, no. 1 (1996): 107.

8 Ronald Inglehart, Neil Nevitte, and Miguel Basanez, *The North American Trajectory: Cultural, Economic and Political Ties among the United States, Canada and Mexico* (New York: Aldine de Gruyter, 1996), 18–19.

9 Inglehart, Nevitte, and Basanez, *The North American Trajectory*, 22.

10 C.B. Macpherson, *The Political Theory of Possessive Individualism: Hobbes to Locke* (London: Oxford University Press, 1962), 3.

11 Number of volunteers from personal communication, Sheila Hagens, Hamilton-Wentworth Volunteer Centre, August 1993. Cited in Howard, *Human Rights and the Search for Community*, 21.

12 Guy Haarscher, 'European Culture, Individual Rights, Collective Rights,' in *Human Rights in a Pluralist World: Individuals and Collectivities*, ed. Jan Berting et al. (Westport, CT: Meckler, 1990), 151

13 Amartya Sen, *Development as Freedom* (New York: Alfred A. Knopf, 1999), first two quotations from p. 261, third quotation from p. 283.

14 Nussbaum, 'Compassion.'
15 Rhoda E. Howard, 'Cultural Absolutism and the Nostalgia for Community,' *Human Rights Quarterly* 15, no. 2 (1993): 338.
16 Ronald J. Berger, *Fathoming the Holocaust: A Social Problems Approach* (New York: Aldine de Gruyter, 2002), 86.
17 For an introduction to the literature on altruism, see Morton Hunt, *The Compassionate Beast: The Scientific Inquiry into Human Altruism* (New York: Anchor Books, 1990).
18 Helen Fein, 'Genocide: A Sociological Perspective,' *Current Sociology* 38, no. 1 (1990): 64–6; and Raul Hilberg, *Perpetrators, Victims, Bystanders: The Jewish Catatrophe 1933–1945* (New York: HarperCollins, 1992), 195–268.
19 The remaining paragraphs in this section draw in part on my 'Identity, Empathy and International Relations,' McMaster University, Institute on Globalization and the Human Condition, Working Paper Series, April 2000, http://www.humanities.mcmaster.ca/~global/global.htm.
20 Helen Fein, *Congregational Sponsors of Indochinese Refugees in the United States, 1979–1981: Helping beyond Borders* (London and Toronto: Associated University Presses, 1987), 52, 116–17.
21 Nancy Sherman, 'Empathy, Respect, and Humanitarian Intervention,' *Ethics and International Affairs* 12 (1998): 104, 105.
22 The phrase 'universe of obligation' is originally from Helen Fein, *Accounting for Genocide: National Responses and Jewish Victimization during the Holocaust* (Chicago: University of Chicago Press, 1979), 33.
23 Rhoda E. Howard and Jack Donnelly, 'Human Dignity, Human Rights, and Political Regimes,' *American Political Science Review* 80, no. 3 (1986): 801–17. See also Rhoda E. Howard, *Human Rights in Commonwealth Africa* (Totowa, NJ: Rowman and Littlefield, 1986), 119–83.
24 On this incident, see Sharon Pond, 'When Rights Collide,' *University Affairs*, December 1994, 6–7; see also Canadian Civil Liberties Association, 'Borovoy Blasts Treatment of New Brunswick Professor,' November 1994. The original article by Yaqzan is reprinted in the McMaster University student newspaper, *The Silhouette*, 11 November 1993, under the heading 'UNB Prof's Rape Article Controversy.'
25 This incident is reported in A. Alan Borovoy, *The New Anti-Liberals* (Toronto: Canadian Scholars' Press, 1999), 62–5. See also Martin Loney, *The Pursuit of Division: Race, Gender, and Preferential Hiring in Canada* (Montreal and Kingston: McGill-Queen's University Press, 1998), 280–4.
26 Two hundred and forty anti-Semitic incidents were reported to the B'Nai Brith Canada League for Human Rights in 1998. B'nai Brith Canada, League for Human Rights, *1998 Audit of Antisemitic Incidents*, http://

www.bnaibrith.ca/publications/audit-98/as98-02.htm, accessed 21 January 2000.

27 Not all Canadian feminists support censorship of pornography. See the essayists in Varda Burstyn, ed., *Women against Censorship* (Toronto: Douglas and McIntyre, 1985), especially Burstyn's own argument in her 'Political Precedents and Moral Crusades: Women, Sex and the State' that 'we may begin [censorship] with very good intentions and end up with very bad results,' 16.

28 Canadian Charter of Rights and Freedoms, Section 25, in Thomas R. Berger, *Fragile Freedoms: Human Rights and Dissent in Canada* (Toronto: Clarke, Irwin and Company, 1981), 278–84.

29 In Berger, *Fragile Freedoms*, 283.

30 United Nations, International Convention on the Elimination of All Forms of Racial Discrimination, General Assembly Resolution 2106 (XX), 21 December 1965, entry into force 4 January 1969.

31 Rhoda E. Howard, 'Women's Rights, Group Rights and the Erosion of Liberalism,' in *Mistaken Identities: The Second Wave of Controversy over 'Political Correctness,'* ed. Cyril Levitt, Scott Davies, and Neil McLaughlin (New York: Peter Lang, 1999), 130–45.

32 Howard, *Human Rights and the Search for Community,* 121.

33 Amitai Etzioni, 'Creating Good Communities and Good Societies,' *Contemporary Sociology: A Journal of Reviews* 29, no. 1 (2000): 188.

34 Etzioni, 'Creating Good Communities and Good Societies,' 192.

35 Joseph H. Carens, *Culture, Citizenship, and Community: A Contextual Exploration of Justice as Evenhandedness* (Toronto: Oxford University Press, 2000), 193.

36 Rhoda E. Howard-Hassmann, 'Gay Rights and the Right to a Family: Conflicts between Liberal and Illiberal Belief Systems,' *Human Rights Quarterly* 23, no. 1 (2001): 73–95.

37 Four years after I finished interviewing the Hamilton civic leaders, a group of extremist Muslims attacked New York's World Trade Center. Four days later in Hamilton, arsonists – apparently confusing Hinduism and Islam – burned down a Hindu temple. Both officials of the city and many civic leaders immediately responded to the arson, however, in an attempt to lend support to the Hindu, Muslim, and other vulnerable communities. Cheryl Stepan, 'Temple Arson Sparked Move to Build Peaceful Community,' *Hamilton Spectator*, 16 March 2002, A4.

38 I owe this point to Bas de Gaay Fortman, in discussion, 27 November 2000.

Bibliography

Abella, Irving, and Harold Troper. *None Is Too Many: Canada and the Jews of Europe, 1933–1948.* Toronto: Lester and Orpen Dennys, 1986.

Abu-Laban, Yasmeen, and Daiva Stasiulis. 'Constructing "Ethnic Canadians": The Implications for Public Policy and Inclusive Citizenship: Rejoinder to Rhoda Howard-Hassmann.' *Canadian Public Policy* 26, no. 4 (2000): 477–87.

Agocs, Carol, and Monica Boyd. 'The Canadian Ethnic Mosaic Recast for the 1990s.' In *Social Inequality in Canada: Patterns, Problems, Policies.* 2d ed., edited by James Curtis, Edward Grabb, and Neil Guppy, 330–52. Scarborough, ON: Prentice-Hall Canada, 1993.

Albinski, Henry S. 'Politics and Biculturalism in Canada: The Flag Debate.' *Australian Journal of Politics and History* 13 (1967): 169–88.

Alford, Robert R., and R. Friedland. *Powers of Theory: Capitalism, the State, and Democracy.* New York: Cambridge University Press, 1985.

Amory, Deborah P. '"Homosexuality" in Africa: Issues and Debates.' *Issue: A Journal of Opinion* 25, no. 1 (1997): 5–10.

Anaya, S. James. *Indigenous Peoples in International Law.* New York: Oxford University Press, 1996.

Anderson, Benedict. *Imagined Communities: Reflections on the Origin and Spread of Nationalism.* New York: Verso, 1991.

Anderssen, Erin. 'Ottawa to Return Ipperwash Land: Deal with Natives Ends 50-Year Feud.' *Globe and Mail*, 18 June 1998, Toronto edition.

Angus Reid Group. *Multiculturalism and Canadians: Attitude Study 1991 – National Survey Report.* Ottawa: Multiculturalism and Citizenship Canada, August 1991.

– 'The National Angus Reid Poll: Tolerance and the Canadian Ethnocultural Mosaic.' February/March 1993.

Angus Reid/Southam News Poll. *Public Attitudes on Specific Gay Rights Issues*. http://www.angusreid.com/pressrel/gayrights.html, 7 June 1996.

An-Na'im, Abdullahi A. 'The Synergy and Interdependence of Human Rights, Religion and Secularism.' Unpublished manuscript. January 2001.

– *Toward an Islamic Reformation: Civil Liberties, Human Rights, and International Law*. Syracuse, NY: Syracuse University Press, 1990.

B'nai Brith Canada. League for Human Rights. *1998 Audit of Antisemitic Incidents*. http://www.bnaibrith.ca/publications/audit-98/as98-02.htm, accessed 21 January 2000.

Baar, Ellen. 'Issei, Nisei, and Sansei.' In *Modernization and the Canadian State*, edited by Daniel Glenday, Hubert Guindon, and Allan Turowetz, 335–55. Toronto: Macmillan, 1978.

Baker, Judith, ed. *Group Rights*. Toronto: University of Toronto Press, 1994.

Barrett, Stanley R. *Is God a Racist? The Right Wing in Canada*. Toronto: University of Toronto Press, 1987.

Barsh, Russel Lawrence, and Chantelle Marlor. 'Alternative Paradigms: Law as Power, Law as Process.' In *Law in Society: Canadian Readings*, edited by Nick Larsen and Brian Burtch, 142–8. Toronto: Harcourt Brace, 1999.

Begin, Patricia, Wendy Moss, and Peter Niemczak. 'The Land Claim Dispute at Oka.' Library of Parliament Research Branch, Background Paper BP-235E. Ottawa: Minister of Supply and Services Canada, 1992.

Belkin, Aaron, and Jason McNichol. 'Homosexual Personnel Policy in the Canadian Forces: Did Lifting the Gay Ban Undermine Military Performance?' *International Journal* 56, no. 1 (2000–1): 73–88.

Berger, Ronald J. *Fathoming the Holocaust: A Social Problems Approach*. New York: Aldine de Gruyter, 2002.

Berger, Thomas R. *Fragile Freedoms: Human Rights and Dissent in Canada*. Toronto: Clarke, Irwin and Company, 1981.

Bergman, Brian. 'A Nation of Polite Bigots.' *Maclean's*, 27 December 1999, 42–3.

Bibby, Reginald W. *Mosaic Madness: Pluralism without a Cause*. Toronto: Stoddart, 1990.

– *Unknown Gods: The Ongoing Story of Religion in Canada*. Toronto: Stoddart, 1993.

Bissoondath, Neil. *Selling Illusions: The Cult of Multiculturalism in Canada*. Toronto: Penguin Books, 1994.

Bohannan, Paul. '*Conscience Collective* and Culture.' In *Essays on Sociology and Philosophy by Emile Durkheim et al.*, edited by Kurt H. Wolff, 77–96. New York: Harper Torchbooks, 1960.

Borovoy, A. Alan. *The New Anti-Liberals*. Toronto: Canadian Scholars' Press, 1999.

- *Uncivil Obedience: The Tactics and Tales of a Democratic Agitator.* Toronto: Lester Publishing, 1991.
Bothwell, Robert, and J.L. Granatstein, eds. Introduction. In *The Gouzenko Transcripts*, 3–22. Ottawa: Deneau Publishers, 1982.
Bowlby, Geoff, and Philip Jennings. 'Youth Employment: A Lesson on Its Decline.' In Statistics Canada, *Education Quarterly Review* 5, no. 3 (1999): 36–42.
Boyd, Monica. 'Canadian, eh? Ethnic Origin Shifts in the Canadian Census.' *Canadian Ethnic Studies* 31, no. 3 (1999): 1–19.
- 'Gender, Visible Minority, and Immigrant Earnings Inequality: Reassessing an Employment Equity Premise.' In *Deconstructing a Nation: Immigration, Multiculturalism and Racism in '90s Canada*, edited by Vic Satzewich, 279–321. Halifax: Fernwood Publishing, 1992.
Boyd, Monica, et al. *Ascription and Achievement: Studies in Mobility and Status Attainment in Canada.* Ottawa: Carleton University Press, 1985.
Bozinoff, Lorne, and Peter MacIntosh. 'Feminist Movement Strongly Supported by Canadian Public.' *The Gallup Report*, 25 June 1992.
- 'Majority Oppose Same Sex Marriage.' *The Gallup Report*, 21 May 1992.
Brems, Eva. 'Enemies or Allies? Feminism and Cultural Relativism as Dissident Voices in Human Rights Discourse.' *Human Rights Quarterly* 19, no. 1 (1997): 136–64.
Breton, Raymond. 'Multiculturalism and Canadian Nation-Building.' In *The Politics of Gender, Ethnicity and Language in Canada*, edited by Alan Cairns and Cynthia Williams, 27–66. Toronto: University of Toronto Press, 1986.
Brooks, Stephen. *Public Policy in Canada: An Introduction.* Toronto: Oxford University Press, 1998.
Brown, Judith K. 'Iroquois Women: An Ethnohistoric Note.' In *Toward an Anthropology of Women*, edited by Rayna R. Reiter, 235–51. New York: Monthly Review Press, 1975.
Bruni, Laura. 'Index Amorum Prohibitorum [Index of Prohibited Love].' *Index on Censorship* 24, no. 1 (1995): 195–204.
Burr, Chandler. 'Homosexuality and Biology.' *Atlantic Monthly* 271, no. 3 (1993): 47–65.
Burstyn, Varda. 'Political Precedents and Moral Crusades: Women, Sex and the State.' In *Women against Censorship*, edited by Varda Burstyn, 4–31. Toronto: Douglas and McIntyre, 1985.
- ed. *Women against Censorship.* Toronto: Douglas and McIntyre, 1985.
Byne, William. 'Why We Cannot Conclude That Sexual Orientation Is Primarily a Biological Phenomenon.' *Journal of Homosexuality* 34, no. 1 (1997): 73–80.

Cairns, Alan C. 'The Fragmentation of Canadian Citizenship.' In *Belonging: The Meaning and Future of Canadian Citizenship*, edited by William Kaplan, 181–220. Montreal and Kingston: McGill-Queen's University Press, 1993.

Campaign 2000. 'Child Poverty in Ontario: Report Card 2000.' http://www.campaign2000.ca.

Canada. Acts of the Parliament of Canada. 'An Act Respecting Employment Equity.' 42–43–44 Elizabeth II, 15 December 1995.

– Canadian International Development Agency. 'Country-to-Country ODA by Country, by Delivery Channel.' 10 March 2000.

– Citizenship and Immigration Canada. *A Look at Canada*. Ottawa: Minister of Public Works and Government Services Canada, 1999.

– 'A Stronger Canada: 1998 Annual Immigration Plan.' 23 October 1997. http://www.cic.gc.ca/english/pub/anrep98e.html.

– *Consensus Report on the Constitution: Final Text*. Charlottetown, 28 August 1992.

– Department of Finance. 'International Monetary Fund, 2000 Article IV Consultation with Canada, Statement of the IMF Mission.' News Release 99–097, 16 November 1999. http://www.fin.gc.ca/newse99/data/99-097_1e.html.

– Department of Indian Affairs and Northern Development. *Comparison of Social Conditions, 1991 and 1996: Registered Indians, Registered Indians Living On Reserve and the Total Population of Canada*. Ottawa: Minister of Public Works and Government Services Canada, 2000. http://www.ainc-inac.gc.ca/pr/sts/hac/socl_e.pdf, accessed 31 January 2001.

– Department of Indian Affairs and Northern Development. *Highlights of Aboriginal Conditions 1991, 1986: Demographic, Social and Economic Characteristics*. Catalogue no. R32–154/1–1986. Ottawa: Information Quality and Research Directorate, October 1995. http://www.ainc-inac.gc.ca/pr/sts/hac/hilts_e.pdf.

– House of Commons. Bill C-23, 'The Modernizing Benefits and Obligations Act.' 2d Sess., 36th Parliament, 48–49 Elizabeth II, 1999–2000.

– House of Commons. Bill C-27, 'An Act to Amend the Criminal Code (child prostitution, child sex tourism, criminal harassment and female genital mutilation).' 2d Sess., 35th Parliament, 45 Elizabeth II, 1996.

– House of Commons. Bill C-41, 'An Act to Amend the Criminal Code (Sentencing) and Other Acts in Consequence Thereof.' 1st Sess., 35th Parliament, 42–43–44 Elizabeth II, 15 June 1995.

– House of Commons. Bill C-93, 'An Act for the Preservation and Enhancement of Multiculturalism in Canada.' 2d Sess., 33rd Parliament, 12 July 1988.

– House of Commons. *Debates*, 20 September 1994.

– House of Commons. *Debates*, 13 June 1995.

- House of Commons. *Debates*, 14 June 1995.
- Indian and Northern Affairs. 'Indian Residential Schools.' Information Sheet no. 46, April 1993.
- Indian and Northern Affairs. 'Status Indians and Taxes.' December 1997. http://www.ainc-inac.gc.ca/pr/info/info113_e.html.
- Indian and Northern Affairs. *White Paper on Indian Policy.* Ottawa: Queen's Printer for Canada, 1969.
- Royal Commission on Aboriginal Peoples. *Looking Forward, Looking Back.* Vol. 1 of *Report of the Royal Commission on Aboriginal Peoples.* Ottawa: Minister of Supply and Services Canada, 1996.
- Royal Commission on Aboriginal Peoples. *Restructuring the Relationship.* Vol. 2 of *Royal Commission on Aboriginal Peoples.* http://www.indigenous.bc.ca/v2/Vol2Ch3s2tos2.2.asp.
- *Shaping Canada's Future Together, Proposals.* Ottawa: Government of Canada, 1991, 3. Quoted in Will Kymlicka, 'Individual and Community Rights,' in *Group Rights*, edited by Judith Baker, 17–33. Toronto: University of Toronto Press, 1994, 24.
- Statement from UN Working Group on the Draft Declaration on the Rights of Indigenous Peoples. 31 October 1996. Obtained privately from Indian and Northern Affairs Canada.
- Statistics Canada. 'Population 15 Years and Over by Sex, Visible Minority Population, Immigrant Status and Total Income Groups.' 1996 Census, 94F0009XDB96057.
- Statistics Canada. *Profile of Census Tracts in Hamilton.* Catalogue no. 95-202-XPB. Ottawa: Minister of Industry, 1999.
- Statistics Canada. *Religions in Canada.* 1991 Census of Canada. Catalogue no. 93–319. Ottawa: Industry, Science and Technology Canada, 1993.
- Statistics Canada, 'Statistical Profile: Income and Work Statistics for Hamilton (Census Metropolitan Area), Ontario.' Accessed 14 January 2000. Available through http://ceps.statcan.ca/english/Profil/PlaceSearchForm1.cfm.
- Statistics Canada. *Statistics Canada Daily.* 4 November 1997. As reported in http://www.acs.calgary.ca/~ponting/SocialFacts.html;#Demography.
Canadian Broadcasting Corporation. 'Homelessness: Canada's Mean Streets.' http://cbc.ca/insidecbc/newsinreview/dec98/homeless/why.htm.
Canadian Centre for Adolescent Research. *Job Statistics.* http://ccar.briercrest.ca/stats/jobs.shtml, accessed 22 June 2001.
'Canadian Charter of Rights and Freedoms.' In Thomas R. Berger, *Fragile Freedoms: Human Rights and Dissent in Canada*, 278–84. Toronto: Clarke, Irwin and Company, 1981.

Canadian Civil Liberties Association. 'Borovoy Blasts Treatment of New Brunswick Professor.' November 1994.

Canadian Council on Social Development. 'Poverty Rates for Selected Nonelderly Family Types, 1980–1995.' Prepared by the Centre for International Statistics. http://www.ccsd.ca/fs_pov95.htm.

Canadian Press Newswire. 'Ontario Workfare Placements Finally up to Snuff: Baird.' 5 June 2000.

– 'Supreme Court of Canada Rules Author of Anti-Semitic Books Can't Teach Children.' 3 April 1996.

Carens, Joseph H. 'Aliens and Citizens: The Case for Open Borders.' In *The Rights of Minority Cultures*, edited by Will Kymlicka, 331–49. New York: Oxford University Press, 1995.

– *Culture, Citizenship, and Community: A Contextual Exploration of Justice as Evenhandedness.* Toronto: Oxford University Press, 2000.

Casavant, Lyne. 'Counting the Homeless.' Government of Canada, Parliamentary Research Branch, Political and Social Affairs Division, PRB 99–1E, January 1999. http://dsp-psd.pwgsc.gc.ca/dsp-psd/Pilot/LoPBdP/modules/prb99–1–homelessness/counting-e.htm.

Center for the Study of Human Rights. *Twenty-Four Human Rights Documents.* New York: Columbia University, 1992.

Champion, Chris. 'In Quest of the Perfectly Modern Mountie: The RCMP Announces This Year's Racial and Female Quotas.' *Western Report*, 2 September 1996, 28.

Chenier, Nancy Miller. 'Suicide among Aboriginal People: Royal Commission Report.' Library of Parliament, Parliamentary Research Branch, MR-131E. 23 February 1995. http://www.parl.gc.ca/information/library/PRBpubs/mr131_e.htm.

Chigbo, Okey. 'Reading, Writing and Racism: Black Ideology Is the Black Child's Most Debilitating Burden.' *The Next City* 2, no. 3 (1997): 32–9, 53.

CJN Staff. 'Jewish Groups Back Bill's Protection of Gays.' *Canadian Jewish News*, 1 December 1994, 4.

Coon Come, Matthew. 'Address to the National Congress of American Indians, Speaking Notes.' 56th Sess. St. Paul, Minnesota, 14 November 2000. http://www.afn.ca/Press%20Realeses%20&%20Speeches/address_to_the_national_congress.htm.

Cox, Christine. 'Hamilton Finishes Last in Workfare Placements.' *Hamilton Spectator*, 19 June 2001, A1, A8.

Cranston, Maurice. 'What Are Human Rights?' In *The Human Rights Reader*, edited by Walter Laqueur and Barry Rubin, 17–25. New York: New American Library, 1989.

Crnkovich, Mary. 'A Sentencing Circle.' *Journal of Legal Pluralism and Unofficial Law* 36 (1996): 159–81.

Crowley, Brian Lee. 'Does Counting Bodies Add Up to Fairness?' *Canadian Business* 66 (November 1993): 71–8.

Daenzer, Patricia. *Regulating Class Privilege: Immigrant Servants in Canada, 1940s-1990s*. Toronto: Canadian Scholars' Press, 1993.

Dalzell, Catherine. 'New Canadians in Search of the Old: Ethnic and Religious Minorities Unite against "Tolerance."' *Alberta Report*, 15 May 1995, 11.

Dankwa, Victor, Cees Flinterman, and Scott Leckie. 'Commentary to the Maastricht Guidelines on Violations of Economic, Social and Cultural Rights.' *Human Rights Quarterly* 20, no. 3 (1998): 705–30.

Davies, Allan. 'The Keegstra Affair.' In *Antisemitism in Canada: History and Interpretation*, edited by Alan T. Davies, 227–47. Waterloo, ON: Wilfrid Laurier University Press, 1992.

De Cecco, John P., and David Allen Parker. 'The Biology of Homosexuality: Sexual Orientation or Sexual Preference?' *Journal of Homosexuality* 28, no. 1–2 (1995): 1–27.

de Gaay Fortman, Bas. 'Religion and Human Rights: Mutually Exclusive or Supportive?' *Studies in Interreligious Dialogue* 6, no. 1 (1996): 98–109.

DeMont, John. 'Beyond Burnt Church: The Lobster War Escalates into a National Debate over Native Traditions and Special Rights.' *Maclean's* 112, no. 42 (1999): 34–5.

Denis, Claude. *We Are Not You: First Nations and Canadian Modernity*. Peterborough, ON: Broadview Press, 1997.

Dillard, Irving, ed. *The Spirit of Liberty: Papers and Addresses of Learned Hand*. London: Hamish Hamilton, 1954.

Donnelly, Jack. *Universal Human Rights in Theory and Practice*. Ithaca, NY: Cornell University Press, 1989.

Donnelly, Jack, and Rhoda E. Howard. 'Assessing National Human Rights Performance: A Theoretical Framework.' *Human Rights Quarterly* 10, no. 2 (1988): 214–48.

Dunton, Chris, and Mai Palmberg. 'Human Rights and Homosexuality in Southern Africa.' In *Current African Issues 19*. Uppsala, Sweden: Nordiska Afrikainstituet, June 1996.

Durkheim, Emile. *The Division of Labor in Society*. New York: The Free Press, 1933 [1st ed. 1893].

Dworkin, Ronald. 'The Coming Battles over Free Speech.' *New York Review of Books* 39, no. 11 (1992): 55–64.

– *Taking Rights Seriously*. Cambridge, MA: Harvard University Press, 1978.

Eady, Robert. 'Homosexuals Battering the Family (Bill C-41 and "sexual orientation").' *Catholic Insight* 3, no. 1 (1995): 14–15.

Edwards, Gary, and Josephine Mazzuca. 'Canadians Favour Decreased Immigration.' *The Gallup Poll* 58, no. 59 (1998).

EGALE. 'Canada Watch: Who's Doing What.' 27 December 1998. http://
www.egale.ca/features/watch.htm.

– 'EGALE Condemns Attempts to Water Down Hate Crimes Bill.' 14 June
1995. http://www.egale.ca/pressrel/950614.htm.

Elkins, David J. 'Facing Our Destiny: Rights and Canadian Distinctiveness.'
Canadian Journal of Political Science 22, no. 4 (1989): 699–716.

Elliott, Jean Leonard, and Augie Fleras. *Unequal Relations: An Introduction to
Race and Ethnic Dynamics in Canada.* Scarborough, ON: Prentice-Hall Canada,
1992.

Elman, Bruce P. '*Her Majesty The Queen v. James Keegstra*: The Control of Racism
in Canada, A Case Study.' In *Under the Shadow of Weimar: Democracy, Law, and
Racial Incitement in Six Countries*, edited by Louis Greenspan and Cyril Levitt, 149–76. Westport, CT: Praeger, 1993.

Emberley, Peter C. *Zero Tolerance: Hot Button Politics in Canada's Universities.*
Toronto: Penguin Books, 1996.

Ernulf, Kurt E., Sune M. Innala, and Frederick Whitam. 'Biological Explanation, Psychological Explanation, and Tolerance of Homosexuals: A Cross-
National Analysis of Beliefs and Attitudes.' *Psychological Reports* 65 (1989):
1003–10.

Eskridge, William N., Jr. *The Case for Same-Sex Marriage: From Sexual Liberty to
Civilized Commitment.* New York: The Free Press, 1996.

Etzioni, Amitai. 'Creating Good Communities and Good Societies.' *Contemporary Sociology: A Journal of Reviews* 29, no. 1 (2000): 188–95.

– 'Social Norms: Internalization, Persuasion, and History.' *Law and Society
Review* 34, no. 1 (2000): 157–78.

Falk, Richard. *Predatory Globalization: A Critique.* Cambridge, UK: Polity Press,
1999.

Fein, Helen. *Accounting for Genocide: National Responses and Jewish Victimization
during the Holocaust.* Chicago: University of Chicago Press, 1979.

– *Congregational Sponsors of Indochinese Refugees in the United States, 1979–1981:
Helping beyond Borders.* London and Toronto: Associated University Presses,
1987.

– 'Genocide: A Sociological Perspective.' *Current Sociology* 38, no. 1 (1990),
entire issue.

Fekete, John. *Moral Panic: Biopolitics Rising.* Montreal-Toronto: Robert Davies
Publishing, 1994.

Felice, William F. *Taking Suffering Seriously: The Importance of Collective Human Rights*. Albany: State University of New York Press, 1996.

FGMNetwork. *Female Genital Mutilation around the World: Population Groups*. http://www.fgmnetwork.org/intro/world.html.

Fish, Stanley. Handout from lecture at McMaster University. Hamilton, Ontario, 22 January 1999.

– *There's No Such Thing as Free Speech ... and It's a Good Thing Too*. New York: Oxford University Press, 1994.

Fletcher, Joseph F., and Marie-Christine Chalmers. 'Attitudes of Canadians toward Affirmative Action: Opposition, Value Pluralism, and Nonattitudes.' *Political Behavior* 13, no. 1 (1991): 67–95.

Foster, Cecil. *A Place Called Heaven: The Meaning of Being Black in Canada*. Toronto: HarperCollins, 1996.

Frideres, James S., with Lilianne Ernestine Krosenbrink-Gelissen. *Native Peoples in Canada: Contemporary Conflicts*. 4th ed. Scarborough, ON: Prentice-Hall, 1993.

Friedman, Lawrence M. *The Horizontal Society*. New Haven: Yale University Press, 1999.

Friedman, Milton. *Capitalism and Freedom*. Chicago: University of Chicago Press, 1962.

Galenkamp, Marlies. *Individualism versus Collectivism: The Concept of Collective Rights*. Rotterdam: Erasmus University, 1993.

Gallant, Mavis. *Home Truths*. Toronto: Macmillan, 1981, xiii. Quoted in Ramsay Cook, 'Nation, Identity, Rights: Reflections on W.L. Morton's *Canadian Identity*,' *Journal of Canadian Studies* 29, no. 2 (1994): 5–18.

Gallup Canada. '74% Oppose Employment Equity Programs.' *The Gallup Poll*, 23 December 1993.

– '86% Favour Making Welfare Recipients Go To Work.' *The Gallup Poll*, 31 March 1994.

Gans, Herbert J. 'Symbolic Ethnicity: The Future of Ethnic Groups and Cultures in America.' *Ethnic and Racial Studies* 2, no. 1 (1979): 1–20.

Giddens, Anthony. *The Consequences of Modernity*. Stanford, CA: Stanford University Press, 1990.

– *The Third Way and Its Critics*. Cambridge, UK: Polity Press, 2000.

Giese, Rachel. 'Hating the Hate-Crimes Bill.' *This Magazine*, November 1995, 7–9.

Glazer, Nathan. 'Individual Rights against Group Rights.' In *Human Rights*, edited by Eugene Kamenka and Alice Erh-Soon Tay, 87–103. New York: St Martin's Press, 1985.

Green, L.C. 'The Canadian Charter of Rights and International Law.' *The Canadian Yearbook of International Law* 20 (1982): 3–23.

Green, Leslie. 'Internal Minorities and Their Rights.' In *Group Rights*, edited by Judith Baker, 101–17. Toronto: University of Toronto Press, 1994.

Haarscher, Guy. 'European Culture, Individual Rights, Collective Rights.' In *Human Rights in a Pluralist World: Individuals and Collectivities*, edited by Jan Berting et al., 149–53. Westport, CT: Meckler, 1990.

Habermas, Jurgen. 'Struggles for Recognition in the Democratic Constitutional State.' In Charles Taylor, with Respondents, *Multiculturalism*. Princeton, NJ: Princeton University Press, 1994.

Haig-Brown, Celia. *Resistance and Renewal: Surviving the Indian Residential School*. Vancouver: Tillacum Library, 1989.

Hall, Michael, et al. *Caring Canadians, Involved Canadians: Highlights from the 1997 National Survey of Giving, Volunteering and Participating*. Catalogue no. 71–542–XIE. Ottawa: Minister of Industry, 1998.

Hamilton, A.C., and C.M. Sinclair. *The Justice System and Aboriginal People*. Vol. 1 of *Report of the Aboriginal Justice Inquiry of Manitoba*. Winnipeg: Queen's Printer, 1991.

Hamilton-Wentworth Catholic District School Board. 'Policy Statement: Family Life Education (Elementary Schools).' Fax. Hamilton, Ontario, 5 February 2001.

Hamilton-Wentworth School Board. Interview by Rina Rodak. Hamilton, Ontario, May 1999.

Hamm, Mark S. 'Conceptualizing Hate Crime in a Global Context.' In *Hate Crime: International Perspectives on Causes and Control*, edited by Mark S. Hamm, 173–94. Cincinnati: Anderson Publishing, 1994.

– ed. *Hate Crime: International Perspectives on Causes and Control*. Cincinnati: Anderson Publishing, 1994.

Hannum, Hurst. *Autonomy, Sovereignty, and Self-Determination: The Accommodation of Conflicting Rights*. Philadelphia: University of Pennsylvania Press, 1990.

Harles, John C. 'Integration *before* Assimilation: Immigration, Multiculturalism, and the Canadian Polity.' *Canadian Journal of Political Science* 30, no. 4 (1997): 711–36.

Hay, Sheridan. 'Blacks in Canada: The Invisible Minority.' *Canadian Dimension*, November–December 1996, 14–17.

Henry, Frances. *The Caribbean Diaspora in Toronto: Learning to Live with Racism*. Toronto: University of Toronto Press, 1994.

– *Forgotten Canadians: The Blacks of Nova Scotia*. Don Mills, ON: Longman Canada, 1973.

Henry, Frances, and Effie Ginzberg. 'Racial Discrimination in Employment.' In *Social Inequality in Canada: Patterns, Problems, Policies*. 2d ed. Edited by James

Curtis, Edward Grabb, and Neil Guppy, 353–60. Scarborough, ON: Prentice-Hall Canada, 1993.

Herdt, Gilbert. *Same Sex, Different Cultures: Exploring Gay and Lesbian Lives.* Boulder, Co: Westview, 1997.

Herek, Gregory M. 'Heterosexuals' Attitudes to Lesbians and Gay Men: Correlates and Gender Differences.' *The Journal of Sex Research* 25, no. 4 (1988): 451–77.

– 'Myths about Sexual Orientation: A Lawyers' Guide to Social Science Research.' *Law and Sexuality* 1 (1991): 133–72.

Hess, Henry. 'Firefighters Face Rights Complaint: Union "Poisoned" Work Environment for Women, Minorities, Commission Says.' *Globe and Mail*, 17 December 1997, Toronto edition, A1.

Heynen, Ralph, et al. (Homosexuality Committee). 'Homosexual Behavior and the Church: A Christian Reformed View, Looking at the Scriptures.' In *A Crisis of Understanding: Homosexuality and the Canadian Church*, edited by Denyse O'Leary, 62–102. Burlington, ON: Welch Publishing Company, 1988.

Hilberg, Raul. *Perpetrators, Victims, Bystanders: The Jewish Catastrophe 1933–1945.* New York: HarperCollins, 1992.

Hobsbawm, Eric. *Nations and Nationalism since 1780: Programme, Myth, Reality.* New York: Cambridge University Press, 1990.

Horn, Michiel. *Academic Freedom in Canada: A History.* Toronto: University of Toronto Press, 1999.

Howard, Rhoda. 'Contemporary Canadian Refugee Policy: A Critical Assessment.' *Canadian Public Policy* 6, no. 2 (1980): 361–73.

Howard, Rhoda E. 'Academic Freedom and Inclusivity in Canadian Universities.' In *Mistaken Identities: The Second Wave of Controversy over 'Political Correctness,'* edited by Cyril Levitt, Scott Davies, and Neil McLaughlin, 172–86. New York: Peter Lang, 1999.

– 'Being Canadian: Citizenship in Canada.' *Citizenship Studies* 2, no. 1 (1998): 133–52.

– 'Black Africa and South Africa.' In *Human Rights in Canadian Foreign Policy*, edited by Robert O. Matthews and Cranford Pratt, 265–84. Montreal and Kingston: McGill-Queen's University Press, 1988.

– 'Cultural Absolutism and the Nostalgia for Community.' *Human Rights Quarterly* 15, no. 2 (1993): 315–38.

– 'Human Rights, Development and Foreign Policy.' In *Human Rights and Development: International Views*, edited by David P. Forsythe, 213–34. London: Macmillan, 1989.

– 'Human Rights and the Culture Wars.' *International Journal* 53, no. 1 (1997–8): 94–112.

- *Human Rights and the Search for Community.* Boulder, Co: Westview, 1995.
- *Human Rights in Commonwealth Africa.* Totowa, NJ: Rowman and Littlefield, 1986.
- 'Human Rights in South Africa versus Human Rights in Black Africa: An Illegitimate Comparison.' *Transafrica Forum* 5, no. 1 (1987): 39–56.
- 'Women's Rights, Group Rights and the Erosion of Liberalism.' In *Mistaken Identities: The Second Wave of Controversy over 'Political Correctness,'* edited by Cyril Levitt, Scott Davies, and Neil McLaughlin, 130–45. New York: Peter Lang, 1999.
Howard, Rhoda E., and Jack Donnelly. 'Human Dignity, Human Rights, and Political Regimes.' *American Political Science Review* 80, no. 3 (1986): 801–17.
Howard-Hassmann, Rhoda E. '"Canadian" as an Ethnic Category: Implications for Multiculturalism and National Unity.' *Canadian Public Policy* 25, no. 4 (1999): 523–37.
- 'Canadians Discuss Freedom of Speech: Individual Rights versus Group Protection.' *International Journal on Minority and Group Rights* 7, no. 2 (2000): 109–38.
- 'The Gay Cousin: Learning to Accept Gay Rights.' *Journal of Homosexuality* 42, no. 1 (2001): 127–49.
- 'Gay Rights and the Right to a Family: Conflicts between Liberal and Illiberal Belief Systems.' *Human Rights Quarterly* 23, no. 1 (2001): 73–95.
- 'Identity, Empathy and International Relations.' McMaster University, Institute on Globalization and the Human Condition, Working Paper Series, April 2000. Available at http://www.humanities.mcmaster.ca/~global/global.htm.
- 'Multiculturalism, Human Rights, and Cultural Relativism: Canadian Civic Leaders Discuss Women's Rights and Gay and Lesbian Rights.' *Netherlands Quarterly of Human Rights* 18, no. 4 (2000): 493–514.
- 'Rebuttal to Abu-Laban and Stasiulis.' *Canadian Public Policy* 26, no. 4 (2000): 489–93.
Howe, R. Brian, and David Johnson. *Restraining Equality: Human Rights Commissions in Canada.* Toronto: University of Toronto Press, 2000.
Hucker, John. 'Affirmative Action Canadian Style: Reflections on Canada's Employment Equity Law.' In *Non-Discrimination Law: Comparative Perspectives,* edited by Titia Loenen and Peter R. Rodrigues, 265–77. Boston: Martinus Nijhoff, 1999.
- 'Antidiscrimination Laws in Canada: Human Rights Commissions and the Search for Equality.' *Human Rights Quarterly* 19, no. 3 (1997): 547–71.
Hum, Derek, and Wayne Simpson. 'Wage Opportunities for Visible Minorities in Canada.' *Canadian Public Policy* 25, no. 3 (1999): 379–94.

Humphrey, John. *No Distant Millennium: The International Law of Human Rights.* Paris: United Nations Educational, Scientific and Cultural Organization, 1989.

Hunt, Morton. *The Compassionate Beast: The Scientific Inquiry into Human Altruism.* New York: Anchor Books, 1990.

Ignatieff, Michael. *The Rights Revolution.* Toronto: Anansi, 2000.

– Speech to the Nexus Instituut, Catholic University of Tilburg, The Netherlands, 24 October 2000.

Ing, N. Rosalyn. 'The Effects of Residential Schools on Native Child-Rearing Practices.' *Canadian Journal of Native Education* 18 (1990): 65–118.

Inglehart, Ronald, Neil Nevitte, and Miguel Basanez. *The North American Trajectory: Cultural, Economic and Political Ties among the United States, Canada, and Mexico.* New York: Aldine de Gruyter, 1996.

International Bank. *World Development Indicators.* 2000.

Ishay, Micheline R., ed. *The Human Rights Reader: Major Political Essays, Speeches, and Documents from the Bible to the Present.* New York: Routledge, 1997.

Jackson, Andrew. 'Social Inclusion/Exclusion of Canadian Children.' *Horizons: Policy Research Initiative* 4, no. 1 (2001): 4–5.

James, Carl E. *Seeing Ourselves: Exploring Race, Ethnicity and Culture.* 2d ed. Toronto: Thompson Educational Publishing, 1999.

Janoski, Thomas. *Citizenship and Civil Society: A Framework of Rights and Obligations in Liberal, Traditional, and Social Democratic Regimes.* New York: Cambridge University Press, 1998.

Jenness, Valerie, and Kendal Broad. *Hate Crimes: New Social Movements and the Politics of Violence.* New York: Aldine de Gruyter, 1997.

Jhappan, Radha. 'Inherency, Three Nations and Collective Rights: The Evolution of Aboriginal Constitutional Discourse from 1982 to the Charlottetown Accord.' *International Journal of Canadian Studies* 7–8 (1993): 225–59.

Johnston, Darlene. 'First Nations and Canadian Citizenship.' In *Belonging: The Meaning and Future of Canadian Citizenship,* edited by William Kaplan, 349–67. Montreal and Kingston: McGill-Queen's University Press, 1993.

– 'Native Rights as Collective Rights: A Question of Group Self-Preservation.' In *The Rights of Minority Cultures,* edited by Will Kymlicka, 179–201. New York: Oxford University Press, 1995.

Johnston, Hugh. 'Komagata Maru.' In *The Canadian Encyclopedia.* Vol. 2, 948. Edmonton: Hurtig, 1985.

Jones, Thomas David. *Human Rights: Group Defamation, Freedom of Expression and the Law of Nations.* Boston: Martinus Nijhoff, 1998.

Kalbach, Madeline A., and Warren E. Kalbach. 'Becoming Canadian: Problems of an Emerging Identity.' *Canadian Ethnic Studies* 31, no. 2 (1999): 1–16.

Kallen, Evelyn. *Ethnicity and Human Rights in Canada*. 2d ed. Toronto: Oxford
    University Press, 1995.
– 'Never Again: Target Group Responses to the Debate Concerning Anti-Hate
    Propaganda Legislation.' In *Windsor Yearbook of Access to Justice, 1991*. Wind-
    sor: University of Windsor Press, 1992.
Kaplan, William. 'Introduction.' In *Belonging: The Meaning and Future of Cana-
    dian Citizenship*, edited by William Kaplan, 3–22. Montreal and Kingston:
    McGill-Queen's University Press, 1993.
Klapp, Orrin E. *Collective Search for Identity*. New York: Holt, Rinehart and Win-
    ston, 1969.
Knights of the Ku Klux Klan. 'Frequently Asked Questions.' 1998. http://
    www.kukluxklan.org/faq.htm, accessed 21 January 2000.
Knopff, Rainer, with Thomas Flanagan. *Human Rights and Social Technology: The
    New War on Discrimination*. Ottawa: Carleton University Press, 1989.
Kymlicka, Will. *Multicultural Citizenship*. Oxford: Clarendon Press, 1995.
Lance, Larry M. 'The Effects of Interaction with Gay Persons on Attitudes
    toward Homosexuality.' *Human Relations* 40, no. 6 (1987): 329–36.
Laumann, Edward O., John H. Gagnon, Robert T. Michael, and Stuart
    Michaels. *The Social Organization of Sexuality: Sexual Practices in the United
    States*. Chicago: University of Chicago Press, 1994.
Lawyers Committee for Human Rights. *Beset by Contradictions: Islamization,
    Legal Reform and Human Rights in Sudan*. New York: Lawyers Committee for
    Human Rights, 1996.
Leenaars, Antoon A., et al. 'Genocide and Suicide Among Indigenous People:
    The North Meets the South.' *The Canadian Journal of Native Studies* 19, no. 2
    (1999): 337–63.
Leets, Laura, and Howard Giles. 'Words as Weapons – When Do They Wound?
    Investigations of Harmful Speech.' *Human Communication Research* 24, no. 2
    (1997): 260–301.
Lewis, David. *Louder Voices: The Corporate Welfare Bums*. Toronto: James Lewis
    and Samuel, 1972.
Lienemann, Wolfgang. 'Churches and Homosexuality: An Overview of Recent
    Official Church Statements on Sexual Orientation.' *The Ecumenical Review* 50,
    no. 1 (1998): 7–21.
Loney, Martin. *The Pursuit of Division: Race, Gender, and Preferential Hiring in
    Canada*. Montreal and Kingston: McGill-Queen's University Press, 1998.
Loury, Glenn C. 'Why Should We Care about Group Inequality?' *Social Philoso-
    phy and Policy* 5, no. 1 (1987): 249–71.
MacIntyre, Alisdair. 'Is Patriotism a Virtue?' In *Theorizing Citizenship*, edited by
    Ronald Beiner, 209–28. Albany: State University of New York Press, 1995.

Mackie, Marlene, and Merlin B. Brinkerhoff. 'Measuring Ethnic Salience.' *Canadian Ethnic Studies* 16, no. 1 (1984): 114–31.

Macpherson, C.B. *The Political Theory of Possessive Individualism: Hobbes to Locke.* London: Oxford University Press, 1962.

Madison, Gary B. *The Political Economy of Civil Society and Human Rights.* New York: Routledge, 1998.

Mahoney, Kathleen. 'The Canadian Constitutional Approach to Freedom of Expression in Hate Propaganda and Pornography.' *Law and Contemporary Problems* 55, no. 1 (1992): 77–105.

Manzer, Ronald. *Public Policy and Political Development in Canada.* Toronto: University of Toronto Press, 1985.

March, Karen. *The Stranger Who Bore Me: Adoptee-Birth Mother Relationships.* Toronto: University of Toronto Press, 1995.

Marchak, M. Patricia. *Racism, Sexism, and the University: The Political Science Affair at the University of British Columbia.* Montreal and Kingston: McGill-Queen's University Press, 1996.

Martin, Paul. 'Citizenship and the People's World.' In *Belonging: The Meaning and Future of Canadian Citizenship,* edited by William Kaplan, 64–78. Montreal and Kingston: McGill-Queen's University Press, 1993.

Martin's Annual Criminal Code 1999. Aurora, ON: Canada Law Book Inc., 1998.

Mbeki, Thabo. 'Statement at the UN Millennium Summit.' New York, 7 September 2000. http://www.anc.org.za/ancdocs/history/mbeki/2000/tm0907.html.

McChesney, Robert Allan. 'Canada.' In *International Handbook of Human Rights,* edited by Jack Donnelly and Rhoda E. Howard, 29–47. Westport, CT: Greenwood Press, 1987.

McIlroy, Anne, and Susan Delacourt. 'Chretien on Attack over Rights for Gays: Reform MP Draws Stinging Rebuke.' *Globe and Mail,* 1 May 1996, Toronto edition, A1, A9.

McLaren, Angus. *Our Own Master Race: Eugenics in Canada, 1885–1945.* Toronto: McClelland and Stewart, 1990.

McLeod, Keith A. 'Multiculturalism and Multicultural Education in Canada: Human Rights and Human Rights Education.' In *Beyond Multicultural Education: International Perspectives,* edited by Kogila A. Moodley, 215–42. Calgary: Detselig Enterprises, 1992.

Meyer, William H. *Human Rights and International Political Economy in Third World Nations.* Westport, CT: Praeger, 1998.

– 'Toward a Global Culture: Human Rights, Group Rights and Cultural Relativism.' *International Journal on Group Rights* 3, no. 3 (1996): 169–95.

Mezlekia, Nega. *Notes from the Hyena's Belly: Memories of My Ethiopian Boyhood*. Toronto: Penguin, 2000.

Moodley, Kogila. 'Canadian Multiculturalism as Ideology.' *Ethnic and Racial Studies* 6, no. 3 (1983): 320–31.

Moodley, Kogila A. 'Multicultural Education in Canada: Historical Development and Current Status.' In *Handbook of Research on Multicultural Education*, edited by James A. Banks and Cherry A. McGee Banks, 801–20. New York: Macmillan, 1995.

Moore, Barrington, Jr. *Injustice: The Social Bases of Obedience and Revolt*. White Plains, NY: M.E. Sharpe, 1978.

Morsink, Johannes. *The Universal Declaration of Human Rights: Origins, Drafting and Intent*. Philadelphia: University of Pennsylvania Press, 1999.

Morton, Desmond. 'Divided Loyalties? Divided Country?' In *Belonging: The Meaning and Future of Canadian Citizenship*, edited by William Kaplan, 50–63. Montreal and Kingston: McGill-Queen's University Press, 1993.

Morton, F.L., and Rainer Knopff. *The Charter Revolution and the Court Party*. Peterborough, ON: Broadview Press, 2000.

Mukerjee, Prabhati. 'Dowry.' In *Women's Studies Encyclopedia: Revised and Expanded Edition, A–F*, edited by Helen Tierney, 387–90. Westport, CT: Greenwood Press, 1999.

National Anti-Poverty Organization. 'NAPO Facts: More Facts about Child Poverty.' June 1996. http://www.napo-onap.ca/nf-child.htm.

– 'Poverty Statistics at a Glance.' April 1999. http://www.napo-onap.ca/glance.htm.

Native Women's Association of Canada. 'Aboriginal Women and the Constitutional Debates: Continuing Discrimination.' *Canadian Woman Studies* 12, no. 3 (1992): 14–17.

Nelson, Jacquelyn, and George Kiefl. *Technical Report: Survey of Hate-Motivated Activity*. TR 1995–4e. Ottawa: Department of Justice Canada, 1995.

Nickel, James W. *Making Sense of Human Rights: Philosophical Reflections on the Universal Declaration of Human Rights*. Berkeley, CA: University of California Press, 1987.

NSERC/Nortel Joint-Chair for Women in Science and Engineering in Ontario. http://www.carleton.ca/cwse-on/statistics.htm, accessed 31 January 2001.

Nugent, Robert, and Jeannine Gramick. 'Homosexuality: Protestant, Catholic, and Jewish Issues; a Fishbone Tale.' *Journal of Homosexuality* 18, no. 3–4 (1989): 7–46.

Nunavut Planning Commission. 'General Information about Nunavut.' http://npc.nunavut.ca/eng/nunavut/general.html.

Nussbaum, Martha. 'Compassion: The Basic Social Emotion.' *Social Philosophy and Policy* 13, no. 1 (1996): 27–58.

Ofuatey-Kodjoe, W. 'Self-Determination.' In *United Nations Legal Order*. Vol. 1, edited by Oscar Schachter and Christopher C. Joyner, 349–89. Cambridge, UK: Cambridge University Press, 1995.

Okin, Susan Moller, with Respondents. *Is Multiculturalism Bad for Women?* Princeton, NJ: Princeton University Press, 1999.

Olsen, Kristin. *Chronology of Women's History.* Westport, CT: Greenwood Press, 1994.

Ontario. Legislative Assembly of Ontario. 'An Act to repeal job quotas and to restore merit-based employment practices in Ontario.' 1st Sess., 36th Legislature, 44 Elizabeth II, 1995.

– Legislative Assembly of Ontario. Bill 79, 'An Act to Provide for Employment Equity for Aboriginal People, People with Disabilities, Members of Racial Minorities and Women.' 3rd Sess., 35th Legislature, 42 Elizabeth II, 1993.

– Legislative Assembly of Ontario. Bill 167, 'An Act to Amend Ontario Statutes to Provide for the Equal Treatment of Persons in Spousal Relationships.' 3rd Sess., 35th Legislature, 43 Elizabeth II, 1994.

– Ministry of Community and Social Services. 'Education Key to Getting Teen Parents Off Welfare: Baird Launches First Leap Program in Ontario.' 27 September 1999. http://www.gov.on.ca:80/CSS/page/news/nr98–99/sep2799.html.

– Ministry of Community and Social Services. 'Ontario Works: Information for Participants.' http://www.gov.on.ca/CSS/page/brochure/owia.html.

– *Official Reports of Debates*. Legislative Assembly of Ontario, 19 May 1994.

– *Official Reports of Debates*. Legislative Assembly of Ontario, 1 June 1994.

– *Official Reports of Debates*. Legislative Assembly of Ontario, 2 June 1994.

– *Official Reports of Debates*. Legislative Assembly of Ontario, 27 September 1995.

Patton, Michael Quinn. *Qualitative Evaluation and Research Methods*. 2d ed. Newbury Park, CA: Sage, 1990.

Pendakur, Ravi, and Fernando Mata. 'Patterns of Ethnic Identification and the "Canadian" Response.' *Canadian Ethnic Studies* 30, no. 2 (1998): 125–37.

Petersen, Cynthia. 'A Queer Response to Bashing: Legislating against Hate.' *Queen's Law Journal* 16, no. 2 (1991): 237–60.

Platt, Ken. 'Volunteering too Costly for the Disabled.' *Hamilton Spectator*, 18 June 2001, A10.

Pond, Sharon. 'When Rights Collide.' *University Affairs*, December 1994, 6–7.

Ponting, J. Rick. 'Public Opinion on Aboriginal Peoples' Issues in Canada.' In Statistics Canada, *Canadian Social Trends* (Winter 1988): 9–17.

Pratt, Cranford. 'Human Internationalism and Canadian Development Assistance Policies.' In *Canadian International Development Assistance Policies: An Appraisal*, edited by Cranford Pratt, 334–80. Montreal and Kingston: McGill-Queen's University Press, 1994.

– ed. *Canadian International Development Assistance Policies: An Appraisal*. Montreal and Kingston: McGill-Queen's University Press, 1994.

Pratt, Renate. *In Good Faith: Canadian Churches against Apartheid*. Waterloo, ON: Wilfrid Laurier University Press, 1997.

Prutschi, Manuel. 'The Zundel Affair.' In *Antisemitism in Canada: History and Interpretation*, edited by Alan T. Davies, 249–77. Waterloo, ON: Wilfrid Laurier University Press, 1992.

Pryor, Edward T., Gustave J. Goldmann, Michael J. Sheridan, and Pamela M. White. 'Measuring Ethnicity: Is "Canadian" an Evolving Indigenous Category?' *Ethnic and Racial Studies* 15, no. 2 (1992): 214–35.

Putnam, Robert D. 'Bowling Alone: America's Declining Social Capital.' *Journal of Democracy* 6, no. 1 (1995): 65–78.

– *Making Democracy Work: Civic Traditions in Modern Italy*. Princeton, NJ: Princeton University Press, 1993.

R. v. Butler. *Canada Supreme Court Reports*. Part 3, vol. 1 (1999).

Radwanski, George. *Trudeau*. Toronto: Macmillan, 1978.

Ragin, Charles C. *Constructing Social Research: The Unity and Diversity of Method*. Thousand Oaks, CA: Pine Forge Press, 1994.

Ramcharan, Subhas. 'The Economic Adaptation of West Indians in Toronto, Canada.' *Canadian Review of Sociology and Anthropology* 13, no. 3 (1976): 295–304.

Rao, Arati. 'The Politics of Gender and Culture in International Human Rights Discourse.' In *Women's Rights, Human Rights: International Feminist Perspectives*, edited by Julie Peters and Andrea Wolper, 167–75. New York: Routledge, 1995.

Rasekh, Zohra, et al. 'Women's Health and Human Rights in Afghanistan.' *Journal of the American Medical Association* 280, no. 5 (1998): 449–55.

Reitz, J.G. 'Statistics on Racial Discrimination in Canada.' *Policy Options* 14, no. 2 (1993): 32–6.

Richmond, Anthony H. *Global Apartheid: Refugees, Racism and the New World Order*. Toronto: Oxford, 1994.

Roberts, Julian V. *Disproportionate Harm: Hate Crime in Canada*. WD1995-11c. Ottawa: Department of Justice Canada, Research, Statistics and Evaluation Directorate, 1995.

Roberts, Julian V., and Anthony N. Doob. 'Race, Ethnicity and Criminal Justice in Canada.' In *Ethnicity, Crime and Immigration: Comparative and Cross-National Perspectives*. Vol. 21, edited by Michael Tonry, 469–522. Chicago: University of Chicago Press, 1997.

Roberts, Lance W. 'Understanding Affirmative Action.' In *Discrimination, Affirmative Action, and Equal Opportunity: An Economic and Social Perspective*, edited by W.E. Block and M.A. Walker, 147–82. Vancouver: The Fraser Institute, 1981.

Roberts, Lance W., and Rodney A. Clifton. 'Exploring the Ideology of Canadian Multiculturalism.' *Canadian Public Policy* 8, no. 1 (1982): 88–94.

Rosenthal, Peter. 'The Criminality of Racial Harassment.' In *Canadian Human Rights Yearbook 1989–90*. Ottawa: Human Rights Research and Education Centre, University of Ottawa, 1990.

Ross, Jeffrey Ian. 'Hate Crime in Canada: Growing Pains with New Legislation.' In *Hate Crime: International Perspectives on Causes and Control*, edited by Mark S. Hamm, 151–72. Cincinnati: Anderson Publishing, 1994.

'Ross Ruling Gives Jews Extra Reason to Celebrate.' *Canadian Jewish News* 36, no. 49 (1996): 3.

Rueschemeyer, Dietrich, Evelyne Huber Stephens, and John D. Stephens. *Capitalist Development and Democracy*. Chicago: University of Chicago Press, 1992.

Rushdie, Salman. *The Satanic Verses*. New York: Viking Penguin, 1989.

Ryan, Allan. 'My Way.' *New York Review of Books* 47, no. 13 (2000): 48.

Sabry, Hesham. 'Freedom of Speech: David Irving versus Salman Rushdi [*sic*].' *Cross Cultures* Magazine 7 (December 1992–January 1993): 6–7.

Sandel, Michael J. 'The Procedural Republic and the Unencumbered Self.' *Political Theory* 12, no. 1 (1984): 81–96.

Satzewich, Vic, and Terry Wotherspoon. *First Nations: Race, Class, and Gender Relations*. Scarborough, ON: Nelson Canada, 1993.

Scheff, Thomas J. 'Shame and the Social Bond: A Sociological Theory.' *Sociological Theory* 18, no. 1 (2000): 84–99.

Schmid, Alex P. *Research on Gross Human Rights Violations*. Leiden: University of Leiden, Center for the Study of Social Conflicts (Publication #30), 1989.

Schneider, William, and I.A. Lewis. 'The Straight Story on Homosexuality and Gay Rights.' *Public Opinion* 7 (February–March 1984): 16–20, 59–60.

Sen, Amartya. *Development as Freedom*. New York: Alfred A. Knopf, 1999.

Shaffer, Martha. 'Criminal Responses to Hate-Motivated Violence: Is Bill C-41 Tough Enough?' *McGill Law Journal* 41 (1995): 199–250.

Sheremata, Davis. '[Allan] Rock's Agenda on the Rocks: Opposition to Ottawa's Progressive Justice Minister Grows.' *Alberta Report*, 10 April 1995, 6–7.

Sherman, Nancy. 'Empathy, Respect, and Humanitarian Intervention.' *Ethics and International Affairs* 12 (1998): 103–19.

Shkilnyk, Anastasia M. *A Poison Stronger than Love: The Destruction of an Ojibwa Community.* New Haven: Yale University Press, 1985.

Shue, Henry. *Basic Rights: Subsistence, Affluence and U.S. Foreign Policy.* Princeton, NJ: Princeton University Press, 1980.

Silvera, Makeda. *Silenced: Talks with Working Class Caribbean Women about Their Lives and Struggles as Domestic Workers in Canada.* 2d ed. Toronto: Sister Vision, 1995.

Simms, Glenda P. 'Racism as a Barrier to Canadian Citizenship.' In *Belonging: The Meaning and Future of Canadian Citizenship*, edited by William Kaplan, 333–48. Montreal and Kingston: McGill-Queen's University Press, 1993.

Simpson, Lee. 'Perception of a Problem: Report on Hunger.' Totum Research Inc., August 2000. http://www.cafb-acba.ca/pdfs/other_documents/totum_e.pdf.

Smith, Miriam. *Lesbian and Gay Rights in Canada: Social Movements and Equality Seeking, 1971–95.* Toronto: University of Toronto Press, 1999.

Sniderman, Paul M., Joseph F. Fletcher, Peter H. Russell, and Philip E. Tetlock. *The Clash of Rights: Liberty, Equality, and Legitimacy in a Pluralist Democracy.* New Haven: Yale University Press, 1996.

Solow, Robert M. 'Guess Who Pays for Workfare?' *New York Review of Books* 45, no. 17 (1998): 27–8, 36–7.

Speisman, Stephen. 'Antisemitism in Ontario: The Twentieth Century.' In *Antisemitism in Canada: History and Interpretation*, edited by Allan T. Davies, 113–33. Waterloo, ON: Wilfrid Laurier University Press, 1992.

Spicer, Keith. 'Chairman's Forward.' In *Citizens' Forum on Canada's Future: Report to the People and Government of Canada, 1991.* Ottawa: Supply and Services Canada, June 1991.

Spinner, Jeff. *The Boundaries of Citizenship: Race, Ethnicity, and Nationality in the Liberal State.* Baltimore: Johns Hopkins University Press, 1994.

Stavenhagen, Rodolfo. 'Ethnic Conflicts and their Impact on International Society.' *International Social Science Journal* 127 (1991): 117–31.

Stepan, Cheryl. 'Temple Arson Sparked Move to Build Peaceful Community.' *Hamilton Spectator*, 16 March 2002, A4.

Stone, Linda, and Caroline James. 'Dowry, Bride-Burning, and Female Power in India.' *Women's Studies International Forum* 18, no. 2 (1995): 125–34.

Strum, Philippa. *When the Nazis Came to Skokie: Freedom for Speech We Hate.* Lawrence, KS: University Press of Kansas, 1999.

Swidler, Arlene, ed. *Homosexuality and World Religions.* Valley Forge, PA: Trinity Press International, 1993.

Tarnopolsky, Walter S. *The Canadian Bill of Rights*. Toronto: McClelland and Stewart, 1975.

– 'The New Canadian Charter of Rights and Freedoms as Compared and Contrasted with the American Bill of Rights.' *Human Rights Quarterly* 5, no. 3 (1983): 227–74.

Taylor, Charles, with Respondents. *Multiculturalism*. Princeton, NJ: Princeton University Press, 1994.

Thompson, Allan. 'Most Think Immigrants Must Adapt, Survey Says.' *Toronto Star*, 14 December 1993, A2.

Toobin, Jeffrey. 'X-Rated.' *New Yorker* 70, no. 31 (1994): 70–8.

Toubia, Nahid. 'Female Genital Mutilation.' In *Women's Rights, Human Rights: International Feminist Perspectives*, edited by Julie Peters and Andrea Wolper, 224–37. New York: Routledge, 1995.

Tougas, Francine, and France Veilleux. 'Quelques Déterminants des Réactions des Hommes et des Femmes a l'Action Positive.' *Revue québecoise de psychologie* 13, no. 1 (1992): 128–39.

Tuns, Paul. 'Three Pro-Lifers Arrested in Toronto Bubble-Zone.' *The Interim: Canada's Pro-Life, Pro-Family Newspaper* XVII, no. 5 (1999): 1–2.

Turpel, Mary Ellen. 'Aboriginal Peoples and the Canadian *Charter*: Interpretive Monopolies, Cultural Differences.' In *Canadian Human Rights Yearbook 1989–90*, 3–45. Ottawa: University of Ottawa Press, 1991.

'UNB Prof's Rape Article Controversy.' *The Silhouette*. McMaster University, Hamilton, Ontario, Canada, 11 November 1993.

United Church of Canada. *Gift, Dilemma and Promise: A Report and Affirmations on Human Sexuality*. Toronto: United Church of Canada, 1984.

United Nations. *Convention on the Rights of the Child*, 1989.

– *Convention Relating to the Status of Refugees*. 1951.

– 'Discrimination against Indigenous Peoples: Technical Review of the United Nations Draft Declaration on the Rights of Indigenous Peoples.' Commission on Human Rights, Sub-Commission on Prevention of Discrimination and Protection of Minorities, 46th Sess. E/CN.4/Sub.2/1994/2/Add.1, 20 April 1994.

– 'International Convention on Civil and Political Rights.' General Assembly Resolution 2200A (XXI), 16 December 1966.

– 'International Convention on the Elimination of All Forms of Racial Discrimination.' General Assembly Resolution 2106 (XX), 21 December 1965. Entry into force 4 January 1969.

'Universal Declaration of Human Rights.' In *United Nations: The International Bill of Human Rights*. New York: United Nations, 1978.

U.S. Department of State. *1999 Country Reports on Human Rights Practices:*

Saudi Arabia. Bureau of Democracy, Human Rights, and Labor, 25 February 2000. http://www.state.gov/www/global/human_rights/1999_hrp_report/saudiara.html.

Valpy, Michael. 'Veil of Tears: Muslim Woman Back on Bus.' *Globe and Mail*, 1 September 1999, Toronto edition.

Ventura, Caterina. 'Racial Discrimination and Affirmative Actions: Canada's Experience with Anti-Discrimination Legislation.' In *Combating Racial Discriminations: Affirmative Action as a Model for Europe*, edited by Erna Appelt and Monika Jarosch, 125–35. Oxford: Berg, 2000.

Verburg, Peter. 'A Paper Crime Wave: Rock's Criminologist Speculates Hate Crime is Rampant.' *Alberta Report*, 4 March 1996, 26–7.

Vizkelety, Beatrice. 'Adverse Effect Discrimination in Canada: Crossing the Rubicon from Formal to Substantive Equality.' In *Non-Discrimination Law: Comparative Perspectives*, edited by Titia Loenen and Peter R. Rodrigues, 223–36. Boston: Martinus Nijhoff, 1999.

Vogt, W. Paul. *Dictionary of Statistics and Methodology*. 2d ed. London: Sage, 1999.

Walzer, Michael. 'Comment.' In Charles Taylor with Respondents. *Multiculturalism*. Princeton, NJ: Princeton University Press, 1994.

– *Spheres of Justice: A Defense of Pluralism and Equality*. New York: Basic Books, 1983.

Waters, Malcolm. *Globalization*. New York: Routledge, 1995.

Weaver, Sally. 'First Nations Women and Government Policy, 1970–92: Discrimination and Conflict.' In *Changing Patterns: Women in Canada*. 2d ed., edited by Sandra Burt, Lorraine Code, and Lindsay Dorney, 92–150. Toronto: McClelland and Stewart, 1993.

Weber, Max. *Economy and Society*. Edited by Guenther Roth and Claus Wittich. Los Angeles: University of California Press, 1978.

Weinberg, Paul. 'Poor Relations: Ontario Workfare is not working.' *Our Times* 18, no. 3 (1999): 37–41.

Weinfeld, Morton. 'The Development of Affirmative Action in Canada.' *Canadian Ethnic Studies* 13, no. 2 (1981): 23–39.

Wickberg, E.B. 'Chinese.' In *The Canadian Encyclopedia*. Vol. 1, 336–7. Edmonton: Hurtig, 1985.

Williams, Melissa. 'In Defence of Affirmative Action: North American Discourses for the European Context?' In *Combating Racial Discriminations: Affirmative Action as a Model for Europe*, edited by Erna Appelt and Monika Jarosch, 61–79. Oxford: Berg, 2000.

Wilson, Beth, and Carly Steinman. *HungerCount 2000: A Surplus of Hunger.*

Prepared for Canadian Association of Food Banks, October 2000. http://
www.icomm.ca/cafb/hc-2000.pdf.

Wilson, Bruce G. 'Loyalists.' In *The Canadian Encyclopedia*, 1041–2. Edmonton:
Hurtig, 1985.

Wilson, James Q. *The Moral Sense.* New York: The Free Press, 1993.

Wilson-Smith, Anthony. 'Canada and the World.' *Maclean's* 110, no. 15 (1997):
12–15.

Winks, Robin W. *The Blacks in Canada: A History.* 2d ed. Montreal and Kingston:
McGill-Queen's University Press, 1997.

Winn, Conrad. 'Affirmative Action and Visible Minorities: Eight Premises in
Quest of Evidence.' *Canadian Public Policy* 11, no. 4 (1985): 684–700.

Wolfe, Alan. *One Nation, After All.* New York: Viking, 1998.

Woodard, Joe. 'Victims at Last: The Prime Minister Promises Special Rights for
Homosexuals.' *B.C. Report*, 19 June 1995, 16–19.

World Bank. *Entering the 21st Century: World Development Report 1999/2000.*
New York: Oxford University Press, 2000.

Yalden, Maxwell. 'Collective Claims on the Human Rights Landscape: A Canadian View.' *International Journal on Group Rights* 1 (1993): 17–25.

York, Geoffrey. *The Dispossessed: Life and Death in Native Canada.* Toronto: Lester
and Orpen Dennys, 1989.

'Youths Banished.' *Windspeaker* 12, no. 21 (1995).

Zundel, Ernst. 'Holocaust 101.' http://www.lebensraum.org, accessed 28 May
2001.

Index

Aboriginal civic leaders: as Canadians, 47–8, 51–2, 121, 168; and employment equity, 136; and freedom of speech, 56–7, 65; and hate crimes, 80–2, 88; and international responsibilities, 204; and limits to multiculturalism, 121; and refugees and immigrants, 206; and unwed mothers, 188; and women's rights, 175

Aboriginal peoples: matriarchy, 174–5; and poverty, 149, 159–60; and residential schools, 167, 171–2; responsibility of Canadians to, 161–3; statistics on well-being of, 158; as vulnerable group, 16

Aboriginal rights: abuses of, 24; advocates of, 8, 17; coded responses to, 158–9; as collectivities, 156–7, 225, 233–4; and conflicts with rights of others, 177; and the Constitution, 27; and economic equity, 153–4, 226; historically, 232; police and justice systems, 171–2, 176, 269n24; and privileges, 161, 167; and self-determination, 168–72; self-

government, 170; and sovereignty, 169–70

abortion, 18, 125, 189, 227

Act to Amend Ontario Statutes to Provide for the Equal Treatment of Persons in Spousal Relationships 1994 (Ontario). *See* Bill 167

Adnan (pseudonym): and Aboriginal rights, 165; and international responsibilities, 203; motivation for activities, 18; and same-sex adoption, 103

adoption: by same-sex couples, 93, 102–4, 111–12; for unwed mothers, 189–90

African Canadians, 24

Africville, 24

age: and attitude to diversity, 38–9; of civic leaders, 216

aging society, 207

AIDS, 95, 105, 108

Alexander (pseudonym): and conflicts to freedom of religion, 123; and freedom of speech, 58; and gay and lesbian rights, 97; and national celebrations, 44; and racism, 47

Al (pseudonym): and being Canadian, 35; and employment equity, 140; and gay and lesbian rights, 94; motivation for activities, 20

altruism, 220–1; definition of, 219; as motivation for activism, 18, 21

Amnesty International, 19

Angela (pseudonym): and employment equity, 141; and freedom of speech, 57; and patriotism, 45

Anglo-Canadian elite, 23

An-Na'im, Abdullahi, 216–17, 245n37

anonymity, 9, 12

Anthony (pseudonym): and Aboriginal rights, 166; and conflicts to freedom of religion, 124; and international responsibilities, 203; and patriotism, 45; and unwed mothers, 189

anti-Semitism, 38, 61, 74, 223–4, 278n26; and feeling Canadian, 46; and hate crimes, 83, 89–90; response to, 80

apartheid, 200–2

Aqil (pseudonym): and economic rights, 181; and employment equity, 140; and freedom of thought, 126; and motivation for activities, 20; and responsibility to Aboriginal peoples, 161; and same-sex adoption, 103

Asian immigrant civic leaders: and Aboriginal peoples, 161–2, 165; and being Canadian, 41; and conflicting human rights laws, 124; and economic rights, 181; and employment equity, 140, 147–8; and freedom of speech, 58, 64; and gay and lesbian rights, 97–101;

and international responsibilities, 203; motivation for activities, 18, 20; and national celebrations, 44; and racism, 46–7; and white social power, 145; and work ethic, 150

assimilation: of Aboriginal peoples, 157, 160, 163–6; and language, 42–3. *See also* integration

Auguste, Arnold A., 223–4

Barry (pseudonym): and being Canadian, 37; and employment equity, 142; and freedom of speech, 68; and refugees and immigrants, 208; and workfare, 195

Basanez, Miguel, 217

Basil (pseudonym): and Aboriginal rights, 170; Canadian characteristics, 39; and refugees and immigrants, 206

benefits of activism, 21–2

Betty (pseudonym): and Aboriginal peoples, 161; and employment equity, 144; and gay and lesbian rights, 122; and hate crimes, 82; motivation for activities, 22; and refugees and immigrants, 211–12; trust in government, 40–1

Beverley (pseudonym): and Aboriginal rights, 159; and being Canadian, 38; and black poverty, 151; and freedom of speech, 67; and gay and lesbian rights, 89–90; motivation for activity, 22

Bill 79. *See* Employment Equity Act 1993 (Ontario)

Bill 167 (An Act to Amend Ontario Statutes to Provide for the Equal Treatment of Persons in Spousal

Coalition of Concerned Canadians, 255n6
collective consciousness, 4
collective rights: and Aboriginal peoples, 166–8, 172, 175–7; and Canadian law, 174–5; definition of, 156–7; and freedom of speech, 54–5; and legal rights, 222; and social order, 182
Colleen (pseudonym): and Aboriginal rights, 170; Canadian characteristics, 40; and freedom of speech, 66; and hate crimes, 78; and limits to multiculturalism, 122; motivation for activism, 21; and refugees, 205; and unwed mothers, 190
colonialism, 159–60, 170
common good, 4
'Common Sense Revolution,' 138
Communism, 25, 46, 58, 181, 213
community, 227–8; and communitarianism, 71, 227; definition of, 228; the promotion of, 66; sense of, 198; social commitment to, 231
community activism: feeling Canadian, 42; motivations for, 17–18, 52
community values: and care of the poor, 197–8; defining community, 228; the existence of, 62–3; and gay marriage, 101. *See also* 'Canadian values'
compassion: definition of, 215; and personal responsibility, 191–2; and poverty, 197, 199; under strain, 233; tone of civic leaders, 23; and unwed mothers, 189, 191
competing values, 53, 222. *See also* individual rights
compromise, 39

Constitution, the Canadian, 23; and Aboriginal rights, 172
corporate profit, 184
Cran (pseudonym): and Aboriginal peoples, 161; and Canadian culture, 127; and white social power, 144–5
Criminal Code reforms, 120
cultural relativism: and multiculturalism, 114; 'weak,' 115–17, 132
culture of human rights, 23, 26–7

Dan (pseudonym): and freedom of speech, 57; and gay and lesbian rights, 96; and hate crimes, 79; on limits to multiculturalism, 114; and refugees and immigrants, 209
data: qualitative, 6–7, 14
date rape, 223
debt (Canada), 211
de Gaay Fortman, Bas, 198, 216–17
democracy: and capitalism, 202; and civic participation, 21; and freedom of speech, 55, 59, 73; and gay and lesbian rights, 107; and public opinion, 15–16; and the social-learning theory, 216; as stable, 233; trust of citizens, 41, 218
Denis, Claude, 177
Depression (1930s), 193, 232
development work, 203, 207, 213
Dickson, Chief Justice, 60
dignity: of Aboriginal peoples, 197; of gays and lesbians, 197; of immigrants, 197; the need for, 221; as part of the Canadian experience, 50; of the poor, 197; and vulnerable groups, 223; and work, 195–7
disabled people, 49, 136, 180, 198
diversity, 110–11, 132